THE NEW CONSCIENTIOUS OBJECTION

From Sacred to Secular Resistance

Edited by

CHARLES C. MOSKOS
JOHN WHITECLAY CHAMBERS II

New York   Oxford
OXFORD UNIVERSITY PRESS
1993

Oxford University Press

Oxford   New York   Toronto
Delhi   Bombay   Calcutta   Madras   Karachi
Kuala Lumpur   Singapore   Hong Kong   Tokyo
Nairobi   Dar es Salaam   Cape Town
Melbourne   Auckland   Madrid

and associated companies in
Berlin   Ibadan

Published by Oxford University Press, Inc.,
200 Madison Avenue, New York, New York 10016

Oxford is a registered trademark of Oxford University Press

Library of Congress Cataloging-in-Publication Data
The New conscientious objection :
from sacred to secular resistance /
edited by Charles C. Moskos, John Whiteclay Chambers II.
p.   cm.   Includes bibliographical references and index.
ISBN 0-19-507954-X. — ISBN 0-19-507955-8 (pbk.)
1. Conscientious objection.   2. Draft resisters.
I. Moskos, Charles C.   II. Chambers, John Whiteclay.
UB341.N49   1993   355.2'24—dc20   92-20615

2   4   6   8   9   7   5   3   1

Printed in the United States of America
on acid-free paper

For Enid Curtis Bok Schoettle
Whose friendly persuasion
made this book possible

Acknowledgments

Principled secular objection to military service and its recognition as an international human right are rapidly growing phenomena. Scholarly exploration of this "new" conscientious objection is the basis for this book.

As a comparative examination in nearly two dozen countries, including much of Europe plus Israel, Australia, South Africa, and the United States, this study owes much to many people. First and foremost the editors and contributors wish to thank the Ford Foundation for its core support of the Inter-University Seminar on Armed Forces and Society (IUS), an international inter-disciplinary network of social scientists committed to the idea that civil-military relations is a subject worthy of sustained scholarly research. The foundation also supported the first international scholarly conference on conscientious objection and the state, a meeting organized by the Inter-University Seminar and held in Utrecht in the Netherlands in March 1990. The three-day workshop, attended by scholars from more than twenty countries, occurred less than four months after the fall of the Berlin Wall amid the ending of the Cold War and nine months before the Persian Gulf War. It could hardly have been held at a more historic time.

We are particularly indebted to Dr. Enid Curtis Bok Schoettle, then of the Ford Foundation and now of the Council on Foreign Relations, whose personal interest in the project propelled us. Our dedication of this volume to Enid is small recognition of what we owe to her.

We also wish to acknowledge the *Stichting Maatschappij Krijgsmacht* or SMK, host oranization in the Netherlands and joint convener of the conference. We are particularly indebted to Dr. Willem Scheelen, then director of SMK, and his staff for the local arrangements.

Although the present study began at the conference, this is an integrated and updated book. *The New Conscientious Objection* has an overarching theme and an internal coherency. The unifying principle evaluates the thesis that religious objections to military service are being augmented and largely superseded by secular motives, and that this phenomenon has contributed to the spread of conscientious objection among those conscripted and also those already within the uniformed services, whether conscripts or volunteers. It is also our thesis that conscientious objection is increasingly becoming recognized as a fundamental human right.

Participants in the conference shaped their papers to bear on key dimensions of conscientious objection: criteria of conscience, patterns of objection, and state policy toward conscientious objectors (COs). To paint such a picture across a broad canvas was a bold task, but it gave the volume an analytical framework and a sustained thesis.

Following the workshop meetings, most of the participants revised and updated the papers included here. The editors also sought to keep the papers abreast of contemporary developments. We are grateful to the contributors who gave willingly of their support and encouragement as we too labored to turn individual papers into integrated chapters of a unified and coherent book. For the sake of thematic unity, we found it necessary to exclude some of the papers presented at the conference, but we were able to incorporate a number of other chapters that were written subsequently.

In addition to the chapter authors, we would like to thank the following conference participants whose active involvement also enriched our understanding of this aspect of the relationship of armed forces and society: Hugo Bedau, Nikita A. Chaldymov, Danuta Kociecka, Miklos Tomka, Fred van Iersel, Jerzy Wiatr, and the late Karl-Heinz Roeder. In our revisions, we frequently called upon and were always informed by L. William Yolton, executive director of the National Inter-religious Service Board for Conscientious Objectors (NISBCO), and Robert A. Seeley, executive director of the Central Committee for Conscientious Objectors (CCCO). We also benefited from information from Amnesty International, the United Nations, and the U.S. Department of Defense.

Charles C. Moskos would also like to acknowledge the Woodrow Wilson International Center for Scholars and the U.S. Army Research Institute for the Behavioral and Social Sciences, whose support at different times gave him the opportunity to develop some of the central concepts that underlie this volume. He also wishes to thank his coeditor, John Whiteclay Chambers II, for his many insightful ideas and his significant contribution to this work. It was truly a mutual effort.

In the final preparation of this volume, the editors wrote jointly the introductory and concluding chapters and divided between themselves editorial reponsibility for the other chapters. Charles Moskos took responsibility for the chapters on Germany, Israel, the Socialist countries, Australia, Bulgaria, Greece, and Italy; John Chambers for those on the United States, Britain, France, Denmark, Norway, South Africa, Switzerland, the Netherlands, and the chapter on Comparative Legal Aspects. The collaboration has been an intellectually stimulating and particularly enjoyable one.

Because the contributors represent such varied institutional affiliations (see the list of contributors), the usual caveat that the authors alone are responsible for the findings and interpretations presented is especially relevant here.

Finally, the editors wish to thank David Roll and Paul Schlotthauer of Oxford University Press for ably shepherding this book through to publication.

Evanston, Illinois   C. C. M.
New Brunswick, New Jersey   J. W. C.
November 1992

Contents

Part IV The Secularization of Conscience Reconsidered

PART I

INTRODUCTION:
THE SECULARIZATION
OF CONSCIENCE

1

The Secularization
of Conscience

CHARLES C. MOSKOS
JOHN WHITECLAY CHAMBERS II

If the citizen soldier can be traced back to the origins of the modern Western state, an equally durable social type is the conscientious objector to military service. Conscientious objection is at the core of the individual's relationship to the state because it challenges what is generally seen as the most basic of civic obligations— the duty to defend one's country. At the same time, allowing the right to refuse to bear arms has become a hallmark of the liberal democratic society.

Although conscientious objection is a long-standing phenomenon, only in recent times has it become a major factor affecting armed forces and society. What we call the "new conscientious objection" differs from the old in motive, size, and extent. The contemporary refusal to bear arms is likely to be more secular than religious in origin, to be a widespread rather than marginal occurrence, and to include service people in uniform as well as conscription resisters. No general account of civil-military relations in liberal industrialized democracies is complete without a reference to principled resistance to military service.

In Western Europe, the numbers of conscientious objectors (COs) soared during the final years of the Cold War: The rate of objection increased about sevenfold from the mid-1960s through the late 1980s (see Figure 1–1). In several countries of Northern Europe, one out of four draftable men was declaring some form of conscientious objection to avoid military service in the early 1990s. In Germany in 1991, the number of conscientious objectors climbed to a new high of 151,000 (about the number who must be taken in to keep the armed forces at planned levels).[1] Conscientious objection has become a new occurrence in the former socialist countries of Eastern Europe and the former Soviet Union and in such diverse

3

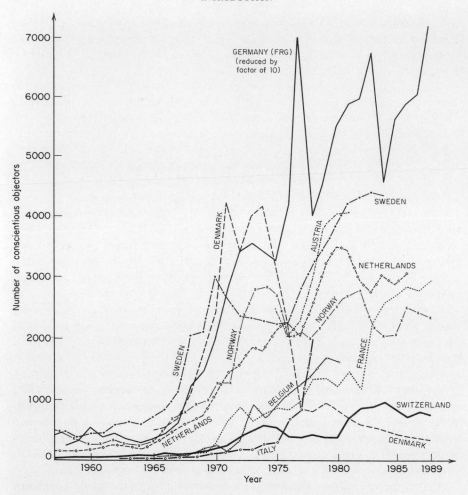

FIGURE 1-1. The rise of conscientious objection in selected Western European countries, 1960–1988. Reprinted with permission from Karl W. Haltiner, *Milizarmee— Bürgerleitbild oder angeschlagenes Ideal?* (Frauenfeld, Switzerland, 1985), p. 14.

societies as South Africa, Switzerland, and Israel.[2] In 1990 the Conference on Security and Cooperation in Europe (CSCE) agreed to consider introducing forms of alternative service for conscientious objectors in lieu of military service among the thirty-five participating states.[3]

In the United States, more young men were being exempted as conscientious objectors by the end of the Vietnam War than were being inducted into the army.[4] Indeed, the widespread resistance to conscription and military service was one of the reasons for the withdrawal of American forces from Southeast Asia and for the end of the draft in the United States in 1973. Conscientious objection also has come to include uniformed members of the All-Volunteer Armed Force (AVF), of whom an average of 150 a year were being discharged as COs in the 1980s. During the buildup and war in the Persian Gulf in 1990–1991, between fifteen hundred and two thousand active-duty members and mobilized reservists applied for conscientious objection status.[5] More than three score of these applicants were court-martialed for refusal to deploy overseas.[6] The peace movement sought to defend them, and in February 1991, the San Francisco Board of Supervisors declared the city a sanctuary for conscientious objectors.[7]

Remarkably, no comprehensive and scholarly treatment of conscientious objection exists.[8] To be sure much has been written about the subject, but most of this writing is a literature of advocacy, often with a low level of conceptual generalization. Moreover, no major cross-national analytical study of conscientious objection has been attempted until now.[9] The aim of this volume is to place conscientious objection in a conceptual context, both historical and contemporary. We seek to correlate the origins and patterns of conscientious objection and the criteria and policies of national governments toward conscientious objectors.

We take care not to subject the reader to an exhausting taxonomy, but for comparative analyses we must begin with common definitions. We define a conscientious objector as a person who refuses either to bear arms or to serve in the military or continue to serve in the military because of religious or moral beliefs that are opposed to killing, or, more recently, are opposed to relying on nuclear weapons for deterrence.

Conscientious Objectors can be classified according to several subcategories: On the basis of their motivation, conscientious objectors can be either *religious COs* (including variously those coming to their beliefs through historic peace sects, through mainline churches, or through nonmainline religious denominations) or *secular COs* (including those with either political or private motives). On the basis of the scope of their beliefs, conscientious objectors can be *universalistic COs,* who are opposed to all wars (these pacifists are the kind of COs most commonly recognized by the state), *selective COs,* who oppose a particular conflict, or *discretionary COs,* who reject the use of particular weapons (primarily weapons of mass destruction, most notably nuclear weapons).[10]

Also distinguishing one type of conscientious objector from another is his (or, more recently, her) degree of willingness to cooperate with the state, specifically represented by the military or the government's conscription agency. *Noncombatant COs* are objectors willing to serve in the military without bearing arms; typically they serve in the branch of the military directly dedicated to saving lives—the medical corps. Such noncombatant COs experience the least friction with the military system because they help the system function. Indeed, several of them have been decorated for valor, including an American medic in the Vietnam War who was awarded the Congressional Medal of Honor.[11] *Alternativist COs* agree to participate in civilian alterative service in public or private agencies, in lieu of military service; most of these COs engage in conservation, health, or cultural work. In many countries, willingness to perform alternative service has become increasingly the de facto measure of the "sincerity" of the conscientious objectors. *Absolutist COs* refuse to cooperate with the authorities in any way in regard to the conscription system. They decline to participate in alternative service programs, even if these programs are unrelated to the military, generally because they reject the authority of the state in this area. Consequently the absolutists are the COs who are most likely to be imprisoned in modern democratic societies.

A gray area of objection exists for persons who refuse to serve in the military for reasons that are based mainly on ethnic, racial, or nationality objections. How would one classify, for example, a Lithuanian draftee during the cold war era who refused to serve in the Soviet Army, but who would be willing, if not eager, to serve in a Lithuanian Army?[12] In the United States since the 1940s, a number of Black Muslims have refused to participate or be drafted in what they denounce as racist conflicts. Black Muslim objectors received prison sentences during World War II and the Korean and Vietnam wars; several were court-martialed during the Persian Gulf War.[13] Ethnic objections to war have been a perplexing issue in a number of countries. But opposition to military participation on grounds of ethnicity, race, or national origins is peripheral to our main focus. General refusal to kill or participate in mass destruction is inherent in our definition of conscientious objection.

The unifying theme of this volume is that even when national singularities are taken into account, a consistent pattern characterizes the social and political evolution of conscientious objection in modern Western democracies. Over time the definition of objector status as recognized by the state shifts from membership in historic "peace churches" to include congregants of mainline religious bodies, and finally those who object to military service on moral and ethical reasons not derived from religious tenets. Although religious conscientious objection continues to exist, it declines proportionately in the face of the dynamic growth of secular COs. We call this pattern *the secularization of conscience*.

As presented in Table 1.1, it is useful to describe fairly distinct and sequential "stages" that generally have characterized the relationship between the state and conscientious objection. In this conceptualization, political-military developments are related to overall socioeconomic trends in Western society. The stages in the evolution of CO-state relations correspond roughly to pre-industrial, early industrial, late industrial, and post-industrial Western societies.

The "proto-stage," characteristic of pre-industrial, premodern seventeenth- and eighteenth-century Western societies, finds conscientious objectors existing in a limbo world. In such a situation states variously and inconsistently permit unofficial objection, allow purchase of exemption, or mete out severe punishment to objectors.

In Stage 1, early modern society, the state formally recognizes conscientious objection but limits such recognition to "historic peace faiths." These are churches that came out of the radical wing of the Protestant Reformation and its aftermath. The main bodies today are the Mennonites, the Brethren, and the Quakers. In the twentieth century, and with less consistency, Jehovah's Witnesses and Seventh-Day Adventists claimed CO status. The initial compromise of the state is to allow conscientious objectors the right to serve in a non-combatant capacity within the armed services. The leadership of the conscientious objection movement is largely in the hands of the traditional peace churches. From the viewpoint of the conscientious objectors, the dominant mood is simply wanting to be left alone.

In Stage 2, characterizing many late modern Western societies, the state begins to accept broad religiously based objection as a criterion; thus objector status now is granted to COs from mainline Protestant denominations, Roman Catholicism, and other religious bodies. This stage sees the appearance of alternative civilian service under some form of the military or conscription system. Such alternative

TABLE 1.1   State and Conscience: A Paradigm

Stage	State Criteria for Conscientious Objection	State Policy toward Conscientious Objectors	Immediate Goals of Conscientious Objectors
Proto-stage Pre-modern Western society	COs exist in a limbo where the state, variously and inconsistently, permits unofficial exemption, allows purchase of exemption, or metes out severe punishment.		
Stage 1 Early modern Western society	Lifelong membership in traditional "peace churches"	Non-combatant military service	Exemption from military service for all religious COs
Stage 2 Late modern Western society	As above, plus any religious objection to military service	Alternative civilian service under military aegis	Exemption from military service for all COs
Stage 3 Postmodern Western society	As above, plus secular objection to military service	Alternative civilian service under civilian aegis	Advocacy of selective conscientious objection

service typically lasts longer and is less well remunerated than military service. In this phase church bodies also may play an intermediary role between the state and the alternative servers. The leadership of the conscientious objection movement expands to include some individuals from mainline churches (which, however, remain internally divided on the issue of conscientious objection). Negotiation between church bodies and the government on the terms of conscientious objection is the prevailing tendency.

In Stage 3, characterizing many post-modern Western societies, a major change occurs: The definition of conscientious objection is vastly expanded to include secular and humanitarian motives. In effect, religion is no longer the sole determining factor. The majority of COs base their objection on nonreligious grounds, and this secularization of conscientious objection is accepted by the state. There is also a definite movement toward regarding civilian service as the functional equivalent of military service, a trend that diminishes the role of intervening church bodies. The conscientious objection establishment, which now includes many secularist organizations, such as human rights and anti-military groups, moves toward advocacy of selective opposition to particular wars. This contributes to the new phenomenon of unprecedented numbers of active-duty military personnel becoming conscientious objectors. Few of the COs, in or out of uniform, in Stage 3 would have met the more stringent tests designed to restrict conscientious objection in the past. The older conscientious objection pattern of limited engagement with the polity gives way to political confrontation with the state military system.

No scheme of broad societal change can be as neat as the stages of conscientious objection presented here. Our concern is to grasp the whole, to underline the salient fact, and to have a framework for further understanding of civil-military relations, broadly conceived. By definition, all cases are different; the key is whether these differences can be accommodated within the framework presented. Broadly speaking it would be fair to say that the historical and cross-national data seem to fit the paradigm well, although some adjustments must be made for differences in the timing of the stages.

The policy of civilian alternative service is an effective measure of the extent of governmental recognition and accommodation of conscientious objection. The overriding trend in liberal democracies has clearly been toward recognition of conscientious objectors and the provision of alternative service for those COs who refuse to participate in the armed forces. Noteworthy in this regard is the fact that Amnesty International, a leading human rights organization, stated in 1990 that it did not regard as a "prisoner of conscience" an incarcerated conscientious objector who *refused* alternative service.[14] National differences in programs of alternative service involve questions of equity and equivalency as well as differences in political-military circumstances. Salient issues are whether conscientious objectors, in comparison with uniformed conscripts, are required to spend a longer period performing alternative service and whether they come under civil law or under military codes. In short, the issue of civilian alternative service has become a major yardstick measuring the degree to which liberal democracies with conscription are able to manage the modern dilemma posed between the conscript and the conscientious objector.

Religious Origins

Conscientious objection in the West originates in Christianity in the form of religious pacifism, the belief that the taking of human life under any circumstance is evil. Of course, pacifist elements are present in non-Christian as well as Christian thought.[15] A number of quietistic Eastern religions, especially Buddhism, decry war and advocate nonresistance to force.[16] Islam has no pacifist tradition, and although Muhammad was a prophet and a teacher "in the path of God," he was also (unique among founders of major religions) a soldier.[17] Judaism is not a pacifist religion either, although it gave the world the commandment "Thou shalt not kill" (perhaps more accurately translated "Thou shalt not murder"). In the Roman Empire, Jews refused to serve in the Roman army because the soldier's oath of allegiance involved the recognition of the emperor as the deified head of state. As a practical matter, the Roman government exempted Jews from military service on religious grounds. Like most other leading religions, Judaism has no major pacifist tradition comparable to that of Christianity.[18]

Religious pacifism has been most fully expressed in elements of Christianity.[19] Jesus of Nazareth proclaimed a gospel of nonviolence unlike that found in any other religion of the ancient world; the Sermon on the Mount contains what is probably the most powerful exhortation for nonresistance to violence ever uttered. Indeed, although some early Christians served in the Roman army, most refused that military service, and were the world's first conscientious objectors. The first known Christian conscientious objector was Maximilian, a twenty-one-year-old from Numidia in North Africa. Called to the Roman army in A.D. 295, he stubbornly refused to perform military service and was executed on orders from the Roman proconsul.[20]

With the state recognition of Christianity by the Roman Emperor Constantine in the fourth century, however, the Christian Church generally accepted the concept of "just war" conducted as a last resort for legitimate causes by legally constituted authorities.[21] This doctrinal justification, enunciated by Augustine in the fifth century, was developed more elaborately by Thomas Aquinas in the thirteenth. In the Eastern Orthodox Church, although the tradition of a pacifist ideal exists among monks and priests, the prevailing standard is adherence to the equivalent of a just-war doctrine.[22] Just war was later accepted by the major Protestant faiths that came into being as a result of the Reformation beginning in the sixteenth century.

This is not the place for an extended history of Christian pacifism and conscientious objection, but certain main currents can be introduced. Some small Protestant sects that emerged from the Reformation, for example, rejected the just-war doctrine, holding instead that any notion of justified violence contradicted biblical commandments and the Christian duties of charity and love.[23] These sects developed well-defined beliefs of nonresistance and, over time, established their own tradition of opposition to military service and warfare. To be sure, compulsory military service was much less widespread in the principalities and monarchies of early modern Europe than it became under the later nation-states. During this period, informal accommodations developed between the ruling sovereigns and the otherwise generally law-abiding dissenting religious sects that sought to avoid military service. In several European monarchies these accommodations, involving payment of fines, commutation of military service into other work, and sometimes the provision of substitutes, became established customs in regard to certain religious pacifist groups. These customs, of course, were not the formal "rights" that developed in modern times.

Within the radical wing of the early Protestant Reformation certain pacifist groups on the European continent drew from a broader "Anabaptist vision," a perspective that was suspicious of the corrupting influence of the temporal world.[24] The main inspiration of the Anabaptists was a literal interpretation of the New Testament. The sixteenth-century Anabaptists emphasized the importance of keeping one's religious conscience inviolate against the state; and, as their name indicates, they endorsed adult baptism, a ceremony linked directly to the maintenance of a community of dedicated believers. In addition to refusal to bear arms, these sects typically emphasized a withdrawal from the larger community, and refrained from government employment or even from engaging in lawsuits. Calling themselves "defenseless Christians," the separatist Anabaptist pacifist groups contained the embryo of modern ideas of separation of church and state.

Although conscientious objection to military service was of secondary importance in Europe until the introduction of the modern concept of the nation-in-arms in the French Revolution, it existed in a variety of forms among the Anabaptists and their continental successors starting in the sixteenth century. The Hutterian Brethren, descended from the Moravian Anabaptist Brethren, refused to pay war taxes or make weapons of war. The Mennonites, who derived their name from the Dutch reformer Menno Simons, originated in Switzerland, but were a much larger and more diverse Anabaptist sect. The Mennonites became especially influential in the Netherlands, where William of Orange granted them formal exemption from military duties in exchange for payment or commutation (they had refused to hire substitutes to take their places).[25]

In the eighteenth century, after centuries of nonresistance, the Mennonite peace testimony gradually lapsed among the more integrated communities in the Netherlands, France, Switzerland, and Germany. The stricter Mennonites began to emigrate to Russia and the New World. In the latter movement, the Mennonites and their more rigorous splinter group, the Amish, began in the 1680s to arrive in Pennsylvania and later in some other American colonies.[26] They came mainly from Germany and Holland. In the 1870s, the American community was replenished by Russian Mennonite arrivals fleeing tsarist persecution.[27]

Another stream of pacifists developed out of the radical wing of German Pietism, which emerged in the late seventeenth century. These Dunkers, so-called because of their belief in full immersion during adult baptism, were later called German Baptists, and still later were known officially as the Church of the Brethren. They brought their pacifism to America mainly in the early 1700s, at about the same time as the Mennonite-Amish immigrants. Although the Brethren and the Mennonite-Amish came from different traditions, they had many similarities: They shared a social class, that of farmers and craftspeople; most were German-speaking pacifists; and they shared a dedication to religious purity and pacifism aimed primarily at saving the individual rather than the corrupt and unredeemable world.[28]

The first pacifist immigrants to the New World, even before the German pacifist sects arrived, were British Quakers, members of the Religious Society of Friends.[29] The Society was founded in England by George Fox in the mid-seventeenth century as the left wing of the Protestant Reformation. Beginning in the 1680s, under William Penn, English and Welsh Friends emigrated to the American colonies in large numbers and governed Pennsylvania for nearly a century. Pacifism was a central conviction of Friends from the beginning. It stemmed primarily from the Quaker belief that the Inner Light of God shone within all persons, and from a biblical and intuitive view of the wrongness of war and violence. In contrast to separatist pacifist groups from the European continent, British Quakers held that the state could be an instrument for positive good if those who governed could be guided by the Spirit. More pertinent, Quakers did not believe in living outside active society and commerce. In the eighteenth century, Quakerism came to be dominated by a membership that was prosperous, middle class, and increasingly urban. Nonviolence and the refusal to bear arms remained cardinal tenets of the Religious Society of Friends throughout the nineteenth and twentieth centuries, as did their practice of enlisting public and private means to alleviate suffering and injustice.

In recent times, one of the most significant religious groups refusing to serve in the military has been the Jehovah's Witnesses, who brought an urban and proletarian element into the objector groups. Founded in the United States in the 1870s by Charles Taze Russell, this millenarian movement grew into a worldwide denomination. From a strictly theological viewpoint, Jehovah's Witnesses are not pacifists, because they intend to fight at Armageddon. They believe the second coming of Christ already has commenced and, accordingly, regard governments as the work of Satan. Jehovah's Witnesses have refused to salute the flag or to participate in government, much less take part in the military. More central is their unwillingness to perform any form of alternative service. The refusal of Jehovah's Witnesses to cooperate with the authorities has made them by far the largest single group among imprisoned objectors to military service.[30] (The millenarian Seventh-Day Adventists, on the other hand, who have a similar social history, do not reject conscription if they can perform noncombatant military service.)[31]

It is fair to say that modern conscientious objection, as we know it, began in the American colonies with the arrival of Quaker, Anabaptist, and German Pietist immigrants from pacifist sects. Such persons called themselves "nonresistants"; that is, they did not resist evil with force. Slowly, in piecemeal fashion, the status of conscientious objection became accepted legally in most of the English American colonies, at least for members of the traditional peace churches. Subsequently the United States also accepted the formal right of conscientious objection, initially through the militia of most of the states and ultimately through the national government itself.[32]

In Europe the pattern was different. The model of mass conscript and reserve armies fashioned by Prussia and then by Germany in the last third of the nineteenth century had been copied by most other major powers by the time of World War I. (In contrast, the Anglo-American nations retained peacetime all-volunteer armies and adopted selective conscription only in major emergencies). It is a historical oddity that the term "conscientious objector" itself originated in the 1890s when it was applied briefly to those who opposed compulsory vaccination. By World War I, however, the term quickly and irrevocably became associated with conscripts opposed to bearing arms and to participating in any way in the military.[33] These conscientious objectors, or "conchies," as they were derisively called in Britain when the military draft was first adopted there in 1916, emerged as an issue of varying intensity, depending upon a nation's political culture and its need for military manpower.

In a world of nation-states in which military duties often were equated with the privileges of citizenship, and in which armies numbering in the millions were mobilizing for total war, immense demands were placed on civic forbearance. A high degree of civic maturity was required to tolerate the claims of citizens who in wartime refused military service for reasons of conscience. In Europe, in the years before the twentieth century, conscientious objector status was granted, if it was granted at all, only to small, mainly inward-looking religious sects that did not represent a direct challenge to the state's ability to mobilize for war.[34] In any event, conscientious objection in Europe was allowed much less often than it had been in the British American colonies and in the United States.

Our brief survey of the beginnings of Western conscientious objection leads to a simple statement: Traditionally, the only acceptable state definition of conscientious objection, if there was any acceptance at all, was based solely on religious grounds, and was limited to the traditional Christian peace churches at that.

The Move toward Secularization

On the European continent during World War I, the major powers, regardless of political tradition, generally denied any legal right of conscientious objection. In Germany, conscientious objectors, religious and secular alike, were placed in mental institutions. France court-martialed dissenters as deserters and sentenced them to as long as twenty years in prison. Tsarist Russia imprisoned conscientious objectors for four to six years. Any COs already in the military were court-martialed and imprisoned, flogged, or shot.

Among the major belligerents in World War I, the Anglo-American nations alone, with their traditions of individual liberty and religious freedom, grudgingly recognized a legal right of conscientious objection. Influenced by the spirit of the times, however, they defined it narrowly to apply only to members of pacifist churches and merely exempted objectors from bearing arms in military service. The clash between the state and conscientious objectors—members of traditional peace churches, and, increasingly, religious pacifists from mainstream faiths, ethical pacifists, socialists, and anarchists—led to some accommodation, particularly with the religious pacifists. However, there was also some severe punishment, particularly for the secular, political objectors. In Britain, some 6,500 COs went to prison, as did 450 absolutist COs in the United States. The number imprisoned in America was smaller because President Woodrow Wilson eventually designated non-combatant service in the military for some COs and furloughed others to do agricultural work.

The intensive European nationalism and mass mobilization during World War I made conscientious objection a significant political issue for the first time there. Religious objectors were joined by anarchist and socialist opponents of the military system, who refused to fight in bourgeois wars. Although there is no intrinsic link between pacifism and socialist thought (many socialists were willing to fight in a revolution to achieve socialism), and although most of the European social democratic parties initially supported mobilization in their individual nations, many socialists opposed the war. They emphasized international worker solidarity in opposition to national wars.[35]

The governments of Denmark, Norway, Sweden, and the Netherlands, under pressure from "consistent antimilitarists" (mainly socialists), as well as from religious pacifists, adopted provisions for religious conscientious objection in the era of World War I. Although these countries remained neutral during that conflict, socialist objectors received much stiffer sentences than religious objectors. A 1922 statute in Norway broadened the religious exemption to include all of those whose objection was based on "serious religious conviction or on other serious grounds of conscience" and also provided for alternative service. This was the first statutory break with the previous tradition of limiting CO status to those whose objection was based solely on religious grounds.

Predating the Marxian socialists in the nineteenth century, many small, middle-class peace societies had appeared in Europe and America. These associations were a varied group and often interacted with concurrent movements for social improvement, including those for the abolition of slavery, prohibition or temperate use of alcohol, creation of prison reform, and the establishment of women's rights. Following World War I, middle-class secular pacifist organizations appeared on a much larger scale as reflected in their names, including the Women's International League for Peace and Freedom and the War Resisters International, an association of national War Resisters leagues. While the direct influence of religious pacifism on the socialist antiwar movement was negligible, some Quaker and other religious influence was evident in many liberal middle-class peace organizations.[36] Neither the socialist parties nor the liberal reformist peace associations, however, was influenced by the more isolated Anabaptist or pietistic peace sects.

In Russia after the abdication of the tsar in 1917, the liberal Provisional government released all imprisoned conscientious objectors. Premier Aleksandr Kerensky prepared a special decree to offer alternative service for all religious objectors, but he was overthrown by Lenin and the Bolsheviks before the directive was issued. During the Russian civil war between 1918 and 1921, the Soviet government experimented with recognition of conscientious objection and provision for alternative service. After 1924, however, such exemptions were restricted to historic peace sects and were increasingly narrowed. In 1939 Stalin's government, after asserting that not a single person had applied for religious objector status in the previous two years, eliminated the conscientious objection provision from the conscription law.[37]

During World War II the United States and Britain again were exceptions among the major powers in allowing conscientious objection. Those who were willing to perform noncombatant military service were inducted into the armed forces. Those who would not serve in military uniform were assigned to work in agriculture, forestry, or health care (a very few were exempted entirely). In contrast to the World War I experience, conscientious objectors performing alternative service in both countries worked under civilian rather than military authorities. In the United States most alternativists worked in Civilian Public Service camps operated by the historic peace churches. Both Britain and the United States recognized sincere religious objectors, whether or not they were members of the historic peace churches. (Among the mainline churches, the Methodists produced the most conscientious objectors.) Yet there remained the absolutists, who were sent to prison for refusing any cooperation. The number reached 3,500 in Britain, including 214 women, after female conscription started in 1942. In the United States, some six thousand absolutists were jailed, the large majority being Jehovah's Witnesses.[38]

After the Second World War, the United States and Britain expanded their definitions of conscientious objection and also set up individual alternative service in various public and private agencies. This policy existed until the end of the use of conscription, which occurred in 1963 in Britain and in 1973 in the United States.

As we have mentioned already, the number of conscientious objectors in the United States grew to such a volume during the Vietnam War as to help cause the end of a conscription system that had been in place almost continuously since 1940. The dramatic increase in the number of legally recognized COs was made possible in large part because of two Supreme Court decisions that greatly liberalized the acceptable standards of conscientious objection. The Selective Service Act had required that objectors believe in a "Supreme Being"; it had excluded "political, sociological, or philosophical views or merely a personal code." In 1965, in *United States* v. *Seeger*, the Supreme Court broadened the criterion to include those with "a sincere and meaningful belief which occupies in the life of its possessor a place parallel to that filled by the God of those admittedly qualifying for the exemption."[39] In 1970 the Court went even further, ruling in *Welsh* v. *United States* that "ethical and moral beliefs" were as valid as religious convictions.[40] Now even atheists could qualify for objector status if they demonstrated a deep moral aversion to war. Despite such liberal decisions the U.S. Supreme Court rejected selective objection to particular wars.[41]

The most dramatic developments came in Germany. In the wake of World War II and the rejection of Nazism, the Germans fundamentally altered their political-military culture and institutions. The guarantee of the right of German citizens to dissent from enforced military service was one of the new protections against a resurgence of Nazism or militarism insisted upon by the West and accepted by the Bonn government. Chastened by the Nazi experience and the Nuremberg trials' emphasis on the moral responsibility of individuals for war crimes and crimes against humanity, the Federal Republic of Germany guaranteed the right of conscientious objection in the Constitution of 1949. After West Germany joined NATO and subsequently reintroduced conscription in 1959, federal legislation specified that "any person who opposes armed conflict between states" would be assigned to alternative civilian service or, if the draftee requested it, to noncombatant service in the military. The law allowed alternative service for any sincere conscientious objector, whether the objection was on religious or secular grounds, whether it was against a specific war or all wars, and whether or not the objector was already in uniform.[42] For particular historical reasons, West Germany thus adopted the most liberal conscientious objection provisions in the world at that time.

For reasons more in keeping with general developments in the West, the Scandinavian countries and the Netherlands reaffirmed the rights of conscientious objection after World War II. In essence these rights allowed for expanded alternative service and the inclusion of secular motives for objector status. In the early 1990s, the former communist countries of Eastern Europe were planning or already had introduced conscientious objection programs based on the Northern European model. Statistics on the subject in Eastern Europe were not tabulated as reliably as in the West, but the growth rate in conscientious objection there over the past decade has been similar to that of the West, if not greater—although, of course, it started from a much smaller base.[43]

The Western provenance of conscientious objection, both religious and secular, is revealed by a startling fact. In 1991 among some forty-three countries outside Europe where conscription existed, virtually none recognized conscientious objection.[44]

Overview

The plan of the book is straightforward. This chapter, which constitutes Part I, sets forth the thesis of the secularization of conscientious objection and concludes with an overview of the volume. Part II deals with a discussion of topics unique to the American case. Part III is a comparative analysis of seven Western countries, along with chapters on the former German Democratic Republic, Eastern Europe, and South Africa. Although the historical background in each country is not neglected, the primary focus is on recent developments in conscientious objection. Part IV comes full circle with a reevaluation of the secularization thesis by incorporating the case studies, examining international legal trends, and taking a look into the future. Appendixes include short reports on the evolution of conscientious objection in Australia, Bulgaria, Greece, Italy, and the Netherlands.

Part II: The United States

John Whiteclay Chambers II traces the evolution of conscientious objection and its relation to the state in America from the colonial period to the present. Objection to military service as a modern phenomenon began in America because of the importance of pacifist religious sects in the founding of the nation. Despite the early legitimation of religious conscientious objection, wartime dissent has often been limited and repressed by intensive demands for conformity to majority opinion. The author, sensitive to changes and continuities in America's political and religious culture, argues that the current recognition of secular conscientious objection goes far beyond past practice and is a direct result of the divisions at all levels of society that occurred during the Vietnam War. Although the use of the draft ended in 1973, conscientious objection continues to be a political and moral issue. Compulsory draft registration resumed in 1980, bringing in its wake new forms of objection. Of special note is the fact that conscientious objection has come to include serving members of the all-volunteer forces during peacetime, and during the 1990–1991 war in the Persian Gulf. In basic respects, Chambers presents the United States as the paradigmatic case of the secularization of conscientious objection.

John H. Stanfield II describes how conscientious objection poses a particular problem for black Americans. In most American wars, many blacks have been willing and even eager to serve in the armed forces to assert their claim to the equal rights of citizenship. Even well into the Vietnam War, many mainline black organizations refused to oppose the war because of their fear of jeopardizing the Johnson administration's support for civil rights. Many African Americans, moreover, view the military favorably as an avenue of career mobility. Stanfield, however, also describes another tradition, one of opposition to war and conscription within the black community. He cites the objection to war by black Quakers such as Bayard Rustin in World War II, the opposition to that war and to the Korean and Vietnam Wars by the more numerous Black Muslims, and the opposition to the Vietnam War on the part of the black Student Nonviolent Coordinating Committee (SNCC). Stanfield suggests that increased African-American opposition to war, pradoxically, will increase with the growing secularization of the black experience in America.

Donald J. Eberly describes the status of conscientious objectors in the event of a future resumption of the draft in the United States. The Military Selective Service Act of 1980, which is the basis of current standby draft procedures, was designed to avoid the conscription problems of the 1960s and 1970s. Judgments about conscientious objector status would be made by local draft boards that are purposefully more inclusive of women and minorities than the boards of earlier years. Conscientious objectors willing to serve in noncombatant positions would be inducted into the military. Those unwilling to serve in the military would be required to perform two years of alternative civilian service. Alternative service would be separated from the supervision of local draft boards and would be administered by alternative service officers. A conscientious objector would have access to computerized lists of alternative service positions. Eberly examines the process for dealing with such "alternative service workers," as these conscientious objectors would be called. He concludes by noting how alternative service for conscientious objectors might play a crucial role in any future program of national youth service.

Part III: Comparative Perspectives

Gwyn Harries-Jenkins describes how Britain's painful experience with conscientious objection in World War I led to major changes in subsequent conscription acts during and after World War II. Legislation recognized conscientious objection based not only on the refusal by the individual to kill, but also on his or her right not to perform work that would assist the military. The author traces the bases of rationales for conscientious objection from exclusively religious to primarily humanistic. In a provocative conclusion, Harries-Jenkins argues that the traditional conscientious objection to compulsory military service in wartime has been transformed: In place of individual men resisting compulsory military service, we now witness organized groups of men and women challenging the legitimacy of war and armed deterrence. The new social movement brings into question the use of armed forces as instruments of state policy, particularly the use of weapons of mass destruction, as demonstrated in the anti-nuclear weapons movements of the 1970s and 1980s. Harries-Jenkins's chapter is especially interesting because it treats gender as a major variable in examining conscientious objection and resistance to war.

In France the concept of the citizen soldier has been a vital part of the nation's tradition since the revolution. Michel L. Martin describes how France has been the slowest of the major Northern European countries to accept the right of conscientious objection. In 1963, after the Algerian War and under pressure from President Charles de Gaulle, Parliament passed the first law in French history allowing a form of conscientious objection. The law was largely cosmetic, however, and applied only to a few pacifist sects and the Jehovah's Witnesses. Increasing challenges to the military, growing out of the turmoil of the late 1960s, produced a new and militantly secular objector, but real change came only in 1983 under the new socialist government. A new law provided for alternative civilian service for conscientious objectors, whether secular or religiously based. The author notes that although current conscientious objection rates are high by French standards, they are still the lowest figures in the West. Martin concludes by suggesting that French exceptionalism may decline under the pressures for integration into the European Community.

Jürgen Kuhlmann and Ekkehard Lippert show how the Federal Republic of Germany represents one of the most liberal forms of accommodation to conscientious objection. Not only is the right of conscientious objection specified in the national constitution, but by the 1980s authorities accepted conscientious objection with little more than pro forma declarations on the part of the objectors. Secular motives are given equal weight with religious motives. No other country approached the eighty thousand young men serving in the German "civil service" alternative program during the late 1980s. Indeed the number in *Zivildienst* will most likely climb much higher in the wake of the unprecedented CO rates in the reunited Germany of the early 1990s. What gives the situation in that country a special meaning is that alternative servers have become an integral part of the delivery of human service to the aged and handicapped in German society. Indeed, the authors argue, the present German social welfare system could not operate without *Zivildienst*. The degree to which civilian alternative service has become the moral equivalent of military service in Germany—even though the original impetus was repudiation of a Nazi and militaristic past—may point to the future in development of conscientious objection in other countries.

Henning Sørensen describes how Denmark in 1917 became the first continental European country to recognize the right of conscientious objection. From the beginning, moreover, objector status could be based either on religious or ethical pacifism. In 1968, political and private rationales were allowed to qualify for conscientious objection. Denmark is also one of the few nations that allows selective conscientious objection. Additional administrative decisions in the 1970s and 1980s made the length of service and the pay of civilian alternative servers equal to that of draftees. In effect, Denmark grants automatic conscientious objector status and the right to perform alternative service to any young man who requests it. Indeed, alternative servers typically work fewer and more regular hours than do draftees, while performing less onerous and less hazardous duties. Sørensen concludes by asserting that a persuasive case can be made that it is the conscientious objector rather than the draftee who enjoys the more privileged position in modern Denmark.

Nils Petter Gleditsch and Nils Ivar Agøy disabuse us of the notion that all Scandinavian countries come from the same mold. Their analysis of Norway points to a strong tradition of egalitarian conscription dating back to the eleventh century and reinforced in the contemporary state. Challenging that tradition has been a strong peace movement in modern times. Norway initiated conscientious objection and alternative service provisions in the early twentieth century for religious objectors and those with "serious conviction." Beginning in the late 1960s, the number of political and selective objectors increased as opposition grew against nuclear deterrence and even NATO membership. With this growth, the main body of conscientious objection has shifted from rather marginal religious objectors, as in previous times, to a group that is well educated, secular, and mainstream. The question of whether purely political and selective objection qualifies for objector status remains an unresolved political and legal controversy in Norway.

Annette Seegers points out that South Africa, with its polarized racial situation and divided dominant white minority, has always had a particular problem with compulsory military service. From the establishment of the Union of South Africa in 1910 to the present, conscription has been applied to whites only. Yet the whites have often been divided sharply. Many Afrikaners refused to serve in wars that they considered beneficial to the British Empire, including the two world wars. The direction of conscientious objection changed in the 1960s when growing numbers of young men refused to serve in the implementation of apartheid or to take part in actions against neighboring countries. In the early 1980s, the government repressed newly emergent CO organizations, but also liberalized provisions to include all religious objectors who believed in a supreme being. Court decisions subsequently have expanded the criteria to include non-theistic religious objectors. Claims for secular objection were being reviewed by the Supreme Court in 1991. The beginning of the dismantling of apartheid has included an initial reduction in the term of military service, but Seegers finds it difficult to predict the ultimate impact of the end of apartheid on conscientious objection.

Karl W. Haltiner deals with Switzerland, the only European democracy that offers no official civilian alternative service for conscientious objectors. De facto, however, the government allows religious and ethical, but not political or personal, objectors to perform civilian labor service. Although the number of conscientious objectors has grown rapidly since the late 1960s with a corresponding increase in tolerance from the public, the principle of universal militia service is still very strong in Switzerland. Swiss voters until now have rejected referendum proposals to legalize conscientious objection and alternative service.* Haltiner sees Swiss conscientious objectors as increasingly "privatistic," rather than religious, political, or even idealistic. He argues the Swiss pattern is part of a general attitudinal change in European society toward increasing secular individualism, a result of higher standards of living and educational levels.

Yoram Peri points out that conscientious objection poses a special problem in Israel because the state's very survival depends on a strong military force. In fact, nearly all able-bodied men in Israel, and many young women, serve in the Israeli

---

*On May 17, 1992, in a radical departure from Switzerland's tradition, Swiss voters approved a referendum that amended the constitution to permit alternative service. Although the terms of civilian alternative service were not yet agreed upon as this book went to press, the Swiss appear to have taken the first step toward liberalizing their position toward conscientious objection.

Defense Force. Officially, conscientious objection is not allowed in Israel, and there is strong public antipathy toward those inclined not to serve. (In a separate category are the ultra-orthodox Jews in yeshivas who are granted exemptions for religious studies.) Yet modes of de facto selective or discretionary refusal exist for those in the military. These forms of objection began with refusals to serve in the occupied territories of the West Bank and Gaza and in Southern Lebanon. Typically, such refusers are handled informally within their units. The number of these so-called "gray COs" is low enough so as not to pose any threat to national security. Yet the phenomenon of selective conscientious objection has become aggravated by the intifada and could theoretically evolve into a systemic problem.

Wilfried von Bredow argues that a key factor contributing to the ultimate collapse of the German Democratic Republic was the regime's inability to adapt to conscientious objection. The basic law of East Germany prohibited conscientious objections as such, except as *Bausoldaten* ("construction soldiers"). Even though they operated under severe repression, the *Bausoldaten* increased in number between the 1960s and 1980s. This form of dissidence was largely motivated by Christian denominations. In time, this resistance to conventional military service by a small and initially powerless minority helped to undermine the East German state. In the last days of the German Democratic Republic, conscientious objection became a recognized right, but too late to save a discredited regime.

Anton Bebler offers a survey of the countries of Eastern Europe. During the Stalinist era, harsh suppression of conscientious objection was the pattern in the socialist countries. Excepting the *Bausoldaten* in East Germany, noted above, conscientious objectors were not recognized officially before the 1980s. At certain times and places, however, the policy of repression was tempered informally by allowing hardcore objectors, almost always religious pacifists or Jehovah's Witnesses, to serve in noncombatant roles within the military, such as the *stoybat* ("construction battalions") in the former Soviet Union. Starting in the 1980s, a rising tide of conscientious objection was linked with opposition movements, notably in East Germany, Poland, Czechoslovakia, and Hungary. Concessions were granted and led eventually to recognition of alternative forms of civilian service. Since 1989 the new reformist regimes in the region have conformed in major respects with those Northern European parliamentary democracies, allowing secular as well as religious objection to military service. Today, Bebler notes, the former socialist states of Eastern Europe treat conscientious objectors more liberally than do the NATO countries of the Mediterranean region.

Part IV: The Secularization of Conscience Reconsidered

In a broad and innovative comparative essay, Michael F. Noone, Jr., evaluates the manner in which the two dozen nations that recognize conscientious objection have approached the issue through their legal systems. Previously most legal scholarship on conscientious objection focused on statute law and neglected the manner in which the law has been applied. Noone rectifies this omission by including actual administration as well as statute law in his analysis. Liberalization and secularization raise difficult problems both for the objector and the government. Noone offers a number of suggestions for amelioration of these problems to achieve a responsible balance between competing claims, including those of service members in uniform. With regard to non-uniformed conscientious objectors, he concludes that although the conscientious objector laws in a number of Western European countries appear to be moderately stringent as written, they are often relatively lax when applied. This factor contributes directly to the increasing number and the growing secularization of conscientious objectors in the West.

The final chapter is a summary perspective that appraises what we term the "new conscientious objection," in which the old religious and communal motives are surpassed in numbers and proportion by the new secular and privatized grounds. The new conscientious objection is a much more complex challenge to armed forces and society than the old. The conscientious objector in uniform also shows that the issue not only is related to conscription, but also exists as a policy question in all-volunteer forces. In the final chapter we evaluate the paradigm put forward in this introduction as it is supported, modified, or refuted by the essays on the various countries. We describe changing perceptions of security threats, secularizing liberal trends in mainstream churches, growing emphasis upon privatism and individual rights in the cultural milieu, and the increasing political legitimacy of the objectors themselves as reflected in concurrent shifts in attitude within governmental, educational, and media institutions.[45]

We finish with a caveat, a speculation, and a conclusion. The caveat is not to take for granted that the steady advance of secularism will continue into the future. The speculation is that we may be moving into an era where in some countries the civilian alternative server may become the principal societal server while the role of the citizen soldier atrophies. Although we do not believe that we are entering a totally warless era, we do think that the end of the Cold War and the events unfolding in Europe and elsewhere augur some meaningful, even momentous, not illusory, change. If this is true, the link between citizenship and military service is becoming more tenuous even while we witness an increase of alternative civilian servers among draftees in many countries in Northern Europe.

The conclusion of this book is that whatever the future holds, we can, for now, confidently state that the secularization of conscientious objection, in and out of uniform, is a major new historical phenomenon, and that it is causally linked to larger socio-political developments that have been part of the evolution of post-industrial, post-modern society in the West.

PART II

THE UNITED STATES

2

Conscientious Objectors and the American State from Colonial Times to the Present

JOHN WHITECLAY CHAMBERS II

Modern conscientious objection first emerged in America. It did so because of the importance of pacifist religious faiths in the settlement of the British North American colonies and because of the significance of ideas of individualism, freedom of conscience, and religious toleration.[1]

Except for some compulsory militia training and occasional temporary drafts in wartime, Americans have mainly had a volunteer military tradition. Whenever American governments have resorted to compulsory military training or service, however, they have also faced dissenters who refused to accept the military obligation that the state sought to impose. Religious pacifists, such as the Quakers, were first known as "nonresisters" (for their refusal to use violent means to resist or defend against violence). In the twentieth century they and others who refused on principled grounds to bear arms were called "conscientious objectors" or COs.[2]

Whatever the label, these objectors posed an important challenge to the military commands of the state. In popular wars, they also stood against the often repressive force of dominant public opinion. The challenges posed by the objectors have varied over the nearly four centuries of American history, but the common result has been a tradition emphasizing the need for a proper balance between the rights and sincerely held beliefs of the individual and the interests of the community.

Secularization of conscientious objection clearly describes the American experience with COs in the twentieth century. The shift began in the early years of the century and has been particularly dramatic in the last thirty years.

For three centuries the emphasis was upon a religious basis of conscientious objection, a belief that in matters of conscience and the taking of human life, one could be loyal to a higher authority than the state. In the last third of the century, however, the U.S. government and a significant element of public opinion have accepted a broadened concept of conscientious objection, one that includes opposition based upon the ethical and moral beliefs of non-religious—even atheistic—pacifists.

Yet even this recent secular definition of conscientious objection, first accepted by the U.S. Supreme Court in 1970, fits at least part of the American tradition: The state continues to demand that in order to obtain CO status, an individual must oppose all wars. The government formally rejects selective objection, which is accepted in some nations, including Britain, Denmark, the Netherlands, and the Federal Republic of Germany. The state also continues to require what might be called "equivalency," the requirement that objectors make some kind of alternative contribution to society. Before the twentieth century, this equivalent could take several forms, including payment of a fine or commutation fee, the hiring of a substitute or the personal performance of noncombatant service in the military. More recently it has taken the form of alternative civilian public service. Absolutism—the refusal to cooperate in any manner—remains illegal in America, as in virtually all other countries, and is punishable by fine and imprisonment.

Although the United States has not gone as far as some nations in recognizing of the rights of COs, it has gone farther than most. Conscientious objection is acknowledged as a long-standing and legitimate tradition in America, almost as old as the country itself.[3]

That tradition—and the relationship between the conscientious objector and the state—has evolved through four major stages. The colonial period was a time of formative recognition of the right of conscientious objection by almost all of the original thirteen colonies. In an extended preliminary national stage, from 1789 to 1940, the U.S. government, the pacifist churches, and other organized bodies groped for a proper national policy. In 1940, a solid national policy was established; it lasted, with only comparatively minor modifications, through the end of the 1960s. Since the early 1970s, a liberal, secularized national policy has been established in the so-called postmodern period by the U.S. Supreme Court, although not yet by Congress. These stages nearly match the larger evolution of American military formats—the methods of raising armies—which (as I have argued elsewhere) were determined as much by cultural attitudes and political decisions as by military needs.[4]

The American experience with conscientious objection began earlier than and evolved somewhat differently from that of many other countries. In part this situation resulted from American federalism, with its division of governmental authority between the states and the nation. Particularly in the early period, this bifurcation of authority offered the possibility of a variety of relationships between conscientious objectors and their governments. Furthermore, the evolution was related less to the economy than to cultural and political developments, which, in the context of war and defense policy, played the most important part in shaping the relationship between the conscientious objector and the state in America.

The Formative Stage: 1660s—1780s

Because no British Army existed to defend them, the English immigrants who came to North America in the first half of the seventeenth century rejuvenated the old local militia system.[5] Each colony except Quaker Pennsylvania enacted laws that declared that every able-bodied male "freeman" (property owner) was to be considered part of the militia and could be obligated to defend his community against attack. The laws generally provided for several days of compulsory militia training on muster days each year, and also required service in the militia when the need arose. As the Indian frontier was pushed westward, however, and as the colonial populations grew in size, it was not considered necessary to train the entire male population in arms. Colonial legislatures modified the militia laws, exempting certain occupations and allowing persons to pay a fine instead of undergoing militia training or to hire a substitute if they were drafted for militia service.

Beginning in the second half of the seventeenth century, the English colonies were also settled by pacifist Protestants—nonresistant Christians, as they were called at the time. These settlers were members of sects that held as a cardinal tenet that the teachings of Jesus of Nazareth and the Bible prohibited them from participating in war or engaging in any violence against other human beings. Most of these pacifists were members of what came to be known as the historic peace churches.

From England in the seventeenth century came members of the Religious Society of Friends, known as Quakers, who held an intuitional view of the wrongness of war and violence, based on the Inner Light of Christ in every person.[6] From Holland, the Palatinate, and Switzerland, also beginning in the seventeenth century, came Mennonites and other successors of the Anabaptists, including the Amish, who maintained the importance of the biblical injunction "Resist not evil."[7] From Germany in the eighteenth century came radical Pietists, known as the German Baptist Brethren or Dunkers, who shared with the Quakers an unwillingness to participate in any kind of military activity, but resembled the Mennonites and Amish in remaining aloof from the world. The same was initially true of the Moravian Brethren who emigrated from Moravia to Saxony and, in the early eighteenth century, to America.[8]

As early as 1658, sheriffs in Maryland began to threaten and then to fine Quakers for refusing to train or serve in the militia. Soon officials in Massachusetts, New York, Virginia, and North Carolina began to mete out fines and jail terms or to confiscate the property of pacifists who would not perform their militia duties.[9]

Yet the leaders of the colonial governments gradually worked out accommodations with the pacifist religious communities. The legislators recognized the economically productive and otherwise law-abiding nature of the members of these pacifist groups—the German-speaking Pietist farmers and artisans, and the English-speaking Quaker bankers, merchants, tradespeople, and agriculturalists. The pacifists' elders were quick to point out to government officials that their refusals, as one of their petitions put it, stemmed not from "obstinate humour or contempt of your authority [but] purely in obedience as we apprehend to the doctrine of our Beloved saviour & the discharge of a good conscience."[10]

Religious pacifists appealed to the primarily Protestant lawmakers in terms of a Protestant (albeit extreme) interpretation of the Bible. The colonies sought additional settlers, especially productive ones like these. The lawmakers and the local militia officers also came to recognize that many of the religious objectors would rather suffer and die than take up arms and kill other humans. Awash in a sea of religious faiths, the colonies increasingly came to accept concepts of freedom of conscience and toleration of religious pluralism, particularly a heterogeneous Christianity.[11] Thus for practical as well as philosophical reasons, a number of colonial legislatures provided exemptions for Quakers, Mennonites, and other sectarian pacifists who were conscientiously opposed to bearing arms (the legislatures used the words "scrupulously," or based upon "religious scruples"). Such provisions were enacted first and reluctantly by Puritan Massachusetts in 1665, then enthusiastically by Quaker Rhode Island in 1673, and eventually by every one of the thirteen original colonies except for Georgia, which was founded specifically as a frontier defense colony.[12]

Although details varied by colony, the legislatures usually specifically exempted the Quakers, Mennonites, and Brethren, as well as members of other smaller pacifist sects. Most of these colonies, however, exempted the religious pacifists only from bearing arms—that is, from militia training and service. From the beginning, a concept of equivalency prevailed. The objectors had to pay a fine for not training, or, like others, they could hire a substitute if drafted into temporary units in wartime. However, in William Penn's Quaker experiment in Pennsylvania, the territory that he obtained from the crown in 1681, Penn guaranteed freedom of conscience in the *Charter of Liberties,* the constitution he formulated for the colony in 1701.[13] During the more than fifty years that the colony was dominated politically by the Quakers (supported by pacifist Mennonites, Brethren, and Moravians who settled there), there was no militia in Pennsylvania.[14]

Rhode Island, which had been founded on Roger Williams's concept of religious freedom, provided militia exemptions for COs and also made probably the earliest provisions for what later would be called alternative civilian service. In 1673 Quaker-dominated Rhode Island enacted the broadest CO provision in colonial history, which included not only members of pacifist faiths but anyone religiously and conscientiously opposed to war. COs were also exempted from paying militia fines; specifically they were exempted from confiscation of property for nonpayment, the penalty for others who refused to serve or pay. Although a non-Quaker government repealed the provision four years later during a war with Native American Indians, subsequent legislatures exempted members of pacifist faiths from bearing arms and allowed them to perform alternative service in wartime.

Under Rhode Island's landmark 1673 CO provision for civilian alternative service, the legislature directed that, in case of enemy attack upon the colony, civil rather than military officials might require the COs, in the phrasing and spelling of that period,

> to conduct or convey out of the danger of the enemy, weake and aged impotent persons, women and children, goods and cattle, by which the common weale may be the better maintained, and works of mercy manifested to distressed, weake persons; and [the objectors] shall be required to watch to informe of danger (but

without armes in martiall manner and matters), and to performe any other civill
service by order of the civill officers for the good of the Collony, and inhabitants
thereof.[15]

The French and Indian War of 1756–1763 (known in Europe as the Seven Years'
War) led the crown to insist that the colonies tighten their militia laws and raise
expeditionary forces to assist British regulars. Under pressure for military manpower
and equality of service—the latter resulting particularly from local resentment of
the prosperous Quakers' and Mennonites' exemption from military service—many
colonial governments stiffened the fines and sometimes forced young pacifist Quakers, Mennonites, and Brethren to march with the militia or provincial forces or be
confined in a military stockade. Mennonites, who were more obedient to governmental authority on this issue than the Quakers, generally paid the fines; some even
hired substitutes.[16]

The Quakers proved more obstinate; many of them viewed any compliance with
the process as a violation of their religious principles. During the war, sheriffs and
county militia lieutenants frequently seized Quaker property to cover the cost of
hiring substitutes. In Pennsylvania in 1755, the majority of Quaker lawmakers
relinquished control of the state government to nonpacifists, led by Benjamin Franklin and numbers of Scotch-Irish Presbyterians.[17] The new majority created the state's
first militia but exempted religious pacifists. In Virginia, the governor arrested a
small group of Quakers for noncompliance with a temporary draft. He ordered them
to be taken forcibly to the frontier, where he directed Col. George Washington to
incarcerate them in a stockade and to put them on bread and water until they agreed
to fight. Washington declined, however, replying, "I could by no means bring the
Quakers to any terms. They choose rather to be whipped to death than bear arms."
Instead, Washington freed them and granted them permission to live with local
Quakers until the end of their militia terms.[18]

Faced with such stubbornness and recognizing the sincerity of the pacifists'
beliefs, many other colonies in the 1750s listened to the petitions of the sectarian
leaders and allowed their members to perform alternative service. In Virginia, for
example, Mennonite objectors were used as teamsters or to care for the sick and
wounded. After the French and Indian War, several colonies in which Quakers and
Mennonites were concentrated—Rhode Island, Pennsylvania, Maryland, Virginia,
and North Carolina—exempted those sects completely from military duty and fines,
although resentment of such exemption, especially for prosperous pacifists, caused
several colonies to reinstate the fines or substitution provisions. By the end of the
colonial period, the militia laws of every colony except Georgia contained some
provision for religious conscientious objectors.[19]

In the American Revolution, although the Christian nonresistant sects regarded
many of the revolutionary leaders' complaints against the crown as legitimate, they
did not condone armed revolution, and sought to remain neutral in the conflict.[20]
The revolutionaries, however, would not let them do so, especially as the war
dragged on and the newly independent state governments needed money and soldiers. In addition, the revolutionary leaders sought to bring Americans together in
support of the cause and to create a concept of a new American peoplehood. A test

of the revolutionary citizenship was a willingness to swear allegiance to the new government and to aid in its defense.

Initially the revolutionary leaders of every state with a sizable pacifist population recognized religious conscientious objection as a valid ground for exemption from bearing arms, although the COs were required to pay a fine or hire a substitute. Several state governments proclaimed in their new constitutions or fundamental declarations of rights that religious conscientious objection was an absolute right. Among these states were Delaware, Pennsylvania, New York, and New Hampshire.[21] Some Quakers and other pacifists served in the patriots' cause and were disciplined by their meetings or churches for supporting violence.[22] Religious pacifist sects maintained discipline among their members through such coercion and also by their renewed emphasis on the sufferings of earlier martyrs in their faith.

With the decline of martial enthusiasm, service in the militia, and voluntary enlistment in the state units of the Continental Army in 1776 and 1777, the new state governments began to tighten their statutes for compulsory militia service. Once again Mennonites proved more willing than Quakers to pay fines and special taxes for exemption from militia service, and they suffered less as a result. Recalcitrant objectors sometimes found themselves harassed. In one of the most extreme cases, a North Carolina Quaker was brutally whipped for refusing to muster with the militia. According to one eyewitness account, "Forty stripes were very heavily laid on, by three different persons, with a whip having nine cords."[23] Most objectors were jailed for only a few days, but property was often seized because of nonpayment of fines. While most of the new state governments adopted militia laws that exempted COs from bearing arms, they also levied fines to be used to hire substitutes for those who would not serve in person. Some states, such as Pennsylvania (then dominated by an anti-Quaker party), asked that prosperous pacifists contribute financially to the state's defense, then levied a special tax on COs and sought to coerce the Quaker and Mennonite pacifists to contribute to a fund "to assist the common cause other than by taking up arms." Lawmakers clearly viewed fines and special taxes as an equivalent to military service.[24]

After the American Revolution, when military defense was no longer a major issue, most state militia laws allowed some form of conscientious objection. Some required payment of a fine or provision of a substitute; a few offered complete exemption. With the end of external threats following the War of 1812, compulsory militia training was terminated in northern states as economically wasteful, undemocratic, and unnecessary.

Preliminary National Policy: 1780s—1930s

Because of the widespread suspicion in America of strong central government and the belief that a large standing army was unduly expensive and potentially tyrannical, the United States did not create a permanently powerful national government until the twentieth century. The first national government, the Continental Congress, relied entirely upon state contributions for revenue and soldiers in the American Revolution. It did not have the power to draft, but, apparently in an effort to reassure Quakers and other pacifists, one of its first measures was the adoption in July 1775 of a statute assuring religious objectors that they would be exempted from performing military duty.[25] After the War of Independence, the new nation virtually disbanded its army, and for the next century it maintained only a small constabulary force in peacetime.

The Constitution of the United States, ratified in 1789, provided for a stronger central government, but still within a federal system in which the states had primary control over their militia. The national government was authorized to establish uniform regulations for the militia and to summon the state forces into national service only for carefully circumscribed purposes. The framers believed that the regular army would be raised, as standing armies were obtained in England and most of Western Europe, through the use of revenue rather than by conscription.[26] Because many Americans feared that a powerful new constitutional government might threaten states' rights and individual liberties, the First Congress in 1790 enacted a series of protective amendments known as the Bill of Rights.

One of the amendments that was seriously considered would have guaranteed the right of freedom of conscience and of conscientious objection to military service. Twelve state constitutions recognized the right of freedom of conscience, and four of the state conventions that ratified the U.S. Constitution had adopted resolutions, or at least strong minority reports, calling for protection of the right of conscientious objection.[27] The primary architect of the Bill of Rights, James Madison of Virginia, guided the proposed constitutional amendments through the House of Representatives in the First Congress. One of his suggested amendments stipulated that military service would not be required of persons with religious scruples against bearing arms. The House added the words "in person" to military service and adopted the amendment by a narrow margin. However, it was defeated in the Senate and thus failed to become part of the Bill of Rights.[28]

No draft occurred in the War of 1812 or the Mexican War, but a nonsectarian peace movement emerged as one of the reform movements of the 1820s and 1830s through new organizations such as the American Peace Society and the New England Non-Resistance Society. Radical nonresistant Christian pacifists, such as William Lloyd Garrison, also a leading abolitionist, were inspired by the ideas of the Enlightenment and the emotions of religious revivalism in the Second Great Awakening. They departed from the quietism of the historic pacifist sects and began to formulate a modern philosophy of activist noncooperation against "evil" institutions such as slavery and war. In 1845, on the eve of the Mexican War, transcendentalist writer Henry David Thoreau went to jail for refusing to pay taxes in support of what he and other abolitionists saw as an immoral conflict to expand slavery. Such secular civil disobedience proved more of a harbinger than the attitudes of most of the historic peace churches of the radical nonsectarian COs and the antidraft movements of the twentieth century.[29]

The Civil War dramatically altered the situation for conscientious objectors as both North and South, fueled by competing nationalisms, mobilized for a long war fought by mass armies. In the second and third years of the war, the Confederate and then the U.S. government adopted national conscription. Both sides also came to recognize the sincerity and stubbornness of the pacifist religious objectors, and representatives of the two central governments soon began to forge accommodations with the historic peace churches. The initial compromise allowed drafted members of those sects to purchase an exemption or to hire a substitute. This arrangement, however, failed to satisfy the consciences of the more radical sectarian pacifists, and it did not include nonsectarian pacifists.[30]

The main core of pacifists in the United States remained the historic peace churches—opposed to both war and slavery and located in both North and South. Differences divided them. Mennonites expressed their willingness to pay war taxes and exemption fees but were split over whether they would hire substitutes. Quakers often declined to contribute directly to the war effort in any way. Religious leaders failed to form a united lobby among the pacifist sects. Nor did they cooperate with the nonsectarian abolitionist peace movement, which on the whole supported a war to end slavery.

In the Confederacy lawmakers in Virginia and North Carolina, long familiar with the sectarian pacifists, responded rather liberally. They excused members of the historic peace churches completely from combat duty and merely required payment or alternative service.[31] The Confederate Congress, however, exhibited less desire to placate these pacifists, who were unfamiliar to most legislators. The first Confederate conscription act made no provision for them, although the COs, like others, were allowed to hire substitutes. In response to the churches' petitions, the Confederate Congress soon adopted the Virginia model of exempting members of the historic peace sects if they paid a five-hundred-dollar commutation fee or provided substitutes.

In the North the sectarian pacifists included more than two hundred thousand Quakers and a smaller community of Mennonites and Brethren. Longtime opponents of slavery and members of the Republican party, these pacifists found responsive Republican officials in state capitals and in Washington. These officials often obtained release of sectarian COs from the army. Many legislators were not so sympathetic, however. As a result, the first federal conscription law of 1863 did not provide specific protection for COs, although for political and industrial reasons it allowed any draftee to escape personal service by hiring a substitute or paying a three-hundred-dollar commutation fee (the equivalent of a worker's annual wages). As in the South, the Mennonite churches in the North recognized the commutation fee as a legitimate tax, whereas the Quaker meetings generally rejected it as contributing directly to military mobilization and war.

In both North and South, drafted COs were sometimes subjected to severe hardships in attempts to make them bear arms and fight. Some objectors were strung up by their thumbs, tied down in a crouch, pricked with bayonets, threatened with execution, or prodded into battle with muskets tied to their backs. One Southern objector was hanged, and another died of debilitation from exposure. Antipacifist sentiment ran high in many areas; in the Shenandoah Valley of Virginia in 1864, the leader of the pacifists there, a Dunker elder named John Kline, was murdered. Although such severe punishment was exceptional, harassment and brief imprisonment were quite common.[32]

These sufferings tended to reinforce the antiwar commitment of the pacifist sects and the sympathy of key governmental officials, including President Abraham

Lincoln and his Secretary of War, Edwin Stanton, as well as Confederate Assistant Secretary of War John A. Campbell. These three officials released almost all religious COs brought to their attention.[33] In 1864 when the U.S. Congress repealed the commutation clause, Stanton helped convince the lawmakers to give objectors from the pacifist sects the option of working in military hospitals, helping the army care for freed slaves, or paying three hundred dollars into a fund designated exclusively for the care of sick and wounded soldiers. When some refused even these options, Stanton acquiesced and ordered the parole of all drafted sectarian absolutists who conscientiously refused either to pay or to serve the army in any way.

Despite the pressure to raise and maintain mass armies suffering enormous casualties and the popular demand for equal sharing of the burden of service, key civilian administrators on both sides had concluded that they could safely release drafted members of the historic pacifist sects. Complete legislative exemption may have been prohibited because of the lawmakers' fears of popular opposition and the danger of abuse, but partial exemption and an executive policy of individual clemency achieved generally acceptable results. The Quakers, Mennonites, and Brethren represented only small and often clannish segments of society, and civilian leaders concluded that these peaceful, middle-class, generally obedient, and economically productive people posed no real threat to the prosecution of the war. Some military officers concurred. Confederate general Thomas J. ("Stonewall") Jackson stated explicitly that the pacifist farmers indirectly aided the war effort by maintaining agricultural production, and that these objectors were more valuable to the government as working farmers than as noncooperators in the army or as inmates in prison.[34]

Steadfast in their commitment to the values of their religious communities, most of the sectarian nonresistants apparently suffered little of the inner loneliness and self-doubt that, in later wars, would plague nonsectarian objectors who found themselves pitted against the state and the views of the majority of Americans. In the mid-nineteenth century, the members of these predominantly rural sects received spiritual, psychological, and physical sustenance from their families and from their tightly knit religious communities, rather than from the national society. In their hour of need, their faith and their sects provided support for their action and helped them define their obligations to God and to the state. None of these sectarian objectors sought to develop his opposition to military service and violence into effective political action to end either the war or the draft, or even to establish a general nonsectarian exemption for conscientious objectors. As sectarian COs attested, they acted not to obstruct government but to heed their religious beliefs, and the U.S. and Confederate authorities responded accordingly.

The real potential threat to governmental war policies in the Civil War and other American conflicts came not from these small sects but from large numbers of nonpacifist Americans who opposed the government's war aims and mobilization policies. The threatening dissenters were the Loyalists in the American Revolution, New England Federalists in the War of 1812, antiwar Northern Whigs in the Mexican War, and in the Civil War, "Copperhead" Democrats in the North and Unionist Democrats in the South. America's first national draft law expired at the end of the Civil War. However, the question of whether a CO exemption might offer an escape for those who simply opposed the government's war aims haunted President Woodrow Wilson fifty years later when he led the United States into World War I.

The Wilson administration recognized that the Civil War experience had not provided the national government with an adequate formula for effective conscription or for dealing with the issue raised by conscientious objectors.[35] The earlier draft had been regarded by many as inequitable and had led to widespread evasion and major draft riots. In 1917 America was again divided politically over the decision about war and conscription. Isolationist, ethnic, or ideological considerations led probably half of the American people to oppose the United States' entry into the European war. Among these opponents were predominantly rural isolationists; ethnic Irish, Germans, Scandinavians, and many anti-tsarist Russians who opposed the Allied Powers; as well as socialists who viewed the conflict as a capitalist's war. They were joined by many religious and secular pacifists. In the first dozen years of the twentieth century there emerged a broadly based mainstream movement for international peace, which included new secular peace organizations, such as the Carnegie Endowment for International Peace, as well as substantial elements of mainline religious bodies—Protestant, Catholic, and Jewish. Not all of these groups opposed U.S. entry into World War I in 1917, but the growth and transformation of the peace movement rendered the historic peace churches a minority among America's pacifists.[36]

President Wilson and Secretary of War Newton D. Baker accepted some of the recommendations of the military and a civilian-led "preparedness" movement, particularly that the wartime army should be raised primarily through conscription and that the modern selective draft should prohibit substitutions and commutation fees as a matter of equity. The administration also adopted the formula of a largely decentralized and civilian-operated conscription agency—the Selective Service System.[37]

In regard to conscientious objectors, Wilson and Baker initially took a conservative view, fearing that such an exemption might be exploited by many opponents of the war. The administration began with a provision quite similar to that of the Civil War draft law. Indeed, Baker specifically asked the House Military Affairs Committee to exempt only members of the historic peace churches, not everyone with conscientious beliefs against bearing arms.[38] On the other hand, Baker defended the right of conscientious objection against ultranationalists such as former President Theodore Roosevelt, who wanted such persons to be imprisoned, deported, or at least deprived of the right to vote.[39]

Baker and Brig. Gen. Enoch H. Crowder, the judge advocate general who became the head of Selective Service, originally envisioned complete exemption for sectarian COs. The Congress, however, wanted them to perform noncombatant military service, and the administration concurred. Thus the Selective Draft Act of 1917 declared only that

> nothing in this Act shall be construed to require or compel any person to serve in any of the forces herein provided for who is found to be a member of any well-recognized religious sect or organization at present organized and existing and

whose existing creed or principles forbid its members to participate in war in any form . . . but no person so exempted shall be exempted from service in any capacity that the President shall declare to be noncombatant.[40]

John Nevin Sayre, Wilson's son-in-law and a leader of the Fellowship of Reconciliation (FOR), a group of mainstream Protestant religious pacifists founded in 1915, appealed to the president, while the conscription bill was before Congress, to base CO exemption on individual belief rather than on organizational membership. Wilson rejected the suggestion, however, stating that "it has seemed impossible to make the exceptions apply to individuals because it would open the door to so much that was unconscientious on the part of persons who wished to escape service."[41]

The government's policy during the first year of the war was to restrict CO provision to sectarians and to try to persuade even these young men to accept some kind of military service—combatant or noncombatant. Thus the largely military national headquarters of the Selective Service System did not give much guidance on the subject to the civilian volunteer members of the four thousand local draft boards, who viewed their primary responsibility as filling their draft quotas as rapidly as possible. In 1917–1918, among the sixty-five thousand young men who claimed CO exemption (other legal exemptions and deferments were allowed on mental, physical, occupational, and dependency grounds), the local boards certified fifty-seven thousand as COs. Of the thirty thousand COs who then passed their physical examinations, twenty-one thousand were inducted into the army.[42]

In World War I, as in the Civil War, the military had custody of drafted COs. Baker had ignored pleas to keep COs out of the military by secular pacifists, such as Oswald Garrison Villard, publisher of the *New York Post* and the *Nation* magazine and grandson of William Lloyd Garrison, the famous abolitionist and pacifist. In the fall of 1917, as the first COs arrived at the training camps, the secretary of war directed camp commanders to separate the objectors from the other draftees and to treat them tactfully.

Although reactions in the military varied, almost all professional soldiers saw the COs as posing a problem among the millions of young draftees. Some camp commanders, such as Maj. Gen. J. Franklin Bell at Camp Upton, New York, succeeded in persuading a majority of the COs to relinquish their claims and to serve in regular duty in the army. Conversely, tensions and brutality were fostered by hostile and coercive critics, such as Maj. Gen. Leonard Wood at Camp Funston, Kansas, who considered COs to be "enemies of the Republic, fakers, and active agents of the enemy." Physical coercion led to numerous instances of injustice and severe, sometimes fatal, brutality. COs who would not respond to military orders in such camps were harangued, beaten with fists or rubber hoses, scrubbed down in cold showers with stiff brushes until their skin was raw, kept in guardhouses or military prisons on diets of bread and water. Perhaps as many as seventeen COs died as a result of such maltreatment.[43]

In all, 80 percent of the twenty-one thousand inducted certified COs decided in the training camps to abandon their objections and to serve as soldiers in the army. One of these, Alvin York from Tennessee, later became famous as "Sergeant

York,'' the American "doughboy" who in a single day killed twenty-five German soldiers and captured 132 others. Nevertheless, four thousand drafted objectors continued to assert their scruples against war and the military. Three quarters of these belonged to the historic pacifist sects, by now all largely middle-class: the increasingly urban and suburban Quakers, the predominantly rural Brethren and Mennonites, and the agrarian German-speaking Russian Mennonites, who had immigrated to America in the 1870s and 1880s. The training camps, however, also contained a few young men from two comparatively new millenarian religious bodies, the Seventh-Day Adventists and the Russellites, both drawn primarily from alienated lower socioeconomic groups.[44] The latter, subsequently known as Jehovah's Witnesses, were openly contemptuous of existing institutions (including the military and the state), refused to fight for them, and unsuccessfully demanded ministerial exemption on the grounds that all members were ministers. The number of uncompromising Jehovah's Witnesses later grew significantly; in World War II, they would pose a major problem for the government's accommodationist CO program.

An additional 15 percent of the conscientious objectors in World War I were religious COs from nonpacifist churches. Mostly young, well-educated, middle-class liberals, they were committed to domestic and international reform and to a concept of love and compassion for humankind. Among them were social gospel ministers such as Evan Thomas, and social workers such as Roger Baldwin. The remaining 10 percent of the COs were nonreligious "political objectors," who included socialists, syndicalists, and anarchists, as well as some young men of anti-Allied ethnic descent who challenged the war aims of the Allies and the United States.[45]

The Wilson administration came under cross-pressures in regard to the COs—on one hand from pacifists, liberals, and such organizations as the newly formed National Civil Liberties Bureau (predecessor of the American Civil Liberties Union), who urged greater leniency; on the other from ultranationalists such as Theodore Roosevelt, who demanded harsher treatment. Reassured by the early signs of success in limiting the number of COs, the administration liberalized policy somewhat in December 1917 by recognizing all COs who opposed war in general. Nevertheless, COs were still required to perform noncombatant service, and in the spring of 1918, the administration finally designated such service as duty in the medical and other noncombat branches of the army. Only thirteen hundred of the four thousand COs ultimately agreed to serve in these army units.

To determine the sincerity of the "absolutists," who refused any military order, and to recommend disposition of their cases, Secretary Baker appointed a board of inquiry. Ultimately the board found 95 percent of the twenty-three hundred absolutists to be "sincere." After obtaining congressional authorization, Baker furloughed fifteen hundred of these men in late summer 1918 to help harvest crops in areas with acute labor shortage. In effect, the COs were assigned to alternative service, although technically they were still in the army. Some 940 COs remained segregated in training camps; but 450 absolutists, including a number of socialists, were court-martialed. They received harsh sentences that averaged over ten years each, although most served fewer than five years in military prison.[46]

The end of the war and the draft led to increased publicity in the press about the suffering of COs in the army training camps and in prison. In one particularly egregious case, the bodies of two Mennonite brothers, who died of pneumonia in federal prison, were sent home clad in the military uniforms that they had steadfastly refused to wear while alive.[47] Wartime repression of COs, as well as of other critics and dissenters, led in the postwar era to a predominant view that authorities had gone far beyond necessity and had endangered American freedoms. The World War I experience made civil liberties a national issue and led to the creation of a major watchdog organization, the American Civil Liberties Union (ACLU).[48]

That experience also convinced groups sympathetic to conscientious objectors that there was no escape from mass mobilization in modern, total war, and that they needed to work together to prevent a recurrence of the repression and suffering among COs in World War I. In the 1920s and 1930s the sectarian pacifist faiths began to cooperate with each other and to look for allies among secular and other religious groups concerned with civil liberties and peace. They found such allies in the Protestant-based Fellowship of Reconciliation (FOR)* and elements in major religious denominations as well as secular organizations, including the American Civil Liberties Union, the Women's International League for Peace and Freedom (WILPF), established in 1919, and the War Resisters League (WRL), the American branch of the completely secular and social-activist War Resisters International, established in 1923.

Harlan Fiske Stone, dean of Columbia Law School, a member of Secretary Baker's Board of Inquiry, and later chief justice of the U.S. Supreme Court, spoke in 1919 for what would become the liberal consensus when he defended wartime exemption of conscientious objectors. According to the traditional common-law view, good motives did not afford a legal excuse for violating the law. This view, said Stone, offered little guidance for policy towards conscientious objectors. Instead, he stated,

> Their evident sincerity and willingness to suffer to the end rather than yield up their cherished illusion make impossible the wholesale condemnation of the conscientious objector as a coward and a slacker. . . . [B]oth morals and sound policy require that the state should not violate the conscience of the individual. All our history gives confirmation to the view that liberty of conscience has a moral and social value which makes it worthy of preservation at the hands of the state.[49]

A Settled National Policy: 1940—1970

The harsh and fumbling experience with COs during World War I contributed directly to a more liberal and humane governmental policy toward conscientious objectors in World War II. Selective Service, which aside from the COs had been largely viewed on successful in World War I, was reestablished in World War II and also functioned during most of the Cold War. In 1940 in the wake of the rapid

---

*Although the Fellowship of Reconciliation became officially non-sectarian in 1930, it remained substantially Protestant and definitely religious.

German conquest of most of Western Europe, isolationists and interventionists debated proposals for America's first prewar national conscription law. Peace organizations, civil libertarians, most religious bodies, and many liberals and conservatives argued in favor of a broader definition of conscientious objection and for authorizing alternative civilian public service for COs. A public opinion survey in 1940 indicated that half the population favored noncombatant service or exemption from military service for COs in case of war.[50]

The CO provision of the Selective Training and Service Act of 1940 has been hailed by some as a "historic compromise" between the state and the peace churches on behalf of conscientious objectors.[51] In this provision, the national government finally reached the position taken much earlier by many American colonial and state governments in officially allowing COs to provide "equivalent" alternative service instead of serving in the military. (In earlier times, however, such an equivalent also could have been the payment of a fine, or the provision of a substitute.)

The 1940 conscription bill, which initially authorized the U.S. government to draft 1.2 million young men for twelve months of military training, was written and lobbied through Congress by civilian interventionists, including many of the former leaders of the World War I "preparedness" movement for compulsory military training and service. In 1940 these civilians and the army's mobilization planners had sought a CO provision exactly like that of 1917, one which recognized COs only from traditional pacifist sects, drafted them into the army, and exempted them only from combat duty. Pacifist, religious, and civil liberties organizations were well prepared this time, however; besides, the country was not officially at war in 1940, as it had been in 1917. The CO support groups coordinated their efforts, as one historian has put it, "in a greater determination to prepare in pacifism a refuge from the floodtide for violence" that was to come.[52]

Recalling the repressive American experience of 1917–1918 and citing as a model the recent British Conscription Act of 1939 that recognized all sincere COs, including selective objectors to particular wars, the American pacifist, civil libertarian, and religious groups that made up a CO lobby in 1940 also sought to protect all conscientious objectors. They wanted the law to cover sincere objectors in mainstream religious, secular COs, and even absolutists. Particularly influential with the Congress were resolutions from nonpacifist mainstream religious bodies supporting pacifist individuals from their denominations—Baptists, Congregationalists, Lutherans, Methodists, Presbyterians, and Unitarians. In the summer of 1940 the Rev. John M. Swomley, Jr., of the National Council of Methodist Youth told a congressional committee that the Methodist Church did not forbid its members to participate in war; "yet by overwhelming conviction its people desire that the right of conscience of those who are conscientious objectors shall be respected."[53]

The CO lobby distrusted both the Selective Service System and the military, and it sought to remove the fate of COs from both organizations. Pacifists hoped that the Justice Department would be made responsible for investigating CO claims and assigning objectors to civilian alternative service, but that agency demurred. The CO groups also failed to obtain formal exemption for nonreligious absolutists, on the grounds that, as an army official said, the exemption might shelter communists and "fifth columnists." In response to prodding the army's draft experts agreed to recognize all sincere religious objectors because such a concession would significantly reduce religious opposition to the conscription bill. Furthermore, Lewis B. Hershey, a career army officer who would head the Selective Service System from 1941 to 1970, assured concerned lobbyists of the peace and religious organizations that in writing the regulations to enforce the conscription act, draft authorities would make every effort to protect absolutist conscientious objectors, even nonreligious ones. In addition, Hershey reportedly confided that if he were put in charge of the draft system, no conscientious objector would ever go to jail.[54]

In a sharply divided vote, the draft bill was passed by Congress during the presidential election campaign and became law in September 1940. The final phrasing of the CO provision exempted from combat training and service in the armed forces any draftee "who, by reason of religious training and belief, is conscientiously opposed to participation in war in any form." It also provided that a certified objector could be assigned either to noncombatant service or, if conscientiously opposed even to that, to "work of national importance under civilian direction" in lieu of induction.[55]

Recognition of CO status for all religious objectors and provision of civilian alternative service, which would keep many objectors out of the military, were major victories for the CO lobby. Although the law did not make recognized conscientious objection entirely a personal matter, it eliminated the requirement of membership in a historic peace church. Thus it opened the way for individual pacifists whose belief in nonviolence stemmed, for example, from Protestantism, Catholicism, or Judaism.[56] In addition, as the leading study of the adoption of 1940 draft act concludes, "the efforts of dedicated pacifists to expand CO protection made for a more equitable bill and may actually have facilitated the enactment of selective service in the end."[57]

After the United States entered World War II in December 1941, the Selective Service Act enabled the government to draft ten million men, who, together with five million volunteers, gave the United States the largest armed force in its history. Fifty thousand draftees were classified as COs. One study estimated that as many as 93 percent of these claimed a religious affiliation.[58] Most of these served as noncombatants in the military, primarily in the medical corps. The most famous and controversial of these pacifist "medics" was film star Lew Ayres, who said his belief in Christian non-resistance had been influenced by his roles as a soldier in the anti-war film *All Quiet on the Western Front* and as a physician in the motion picture *Doctor Kildaire*.[59] Some twelve thousand of the noncombatants were Seventh-Day Adventists.[60] Another twelve thousand COs refused to aid the military in any way, but agreed to work without pay on such nonmilitary projects as soil erosion control, reforestation, and agricultural experimentation in one of the seventy Civilian Public Service (CPS) camps.[61]

The CPS camps were operated for the Selective Service System by the historic peace churches, which formed a coordinating body known as the National Service Board for Religious Objectors (now NISBCO, the National Interreligious Service Board for Conscientious Objectors). The churches were placed in this unusual position as a private instrument for a quasi-military public body because of their justifiable fear that President Franklin D. Roosevelt was considering placing the camps under the control of military officers.[62] Some two thousand COs worked in mental hospitals; and another five hundred volunteered to be human guinea pigs in medical experiments on malaria, hookworm, typhus, and infectious hepatitis. More than two thirds of the COs in the CPS camps were members of the historic peace sects.[63]

Five thousand objectors went to federal prison during World War II. They included some secular objectors excluded from exemption because their claims rested on nonreligious grounds.[64] They also included absolutists—secular or religious—who refused to register or cooperate with the government in anyway. The majority of nonpacifist absolutists came from alienated, lower socioeconomic, mainly urban religious groups. A small number, nearly two hundred, were Black Muslims, critical of America's racial and foreign policies, who declared that the war was not a "holy war" as defined by the Koran.[65] The great majority of imprisoned objectors, more than three thousand (thus 60 percent), were Jehovah's Witnesses. Members of this millenarian, nonpacifist sect were contemptuous of worldly government and the established churches, and refused to seek CO status. (They were willing to fight for God at the prophesied battle of Armageddon but not for worldly governments.) Nor would they perform alternative service which would interfere with their preaching. They demanded complete exemption as ministers, but the government recognized as ministers only those clergy who had no gainful secular employment. Most draft objectors who were Jehovah's Witnesses also refused alternative service. Consequently, they were imprisoned, generally for terms of up to five years.[66]

Also in prison were a number of radical activist COs. Among these were A. J. Muste of the Followship of Reconciliation, whose influential pamphlet, *Of Holy Disobedience,* advocated Gandhian civil disobedience protest tactics against injustice in the camps and in society. Many of these political activist COs later played important roles in direct action civil rights and peace organizations such as the Congress of Racial Equality (CORE) and the Committee for Non-Violent Action (CNVA).[67]

The Selective Service model, as developed in 1940, accepted all religious pacifists, and it formally authorized civilian alternative service. With some modifications, this model remained, the basis for the relationship between COs and the state throughout World War II and most of the Cold War. The major change was the termination in 1946 of the Civilian Public Service camps, which had proved unacceptable to many COs. Thereafter conscientious objectors were allowed to perform individual rather than collective alternative service.

Between 1945 and 1952, the army, the Truman administration, and some foreign policy groups sought repeatedly to go beyond a selective draft and to develop a program of short-term universal military training (UMT) and long-term reserve service. Their proposals included provisions for COs; persons with sincere conscientious objections would undergo some kind of nonmilitary training. UMT, however, was too radical a departure from American tradition to be adopted. Instead Congress extended the selective draft through 1947. Then, after a fifteen-month hiatus, selective conscription was re-enacted in June 1948, during a period of heightened tensions between the United States and the Soviet Union over the events leading to the Berlin blockade.[68]

The Selective Service Act of 1948 became the basic draft law of the Cold War era. Indeed, it remains on the statute books today, albeit with a different name and currently without the authority for induction and without appropriations for an extensive Selective Service System. In regard to conscientious objectors, the 1948 law authorized exemption from combatant service—and provided alternative civilian service—but only for religious COs opposed to participation in war in any form. It used the same wording as the 1940 law—"by reason of religious training and belief"—but specifically emphasized that this meant "an individual's belief in a relation to a Supreme Being involving duties superior to those arising from any human relation." The law stated specifically that this position did "not include essentially political, sociological, or philosophical views or a merely personal moral code."[69] This law was intended to end the confusion created by two different and contradictory federal appellate court decisions regarding World War II objectors: One decision had allowed a purely ethical objection by an atheist; the other had insisted that a CO's pacifism include a belief in God. The 1948 congressional definition, reached in the intensity of the early Cold War, sought to remove the possibility of liberalizing the CO exemption beyond explicitly religious grounds.[70]

For COs' alternative public service duty, the 1948 draft law, as amended in 1951, provided that individual objectors might be assigned to perform "such civilian work contributing to the maintenance of the national health, safety, or interests as the local [draft] board may deem appropriate."[71] Accordingly, COs found or were assigned work in public employment or nonprofit organizations benefiting society. Most of the thirty thousand COs performing alternative service between 1951 and 1965 (most of whom were members of the historic peace churches) worked in hospitals or mental institutions. The typical CO performed two years of alternative service, the same length of time as a draftee's tour of duty in the military. COs' entry-level wages also were comparable to the compensation received by draftees. Civilian alternative service worked rather smoothly, with no major complaints from the COs or the general public, and did not become a major public issue in the Cold War.[72]

During the Korean War (1950–1953), the draft obtained 1.5 million men (an additional 1.3 million persons volunteered, most for the Navy and the Air Force). Mounting discontent with that war led to an increase in conscientious objectors. The percentage of inductees exempted as COs grew to nearly 1.5 percent, compared to .15 percent in each of the world wars.[73]

The Vietnam War in the 1960s and 1970s posed the most dramatic confrontation in American history between the government's demands for military service and objection of individual citizens to war. After President Lyndon B. Johnson committed American combat units in 1965, draft calls soared from one hundred thousand in 1964 to four hundred thousand in 1966. Conscription enabled the United States to increase its forces in Vietnam from twenty-three thousand military advisers in 1964 to 543,000 combat and support troops by 1968. Casualty rates rose accordingly. By 1973, fifty-eight thousand Americans had died in Vietnam.

Although draftees were only a small minority (16 percent) of the U.S. armed forces, they made up the bulk of the infantry riflemen in Vietnam (88 percent in 1969) and accounted for more than half of the U.S. Army's battle deaths there. Because of student and other deferments, such as the National Guard (which remained at home), the draft and the casualties were borne disproportionately by working-class youths, black and white. Black Americans, 11 percent of the U.S. population, accounted for 25 percent of U.S. Army battle deaths in Vietnam in 1965 and 1966 (reduced to 14 percent for the entire war).[74]

Opposition mounted along with the rising draft calls and casualty rates. Supported by an antiwar coalition of students as well as by pacifist, religious, civil rights, and feminist organizations and many other liberal and radical groups, a draft resistance movement grew in strength, particularly at the local level. It encouraged COs and resisters, and generated demonstrations, draft card burnings, and sit-ins at draft and induction centers. In a few instances opponents turned to the so-called "ultra-resistance," specifically, break-ins and destruction of records at dozens of local draft boards.[75]

In the Vietnam War, the comparatively small group of mainly religious objectors of previous wars was replaced by massive numbers of secular or religious young men applying for CO status or simply refusing to register or cooperate with the draft. The new COs tended to come from better-educated socioeconomic groups and include young men with nonreligious as well as religious views about war. They were aided by a broad range of CO counselors, from local lawyers and clergy to special agencies established by the historic peace faiths. The pacifist sects now were joined by mainline religions—Protestant, Jewish, and Catholic, the last particularly after the search for peace received emphasis from Pope John XXIII and the Second Vatican Council. Also assisting were specific CO support organizations such as the National Interreligious Service Board for Conscientious Objectors (NI-SBCO), created in 1940, and the Central Committee for Conscientious Objectors (CCCO), established in 1948.[76]

An even greater challenge to Selective Service was the emergence of a massive campaign of public civil disobedience. Often this was locally based. However, it also drew upon national organizations such as the Committee for Non-Violent Action, the War Resisters League, the Student Peace Union, and the Students for a Democratic Society (SDS).

For the first time, large numbers of African Americans actively resisted the draft. In the past most black leaders had encouraged African Americans to serve in the military as a step toward obtaining full rights of citizenship. But beginning in 1965 the Student Nonviolent Coordinating Committee (SNCC) denounced both the war and the draft as racist. Two years later, the Rev. Martin Luther King, Jr., denounced the war as immoral, and urged young people to become conscientious objectors. His civil rights organization, the Southern Christian Leadership Council, endorsed the plea; the more radical black organizations, such as the Congress of Racial Equality (CORE), the Black Muslims, and the Black Panther Party, called for active resistance to the draft. Muhammad Ali, an American Black Muslim and the heavyweight boxing champion of the world, filed as a conscientious objector. The government, however, rejected his claim, and a federal court sentenced him to five years in prison, a conviction later overturned by the Supreme Court.[77]

Faced with well over 100,000 apparent draft offenders, the federal government between 1965 and 1975 indicted 22,500 persons for draft law violations (including draft card burning, which Congress declared to be a crime in 1965). Eight thousand of these individuals were convicted and four thousand imprisoned. The most common form of draft protest was evasion: of the twenty-seven million young men who reached draft age between 1964 and 1973, sixteen million (60 percent) did not serve in the military. Of those who did not serve, fifteen million received legal exemptions or deferments, and perhaps 570,000 evaded the draft illegally. Among the illegal draft evaders, 360,000 were never caught, another 198,000 had their cases dismissed, 9,000 were convicted, and 4,000 were sent to prison. In addition, an estimated 30,000 to 50,000 fled into exile, most to Canada, Britain, and Sweden.[78]

Because the draft was so controversial, Congress came under increased pressure either to reform it or to eliminate it. The longtime director of Selective Service, Gen. Lewis Hershey, supported by many conservatives, blocked any reforms until 1969. By the time of the 1968 presidential election, the Vietnam war and the draft had become major political issues. It was clear that significant changes would have to be made in the means of raising America's armies, as well as in the state's relationship to conscientious objectors.

The legislative and administrative mechanisms were blocked, but the federal judiciary, prodded by sweeping new currents of opinion, greatly liberalized the rights of draft law protesters and violators and the legal definition of conscientious objection. This judicial intervention represented an important departure from the federal courts' previous relationship with the draft, which had included upholding the constitutionality of national conscription in 1918 and subsequently refusing to interfere in the operation of the draft or the decisions of the Selective Service boards, except to ensure due process. Before the mid–1960s, the federal judiciary had generally been quite willing to sentence draft violators to stiff prison terms. But in the late 1960s juries became increasingly unwilling to convict, and judges imposed reduced sentences on those convicted. The federal courts expanded the due process rights of draft registrants in the systems even against government attempts to terminate the deferments of antiwar demonstrators.[79]

Between 1965 and 1972, some 22,500 young men—absolutists and other resisters—were indicted for draft law violations, and 8,800 were convicted (4,000 were imprisoned). For the first time in the country's history, the overwhelming majority (about 72 percent) of those convicted were either nonreligious objectors or members of a nonpacifist church. In addition, twenty-one percent were Jehovah's Witnesses. Only 7 percent came from the historic peace faiths.[80]

Greater attention to civil liberties, due process, and equality characterized the direction of the Supreme Court of the United States in the post–World War II period. This movement intensified during the civil rights revolution of the 1950s and 1960s. Draft registrants, antiwar protesters, and conscientious objectors also benefited from this more liberal interpretation of due process, civil rights, and the protection of minorities and dissenters. In line with this development and with significant elements of public opinion that opposed the war and supported recent developments in liberal theology and secular humanism, the Supreme Court expanded the criteria for conscientious objector status from religious to nonreligious

TABLE 2.1   Exemption Rates for Conscientious Objectors in the United
States in the Two World Wars and during the Vietnam War

War/Year	Ratio of CO exemptions to actual inductions (per 100 inductions)
World War I	.14
World War II	.15
1966	6.10
1967	8.10
1968	8.50
1969	13.45
1970	25.55
1971	42.62
1972	130.72
1973	73.30

Sources: Ratios compiled by Stephen M. Kohn, Jailed for Peace: The History of American Draft Law Violators, 1658–
1985 (New York: Praeger, 1986), 93. Copyright © 1986, 1987 by Stephen M. Kohn, Praeger Publishers, an imprint
of Greenwood Publishing Group, Inc., Westport, CT. Reprinted with permission. See also U.S. Selective Service
System, Annual Report of the Director of Selective Service, periodically between 1946 and 1967; and Semi-Annual
Report of the Director of Selective Service, since 1968. Especially valuable are the tabular compilations from 1952 to
1973 in Semi-Annual Report of the Director of Selective Service for the period January 1 to June 30, 1973 (Washington,
D.C.: Government Printing Office, 1973), 55, Appendixes 12 and 13; and U.S. Selective Service System, Special
Monograph No. 11; Conscientious Objection (Washington, D.C.: Government Printing Office, 1950), 53, 314–15.

moral or ethical objection. In two major decisions, the Court essentially rewrote
part of the draft law to accept completely secular COs.

In the first case, United States v. Seeger (1965), the Court, in direct opposition
to the wording of the 1948 draft law, held that a recognized CO no longer had to
show belief in a god or a supreme being, but instead only had to demonstrate
"sincere or meaningful belief" that occupied a place "parallel to that filled by
God."[81] In the second case, Welsh v. United States (1970), the Court went even
farther and declared that even strongly held atheistic beliefs against war could meet
the test of CO status as long as they were "ethical and moral beliefs."[82] Although
the Court continued to reject selective objection, thus requiring opposition to all
war, it had declared that despite the statute's language, the principles of conscientious objection could be based entirely on secular grounds.[83]

As the courts expanded the definition of conscientious objection, and as many
local boards became increasingly responsive to CO claims, the number of objectors
grew enormously during the Vietnam War. Between 1965 and 1970, more than
170,000 registrants obtained classification as conscientious objectors. Because the
Selective Service System was overwhelmed by the growing numbers, perhaps only
half of these COs actually performed alternative service. In relation to actual inductions, CO exemptions soared from 8 percent in 1967 to 43 percent in 1971, and
to an incredible 131 percent in 1972 (see Table 2.1). In the year before the draft
ended in 1973, more registrants were classified as COs than were inducted into the
army. Such a phenomenon was unprecedented in American history.[84]

In addition, thousands of members of the armed services applied for noncombatant status or discharge as conscientious objectors during the Vietnam War.
Department of Defense figures show that between seventeen thousand and eighteen
thousand such applications were processed by the various branches of the military

between 1965 and 1973. In-service applications for conscientious objection for all four services increased from 829 in 1967 to 4,381 in the peak year of 1971, before declining to 2,056 in 1973.[85] Conscientious objection within the military appeared to be closely related both to patterns of military involvement and to political and other activities in the military and in civilian society. Most notable was opposition to the war by "GI-movement" activists, many Vietnam veterans, and the antiwar movement as a whole.[86]

The Postmodern Stage: Early 1970s to the Present

Public divisions led to the abandonment in 1973 of the draft, which had existed almost continuously in the United States since 1940. In the face of criticism, resistance, and direct assault, the Selective Service System buckled; reforms came too late and failed to defuse the criticism and protest. By 1973 a new policy had been adopted—an All-Volunteer Armed Force (AVF).[87] Although the amended 1948 draft law remained on the statute books, Congress ended the president's induction authority.[88] The lawmakers provided only for a standby draft, and they reduced the Selective Service System merely to a headquarters organization that would register and classify young men by mail. In 1975 President Gerald R. Ford terminated the remaining requirement of compulsory draft registration.

Compulsory draft registration was resumed by President Jimmy Carter in 1980 in reaction to the Soviet invasion of Afghanistan. President Ronald Reagan extended it in 1982 and prosecuted a few of the absolutist objectors who publicly refused to register (an estimated five hundred thousand young men failed to register between 1982 and 1984).[89] Several of those convicted, however, were sentenced by federal courts to perform community service work instead of being sent to prison. There was not much public support for imprisoning young men who refused to register for the draft when conscription itself did not exist and the nation was not at war. President George Bush's administration did not continue the policy of public prosecutions during peacetime. However, in the mid to late 1980s the federal government (through the efforts of Rep. Gerald Solomon [R., N.Y.] and Sen. Strom Thurmond [R., S.C.]) and thirteen states have penalized nonregistrants by denying them student financial assistance from public funds and, in four states, prohibiting them from enrolling in state colleges or universities.[90]

Within the armed services, even without conscription and without a war, there were each year in the 1980s small numbers of uniformed personnel who obtained discharges as conscientious objectors from the All-Volunteer Armed Force (AVF). With an AVF that averaged 2.1 million persons, the application and discharge of uniformed COs—between ninety and 240 annually from the four services between 1985 and 1990—did not become a major internal problem or even a public issue.[91] The Persian Gulf War, however, made the situation of COs in the military a significant issue once again in the United States.

The Bush administration deployed more than five hundred thousand servicemen and servicewomen in the Persian Gulf in 1990–1991. The U.S. millitary deployment, which began after the Iraqi invasion of Kuwait in August 1990, culminated in "Operation Desert Storm," an air and ground war in January and February 1991. This conflict, the largest U.S. military action since the Vietnam War, again raised dramatically the issues of conscientious objection and conscription. In anticipation of a long and bloody ground conflict, the possibility of resuming the draft was discussed, particularly because of the equity issue raised by the racial and socio-economic composition of the All-Volunteer Armed Force.[92] More immediately, probably between fifteen hundred and two thousand persons in reserve and regular military units had applied for discharge as COs.[93] Churches in Atlanta, Boston, New York City, San Francisco, and Seattle as well as city councils in San Francisco, Oakland and Berkeley formally offered sanctuary for uniformed COs seeking to avoid deployment to the Persian Gulf.[94]

After initially refusing to process any more CO applications until the American troops arrived in the Gulf, the U.S. military divided in its response to the in-service COs. The U.S. Army, although incarcerating a few COs and coercing many more, eventually worked out an accommodation at the local unit level, reassigning the COs or discharging them from the service in various manners. In contrast, the Marine Corps sought to maintain its image as a disciplined and fighting unit by intolerantly court-martialing and imprisoning nearly fifty Marine COs in the glare of considerable publicity.[95]

Responding to this development, Rep. Ronald V. Dellums, a liberal Democrat from Berkeley, California, and a member of the House Committee on Armed Services, introduced on May 5, 1992, a measure prepared in cooperation with CO organizations and various religious denominations to reform the procedures for dealing with COs in the military. He was joined initially by seventeen cosponsors, a number that by July reached twenty-five and included such influential legislators as Patricia Schroeder of Colorado and Leon Panetta of California. In introducing the "Military Conscientious Objector Act of 1992" Dellums declared that the right to refuse military service as a result of profound conviction was considered in America "a legitimate exercise of the right to freedom of thought, conscience, and religion." He also cited international recognition of the right of conscientious objection by the United Nations Universal Declaration of Human Rights and the International Covenant on Civil and Political Rights, and he noted that in 1991, for the first time since the 1960s, Amnesty International had declared that there were "prisoners of conscience" in the United States—specifically three dozen military COs incarcerated improperly during the Persian Gulf War.[96]

In addition to uniformed personnel who applied for CO status during the Persian Gulf deployment and conflict, perhaps as many as twenty-six thousand reservists and young draft registrants queried churches and CO organizations during the winter of 1990–1991 about obtaining conscientious objector status. One organization, the East Coast Central Committee for Conscientious Objectors (CCCO), received 8,662 requests in January 1991 for its "CO card," a form for listing oneself as a conscientious objector. Even the National Interreligious Service Board for Conscientious Objectors (NISBCO), whose estimates tend to be more conservative, predicted that among the draft-eligible young men who were twenty years old, probably 10 to 20 percent (160,000 to 320,000) would have sought CO status if a draft had been reinstituted during the Persian Gulf War.[97] These events demonstrated that war, conscription, and conscientious objection had not ended for Americans with the Vietnam War.

Conclusion

Conscientious objection, like conscription, evolved in stages in America. The formative stage occurred in the late seventeenth and the eighteenth centuries, when the religious pacifists arrived and when the colonies, and later the newly independent states, established their policies towards the objectors. Subsequently, in the preliminary national stage, which lasted from the 1780s to World War I, the federal government sought sporadically to define an appropriate CO policy to accompany periodic conscription. Such a policy was not determined until the era of World War II; that third stage, of established national policy, lasted from 1940 until the end of the 1960s. Since the 1970s the United States has entered a fourth stage, groping once again for an appropriate national policy concerning conscientious objectors, particularly in the 1990s toward COs in the All-Volunteer Armed Force.

In part these stages have been characterized by altered definitions of conscientious objection as well as by changes in the nature of the political culture and the branch of government that has dealt with the COs. From restriction to members of the historic peace sects—Quakers, Mennonites, and Brethren—during the period extending from colonial times to the Civil War, the definition expanded in the first half of the twentieth century to include all sincere religious objectors. This expansion was accomplished informally by administrative action in World War I and formally by congressional statute in World War II and the Cold War. Since the late 1960s the federal judiciary has enlarged the legal definition to include secular objectors as well. Neither the courts nor the other branches of the federal government, however, has yet recognized the right of COs to object merely to a particular war, or to refuse to register, or to decline to perform alternative civilian service when assigned by the Selective Service System.

Similarly, the state's requirement imposed upon COs has evolved gradually. Over time this "equivalency" has changed from arrangements for payment of fines or commutation fees or the provision of a substitute (all of which were disallowed as undemocratic in the early twentieth century) to the provision of noncombatant service in the military or alternative service in civilian society. Alternative service was first organized under army supervision in World War I, then under the direction of the peace churches in World War II, and finally, beginning in 1951, by individual employers involved in approved public service work.

These changes in the relationship between COs and the American state occurred for a number of reasons. Most directly they were stimulated by events, beginning with the creation of colonies such as Rhode Island and Pennsylvania as havens for dissenters seeking religious freedom and peace. During the Civil War, when the U.S. government first adopted national conscription, the Quakers, Mennonites and other COs were primarily antislavery Republicans; not surprisingly the Lincoln administration responded favorably to them. The two World Wars and the Vietnam War proved the impetus for reevaluating the nation's position towards conscription and conscientious objection. The Persian Gulf War and the end of the Cold War in the 1990s may have provided another such opportunity.

It is also within the context of American political and religious culture that the evolution of conscientious objection in the United States and the state's policy toward it must be understood. That culture evolved to include religious toleration, individualism, and an acceptance of freedom of conscience. It also included an ingrained suspicion of central government and large standing armless. American federalism encouraged the development of governmental recognition of conscientious objection because the early sectarian pacifists were able to gain strong legislative recognition in a number of colonies and states in which they were influential: Rhode Island, New Jersey, Pennsylvania, Virginia, and North Carolina. They were almost able to obtain national recognition of conscientious objection in the Bill of Rights.

In the twentieth century, the sectarian pacifists gained allies among mainstream churches, among civil libertarians, and from the secular peace movement. The CO lobby won support from liberal—and other libertarian—elements of both major political parties, particularly the Democratic party. In the 1960s and 1970s, during the Vietnam War era, the judiciary included conscientious objectors in its expanded protection of the civil rights of dissenters and minority groups.

In contrast, another aspect of American civic culture has been intense periodic campaigns for allegiance and conformity to national norms. This is partly a result of insecurities in a relatively new country composed of diverse ethnic, racial, religious, and cultural groups. Conscientious objectors, like other dissenters, have suffered accordingly in these phases of patriotic nationalism, particularly in periods of war and cold war.

The role of the COs themselves—and of their resistance to the ultimate power of the state—has been vital to the evolution of the American tradition of conscientious objection. So has the support given by the religious and secular bodies that have encouraged and defended them. Certain traditions have provided a favorable context: first, religious toleration and later, the protection of civil liberties. As a result, the liberal state in the United States, despite much justified skepticism toward it, has recognized a continuing and even an expanding basis for conscientious objection through legislative, executive, or judicial response.[98]

The current status of the right of conscientious objection in the United States, including recognition of secular COs in or out of uniform, goes beyond past practice and is the direct result of divisions at all levels of society during the Vietnam War. It is not at all clear how long the decisions made then for raising America's armies and evaluating its COs will remain the policy in the future. The Persian Gulf deployment and conflict and the end of the Cold War have raised these questions anew. It is undisputed, however, that conscientious objection, to compulsory military service is a long standing and continually evolving part of the American tradition.

3

The Dilemma
of Conscientious Objection
for Afro-Americans

JOHN H. STANFIELD II

Conscientious objection has posed a particular problem for Afro-Americans. The military has offered an area of opportunity for blacks and other members of lower-income groups. In addition, many black Americans have been willing and even eager to serve in the armed forces of the United States in most of the nation's wars in support of their claim to equal rights and opportunities of citizenship. Nevertheless, a lesser-known tradition of opposition to military service and war also exists within the Afro-American community.

The current literature about conscientious objection in America and abroad is quite Eurocentric. Whether these writings are content analyses of pacifist biographies, peace church statements, or government reports, Eurocentric moral, political, and social definitions and policy analyses enjoy an uncritical dominance.[1] In view of the historical and the growing contemporary demographic presence and political-economic importance of American racial minorities and Third World populations in the world system, there is a critical need to examine systematically the attitudes and actions regarding peace and war resistance among nonwhites.

In this essay I explore the importance of ethnic diversity in historical and sociological analyses of conscientious objection. The essay begins with a discussion rooted in the sociology of knowledge, explaining why scholars have virtually ignored the existence of conscientious objection in Afro-American communities. I also attempt to explain sociologically why, when we consider dominant Euro-American definitions of conscientious objection (namely, opposition to war and military service for moral and religious reasons), we find only a few Afro-Americans publicly claiming and being recognized as conscientious objectors. In the next portion of the essay I put forward a theoretical argument about the need to expand Eurocentric definitions of conscientious objection to include multiracial, multicultural concepts of objection to compulsory military service and war.

Institutional Afro-American History

To understand why Afro-American conscientious objection has been ignored by scholars and others, such as persons in the mass media, we must consider the genesis and the functions of Afro-American history as a subfield in American history, because this subfield produces the core of public knowledge about Afro-Americans and their historical institutional and community development.

Afro-American history as an intellectual enterprise can be traced in part through the professional careers and writings of late-nineteenth- to mid-twentieth-century pioneers in Afro-American history, such as George Williams, William E. B. Du Bois, Carter G. Woodson, Charles Wesley, and Anna Johnson, and through a post–World War II generation of historians, including John Hope Franklin, Rayford Logan, John Blassingame, August Meier, Louis Harlan, Mary Berry, and Kenneth Stamp. In constructing and transforming the normative paradigm of Afro-American history, scholars have maintained three intellectual traditions that have influenced the presentation of conscientious objection as a historical and social occurrence in Afro-American communities.

First, Afro-American historical writing developed primarily as an intellectual response, particularly by blacks, to the exclusion, marginalization, and distortion of blacks' experiences in American history. One significant consequence of this rationale is the *celebration complex* of much Afro-American historical literature. This complex is an attempt to set the record straight about contributions by blacks to the American past. It is most evident in the efforts to celebrate the many times when Afro-Americans have demonstrated their patriotism and loyalty to America, particularly in the military.[2] This celebration is a response to popular assumptions that blacks have contributed little to the nation's defense and wars.

Celebration of Afro-American war heroes also has been designed to quell public fears about possible Afro-American disloyalty to the nation, especially during wartime. In light of the tendency of the dominant American culture to equate opposition to war, as well as opposition or resistance to military service, with disloyalty to the nation, it is not surprising that students of the Afro-American past, obsessed with the celebration complex, have displayed little interest in studying draft evasion, war resistance, or conscientious objection in Afro-American communities. Furthermore, most of the architects of Afro-American history either have been conservative cultural assimilationists, many of them overly patriotic, or have preferred to keep their dissenting pacifist perspectives out of their scholarship. In either case, "conventional Afro-American history" has been silent about the issue of black conscientious objectors.

A second characteristic of Afro-American history is its stifling fixation on race relations and on race-related contributions of prominent Afro-Americans. As a result, there is a wealth of scholarly information on the racial philosophies of Frederick Douglass, Booker T. Washington, William E. B. Du Bois, Marcus Garvey, George Washington Carver, A. Philip Randolph, Ida Wells-Barnett, Alain Locke, Bayard Rustin, Jean Toomer, and Martin Luther King, Jr. Most people, however, know little, if anything, about other issues that concerned these and other Afro-Americans. Three such neglected issues are war resistance, pacifism, and conscientious objection by black Americans.

A notable case in point is Booker T. Washington, the most powerful Afro-American leader and educator from 1895 until his death in 1915. Washington's industrial education and accommodative philosophies of relations have been written about extensively. Yet to be studied, however, are his pacifist views and how they were related to the Spanish-American War and World War I. Washington's pacifism was known within the large American peace movement in the early twentieth century. In 1913 he was invited to give a keynote address on peace and disarmament before the Fourth Annual Peace Congress in St. Louis.[3] Yet few people know of this today.

Martin Luther King, Jr., is a more recent example. In the celebration of this Afro-American leader in school textbooks and on the commemoration of his birthday as a national holiday, he is remembered for his championing of civil rights for blacks rather than for his staunch opposition to the Vietnam War. Yet opposition to the war became vitally important to him in the two years before his assassination in 1968. In opposing the Johnson administration's conduct of the war, King faced harsh criticism from the national media, which could not understand the intrinsic political and sociological connections between the civil rights and the peace movements (let alone how both movements related to the federal government's "war on poverty" programs). Because King was so early in voicing his anti–Vietnam War sentiments (in 1966), his pacifist remarks were criticized even more hotly. Even King's own organization, the Southern Christian Leadership Conference, was lukewarm about his antiwar stand. The more traditional black organizations were even more critical.

Two other important blacks took a stand in support of conscientious objectors in earlier wars, in part because both had become pacifist Quakers. Jean Toomer, a black writer who became famous in the Harlem Renaissance of the 1920s, later became a Quaker, and in the 1970s wrote impassioned pacifist articles that deserve closer study.[4] Bayard Rustin, a civil rights and labor activist and a close colleague of Martin Luther King, Jr., and of labor militant A. Phillip Randolph, went to prison during World War II as a conscientious objector. In the postwar period, he worked with the War Resisters League as well as with civil rights organizations such as the Congress of Racial Equality (CORE). During the 1960s, Rustin became quite disturbed about the split that developed between the peace movement and the civil rights wing of the labor movement, which argued that blacks' prosperity depended on progressive economic programs and the eradication of poverty.

A third tradition related to Afro-American history's fixation on the racial views and contributions of prominent blacks, is the concentration on indigenous institutions of Afro-American communities, such as religious organizations, fraternal orders, and families, or on white institutions that affect Afro-American communities, such as corporations, public schools, the media, and welfare systems. This conventional focus has distracted attention from the statistically rare, though sociologically relevant, involvement of Afro-Americans in historically white institutions and communities such as peace churches, radical Eurocentric political parties, and American foreign service communities abroad. Because the number of Afro-Americans in such organizations is so small, authorities have ignored them or have discussed their activities only in passing.

The Historical Patriotism of Afro-American Elites

Conscientious objection is sustained as a movement and as an opposition to the warmaking motives of central state elites only when war resisters are integrated into durable social support systems. The more the members of such a system gain entry into central state policy circles, the more the form of conscientious objection that they advocate has the potential to be recognized as legitimate by the central state.

The most significant historical example of such penetration is the American experience with conscientious objection during World War II. The COs who were affiliated with the major peace churches that operated the CO camps for the federal government stood a much better chance of being exempted from military service than men who did not belong to such religious bodies or who offered nonreligious reasons for claiming CO status. Men who could demonstrate lifelong, if not multigenerational, membership in a recognized peace church community had the greatest chance of obtaining recognized CO status.[5]

Eurocentric forms of conscientious objection have never had significant organizational foundations in Afro-American communities. For this reason, even if an enterprising historian of Afro-American experiences took an interest in Eurocentric forms of Afro-Americans' conscientious objection, that historian would find little indigenous support.

This historical lack of significant support can be traced to the promilitary and prowar positions of most national and local black leaders. With the exception of Booker T. Washington and Martin Luther King, Jr., mainstream Afro-American political leaders have viewed military service and wartime as socioeconomic opportunities for Afro-Americans and even as areas for reinforcing their claims to equal rights. Frederick Douglass at the outbreak of the Civil War and William E. B. Du Bois at the U.S. entry into the First World War criticized discrimination against Afro-Americans in and out of uniform, but they both urged blacks to participate in the war effort in the armed forces and at home.[6] During World War II, black leaders in various organizations, from moderate groups such as the Urban League to more radical bodies such as the Socialist Workers Party, criticized the federal government for not doing enough to end discrimination at home, but ignored the moral atrocities involved in warmaking.[7]

Traditional civil rights organizations, black churches and denominations, and black colleges are the institutional foundations of the old-line mainstream Afro-American social and cultural leaders. Few of the leaders of these institutions and few black political leaders have spoken out against American participation in war. They, too, have viewed wartime as an opportunity for Afro-Americans to advance economically and politically. Like scholars of Afro-American history, these leaders consider blacks' participation in war as concrete evidence of Afro-American loyalty to the United States.

Indeed, black leaders have been particularly anxious to demonstrate Afro-American patriotism during wartime. This is the case because white elites and the government historically have feared the possibility that Afro-Americans, as a racially oppressed class, might not support the United States during time of war, and might even be won over by enemy propaganda that focused on the racism and oppression in American society.[8] Thus it is hardly surprising that the staunchest supporters of the government in wartime often have included prominent Afro-American leaders from traditional civil rights organizations and from black churches, media, and colleges. In addition, black colleges, largely unscathed by anti-ROTC and antiwar movements, historically have had a promilitary orientation.

Black leaders criticize warmaking only when Afro-Americans suffer brutal discrimination at the home front or on the battlefield. After government officials have offered assurances that Afro-Americans will be recruited equitably and promoted fairly, and that black civilians will be given equal access to jobs in defense industries, Afro-American leaders have tended to be satisfied. Paradoxically, in every postwar era, the same leaders usually have become disillusioned with the lack of significant socioeconomic progress for blacks. The government seems willing to make only superficial gestures toward formulation and implementation of racial equality policy. The cycle of black leaders' attitudes is apparent in the social history surrounding the American Civil War, the Spanish-American War, the two World Wars, and, to a lesser extent, the Korean War and the Vietnam War.

The persistent promilitary stance of mainstream Afro-American leaders and the convergence of their community-based institutions with promilitary values in the dominant American culture have contributed to Afro-Americans' views about military service and war.[9] Practically, although blacks, like most Americans, deplore war in general and the Vietnam War in particular because it took the lives of a disproportionate number of blacks, they also recognize that the armed forces have become a major employer of Afro-Americans. In addition, since the 1950s the military rather than the civilian sector has taken the lead in fair employment practices and has provided opportunities for black leadership. Gen. Colin L. Powell, chairman of the Joint Chiefs of Staff during the Persian Gulf War of 1991, is the most striking example of such opportunity.[10]

The ambivalence of many Afro-Americans toward military service and war was illustrated in the tensions that developed over the Vietnam War between Depression-generation black fathers and their postwar "baby boom" sons. Many sons who opposed the Vietnam War were deeply shocked when their fathers, who had complained so much about the discrimination they had experienced in World War II, came out in support of the war in Vietnam. The fathers reasoned that despite the discrimination they experienced and the harm caused by war, America's honor had to be defended. Their sons disagreed. More research is needed on the complex dynamics of the tensions between these two generations of black men as an illustration of the ambivalence among male Afro-Americans about military service and war.

Historically, blacks who have been involved in sustaining Eurocentric forms of conscientious objection have belonged to institutions and movements marginal, or even external, to Afro-American communities. Among these external institutions were the historic peace churches and pacifist religious communities, all of which are mainly white. The Afro-American COs included A. Philip Randolph and Chandler Owen in their early Socialist Party days; Louis Gregory of the Baha'i Faith community; historian C. L. R. James of the Socialist Workers Party; anthropologist St. Clair Drake, a member of the World War II Conscientious Objectors against Jim Crow organization; and Afro-American Quakers Bayard Rustin and Jean Toomer.

In view of the importance of religious conviction in traditional conscientious objection, it should be noted that institutional religious support for conscientious objection in Afro-American communities has come largely from marginal sects and churches, including the Black Muslims, the Pentecostals, and the Jehovah's Witnesses. For the most part, mainline Afro-American denominations have been pro-military or at least silent about conscientious objection, especially during wartime.

Conscientious Objection on Grounds of Racial Injustice

Afro-Americans have internalized many national values and have conformed to numerous norms usually associated with dominant white society and culture. Yet Afro-American communities are also distinctive entities. After the official end of slavery in America in the 1860s, and indeed long before that time, Afro-Americans developed communities with a unique cultural base, in many ways incorporating features retained from African cultures, the cultural baggage of West Indian and African immigrants, and intergenerational geographical segregation.

The historical and sociological origins and dynamics of Afro-American subordination have been a major impetus, if not the most important force, behind Afro-American cultural expression, political styles, and moral character. Insofar as there exists an identifiable indigenous form of Afro-American conscientious objection, it emanates from the contradictory political history of racism practiced by state and national governments. The contradiction in this history is the divergence between liberal democratic ideology and the systematic oppression of Afro-Americans by the American polity and society.[11] This deep-seated contradiction becomes acutely apparent during times of war. From the American Civil War to the war in Vietnam, prowar advocates argued in different ways that although war was a horrible human experience, it was necessary in order to save democracy. These advocates, however, did very little to eradicate the structures of racial inequality that challenged democracy at home.[12] During World War II, there were well-publicized cases of Afro-American draft resisters who refused to bear arms on grounds of racial injustice.[13] Research is needed into the social organization, if any, supporting their positions. Attempts also should be made to identify similar patterns of Afro-American conscientious objection in earlier wars.

The most vivid and most highly politicized example of Afro-American conscientious objection on racial and civil rights grounds was the black student movement against the war in Vietnam in the 1960s. The prominent and powerful Afro-American student organization, the Student Nonviolent Coordinating Committee (SNCC), became the first civil rights organization to advocate draft resistance against the Vietnam War. More traditional civil rights organization leaders, such as those of the National Association for the Advancement of Colored People and the National Urban League, refused to oppose the draft and the war, fearing retaliation from the powerful white interest groups on which they depended for support for civil rights and antipoverty programs. Radical white student organizations, principally Students for a Democratic Society (SDS), opposed the war quite early but did not begin to mobilize an antiwar movement until they were prodded by SNCC leaders to join them in their organizational efforts.

Although SNCC eventually developed broad humanitarian arguments for conscientious objection, its original and most fundamental concern was racial injustice involved in the war. The black students' concern was twofold. First, statistics of U.S. casualties at the beginning of the U.S. ground war in Vietnam revealed that a substantially disproportionate number of Afro-Americans were being killed in battle. Second, the national government's enthusiastic war-making ideology stood in opposition to its gradualistic, limited interest in civil rights at home and human rights of persons of color abroad. In a 1965 leaflet issued in Mississippi, blacks who opposed the war listed reasons why Afro-Americans should not be involved in the war in Vietnam, or in the concomitant U.S. military intervention in Santo Domingo. This leaflet was the first call to draft resistance within the civil rights movement:

No Mississippi Negroes should be fighting in Viet Nam for the White Man's freedom, until all the Negro People are free in Mississippi.

Negro boys should not honor the draft here in Mississippi. Mothers should encourage their sons not to go.

We will gain respect and dignity as a race only by forcing the United States Government and the Mississippi Government to come with guns, dogs, and trucks to take our sons away to fight and be killed protecting Miss., Ala., Ga., and La.

No one has a right to ask us to risk our lives and kill other Colored People in Santo Domingo and Viet Nam, so that White Americans can get richer. We will be looked upon as traitors by all the Colored People of the world if the Negro people continue to fight and die without a cause.[14]

This perspective was echoed by many Afro-American soldiers who attempted to organize antiwar protests within the army.[15]

This movement was a product of the changes in national political environment and of the often divisive relations among the civil rights, student, and peace movements. Its visibility on the national level was symbolized by the antiwar positions of Martin Luther King, Jr., Stokely Carmichael, and Julian Bond. Their dramatic actions were made possible by the expanding mass media and by movement leaders who knew how to use such technological development to their advantage.[16]

The classic example of conscientious objection on grounds of racial injustice is the Nation of Islam (Black Muslims). As a mass-oriented Afro-American religious movement organized in the urban Midwest during the 1930s, the Nation of Islam is a cultural institutional response to the dynamics of dominant-group oppression of Afro-Americans. Until very recently, the Nation of Islam was a nationalistic movement emphasizing the doctrine of the superiority of blacks and other people of color to whites; this doctrine regards characteristics of European-descended populations as satanic.

These beliefs have caused leaders of the Nation of Islam to discourage their followers from joining in white society in areas such as electoral politics, education, and business. They also discourage their followers from participating in what they call the "wars of white men." Many Black Muslims accepted this position, but the U.S. government rejected it adamantly. Black Muslim draft resisters were imprisoned during World War II and the Vietnam War, including heavyweight boxing champion Muhammad Ali, who refused to be drafted to fight in Vietnam. Although the Black Muslims liberalized their racial views in the mid–1970s, after the death of Nation of Islam leader Elijah Muhammad, they have not found it wise or necessary to take a position on American military actions since that time.

In the Persian Gulf War, with Afro-Americans making up a disproportionate percentage of enlisted ranks in the U.S. military, it was not surprising that many of those uniformed personnel filing CO claims were black. Within the U.S. Marine Corps, for example, of the forty-six COs, most of them reservists, convicted for refusal to serve in the war, twenty-four were black (three were Hispanic, one was Asian, the rest were white). Among these Afro-American COs, ten gave their religion as Baptist, four identified their religion as Protestant, and three as Pentecostal. There were also two Muslims, two Catholics, two Methodists, and one who listed himself simply as "Christian." There were similar refusals in the other branches of the armed forces.[17]

As a consequence of the government's reluctance to grapple with the realities of racial inequality, conscientious objection claims on grounds of racial injustice have been reduced to "nonissues" or, at the most extreme, to an issue of military disloyalty. Scholars need to examine more closely the claims of racial injustice by the relatively few Afro-American COs who have dared to articulate what many blacks are thinking. Is the resistance of Afro-Americans who refuse to go to war on these grounds merely a political fluke or is it based on moral arguments against bearing arms, rooted in the ways in which Afro-Americans view their oppression and express it culturally? This question cannot be answered by reference to the present literature on conscientious objection because that scholarship is virtually silent about Afro-American issues. Scholars must consult archival collections and biographical sources pertinent to the study of Afro-Americans. In addition, rather than depend on governmental public opinion literature and the public relations information of civil rights organizations, they should conduct their own field studies. In-depth interviews and oral histories of Afro-Americans from various walks of life and different generations would reveal a great deal about how blacks *really* feel about war, peace, military service, and other issues related to conscientious objection.

We should proceed to examine the social history and historical sociology of conscientious objection styles in Afro-American communities. We need to do so with the hope of demonstrating the importance of pluralistic perspectives, including comparative work among Hispanic Americans, Native Americans,[18] and Asians, as well as Afro-Americans. We also need to examine trends among persons of color living in other Western and non-Western societies and regions. Only then will we come to appreciate the complexities of conscientious objection as expressed in varied cultural forms and ethnically based social organizations.

Conclusion

Future trends in Afro-American conscientious objection will be linked to the general theme of this volume, the secularization of conscience. Most of the contributors to this book have applied the concept of secularization of conscience to understand the states' contemporary tendencies to accept secular rationales for conscientious objection and to establish civilian alternative service programs for COs. In this case, however, we must refer to the consequences of the secularization of Afro-Americans as a population.

The coming of age of the Afro-American "baby-boomer" generation in the 1960s helped to create the militant black student protest movement. This generation experienced a profound secularization process when unprecedented numbers of young black people attended and graduated from colleges, moved into desegregated communities, and participated in integrating professional and technical occupations outside of traditional black communities.

The same generation, particularly members of the middle classes, also turned away from traditional Afro-American churches. More than their parents, these young Afro-Americans attended integrated services, and also were attracted to individualistic, meditative philosophies. Jesse Jackson is the hero of many baby-boomer–aged and younger Afro-Americans because, like Martin Luther King, Jr., he advocates a politicized moral philosophy from a theological standpoint that is outside the confines of the traditional black churches. Jackson's signal to Afro-Americans in general is that one need not be a devout churchgoer to be a morally committed person.

The secularization of Afro-American culture is also seen in the embracing of professional pursuits, mass consumerism, even health food fads, and also the dependence on social service agencies instead of traditional black churches for emotional and spiritual (and, to varying degrees) material needs. Secularization in this sense has *individualized* black people and has detached them from traditional institutional and community bonds.

In the future, Afro-Americans, particularly those with resources for living and working outside traditional black communities and institutions, will become more openly attracted to Eurocentric as well as Afrocentric forms of conscientious objection. Because of their wider exposure to national media and to historically white schools and colleges and residential communities, Afro-Americans probably will not go so willingly to a future war. In this sense, they will be under less internal and external pressure than in the past to prove their loyalty to America.

Catalytic leaders such as Jesse Jackson will be successful in galvanizing antiwar sentiment among Afro-Americans, even across class lines, because they are aware of the usual discrepancies between state rhetoric and the realities of racial inequality. Because so many black troops became casualties in Vietnam—a memory stamped in the collective mind of Afro-American communities—blacks will be more likely to resist going to war. At least they will resist fighting in long, bloody wars of attrition involving heavy casualties among American ground troops, who are disproportionately Afro-American, particularly if the domestic condition of blacks continues to decline.

This widespread resistance among Afro-Americans probably will occur because the traditional black leaders no longer have their former monopolistic hold on Afro-American community life or on black public opinion. The secularization of Afro-American culture (and the growing alienation from traditional black leaders among the Afro-American underclass as well as in the new middle classes) will do much to encourage blacks to challenge white America.[19] Such war resistance probably will include the development of culturally distinctive organizations as well as involvement in traditional Eurocentric organizations for conscientious objection.

4

Alternative Service in a Future Draft

DONALD J. EBERLY

If a draft is instituted again in the United States, under the present formula it will include a system for handling conscientious objectors among those drafted that was created in the 1980s to avoid the problems of the 1960s and 1970s. The Military Selective Service Act of 1980 and the regulations established by the various directors of the Selective Service System in the past dozen years form the basis for the operation of the draft system. In such a system, judgments about CO status would be made by local draft boards that would be more representative of a pluralistic community, when activated, and would apply more uniform standards than the draft boards of past years.

Under such a draft, registrants would be able to apply for CO status if they were conscientiously opposed to war in any form and to *combatant* training and service. Those COs who could accept noncombatant training and service, if they met the other requirements, would be drafted into the armed forces and given noncombatant duties. Those COs who were conscientiously opposed to any participation in military service would be required to meet their service obligation by completing a period of alternative civilian service. If this scenario materializes, the major figures will be the COs themselves, a number of CO-oriented religious groups, and the U.S. Selective Service System.

It is useful to conceive of conscientious objectors as comprising two categories. One group, the traditional, consists of the pacifists, who are opposed to killing and to war under all circumstances and are willing to accept severe sanctions in defense of their beliefs. The largest number of traditional pacifist COs has consisted of members of the historic peace faiths—Mennonite, Brethren, and Quaker. Although no statistical breakdown is available, it is very likely that the number of potential COs from these and other traditional peace churches has remained fairly steady for the last two decades, while the number from mainline churches has increased markedly. The traditional pacifist considers himself a CO whether or not a draft is in effect, and whether or not he has been judged by a panel to be a CO.

In contrast, the *selective* COs claim CO status on a narrower basis, including belief in the "just war" concept, which differentiates unjust wars from morally acceptable wars. The steep rise in the number of COs during the Vietnam War probably was attributable less to a rise in the number of traditional COs than to an increase in the number of selective COs, despite the Supreme Court's criterion that a CO had to oppose war in general. There is no way to determine the cause for certain, however, because of the masking effect created by the fact that selective conscientious objection was not a legally acceptable reason to claim CO status.

Whether COs are traditional or selective, there is little point in attempting to compare the views of young men at a time when there is no war and when no draft is in effect with those of young men in the presence of a war and a draft. A question about beliefs that might be answered casually under the former conditions becomes an intensely personal matter under the latter. Circumstances are important: Many of the hundreds of thousands of Americans who signed the so-called Oxford Pledge of the 1930s not to fight for their country served later in World War II. An eighteen-year-old who previously may have been allowed to make few (if any) important decisions is suddenly faced with a life-and-death decision. Many young men in these two circumstances would not only reverse their previous views; but would also develop an intensity of conviction about the issue greater than any they had experienced while growing up.

The pacifist church groups that provide the religious background of most traditional COs agreed only reluctantly to a government-mandated program of alternative service for COs. They prefer that there be no war, that there be no armed forces, that their young people voluntarily contribute a period of service to others as an expression of their religious faith. When faced with no alternative to military service, many of their young men have gone to prison or emigrated. Given the middle ground of conscription with an alternative service option, the pacifist churches tend to cooperate, but they prefer to be entrusted with operating an alternative service for their COs with a bare minimum of governmental direction.

The National Interreligious Service Board for Conscientious Objectors (NISBCO) is the major voice of the pacifist CO community in regard to the alternative service program. Since its founding in 1940 it has been dominated by the Mennonites, the Brethen, and the Quakers. Not until 1984 was NISBCO led by a person chosen from another denomination, the Rev. L. William Yolton, a minister of the Presbyterian church. It worked with the government's alternative service program from 1940, when the draft was established, until the draft was terminated in 1973.

As a legislatively mandated federal program, alternative service has been and would be atypical both in regard to the public employees who operate it and the individuals who participate. Federal programs in such areas as agriculture and education, for example, are administered by bureaucrats who are basically in sympathy with their clients interests, and by clients who generally work closely with the bureaucrats, and yet who are assertive if they believe their interests are in jeopardy. In the Selective Service System, the military reservists, who would direct alternative service at the local level for the first several months in a restored conscription system, generally have little sympathy with COs. Meanwhile the traditional religious pacifist CO, although firm in his beliefs, tends to hold these beliefs quietly and not become engaged in the political process.

Background

The operation of alternative service in the 1990s if a draft is introduced will largely be a reaction to the way in which it operated under Gen. Lewis B. Hershey, the director of the Selective Service System from 1941 to 1970. A folksy Hoosier and a career military officer, Hershey demonstrated for much of his career a combination of intuitiveness and ambiguousness.

Although the president's power to induct young men into the armed forces expired on June 30, 1973, registration for the draft continued until 1975, when it was ended by President Gerald Ford. At that time local boards were closed down and Selective Service was placed in ''deep standby,'' with only a skeletal Selective Service Headquarters in Washington. In 1980, motivated by the Soviet invasion of Afghanistan in 1979 and by the failure of some branches of the armed forces to meet their enlistment quotas, President Jimmy Carter sought and obtained congressional approval to reinstitute compulsory draft registration. He also directed Selective Service Headquarters to modernize the processing of registrants and to construct a potential alternative service program that would be fair and equitable. To direct the Selective Service Carter appointed Bernard Rostker, a methodical computer expert and Hershey's opposite.

In accordance with President Carter's instructions and a new climate of opinion about the draft, Rostker made decisions that ensured that a future military draft would differ from Hershey-era conscription in several important respects. Local draft boards would include more women and members of minorities and fewer veterans; this makeup would be more representative of the general population than under Hershey. Board members would receive more uniform training in the policies that would apply to making judgments about CO claimants; thus they would avoid the widely varying judgments typical of the Hershey era, when local boards had great autonomy.

In organizing alternative service, Rostker decided to separate the administration of an alternative service program from the local draft boards. Alternative service offices (ASOs) would be created and would follow a set of regulations issued by the national headquarters of the Selective Service System. Typically the jurisdiction of an ASO would coincide with that of several draft boards (served by area offices). In a parallel decision, Rostker decided that conscientious objectors who entered the program would be designated alternative service workers (ASWs).

Issues in Alternative Service

Several matters were at issue as Selective Service began to modernize the alternative service program: Should the registration form include a check-off box where registrants could indicate their intention to apply for CO status if the draft were restored? What could be done to make sure that all registrants who received CO status would actually perform alternative service? How much authority would be given to the historic pacifist churches in conducting alternative service?

Selective Service resisted the desire of the CO community to permit ASWs to serve with organizations—such as church groups—that insisted on a religious affiliation or belief. Citing the 1964 Civil Rights Act provision that prohibited employment discrimination on the basis of race, color, or creed, Selective Service asserted that ASW employers were covered by this statute because they would be employing someone in accordance with a federal law (in this case the Military Selective Service Act). In 1987, however, the Supreme Court ruled that church organizations could require religious beliefs and still employ COs.[1] Shortly thereafter Selective Service gave up its attempt to constrain ASW employers in this way.

The most controversial CO issue in Selective Service in the early 1980s was ensuring that all COs fulfilled their obligation to perform alternative service. During the Vietnam War draft, the failure to place all, perhaps even half, of the COs had been a significant problem. As the Director of Selective Service noted in 1971, "It is evident . . . that men are being classified by local boards into 1–0 [the CO classification] faster than alternate service work is found for them."[2] In California, then Gov. Ronald Reagan helped to relieve the strain in 1971 by creating the California Ecology Corps, whereby the state paid COs to do conservation work. During President Ford's 1974–1977 program, which granted amnesty on condition of a period of alternative service, placement failures caused by the absence of stipends were a major difficulty. A case was made in favor of paying ASWs on the grounds that it was the only way to ensure that all would be placed, and thereby would help to make the system equitable.

The argument against federally supported stipends was that in view of the expanded definition of CO, the administration of alternative service likely would become the dominant part of Selective Service. At some point, perhaps when the number of ASWs reached fifteen thousand, the government would be spending more money on alternative service than on military conscription. In Selective Service, which was staffed heavily with former military officers and current military reservists, there was also an undercurrent of resentment at the idea that ASWs would receive government pay, just like the GIs. Rostker had been open to the idea of federally supported stipends for ASWs, but his successor, Gen. Thomas Turnage, appointed by President Ronald Reagan, opposed such stipends and made the decision not to include them.

In a related decision, Selective Service designated as "preaccepted placement positions" those jobs for which an employer was willing to accept an ASW without interviewing him. Insofar as employers might agree to fill such positions, this arrangement would expedite the placement of ASWs.

A CO check-off box at the time of registration was very much desired by the CO community. The CO organizations believed that in the event of a draft, the evidence of having asserted CO status at the time of registration would fortify subsequent CO claims by registrants. Their case was strengthened by previous experience: Draft board members often had given great weight to various forms of evidence that CO claimants' belief and behavior was consistent with their claims.

Selective Service took the view that the decision of a draft board was to be based on the claimant's belief at the time of his appearance before the draft board. This view was supported by Sen. Sam Nunn, chair of the Senate Armed Services Committee, who opposed a Senate amendment that would have instituted a CO check-off box at the time of registration. Young men registed by completing and mailing a form obtained at the post office; the form did *not* include a provision for checking off conscientious objection as an option. Selective Service maintained that an expressed preference for CO status at the time of registration was irrelevant to the evaluation of a registrant's later claim for CO status. The amendment was defeated; Selective Service did not include a CO check-off box on the registration form.

The Alternative Service Process

The right of conscientious objection in the United States is not granted constitutionally, as it is, for example, in the Federal Republic of Germany. The legal authority for conscientious objector status and for alternative service is based instead on a congressional statute, most recently the Military Selective Service Act (MSSA) of 1980.

By the provisions of this law, there are two classes of CO status under a draft. The first recognizes men who are conscientiously opposed to participation in war in any form and to *combatant* military training and service in the armed forces. Those who establish this claim before a draft board are given 1-A-O status. They can be inducted into the armed forces and can receive training and service assignments, but only of a *noncombatant* nature, such as in the medical corps.

The second category of COs recognizes men who are conscientiously opposed both to any war and to any participation whatever in the armed forces. Persons establishing this claim receive 1–0 status. The MSSA instructs the director of Selective Service to place registrants designated 1–0 in civilian positions that contribute to the maintenance of the "national health, safety or interest." This is the basis for alternative service programs.

Alternative service offices are responsible for recruiting employers and placing ASWS in specified geographic areas. An employer can be a private nonprofit organization or a public agency. Typical employers are hospitals, nursing homes, state departments of natural resources, and the U.S. Forest Service. Employers are allowed to interview ASWS before agreeing to hire them. Information about employers is kept on file in the Alternative Service Program System (ASPS). If and when a draft becomes imminent, employers are asked to specify job openings for ASWS; these openings then are entered in a job bank. Employment agreements between employers and Selective Service may be terminated if the employer ceases to operate an approved program, violates the employment agreement, or requests termination by means of a thirty-day written notice to Selective Service.

A CO is designated an ASW upon issuance of the order to perform alternative service, which is signed by the chair of the local draft board. This order is a signal to the area office to notify the CO that he is now classified 1-W, that he is ordered to perform alternative service for two years, and that his performance will be monitored by a designated ASO. In addition, the area office sends him an ASW guide and skills questionnaire. Responsibility for the alternative service worker then passes from the area office to the alternative service office.

The alternative service office then orders the ASW to report to a job-counseling session where he is informed of the major provisions of alternative service, and reviews job openings for which he qualifies. If he wishes to work for an organization not on the approved list, he may ask that organization to seek "approved employer" status with Selective Service. He interviews for one job or more; when accepted by an approved employer, he relays this information to the ASO, which issues a job placement order. If this process does not produce a job for the ASW within thirty days of the issuance of the order to perform alternative Service, the ASO normally assigns the ASW to a guaranteed job.

Alternative service workers may seek overseas positions. In such cases, the ASW is responsible for finding an acceptable position. The ASO may approve an overseas assignment once it is satisfied that the job contributes to the national health, safety, or interest; that the employer has the capability to supervise and monitor the ASW's work while overseas; and that adequate provision is made for such matters as international travel and inoculations.

The order of priority for placing ASWs is (1) a position that the ASW specifically requests; (2) a position in the job bank that the ASW prefers; and (3) any other position for which the ASW is qualified.

All ASWs are required to perform twenty-four months of alternative service. Normally they do so in a two-year span but in cases of failure to serve due to extended illness or negligence on the part of the ASW, the time could be extended to make the *cumulative* service period twenty-four months.

The "clock" on the ASW is maintained by the award of creditable time to the ASW. Creditable time is linked closely to the individual employer's policies on such matters as holidays, sick leave, vacation time, and training periods, and thus it is not uniform among ASWs. Creditable time is not granted when the ASO determines that the ASW's work is unsatisfactory (as measured against the employer's reasonable requirements), while the ASW travels to or from an overseas assignment, and for the processing time during the first thirty days after issuance of the order to perform alternative service.

A number of provisions cover postponements, grievances, suspensions due to hardship, illnesses, and the early release of ASWs. The most important is the provision that enables an ASW to appeal his job assignment if he believes that it violates his "religious, moral or ethical beliefs or convictions as to participation in war which led to his classification as a conscientious objector."[3] Such a situation might arise if an ASW were working in a state park and was told to deliver some surplus equipment to a military base. He would first appeal to the ASO; then, if not satisfied with its decision, he could obtain a hearing before a civilian review board. After

TABLE 4.1   Military COs, 1983–1988

Year	Number of CO Applications Approved
1983	155
1984	163
1985	191
1986	188
1987	173
1988	175

Sources: Letters from the Army, Navy, Air Force, and Marine Corps. A Letter from the Department of Defense implies that it does not keep central records of COs.

hearing the case, the civilian review board would either confirm the ASO's decision or order the reassignment of the ASW.

When the ASW completes his assigned period of service, the ASO issues him a certificate of release and transfers him to the jurisdiction of the area office, which then changes his classification from 1-W to 4-W.

Conscientious Objectors Today

Without compulsory induction of civilians into the military, the only legally recognized conscientious objectors today are those members of the military who have applied for and received status as COs. The Department of Defense defines a CO as a person holding "a firm, fixed and sincere objection to war in any form or the bearing of arms, by religious training or belief," or whose moral and ethical beliefs are as strongly held as traditional religious beliefs.

The Department of Defense recognizes the same two classes of conscientious objection as the Selective Service System. Persons in the military who receive 1–0 status are discharged from military service; those receiving 1-A-O status are reassigned to noncombatant duties within the service.

In the years before the Persian Gulf crisis of 1990–1991, the number of military COs had been fairly steady, as illustrated in Table 4.1.

Approval rates for CO status appear to be fairly uniform among the services: 80 percent for the Army; 76 percent for the Navy, and 73 percent for the Marine Corps (the Air Force reported that information on the number of applicants for CO status was not available).

Probably the number of military persons who might be called unofficial COs is greater than the number of those actually awarded that status.[4] For example, some potential CO claimants receive administrative discharges. Others simply are assigned noncombatant duties.

Future Prospects

The likelihood of a return to conscription is highly remote under present conditions. From a plateau of some two million persons on active duty the 1980s, levels of the U.S. military force are expected to fall substantially throughout the 1990s.

A return to the draft is a possibility, of course. If it should occur under circumstances in which all but the traditional pacifist COs were willing to volunteer or be drafted for military service, Selective Service probably could manage alternative service as presently planned.

If the country should return to the draft, however, under conditions in which significant numbers of secular objectors and young men from mainline churches declare their CO beliefs—conditions that I believe prevailed throughout the 1980s— Selective Service soon would be overwhelmed with the processing of registrants claiming to be COs and with the placement of alternate service workers. Selective Service would be particularly hard pressed to find a sufficient number of organizations willing to pay those workers.

In that event, Selective Service likely would adopt the approach taken by the Federal Republic of Germany (see the chapter by Kuhlmann and Lippert in this volume), whereby the government reimburses employers for the stipends paid to COs and young men essentially choose the civilian service option without having to prove the sincerity of their beliefs relating to war and military service.

In the last decade of the twentieth century or the first decade of the twenty-first century, a more likely scenario in the United States might be the introduction of some form of national service in which all young men, and probably young women as well, would be encouraged to perform a period of civilian or military duty. It is unlikely that the sanction for failure to serve would be as severe as a prison sentence. Probably there would be a reward to those who serve, such as financial support for further education and training, and a penalty to those who do not, such as adding two or three years to the age of eligibility for drivers' licenses.

In the event of such large-scale national service, many of the selective COs— as well as a large number of non-COs—would choose the civilian national service option. Many of the pacifist COs would declare themselves COs, gain objector status through their draft boards, and serve as alternate service workers within the system planned by Selective Service. A small number of absolutists would choose to make a statement of their noncooperation with any system supported by a government that also supports military service. Some could be expected to manifest their beliefs through legal means, others to assert themselves by assuming civilian service positions independent of any governmental authority.

PART III

COMPARATIVE PERSPECTIVES

5

Britain: From Individual Conscience to Social Movement

GWYN HARRIES-JENKINS

Britain has relied upon a volunteer army more often than upon compulsory military training and service, but in its experiences with conscription—particularly during the two world wars and the first dozen years of the Cold War—it witnessed a progressive liberalization of conscientious objection. Britain's experience also had a significant influence upon conscription and conscientious objection in the United States.

In essence, conscientious objection is the articulation by an individual of a set of highly internalized attitudes in response to a particular stimulus. Expressions of conscience theoretically can reflect a wide range of stimuli: environmental pollution, gender inequalities, racism, penal policy, and so on. The term "conscientious objection," however, is more limited in its scope. Conceptually it can be identified with a continuum of *war resistance,* the characteristics of which can be equated, in the words of one scholar, "with anti-militarist and anti-conscriptionist movements in peace time, with pacifist conscientious objection, with nationalist and socialist resistance and ethical and religious withdrawal from a given state and indeed with revolutionary opposition."[1]

War resistance is a complex phenomenon, whose origins can be attributed to the democratization of war in the context of the growth of the nation-state. It comes into prominence with the emergence of the mass army and with the concomitant introduction of compulsory systems of military service. It rejects the synthesis of popular sovereignty and territorial identity, which justifies the introduction of conscription. It draws heavily on the older traditions of religious pacifism but adds to them a refusal to engage in war for a broad variety of political, social, cultural, and economic reasons. Conscientious objection is thus a subtle mix of the religious and the secular. It embraces both opposition to a specific war and opposition to war in general. It can, however, be distinguished sharply from pacifism. The latter represents a doctrine or belief that the total abolition of war is both possible and desirable. Conscientious objection, in contrast, is neither a policy nor a doctrine. It is the basis of the legal status conferred by the state upon an individual when it is accepted that the individual's articulation of personal values, attitudes, and norms is in accordance with the "conscience clause" that has been incorporated into national legislation governing conscription and/or military service. As Judge Wethered, chairman of the South Western Appeal Tribunal in Britain, acknowledged in 1942, it is "a conscientious objection to military registration or service, based on religious or ethical convictions honestly held."[2]

Conscientious objection is essentially a *negative* concept, whose primary identifying characteristics are encapsulated in national legislation. For the United Kingdom, these can be inferred from three specific Acts of Parliament: The Military Service Act (2) of 1916; The National Service (Armed Forces) Act of 1939 (2 & 3 Geo. VI, c. 81); and the National Service Act of 1948 (11 & 12 Geo. VI, c. 64). Section 173(2) of the 1948 Act repeats the provision of the two earlier Acts when it lays down the following:

> If any person subject to registration claims that he conscientiously objects—
> (a) to being registered in the military service register, or
> (b) to performing military service, or
> (c) to performing combatant duties,
> he may, on furnishing the prescribed particulars about himself, apply in the prescribed manner to be registered as a conscientious objector in a special register to be kept by the Minister (in this Part of this Act referred to as "the register of conscientious objectors").

In referring to the process of registration in "the register of conscientious objectors," the Act recognizes that conscientious objection is the refusal on the part of an individual to kill or to bear arms (performing combatant duties), to join the military organization (performing military service), or to undertake civilian work that frees other individuals to join the military (being registered in the military service register).

The legal definition of conscientious objection is thus relatively straightforward;[3] its social science implications, however, are much more complex. This essay explores such implications more fully, using the British experience of conscientious objection to support the general conclusions that I draw.

The Legal Basis of Conscientious Objection

The incorporation of a "conscience clause" into the conscription Acts of Parliament of 1916, 1939, and 1948 ensured that all who objected to their conscription for military service were entitled to appear before a specially constituted local tribunal and to voice their objection. If the members of the tribunal were satisfied that the applications were genuine, the tribunal could enter the applicant on the register of conscientious objectors without conditions—that is, with *complete exemption*. Alternatively, the individual could be registered on condition that he undertook civilian work under civilian control. This *conditional exemption* often was termed the "B" decision. A third possibility was that the individual's name was removed from the register so that he could be called up for *noncombatant duties* in the armed services (the so-called "C" decision). Finally, if the tribunal was not satisfied that the application was genuine, it could direct that the applicant's name be removed from the register of conscientious objectors and that he be liable for military service (the "D" decision).

In the First World War, Britain's first experience with national conscription, tribunals composed of men unsympathetic to applicants' claims often refused to grant any exemption. Individuals then were enlisted forcibly into the military and were liable to court-martial if they refused to accept military orders.[4]

Subsequent tribunals continued to exercise a positive, if less Draconian, jurisdiction. In 1939 tribunals were set up to hear claims to exemption from military service made on grounds of conscience, and operated in fifteen areas throughout the country. Each was chaired by a county court judge, who was joined by a trade union representative, an academic, and two others.[5] As in 1916 tribunals had power to dismiss an application, to recommend noncombatant service in the armed forces, or to grant exemption from military service, with or without conditions. Tim Evens stresses that unconditional exemption was rare and was granted proportionally less often than the other exemptions.[6] Barber notes that during the Second World War, unconditional exemptions proved to be highly controversial, both within and outside the tribunals.[7] Of all objectors in 1939, some 14 percent (669 from a total of 4,812 applicants) were granted unconditional exemption.

As World War II progressed, the pattern of exemption changed radically. In 1940 only 5 percent of applicants were given unconditional exemption. In 1947, after the war, the figure had fallen to 2 percent. From a total of 59,192 CO applications to local (as opposed to appellate) tribunals between 1939 and 1945, only 6.04 percent were granted unconditional exemption. By the end of 1948, 2,937 of 62,301 applications, or 4.7 percent, had been registered unconditionally.[8]

Most CO exemptions were conditional on the claimant's taking up specified civilian work; normally this was work of national importance. Between 1939 and 1945, 48.52 percent of applicants were so registered. This category was recognized in the second set of subsections of the three conscriptive acts, and an elaborate set of conditions was established to ensure their control. First, individuals were "conditionally registered" in the military service register; the condition was that they undertook work specified by the conscientious objection tribunal, "of a civil character and under civilian control."[9] Second, they were to undergo such training as the minister of labour thought necessary for preparing the applicants. Much of that work was "medical," but as a 1919 leaflet of the Friends' Service Committee pointed out, while some 3,000 objectors during the 1916–1918 period had been engaged in such work, a larger number (4,000) had been employed in other work, "considered of national importance."[10]

The logic of the argument put forward to rationalize this treatment of these CO applicants is seemingly irrefutable. Historical evidence suggests that in no circumstances—not even in Germany and the Soviet Union in periods of great danger—has a nation-state sought to conscript all of the manpower theoretically available—that is, all the nation's adult males. Accordingly there would seem to be no reason why a principle of *occupational exemption* should not prevail. This idea was accepted in the past in both the United States and the United Kingdom; moreover, it has the possible merit of shifting into civilian employment those who can make a more substantial contribution to the war effort in civil than in military specialties. Against this argument, such a policy of exemption has drawn considerable criticism from those who identify this facet of conscientious objection with the abrogation of individual civic responsibilities.

The third decision given by the tribunals, whereby the objector was registered as liable to be inducted for noncombatant duties only, invited a highly politicized discussion about the definition of "noncombatant." In the First World War, it referred primarily to work in the Royal Army Medical Corps. Even then, however, there was some uncertainty as to whether service with the Medical Corps was "combatant" or "noncombatant." The issue was raised again in 1940 by the pacifist organizations. The position was clarified by a decision of March 1940 that a man performing *noncombatant* duties in the Armed Services would never be required to drill with or to handle lethal weapons. The subsequent creation of a distinctive *Non-Combatant Corps* in mid–1940 also obviated many of the problems faced by individuals during the First World War.

A Typology of Conscientious Objectors

To facilitate analysis of the social science implications of conscientious objection, we can propose a number of working hypotheses. First, conscientious objection is not a single unitary concept. On the contrary, it is the expression of wide-ranging and diverse normative attitudes that include, among other things, reactions to militarism, to fighting, to war, to killing, and so on. Second, the value system that underlies the expression of conscientious objection is derived not only from religious beliefs but also from political ideologies. Third, such objection is no longer gender-specific. Finally, the very basis of conscientious objection is materially affected by contemporary reaction to the question of the inevitability of war.

The provisions of the three British conscription Acts of 1916, 1939, and 1948 can be used as the basis of a typology of conscientious objectors. This application confirms the initial hypothesis that a single, unitary concept does not exist. Objectors can be grouped into three categories, each of which mirrors the distinctive characteristics of a subsection of that legislation.

The first category is that of the *absolutists*—that is, the group that objects even "to being registered in the military service register." This stance is a total opposition to any form of cooperation with the military system, either directly or indirectly. When given the option to undertake noncombatant duties, these absolutists responded that they were unable to distinguish between combatant and noncombatant service. In 1916 this group was identified most closely with the No-Conscription Fellowship.[11]

In the Second World War many organizations expressed an interest in conscription and conscientious objection. One of these, the Central Board of Conscientious Objectors (CBC), became a coordinating body that linked other interested groups and provided a specialized service for those who were affected by the provisions of the draft act. Other interested groups included the Peace Pledge Union, the Fellowship of Reconciliation (a Christian organization that had done much to help objectors in the First World War), the No-Conscription Fellowship, and many denominational pacifist groups, including the Methodist Peace Fellowship and the Anglican Pacifist Fellowship as well as the Fellowship of Conscientious Objectors formed at the beginning of the war. The Fellowship of Conscientious Objectors was the only organization that attempted to create a movement of objectors.

Although the absolutists did not suffer as severely in 1939–1945 as did their predecessors in 1914–1918, many still were subject to arrest and imprisonment.[12] After the end of the Second World War, the 1948 National Service Act continued to spell out in considerable detail the interplay between court-martial procedures and more conventional legal processes in dealing with the specific issue of absolutist claims. The environment in which individual attitudes to the forms of conscientious objection were expressed was distinguished by the constraint of the accompanying legal structure and by the manner in which military, rather than civil, law was accepted as the governing mode.

The second category of conscientious objectors comprises a group of men who refuse to perform military service but are prepared to accept alternative civilian employment. In the United Kingdom the basis of the individual objection of these *alternativists* was very clearly expressed in a 1916 leaflet outlining the position of the conscientious objector: "We cannot undertake [such] duties under a military oath which necessitates obedience to all orders and makes us part of the military machine."[13] As has been noted, an elaborate set of conditions evolved so as to ensure that these alternativist conscientious objectors could be properly employed in a civilian role.

The number of alternativists was comparatively large. During the Second World War, 7,452 COs had been registered "conditionally upon undertaking civilian work" by the end of July 1940. In the spring of 1943, the cumulative total had reached 23,538. This number included 501 women, because the government had begun conscripting women for essential jobs in the economy, including war industries. By the end of March 1945 the total was 24,625, of whom 732 were women. Identifying appropriate work was a persistent problem. In 1939 the tribunals seemed to conclude that agriculture and forestry were the two nonwar-related industries that could most readily employ extra workers. In the absence of a structured national manpower planning policy, however, criticism was bound to attend any attempt to divert human resources on the grounds of rationality rather than on the grounds of recognizing what Prime Minister Neville Chamberlain had termed the "useless and exasperating waste of time and effort to attempt to force such people [the COs] to act in a manner which was contrary to their principle."[14]

No such criticism, however, can be leveled against the members of the third group of COs. This final category comprises those individuals who, in the words of the relevant sections and subsections of the draft Acts, object "to performing combatant duties." Although unwilling to fight or to bear arms, some COs always have been willing to fulfill a military obligation by enlisting in national armed forces. Accordingly the underlying value system of these *noncombatant conscientious objectors* is very different from that of the absolutist or the alternativist COs. Their willingness to accept noncombatant duties, often in situations as hazardous as those faced by combat troops, gives them a general status that differs radically from that accorded to other conscientious objectors. The insulting term "conchie," thrown at the latter, contrasts markedly with the acceptance given to noncombatant COs who were members of units such as the Royal Army Medical Corps.

Many Quakers avidly joined what they saw to be life-affirming service organizations for men of peace. One of the most/prestigious of these was the Friends' Ambulance Unit. This unit had an unofficial origin, and during its earlier history was not officially "recognized" by the Religious Society of Friends. Indeed, some Friends thought its work was too closely connected with the army to be free from military involvement. Many of the conditions under which the Friends' Ambulance Unit worked were comparable with those experienced by soldiers in the Royal Army Medical Corps. The unit was necessarily in constant contact with the military authorities in the field, and under their orders. Ultimately, for the sake of convenience, leaders of the Friends' Ambulance Unit were granted commissions as officers.

Even so, the attitudes and the normative perceptions of these noncombatant COs differed materially from the values of those who willingly and unreservedly enlisted in the military. The view of these Quakers was epitomized in the January 1916 minutes of the Meeting for Sufferings of the Religious Society of Friends:

> War in our view involves a surrender of the Christian ideal and a denial of human brotherhood. . . . We regard the central conception of the [Conscription] Act as imperiling the liberty of the individual conscience—which is the main hope of human progress—and entrenching more deeply that Militarism from which we all desire the world to be freed.[15]

The Ideologies of Conscientious Objection

The legal aspects of conscientious objection, as reflected in the identified typology of objectors, are a manifestation of deeply held ideological perspectives. Broadly speaking, two different views can be identified: attitudes based on *religious* beliefs, and attitudes derived from *political* ideologies. In the United Kingdom, as elsewhere in Western society, conscientious objection founded on religious beliefs has a lengthy history. It can be traced to the emergence in the late seventeenth and early eighteenth centuries of a form of religious pacifism. The central theme, "Thou shalt not kill," was particularly equated with the beliefs of the Religious Society of Friends (the Quakers), which emerged in England in the mid–1600s. Later, other groups such as the Plymouth Brethren and (in the twentieth century) the Jehovah's Witnesses also became conscientious objectors on religious grounds.

In Great Britain adherence to this central theme was also a feature of objection to war and militarism by members of religious groups outside the established Church of England. Wartime dissent by these so-called "Non-Conformists"—persons not conforming to the Anglican Church—was very marked in the Boer War in the late nineteenth century. It was also a consistent feature of conscientious objection in the Second World War. One CO in World War II explained the origins of his position in the following words:

> I came to Cambridge as a freshman . . . in October 1938. I came under strong Christian pacifist influences. . . . The Fellowship of Reconciliation was strong amongst undergraduates and I got involved in it and other pacifist groups. . . . [T]he threat of conscription forced me (and many of my contemporaries) to decide "where I stood."[16]

The basis of this value system is highly complex. In one of the few comparative analyses of conscientious objection based on religious belief, it is suggested that "Christian piety" is of critical significance.[17]

Even so, it must be acknowledged that conscientious objection has always been motivated largely by political rather than religious considerations. Thus in Holland, most of the seven hundred objectors who went to prison during the World War I era were working-class International Socialists, notwithstanding the presence in that country of a great many pacifist Mennonites.

Occasionally the distinction between the religious and the secular CO is blurred. Pacifists who met in 1916 in England to stimulate the development of a peace campaign soon encountered a serious division within the Religious Society of Friends. On the one hand, a group of politically radical Quakers argued that international conflicts were the outcome of defects in the existing social order and that individuals would have to decide which side to take in what they called "the approaching culminating struggles in the age-long war of the classes."[18] On the other hand, this view that nothing would preclude war except the abolition of capitalism was strongly criticized by many other Friends, including John W. Graham, the author of *Conscription and Conscience,* who was a prominent Quaker of the old school that opposed all violence.

The interrelated coincidence of political and religious ideologies can also be seen in reference to specific issues. It is questionable whether a refusal to serve on the grounds that a government's policies are contrary to international law is based on religious or political grounds. On a political basis, individual attitudes may be associated with either selective or general conscientious objection. *Selective* objection reflects an individual's reaction to a particular stimulus. Thus one might refuse to fight to defend what is regarded as an unjust regime, or to support an odious political policy such as racial apartheid. *General* conscientious objection, however, which is motivated by political considerations, is much more wide-ranging. It includes, for example, a marked opposition to the growth of militarism, a phenomenon which in this context is identified with the subordination of societal values to the needs of war. It also reflects a fear of the social effects of the introduction of compulsory military service.[19]

The persistent feature of general conscientious objection, however, is the considerable extent to which individual reaction is concomitant with perceptions of the legitimacy of the military. The basic conceptual framework of military legitimacy identifies two highly divergent interpretations of the status of armed forces within the parent society.[20] First, the military is viewed as a cohesive force axiomatically endowed with legitimacy. Where armed forces are identified as the synthesis of the nation and as part of the image of the state, the relationship between the military and the population as a whole is characterized by enthusiasm rather than compulsion. Where this relationship begins from the presumption that the military is legitimate only insofar as its existence and its use of power have been accepted by society as a whole, the central core trait is consent. The generally reached conclusion is that because the legitimacy of the military is not questioned, any call upon individuals to support the armed forces in the defense of the nation and the social order is legitimate. This means, in practice, that it is the *duty* of individuals to assist the military in maintaining policies defined in terms of the basic needs of the state.

Within this situation, selective objection to military service nevertheless may occur if individuals are materially affected by a specified stimulus. A classic example occurs when individuals, on the grounds that armed forces are no longer able to defend their particular interests, wish to withdraw their consent to the military's enjoyment of special privileges and a special status within society. This wish may arise in situations such as that in Ulster (Northern Ireland), where some are convinced that the military, the British Army, does not protect them. The result is a selective objection to the maintenance of the military. Concomitantly, as events in 1914–1916 demonstrated, such objection may quickly disappear in the face of alternative pressures and stimuli. This particular example illustrates the operation of the consent model; the identification of armed forces as the synthesis of the nation, on the other hand, produces no greatly differing conclusion.

Second, the military can be identified as a divisive element within society. In this view, armed forces are thought to perpetuate inequality and injustice. As a result, the military system at best secures only the partial support of members of that society. This attitude encourages the emergence of a general conscientious objection, which is effectively antimilitary. The classic example is the reaction during the First World War of members of the socialist-oriented British Independent Labour Party (ILP), which persistently criticized British participation in the war.[21]

At the annual ILP conference a resolution was passed unanimously "that the ILP should at once take action with the Socialists of other countries to bring the war to a close and to establish the International on a broad, lasting basis." These and comparable comments reflected the conclusion that the military were the upholders of one social class against the interests of another: the elitist middle or upper class against the British working class, which was viewed as part of an international movement of workers. At a May Day meeting in London's Hyde Park in 1915, the ILP adopted a resolution "that the workers of Europe have no quarrel with one another" and "that the real enemy of the proletariat is the Capitalist

TABLE 5.1   Conscientious Objectors Who Appeared before
a Tribunal, United Kingdom, 1914–1918

Arrested		
Absolutists		1,543
Alternativists		3,750
Combatant/Noncombatants		351
Those medically discharged		267
Others		350
	TOTAL	6,261
Not Arrested		
Assigned to:		
Work of National Importance		3,964
Friends' Ambulance Unit		1,000
War Victims Relief Company		200
Directed Work		900
Non-Combatant Corps		3,300
Royal Army Medical Corps		100
	Total	9,464
Evasions of the Act		175
	GRAND TOTAL	15,900

Source: John W. Graham, *Conscription and Conscience: A History, 1916–1919* (London: Allen and Unwin, 1922; New York: Garland Publishing, 1971), passim.

Class.''[22] This ideologically based opposition to military service thus differed markedly from the attitudes exhibited by those who objected on religious grounds.[23]

Whether conscientious objection is derived from religious beliefs or from political ideologies, the relatively limited number of COs in Britain during wartime always must be borne in mind. The most vigorous and most important organization to oppose the introduction of conscription in the First World War was the No-Conscription Fellowship. This body consisted of young men of military age drawn in part from those who refused on religious grounds to perform military service. Although by 1915 its membership had increased to such an extent that the Fellowship was able to open an office in London, its size (thirteen thousand members) should be related to the much larger number who had voluntary joined the military. In July 1914 the British Army comprised 164,000 officers and men. Although the rate of volunteering had fallen off by the end of 1915, more than two and one-half million men had willingly stepped forward by February 1916.[24] In contrast, as Caroline Moorehead notes, within weeks of the passing of the Military Service Act at the end of January 1916, some two thousand young men of military age representing 165 branches of the No-Conscription Fellowship gathered at Devonshire House, the Quaker headquarters in London.[25]

By the time the war ended, some 16,000 COs had appeared before a conscription tribunal (see Table 5.1). Of these, 6,261 were arrested, 819 of whom spent more than two years in prison, much of it in solitary confinement.

Figures produced in World War II by the Central Board for Conscientious Objectors show that in 1939–1945 there were 62,301 COs in Britain out of a call-up of about 5 million; that is, a rate of about 1.2 percent. Of these COs, 1,704 were women, who had been liable to conscription after 1942.[26] For the period 1939–

1941, more than fifty thousand men were registered as conscientious objectors; of these, 18 percent received unconditional exemption, 45 percent received conditional exemption, 20 percent were registered for noncombatant duties, and 17 percent were refused exemption.[27]

Nevertheless, despite the relatively limited number of objectors in Britain in both world wars, they always attracted considerable attention. Although members of the No-Conscription Fellowship were very much in the minority, they consistently waged a vociferous campaign in support of their beliefs. At the first national convention of the Fellowship, held in November 1915, its president, Clifford Allen, declared that if the Military Service Bill were passed by Parliament, the members would vigorously "resist the operation of that Act." Allen also said that the Fellowship was "considering the most vigorous possible forms of opposition" and that they were willing to suffer all the "penalties that the state may inflict—yes, even death itself—rather than go back upon our conviction."[28]

Even so, we must note a conceptual difference between individual COs' refusal to serve in combat or in the military and opposition to conscription as a system. This distinction is particularly relevant in countries such as the United States and the United Kingdom, where the military system traditionally has been identified with a volunteer army. In both countries conscription has generally been regarded as a violation of individual rights and liberties, which, at best, can be tolerated only for substantial reasons and for a limited period. During such a time opposition to conscription becomes manifest; for the remainder of the time it is latent. Consequently, for long periods in the United States and the United Kingdom, there is little, if any, evidence of a manifest opposition to conscription based on highly internalized religious or political ideologies.

Essentially this is a classic example of the selective form of conscientious objection. It is a limited form of objection in that it arises only in response to the particular and very specific stimulus of the existence or the occasional introduction of conscription. The differences between this and the more general form of conscientious objection are asserted by James Burk in an essay on the debate about conscription in the United States in World War II and in the Vietnam War. Burk argues that a central feature of the debate in 1940 was a fear of militarism and a belief that conscription "would militarize society, eroding basic freedoms that would be difficult to restore."[29] Issues of religious conscience, Burk asserts, never figured prominently in this debate.[30]

Gender and Conscientious Objection

Conventional accounts of conscientious objection tend to accept that the concept is gender-specific in that it relates only to males' objection to military service. This idea presumes that war resistance in general is an expression of specific gender attitudes. Accordingly, opposition to war was identified exclusively with the reactions of males who either opposed conscription for the specific war (selective objection) or were more generally against war and the state's use of violence (general objection).

Such a simplistic conclusion, however, overlooks the nature of the more general expression of conscientious objection, which begins from a position of quiescent passivity and projects individual attitudes derived from a complex amalgam of rationalist political nonconformity, radical secular pacifism, and antimilitarism. This form of conscientious objection can be identified with a "women's attitude," which is located very precisely on a continuum of war resistance. This position is clearly summarized in the attitude of some British women in the First World War. In Britain women were involved in the antidraft and antiwar activities largely from the sidelines. Those women's suffragists who had gone over to the pacifist cause had been able to do little more than lend their help to organizations such as the No-Conscription Fellowship.[31] In contrast, many more women actively supported mobilization, even seeking to humiliate "shirkers" by giving them a white feather.

Both of these views, however, are very different from the attitude toward conscientious objection displayed by some women in the United Kingdom in the Second World War. Unlike the situation in the 1914–1918 period, when women were not subject to conscription, single women between the ages of twenty and thirty were liable to conscription after December 2, 1941. This measure, which was first implemented in 1942, produced a strong reaction, albeit among a small number of eligible women. By 1945, of the 62,301 people who had appeared before a conscientious objection tribunal, 1,704 (2.74 percent) were women.[32]

The typology among women COs is quite similar to that among male COs. For refusing a "directive" to work, 257 women were prosecuted, and 214 of these were sent to prison. These absolutist female COs were complemented by a large number of alternativists and by some noncombatant COs.

Although this facet of conscientious objection is in no way unique, the underlying conceptual base has certain distinctive features. First, the basis of objection among the women is almost exclusively pacifist in origin. It is derived from the model of general conscientious objection, with its wide humanitarian, social, economic, and political bases. Second, this gender-specific form of objection is identified with a unique and very specific form of committed pacific opposition to war, which has persisted into the 1990s. The extreme example is the opposition to the military as epitomized by the actions of women who participated in the antinuclear peace protests in the 1980s at Greenham Common in England.

The Inevitability of War

The most significant feature of this new, or alternative, form of protest is the manner in which it has greatly extended the traditional typology of conscientious objection. The latter has always been gender-specific and draws heavily on the legal ramifications of specific governmental policy. It has a conceptual integrity that from 1916 onward had a general rather than a uniquely national significance. One of its primary distinguishing features has been its identification with a specific opposition to a policy of conscription. Yet the principle of conscientious objection goes beyond this. It is a set of highly internalized values and norms that reflect the opposition of individuals not to the specific constraint of conscription but to the wider issue of the legitimacy of the military, to the recognition of the state system's reliance on violence, and ultimately to the very nature of war itself.

Even so, there is a danger that a too hasty identification of conscientious objection with a traditional and limited typology restricts the significance of such opposition in the context of contemporary norms and values. Nowhere is this opposition more important than in the context of contemporary political movements in Europe in the 1980s and early 1990s, where it can be regarded as a general form of "war resistance." In contrast, traditional conscientious objection is an expression of highly internalized attitudes in response to specific stimuli. These stimuli generally have been associated with the prosecution of war, but they have also been identified more specifically with a personal and highly individual opposition to conscription, as in the United Kingdom in 1916 and in the United States during the Vietnam War.

Contemporary political development encourages a critical evaluation of past experience. If, for example, war is no longer to be viewed as an inevitable concomitant of foreign policy, then we must question whether conscientious objection based on a general opposition to war is to be expected. The British evidence drawn from the activities of the Greenham Common women in the 1980s suggests that while males' conscientious objection in the absence of conscription becomes less and less an issue of concern, many women's attitudes continue to be based on such general opposition to war and the military. Conceptually this position is a continuance of a form of conscientious objection that is based on pacifism.

Therefore it can be concluded that until certain issues such as war and peace, violence and nonviolence, freedom and obligation have disappeared from the contemporary world, this type of conscientious objection will continue to be prevalent. Indeed, the hypothesis can be taken a stage further. Whereas conscientious objection based on a rejection of conscription is inextricably identified with *military* service, more general opposition to war and weaponry, of the type epitomized by the Greenham Common reaction, may more properly be identified with a generic rejection of violence. If this position is identified with a continuum of protest, we can begin to locate recent events within a specific structural framework.

Conventionally conscientious objection is related to anticonscription movements or to opposition to a specific war. An underlying thesis of this essay is that the legitimation of armed domination of a given territorial area by a ruling group was the crucial moment in the founding of all states. War, mobilization, conscription, the loyalty of the armed forces remain the most crucial test of sovereignty. Accordingly the traditional mode of conscientious objection has been formulated on a continuum of the processes associated with the maintenance of that sovereignty.

It can now be suggested that the contemporary phenomenon of conscientious objection is much wider-ranging. A continuum of protest suggests that it continues to incorporate reactions to such issues as the irrationality of the arms race, technological determinism, and natural aggression. Contemporary political movements in Western society may materially affect the conventional and traditional interpretation of the role of the military and the characteristics of the phenomenon of war resistance. Political change, however, is unlikely to affect that form of conscientious objection in which a set of highly internalized values reflects a religious or secular pacifism that opposes the power of the bureaucratized and centralized state. Here the almost inevitable conflict of national coercion with individual freedom continues to attract the attention of those whose conscience reacts to the stimuli of state control, coercion, and conscription. The British experience suggests that conscientious objection is not simply a legacy of the past; rather it is a significant characteristic of future responses to the existence of violence, war, and military forces within society.

6

France: A Statute but No Objectors

MICHEL L. MARTIN

In France, the concept of the citizen soldier and the obligation of male citizens for military service through universal conscription have been vital parts of the nation's tradition ever since the French Revolution linked democracy and universal service. In the French view, conscription contributes to the republican tradition and national unity as well as to national defense: Those who refuse to serve are seen as directly challenging a unifying and primary principle that underlies the nation and the state itself.

Objection to armed service is a perennial phenomenon. It takes various forms, from lack of discipline and disobedience to draft dodging and desertion. Its causes are complex—at the same time psychological, economical, and social. They can also be idealistic, related to the domain of conscience. Weapons are rejected because they suggest the inflicting of death on others; bearing arms is refused because it prefigures the resort to violence. In a less holistic fashion, military service is denied because it operates in an unjust or questionable sociopolitical order.

This type of pacifist conduct is undoubtedly rooted in the instinct of self-preservation, but it becomes socially legitimate in particular cultural contexts, as in the West under the impact of Christianity relayed on a secular level by all political ideologies centering on individual freedom and human rights.[1]

Such eminently personal behavior of a normative nature is, however, problematic when it conflicts with other legitimate claims linked to the perennial quality of the sociopolitical order. The resulting tension is still more acute when, as in France, the demand for military service is the basis of the reality of the state and the integration of the nation, and is greatest when military service is equated with citizenship and liberal political institutions.[2]

Dilemmas created by conscientious objection are manifest. Even at its most restrictive and conventional level—the refusal to bear arms—conscientious objection appears as an asocial attitude since it results in rejecting the collective responsibilities of national solidarity. Given the symbiotic relationship of military service and citizenship, it amounts to a form of political self-disfranchisement. Since, in the name of a higher moral ideal, it claims to be above the rule of the majority, it goes against the establishment; in any case, it appears as undemocratic in that it violates the principle of the equality of all before the state as well as the sociopolitical consensus founding the democratic system.

Questioning the validity of conscription, which has long been seen as central to the very essence of the state, is anti-institutional. This is especially true when conscientious objection is secularized and proceeds from political motivations that are expressed in a militant manner, rather than in the traditional contemplative way, and it goes beyond the questioning of only armed service to encompass all the obligations related to the integration of the individual in the polity. Conscientious objection could easily meld with anarchistic, if not nihilistic, currents of civic disobedience.

Conversely, at least in a democratic context, it is difficult to deny a position that derives naturally from the philosophy of a society based on the perennial Christian dichotomies between the individual and collective, and the public and private.[3] Moreover, the continuous extension of citizens' rights to the extreme peripheries of the social system has helped to bring conscientious objection, even in its most radical and comprehensive manifestations, into the mainstream.[4] This evolution has reinforced the legitimation of conscientious objection, not only in its traditional religious configuration but also in its contemporary secularized forms.

Sociopolitical responses to conscientious objection vary according to the conflicting demands of individualistic and collective ideals. Societies that put a premium on individual values are generally more permissive than those that give priority to the public norm, a dichotomy which used to coincide with Protestant and Catholic cultures. Today such an opposition is less pronounced, and the increasing interdependence of modern societies and the declining role and power of the state in contemporary democratic systems tend to evince similar responses to problems. In the case of conscientious objection, it tends to take a more liberal and secular view of it.

In this regard, France constitutes a unique case. Despite its historical claim as a pioneer in the rights and liberties of citizens, but because of its strong tradition of upholding the state, it is only recently that France has approached conscientious objection in a manner that can be considered liberal, and this is true only when compared with past policies. Fully institutionalized in France since 1983, the liberalization seems especially limited when compared to objectors' expectations or to practices in other Western countries.

This chapter is devoted to a description of the historical evolution of conscientious objector status in France, and related issues such as a sociological profile of conscientious objectors and prevailing social attitudes toward this type of conduct.[5]

The Heritage of the Revolution

Refusal of military service in France became an issue when such an obligation was institutionalized. The recourse to a compulsory military service, reflecting the centralizing logic of the absolutist monarchy and accentuated later during the Revolution, was massively opposed. This began with the establishment in 1688 of the royal militia, set up beside the more traditional local communal forms of military service, and with systematic utilization of the royal militia during the second half of the eighteenth century.[6] It accelerated during the Revolution, when—following the call for volunteers in 1791–1792—there were successive call-ups, and again during the Consulate and the Empire, when national conscription was introduced with the 1798 Jourdan-Delbrel law. After that, the numbers were increased every year.[7] Between 1791 and 1810, more than 2,500,000 men were drafted. But except during brief periods of patriotic enthusiasm, objection was endemic, as shown by the high rate of draft dodging and desertion among more than a third of the men called up, not counting the various, more clandestine modes of evasion.

Statements from various military authorities and judicial documents show that objection to military service was based on the rejection of a system that separated the individual from his communal loyalties, his economic attachments, and his family obligations. It was, to refer to a somewhat overused distinction, the resistance of the *Gemeinschaft* (community) to the emerging imperium of the *Gesellschaft* (society). However, considerations of an ideal or ethical nature were absent. There was no trace of religious pacifism or moral or political objection.[8] This absence of idealistic objection is probably related in part to the rural bases of military recruitment and the recruits' general lack of education. It is also related to the fact that local French culture was still largely influenced by Catholicism, which had abandoned the original Christian pacifism at the Council of Arles in 314, and did not consider a legitimate resort to armed violence immoral. Consequently, conscientious objection in France was circumscribed to a small number of dissenting Christian sects, such as the Anabaptists in the eastern areas.

Conscientious objection was tolerated by the French revolutionary government probably because it was marginal, rather than out of a libertarian concern. This decision of the Committee on Public Safety in favor of Anabaptists is usually cited as the first indication of tolerance, but in fact it goes back to the *ancien régime:*

> "[for] the citizens whose religion and morality forbid [them] to bear arms . . . [the decision has been made] to prevent them from being persecuted and to grant them the service they ask for in the armies . . . or to allow them to redeem this service in money."

The status of objectors in the beginning was ill-defined and precarious. It was only afterwards, under the Consulate and Empire, that it would be formally recognized.

In many ways the ideals of freedom advocated by the French Revolution competed with another emerging moral demand, no less imperious, that of service to the nation. Early measures in favor of conscientious objection were abandoned, though, as France entered a peaceful period, modes of military recruitment, derived from the laws of 1818 (Gouvion Saint-Cyr), 1832 (Soult), and 1856 and 1868, were based on only partial forms of compulsory military service.

Systematization of the citizens' military participation with the development of the mass-army model, introduced by the laws of 1889 and 1905 and articulated through active and reserve forces in peace as well as war, did not produce a wave of evasion similar to that in the early nineteenth century. Conscientious objection appeared almost nonexistent, limited to a small number of sectarians, until after World War I. It was challenged only by the emergence, after the Dreyfus affair at the turn of the century, of an antimilitarist current on the part of literary figures, anarchists, and the extreme Left, which branded the army an instrument of social repression and which advocated refusal to serve in it.

The patriotic fervor born from the spirit of revenge after the Franco-Prussian War of 1870 is one explanation for the general acceptance of conscription. The most important factor, however, was the success of the new religion of civic nationalism advocated by the modern and consolidated nation-state. The lack of interest in, and even outright public animosity toward, draft evaders demonstrates the legitimacy and the strength of this evolution. The severity of sentences against draft evaders is noteworthy: Defaulters and conscience objectors, even into the late 1950s, were treated as common deserters and given harsh sentences. It was commonly one year in jail (often with hard labor) after the first refusal to respond to a draft call, followed by additional two-year periods each time the objector subsequently refused to join his unit. This could last until the objector reached the age of 50.

There was some change after the First World War, led by the action of pacifist movements, Christian and secular, national and international, including the International War Resisters League, the International Movement of Reconciliation, and the Reformed Church of France, whose antiwar position was opposed by the Roman Catholic Church. In 1920 the Committee for the Defense of Conscientious Objection was created, followed later by the League for the Recognition of Conscientious Objection. However, this evolution did not go very far.

Conscientious objection remained a poor mobilizing issue in France. There were only about forty COs, some of whom made no public appeal, almost wishing, it appears, to assume the consequences of their actions. In the interwar period, only one proposal advocating legal recognition of conscientious objection (the Richard Georges bill of 1931) was introduced in the National Assembly, and it was largely ignored. In a rigorous response to a campaign supporting COs and advocating destruction of draft records, the government in 1934 ordered the dissolution of the League for the Defense of Conscientious Objection.

This harsh governmental attitude toward conscientious objection continued until the 1960s. But society's relationship to conscientious objection became gradually more moderate, as most COs, not seeking to pose as martyrs, asked for no particular exemption; they were willing to accept any alternative service rather than demand, in the "absolutist" perspective, a full dispensation of service. In 1948 the Reformed Church of France recognized the legitimate character of this behavior and claimed it should be admitted officially. The League of Human Rights, as well as members of leftist parties and trade unions, adopted a similar position. The Socialists thus initiated a proposal to establish an alternative civic service program for COs. Put forward by André Philip in 1949, it was reintroduced by the Christian Democrats in 1952 and again by the Socialists in 1956. French Communists in May 1950 proposed a measure to free imprisoned COs. In 1953 an amnesty bill defended by the Socialists with Daniel Mayer was carried in the National Assembly but failed in the Senate.[9]

From this point on, the issue of conscientious objection took on a growing importance. On the one hand, it continued to develop on a religious basis, as the members of sects grew; there were 20 Jehovah's Witnesses in 1952, 50 in 1957, and 150 in 1964.[10] On the other hand, it took on an increasingly secular dimension; earlier pacifism grew into political opposition against the Algerian war, when draftees were called up and sent to North Africa. Secular conscientious opposition was encouraged by various antiwar and antimilitary organizations, such as the Jeune Résistance Movement, and it was supported by the signatories of the "Manifesto of the One Hundred and Twenty-One." Although there were fewer than one hundred COs between 1945 and 1955, their number reached more than two hundred in the early 1960s. Consequently, though still not strong, they succeeded in mobilizing themselves. Under the aegis of Louis Lecoin, a CO and an anarchist, objectors established the organization Aid to Conscientious Objectors and the journal *Liberté;* they also created the Center of Defense of the Objectors, directed by Emile Véran.

Nevertheless, Parliament did not adopt any of the reform proposals until 1958, when it granted COs the option of serving as paramedics in a paratroop unit. This concession satisfied few, since it still meant service in a military, indeed a combat, unit. The government decided, for humanitarian reasons—and actually in contradiction to the law—to limit the jail sentences for COs to five years; this was further reduced to three years after 1962.

The 1963 Legalization of Conscientious Objection

The government of General Charles de Gaulle decided in 1962 to overcome the opposition of an obstinate Parliament that had rejected a fifth proposal to accept the legalization of conscientious objection. The cessation of war in Algeria meant that the traditional rigidity was no longer justified. Furthermore, most major Western nations had already recognized conscientious objection. As President de Gaulle explained: "It is absurd and undignified to let conscientious objectors be treated as delinquents." In July 1963, at the direction of Prime Minister Georges Pompidou, a bill to legalize conscientious objection was introduced in Parliament.[11]

The 1963 bill, inspired in many particulars by André Philip's 1949 proposal, was liberal enough, though not as advanced as the first governmental proposal. Recognition as a CO was not granted automatically, but rather had to be conferred by a commission. But there were no limiting specifications regarding the principles of those opposed to bearing arms. Candidates had a month after the *conseil de révision* to submit their request. If granted CO status, they had to serve either in an unarmed military unit or in a civilian group performing alternative service in the public interest. The length of alternative service was to be one and one-half times that of normal military service. The proposal's aims were to decriminalize the conduct of the relatively small number of COs by recognizing their action, and to organize their participation in civic duty without breaching the principle of national service.

The bill proved extremely controversial, especially among the Gaullist majority in the Parliament. Unable to reject a proposal supported by the president, the National Assembly sought to modify it through numerous restrictive amendments.[12] The Senate was adamantly opposed. After nearly six months of tumultuous debate and much pressure from the executive branch, Parliament adapted the reform law by a narrow majority of 204 on December 11, 1963. Passage came despite dissent from both the Right and the Left; the latter, although favoring legal recognition, was disappointed in the limited liberalization.

The law, which went into effect December 21, 1963, was indeed an adulterated version of the original proposal.[13] In the law's twelve articles, the words "conscientious objection," and "conscientious objector" are never even mentioned as recognized status. Rather, the document refers only to a method of accomplishing military service. Even the 1959 ordinance had recognized the comprehensive notion of defense and anticipated the extension of the citizen's service outside the sole military domain. Furthermore, article 11, resulting from an amendment introduced by Gaullist deputy Hubert Germain, forbids any "propaganda under any possible form, intending to incit[e] anyone to benefit from the stipulations of the present law.... " It imposes severe sanctions for such "propaganda," jail terms of six months to three years and fines from 360 francs to 10,000 francs. Indeed, the purpose was to punish propaganda that had as its aim "the exclusive goal of avoiding one's military obligations." Deliberately left unclear was how to distinguish between information and propaganda thereby allowing a wide application of the measure. The aim clearly was to cloak the statute in secrecy.

The dissuasive nature of the 1963 law is also evident in the constraints on obtaining CO status, insofar the objector could be aware of the statute—circumstances made more difficult by article 11. The objector was to file an application within fifteen days following publication of the decree calling the contingent to which he belonged to join the armed forces. This is very short notice, with a rather confidential quality, since the decree is published in the government's *Journal Officiel* and may or may not be published by the press.[14] Furthermore no provision was made for CO requests after entering military service.[15]

A CO request, addressed to the minister of national defense, would be transmitted to a jurisdictional commission composed of a magistrate designated by the minister of justice, three officers nominated by the minister of national defense, and three persons named by the prime minister. The commission would meet privately and make the decision without the objector present. There were only limited grounds for an appeal, which would be heard by the minister of national defense, and in any case the appellant's entrance to the armed forces would *not* be delayed during the course of the appeal.

The legislators also increased the burden of proof for the objector and gave great discretionary powers to the commission. Several subjective qualifications were required for refusal to bear arms: opposition must be grounded upon sincere "convictions," these must be "religious or philosophical," and they must apply in "all circumstances."

These conditions implied at the same time the demonstration of the depth, the perennial quality, the intimate and personal nature, and the specificity of the objection. Such requirements considerably limited the scope of legitimate objection. They excluded secularized (purely moral or political) and circumstantial requests. Judging subjectively on the sincerity of these beliefs, the commission was given wide discretion and its composition warranted that each condition be strictly applied. As a result, between 1963 and 1978, 5,655 CO requests were accepted out of 7,251, a rejection rate of 23 percent. Between 1974 and 1979, this rejection rate increased to nearly 30 percent.[16]

Two other elements reinforced the dissuasive nature of the 1963 law. Article 8 forced COs to serve for a period nearly double that of regular military service. This was partly a way to preserve the equality of public duties, the objector compensating with additional time for the more dangerous tasks assumed by draftees. However, considering that the CO might serve in an unarmed but nevertheless military unit and that in a general mobilization he would be assigned to defense duties, the disposition cannot be justified only in terms of equity. Article 12, even though it has not been enforced, sought to forbid access by COs to many governmental jobs. It indicates the dissuasive intention of the lawmakers; the limited number of satisfied requests—around sixty per year between 1965 and 1975—is proof of it.

The fact that practically nothing had been organized for the objector's service, except its duration and the provision that it be done in an unarmed unit or a civilian formation engaged in tasks of national interest, added another element of uncertainty. "The history of the application of the statute of December 1963," declared Joël Le Theule, member of the Assembly's national defense commission, in 1970, "is that of a succession of failures."[17]

Concerning the places of service, several policies had been developed under a succession of unenthusiastic bureaucratic agencies that failed to provide an adequate situation for the certified COs. Between 1964 and 1968 COs served with the Civil Safety service placed under the Ministry of Interior. But the peculiar nature of this organization, which was a part of the defense system, as well as its disciplinary and command rules, defined it as a paramilitary service, making it unacceptable to COs. In 1969, now under the Ministry of Social Affairs (later the Ministry of Public Health), objectors were assigned to hospitals as paramedical personnel, but this program also failed. Moreover, it was not clear whether COs, even in their civilian alternative service, came under military or civil law. The legal vacuum left by the text of 1963—later partially rectified by a decree in 1972—caused unending conflicts between COs and their superiors, and was the object of several lawsuits.

Such conditions were of no serious consequences, since the number of COs remained circumscribed. But in the early 1970s the situation began to deteriorate rapidly. While the 1963 statute and its applications appeared everyday more inadequate, the nature and the extent of conscientious objection evolved significantly.

The National Service Law of June 10, 1971, which regrouped all dispositions concerning national service and introduced various important reforms, touched only marginally on conscientious objection.[18] The term "conscientious objectors" was used (though not the term "status"), the filing time for a request was extended from fifteen to thirty days, and the stipulation about forbidden jobs was abolished. Moreover, the civilian law courts were declared competent to deal with contraventions of a military nature, such as default and desertion by certified objectors. However, the issue of "propaganda," or publicity about the CO provision was untouched. Many aspects of CO service continued to be subject to military disciplinary regulations. And although civilian courts were allowed to handle certain military offenses, they were required to apply the Code of Military Justice: thus COs were largely assimilated as draftees in the armed forces. The parliamentary debates and reports, particularly those of the Senate, demonstrate that these conservative positions derived from a fear both of mounting conscientious objection and a desire for stricter control.[19]

The subjugation of COs under the 1971 Act was, at least initially, even stricter than under the 1963 law. On August 31, 1972, under the so-called decree of Brégançon inserted into the Code of National Service, objectors had to obtain administrative authorization to express themselves on political and international issues.[20] They could not participate in any political or trade union activities or meetings, or petition, demonstrate, or strike. Any violation exposed the CO to sanctions prescribed under general military discipline.

For their first year of service, COs were assigned to tasks by the Ministry of Agriculture, the new tutelary ministry. Until 1975, assignments were made in several different agencies dealing with forestry, social welfare, and culture. These assignments provoked strong opposition among objectors (as well as discontent among these agencies' employees). The COs objected to their arbitrary character, to the limitations imposed on their political freedom, and to their living conditions and the tasks to be performed.[21] Although after 1977 they were allowed to perform service in an enlarged and more diverse spectrum of organizations—including groups linked with youth and sports, health and education, and various private associations—their protests continued. Many refused to join their posts. The number of young men admitted as COs but refusing their assignment (such action was called "civil service dodging") grew significantly—to twenty-three hundred in 1979. Between 1979 and 1980 such evasions increased from 32 percent to 59 percent.[22]

This mounting protest derived in part from the restrictive character of the conditions surrounding objectors' service, but it was also linked to the changing nature of conscientious objection that developed in the late 1960s.

The Transformation of Conscientious Objection

From the late 1960s to the 1970s, conscientious objection in France both changed and increased dramatically. Previously representing largely passive and introverted behavior, it had been motivated by a belief of deeply ethical and philosophical, if not fully religious, convictions. But as with many other social and individual attitudes in those decades under the effect of the liberalization of values and beliefs,[23] conscientious objection became collective, secularized, and extreme. The new con-

scientious objection was more ideological, operating on a more militant and an-
tiestablishment level. Objectors not only protested against the conditions of service
but also refused the very idea of a service to the state. Conscientious objection in
this uncompromising stance is a means of denouncing the societal status quo, of
rejecting what is seen as oppressive authority in general, be it military or civilian.

In addition, COs began to become organized and politicized. The Secretariat
of the Conscientious Objectors was succeeded by organizations more anti-militarist,
such as the Committee for the Support of Conscientious Objectors and the Committee for the Objectors' Struggle. Others—the Groups for Total Defaulting (meaning refusal to respond to a call-up), the Groups for Collective Defaulting, and the
very active Group of Action and Resistance to Militarization, which appeared in
the early 1970s—advocated resistance. An analysis of the content of the CO organizations' main publications confirms this politicization.[24] Thus, alongside legal
conscientious objection, a militant new secular objection directly challenged both
the military and the established system of national defense.

Expansion of the new conscientious objection was related both to organizational
growth and external events. Requests for recognition as a CO grew more than eight
times, from 150 in 1969 to 1,208 in 1978.[25] The number of conventional requests
(that is, religious and philosophical-ethical) also increased—from 196 in 1973 to
340 in 1980 (largely because of the growth of Jehovah's Witnesses). More important, however, was the appearance in the 1970s of requests motivated in explicitly
secular political or ideological terms, for example denouncing specific defense
policies, such as French military intervention in Africa or the modernization of the
French nuclear force in Europe. Such requests were often less individualized than
stereotypical. The prototype is a model request nicknamed "*pelles-ploches*"
("shovels-picks") drafted in 1971 by a group of protesting objectors, known as
"O.P. 20." The number of such COs grew from 16 in 1971 to nearly 260 in 1978,
to more than 20 percent of the total.

Resisting authority has also increased. Dodging of civilian alternative service,
called "total defaulting" (an absolutist position), was advocated by various anti-
militarist movements and has become an alternative chosen by COs. This new
behavior is a contributing factor to the general increase in the number of draft
dodgers, which quadrupled between 1968 and 1978, from 906 to 3,969. This growth
also correlates with higher desertion rates—from 1,832 to 4,856 cases between
1968 and 1978.[26] It was during this period that conscientious objection penetrated
the military profession itself, affecting enlistees—even some NCOs and commis-
sioned officers—though there are no precise figures regarding this particular aspect.

Embarrassed authorities have reacted inconsistently. On the one hand, draft
dodgers have been sued or the recognition process has been slowed down. In this
regard, the jurisdictional commission has maintained its firmness. On the other
hand, amnesty has been granted regularly, for example, just after presidential
elections in 1969, 1974, and 1981. Further, through medical, psychiatric, and other
dispensations, a few cases have been removed from the jurisdictional framework
of penal repression. Nevertheless, in 1981, 628 COs were imprisoned. Finally, the
government has sought to alleviate discontent by making alternative service more
acceptable. Arbitrary direction has been reduced, a more diversified context estab-

lished, and, following a bill in August 1975, obligations during service were liberalized by allowing political and union activities.

By the late 1970s, however, the highly polarized approach to the issue declined, and the debate about conscientious objection grew more moderate. Absolutist refusal, denying the essence of conscientious objection, had isolated the radical movement from attracting interest and support from institutional political organizations.[27] New associations now appeared, such as the Federation of Conscientious Objectors (FÉDO) succeeded by the Movement of Conscientious Objectors with far less ideological positions. Even the O.P. 20 became less radical. By the end of the 1970s, advocacy of "defaulting" and the antimilitarist denunciations were, if not abandoned, at least lessened and circumscribed to such specific formations as the Group for Deserter Solidarity.

This is evidenced by the decline in dissident tendencies in the late 1970s and early 1980s. Draft dodging, after reaching a peak of 3,969 cases in 1978, fell to 2,504 in 1979 and 1,877 in 1980. Desertions decreased from 4,856 in 1978 to 3,685 in 1979. The proportion of certified objectors who were draft dodgers or deserters dropped from 40 percent in May 1981 to 19 percent in late 1982. Requests for CO recognition, which reached 1,312 in 1981, declined slightly—to 1,147 in 1982 and 1,100 in 1983. The ratio of secular to religious COs reversed, at least temporarily: More requests were now put in terms of religious or philosophical opposition (the kind required by the statute). Requests based on strictly religious grounds, which composed 44 percent of the total in 1978, grew to 74 percent in 1981.[28]

These changes contributed to a climate more favorable to conscientious objection in the public opinion as well as in the political class now aware not only of the restrictive nature of the CO provisions of the 1963 law but also of the necessity to amend it, as witnessed by the various propositions of reform introduced.[29] That position was enhanced by the arrival in power of the Socialists, who had always evinced a more liberal attitude toward conscientious objection, and whose campaign platform contained a number of specific reforms touching on the national service.[30]

The 1983 CO Status and the Limit to Liberalization

The Socialist government of President François Mitterrand moved the status of conscientious objection to a new level in France. That change was achieved with the passage of the law of July 8, 1983, modifying the Code of the National Service, and completed by Article R. 227 of the decree of March 29, 1984.[31] Compared with the 1963 CO bill, the new provisions are clearly more liberal. Conscientious objection appears now as a genuine right, guaranteed by statute, in the system of public liberties. The 1983 law strips away previous stipulations designed to prevent the dissemination of information about conscientious objection. The service of conscientious objectors is now one of the four forms of civilian service that, along with military service, constitute the national service. It is defined as "civilian service with a social and humanitarian vocation."[32]

The process of obtaining CO status has also been facilitated. A request is possible "at any moment" before the objector's age group is actually called up and until the thirtieth day afterward. In an important further innovation, the request for admission to conscientious objector status may be accepted after completing active military duty, including even active reserve service.[33]

Requirements for certification are now far less restrictive. Considering the term used in the text, "motivations of conscience," there is no special qualification regarding the content, sense, or duration associated with the opposition to the bearing of arms. Authorities' power of appraising the claim can function only marginally, notably with respect to requests formulated in too unorthodox a fashion. In essence a person obtains the right to be a CO if he accepts the conditions defined in the law, especially the requirement to provide alternative service for twenty-four months, twice the length of regular military service. Acceptance of alternative service constitutes the test of the sincerity of his convictions, a "proof by action," in the words of Charles Hernu, minister of national defense in 1983.[34]

The new system bypasses the previous jurisdictional commission, whose role was to judge the legitimacy of the request. Instead, under the 1983 law, CO requests are sent directly to the minister of national defense. That official's role is limited to verifying that deadlines are respected and to refusing requests that do not fulfill the conditions. An objector may appeal to an administrative court that makes the final ruling; however, the Council of State is authorized to annul judgments made by the administrative courts. In contrast to the 1963 law, the claimant's military service is postponed pending outcome of the appeal.

More attention has been given to organizing the objectors' alternative service, though some aspects remain restrictive. The nature and variety of assignments are aimed to satisfy most objectors' expectations. The plan of "a civilian service with a social and humanitarian vocation" is in this regard indicative of a rather open-minded concept of COs' service. It is demilitarized; the former largely unused option of an unarmed military service was abolished. The range of civilian service areas is greatly diversified, encompassing the public sector (national and local) and private organizations "with a social or humanitarian vocation ensuring a mission of general interest." The number of these institutions has almost tripled, from 666 in 1985 to 1,803 in 1988.[35] They include town halls, museums, universities, associations for solidarity, even private radio stations and the like.[36] Further, the CO may choose the general trade of his service as well as the administration or the organization to which he wishes to be assigned—all from a list prepared by the minister that considers the organizations' needs.

The 1983 law also expanded the rights of the COs performing alternative service, completely "demilitarizing" it. No longer under military regulations and discipline, COs are now governed mainly according to the regulations of the employing agencies. Except for being prohibited to strike, COs can participate in all political and trade union activities. For failure to participate in an assignment, COs are subject to the Code of Military Justice; otherwise they come under the authority of the minister of social affairs and national solidarity.

Without doubt, the law of July 1983 considerably liberalizes conscientious objection in France, bringing it into the mainstream and out of the military realm, making it a new right. Still the system is restrictive, especially when compared with those of other Western democracies, and with the expectations of the objectors themselves. Conscientious objectors denounced first the slowness of the reform, then its timidity.[37]

Many—including O.P. 20 and other organizations and individuals—have railed against continuing restrictions, accusing the Socialist government of having reneged on the liberalism of its 1979 proposals. In considering some of these complaints, it must be remembered that if the recognition of conscientious objection is a right, it is one nonetheless obtained by agreement, though there are no real obstacles against this recognition: The filing of a request presumes the motivation of conscience. In the mid- to late 1980s, conscientious objection increased again. The number of CO requests and acceptances more than tripled, growing from 906 in 1982 to 2,951 in 1988.[38] This also testified to the smoothness of the new procedure.

However, the granting of CO status remains non-automatic in principle, and it gives, in theory, considerable discretion to the minister of defense. Because of his functions and involvement with the military, the minister is at the same time judge of and party to the dispute. For many COs a jurisdictional commission, as before, with its collegial structure, offers perhaps greater assurance of objectivity, being more distinct from the military authority. Further, although recognition of conscientious objection can now occur after, as well as before, military service, it remains impossible *while* the individual is on active duty, and it is not open to enlisted personnel. Finally, CO recognition can be withdrawn for insubordination or desertion.

While objectors' service is largely demilitarized, compared with the former system, in some regards it is still derived from military duty. Obligations of objectors as well as some aspects of their rights are reminiscent of those of draftees in the ranks, and the COs are subject to the Code of Military Justice if they default or desert. Also, the two-year alternative service period appears particularly discriminatory as it is longer than the duration of other civilian forms of service, which are already longer than military service. One member of Parliament has labeled it a "vexation [or] punitive measure,"[39] and a disguised means of dissuasion. The objector's choice of assignment is not completely free either since it is selected from a list compiled by the military. And in time of war, COs then assigned to "missions of service and rescue of general interest" could find themselves in situations of armed violence, where the demand has been made in the name of "equality of all in front of the common danger."

There is no need of further evidence of the law's limitations. Every such system, no matter how liberal, will exert some restraint. But clearly the authors of the 1983 reform never sought to create a totally unrestrained framework (which would have been almost impossible), but sought mainly to change the negative and penalizing nature of the 1963 law. It was not their intent to encourage the notion of conscientious objection as commonplace, a concern frequently aired in the debate. "Any particular clemency in favor of conscientious objectors would be inadmissible because it would be unjust," declared one participant in the parliamentary debate, adding that "routinizing objection will nip it in the bud."[40]

Never was there the desire to place France in the forefront of the European movement for liberal recognition of conscientious objection. Indeed, in France the various resolutions of the European Council in favor of liberalization were inter-preted in a restrictive sense, probably contrary to what they intended.[41] During the debate in May 1983, Charles Hernu, French minister of national defense, said that the European Council's 1983 liberal decision on COs "did not have the force of the law." Succeeding ministers of national defense in France agreed.[42] The author of the reform and the government had chosen to remain ambiguous, as many have pointed out. Conscientious objection was recognized as a right, and the policy toward COs was somewhat liberalized. But conscientious objection was certainly not seen as normal conduct, and the terms of alternative service—especially the extended duty period—were designed to discourage significant interference with conscription in France.

The Citizen Soldier in France

The concern with restraining the liberty of COs and facilitating access to CO status might appear surprising. At this time the governing Socialists still viewed their political mission in rather radical terms. Of course, there was the hostility of the former conservative majority and that of the military. But opposition to a greater liberalization of conscientious objection came also from many Socialists, the Com-munists,[43] and other Leftist groups. This wide spectrum results from a prevalent attitude in France, that is, the transcendence of the principle of national and universal conscription. This powerful principle plays the role of a "primary" and axiomatic norm, when various defense issues are considered. This is why France's strategy of nuclear deterrence, which rejects the doctrine of flexible response with its initial stage of ground combat against the enemy, is not seen as contradictory to keeping a large conscript army. It also explains the very small place given to alternative civilian service, and, above all, the view that a fully professionalized military would have no virtue, even if it were considered politically moral. Any military reform, in other words, is always evaluated in light of the basic principle of a national army of citizen soldiers. Politically, the Right as well as the Left share this view, each seeking to appear as custodian of this tradition and accusing the other of violating it. The various interventions of Socialist Defense Minister Charles Hernu against considering reduction of military service or uncontrolled multiplication of oppor-tunities to escape the draft, are telling. As a partisan of the idea of citizen-soldier in the Jaurès tradition, Hernu was responsible for the abandonment of the old antimilitaristic opinion by the Socialists.[44] Military service remains a priority, and in France national service is identical with military service. In 1989, for example, civilian forms of service concerned less than 6 percent of the draft-eligible men. It is noteworthy also that such forms remain justified only in terms of national defense.

The highly normative character of the principle of the citizen-soldier in France derives from its origins and in particular from its linkage with the genesis of the democratic nation-state. More than anywhere else, this development was long and difficult in France because of the vitality and the resistance of the country's various regions, the *Gemeinschaften*, to use Tönnies' word, to their integration in the rising *Gesellschaft*'s center. In this struggle, initiated under the *ancien régime* and continued during the Revolution and by Napoleon, military conscription played a decisive role to the advantage of the center *imperium*. It was an older role, for that matter, than that played by other institutions, such as the *école publique*. The first instance of real contact between the state and civil society, conscription at first produced massive evasion and resistance to which the state responded coercively.[45] But with the consolidation of the state organizations, created by the setting up of the administration and control of the mass armies, military service eventually became the main vehicle for the integration and acculturation of the peripheries to the nation-state. Conscription provided also other material advantages by offering an opportunity to break away from familial, religious, and occupational constraints, as well by inculcating modern standards of hygiene, nutrition, and health.[46]

But this process operated also in a revolutionary way in that the institutionalization of military service came to be associated with the emergence of democratic ideology and structures; it was in 1793, the year the *levée en masse* was decreed, that universal suffrage was declared for the first time. The arming of the masses introduced by the Revolution was the essential element of the transfer of the sovereignty to the nation. It was at the same time a way to obtain citizenship and the test of the loyalty toward the new regime. This, with the institutionalization of the *levée* into a regular conscription, the revolutionary regime and its successors have regenerated through a sort of "political sublimation" a compulsory military service that was previously condemned as a form of enslavement. Machiavelli and Rousseau actually were the first to anticipate the interaction between democratic development and conscription, something that Engels, Mosca, and later Janowitz fully demonstrated in their analyses of the political function of military service in the West.[47]

Because of its linkage with these two decisive moments in French history, conscription ended in subsuming the ideals of the nation-state and democracy. Ideology, afterwards, contributed to mythologize this union in the national belief system, as shown by the way the historical past is viewed in France. The political and military discourse took on these themes, giving conscription a superior military value in addition to its political and social advantages. Even partisans of an all-volunteer force have to present their goal not as a means to displace the conscript-army but as a way to complement it.

An analysis of French *mentalité* since the end of the nineteenth century testifies to this attachment to the institution of the citizen army. For a long time anyone who did not perform military obligations faced a certain ostracism. It was perhaps temporary, but it was not without consequences, notably in lower and middle classes—resulting in difficulties, for example, in finding a wife or a job.[48] Things have changed somewhat, but in some milieus at least vague reprobation still surrounds a man who is exempted from military service. Conscription may seem a disturbing obligation and it is often criticized, but no one would oppose its existence. Until quite recently between 60 and 70 percent of the French public were favorable to it. Actually this was one of the rare instances of the national consensus. Indeed, although among young men it is seen as disturbing, often absurd, they do not seek to escape it even if they verbally question it. The rate of defaulting remains insignificant, less than 0.50 percent of the draft, and fraud is allegedly nonexistent. Of course, many are happy to be exempted within the officially defined medical or social criteria. It is also possible to choose among the various paramilitary or civilian options offered in place of military service. However, these options continue to be justified as normal forms of citizen defense participation. Moreover, they concern only a small proportion of the call-up contingent: in 1988 they involved 8,781 cases, about 2.5 percent of all draftees.[49]

The Marginal Character of French COs Today

Despite the liberalization of conscientious objection, absolutist objection, which refuses any service even indirectly linked with the military, remains a rather infrequent phenomenon in France. The 1983 law did not produce a flood of CO applications, as some had feared. Rather, between 1983 and 1986, the number of requests grew from 1,707 to 2,737, then stayed stable with 2,950 in 1988 and 2,861 in 1989.[50] In February 1989, French COs totaled 5,300—low in terms of statistics for Western countries—nowhere near the wild fears that it would reach 100,000 cases or possibly even emulate the West German situation, in which there is one objector out of every four draftees.[51]

It seems that the conscientious objector has still a rather negative image in France. A member of the Coordinating Committee for Civilian Service declared in 1989 that "still today objectors are suspected of some kind of uncivic behavior that would endanger the society." Many associations hide the fact that they employ objectors, as though "they would be ashamed of it."[52] And some express fear that conscientious objectors who are involved with educational institutions might corrupt the views of young people.[53] Likewise, the legal sanctions for which defaulting objectors are liable—in 1988, more than five hundred were jailed with some sentenced up to fourteen years—indicate the implicit social reprobation that the judges were representing.[54]

A current statistical profile of COs in France reflects their marginality, although the data are often scarce and imprecise. Excluding COs with religious motivations (essentially Jehovah's Witnesses, who are not a small proportion of the total), the secular objectors appear to be asocial, refusing obedience in general and emphasizing self-autonomy and disengagement from the world; they represent extreme forms of the general tendency toward individualism.[55]

Geographically, in 1981 the secular COs came disproportionately from two regions, Rhône-Alpes (17.4 percent) and the Île de France (17.2 percent), although these proportions have slightly declined since 1979. In Brittany, however, the number of objectors increased somewhat (from 5.7 percent in 1979 to 7.6 percent in 1981). The average objector is slightly younger than he used to be (twenty-one-and-one-half-years-old in 1981, opposed to more than twenty-two years of age in 1979).

The secular CO is also better educated than the average draftee. Yet conscientious objection does not appear to be a phenomenon linked to the intellectual stratum as it was some years ago. Although students still represent an important segment, their percentage has declined—from 36.4 percent in 1979 to 27.8 percent in 1981—evidence of an apparent depoliticization of conscientious objection (at least of the reasons given for objection) in that period. Similarly, the number of working-class objectors has dropped—from 15.8 percent to 9.3 percent between 1979 and 1981.[56] Symptomatic of this new profile is the increasing proportion of COs coming from low-level clerical and support positions, and from educational white-collar occupations: from 7 to 12 percent between 1979 and 1981. These are social groups where an individualistic or radical outlook are the most prevalent.

The history of conscientious objection in France shows that after long being outlawed, it was first recognized—if within a rather constraining framework—in 1963, then liberalized in 1983. There continue to be more restrictions and opprobrium, however, in France than in other major Western nations. Yet such particularism is not incongruent with the current social thought. In a way, the phrase attributed to General de Gaulle in 1962 when president of the Republic—"I want a statute but no objectors"—seems essentially realized.

The Future of Conscientious Objection in France

Students of French society today tend to agree that most salient and representative elements of France's uniqueness or "exceptionalism"[57] have changed. As for conscription, and connected issues as conscientious objection, such a prediction, taking into account the trend described in the preceding section, might appear excessive. Yet it is not impossible that it may be only premature.

On a general level, integration into the European Community will certainly accentuate the movement toward general norms and toward thinking that is more akin to the dominant pacifist tendencies in Europe, thus reducing the singular quality of conscientious objection in France. At the same time, the decline of Catholicism and the growth of Anglo-Saxon and Americanized values will contribute to the revival of individualism and the devaluation of both public norms and the exaltation of the state. New manifestations of civil life operating on more material and individualistic levels will displace traditional collective forms of citizenship epitomized by the military service. This focus on libertarianism will help to justify individualist and noninstitutional behavior such as conscientious objection.

Evolution on the international scene, moreover, could accelerate these trends. The collapse of the communist order has changed the kind of threat that determines the organization of national defense. If the emerging world system is not threat-free, as shown by the Persian Gulf conflict and the violent disintegration of Yugoslavia, the evolution has nevertheless created an equivocal demobilizing climate that has rendered obsolete the defense institutions in their traditional configuration.

A poll conducted in 1989 found that the French public put risks of war last (22 percent of responses) after ecological dangers (48 percent), terrorism (45 percent), and economic threats (27 percent). Even the French spirit of defense is undergoing modifications. While 57 percent favor a nuclear capability, many, nevertheless, oppose the use of nuclear arms. In the hypothetical case of a Soviet invasion, negotiation was seen in 1989 as preferable (56 percent) to the use of nuclear weapons (6 percent) and even to the use of conventional forces (25 percent). Significantly, French respondents (56 percent) felt that funds expended for nuclear forces would be better employed for educational and health benefits.[58] France has probably been less affected by pacifism than any other major Western nation, but its sentiment could evolve in that direction.[59] On the Left, the French Communist party served to hinder the development of pacifist tendencies, but its current credibility problem could result in effecting such a change.[60]

Above all, the principle of conscription seems to be losing its characteristic salience in France. Although the public does not yet believe it is possible to abolish it, French citizens are less persuaded that it is the best means to structure a modern military institution. There is growing debate about the increasing inequality of conscription. Above all, the idea of an all-volunteer force is becoming more popular. A survey in early 1989 showed that 49 percent of the French people were in favor of an all-volunteer system. This was up from 32 percent in 1981. In 1991, it reached a national average of 66 percent (with, as always, a higher figure among young people).[61] Support for an all-volunteer force came from the Right as well as the Left.

The trend toward popular support for an all-volunteer force also reflected official discourse, military and civilian. Although President Mitterrand has reaffirmed regularly the "indispensable character" of conscription in France, he also promoted a reduction in its length. Since the end of 1991, military service is down to ten months. Others, such as former president Giscard d'Estaing, former premiers Pierre Messmer, Jacques Chirac, Laurent Fabius, defense ministers Jean-Pierre Chevènement and Pierre Joxe, have declared their preference for the all-volunteer system. It is noteworthy that sympathizers with the Left have become less favorable to conscription than people of conservative opinion. In 1989, 49 percent of respondents with Socialist outlook were partisan of the all-volunteer force. In the military establishment, traditionally attached to conscription, at least in the army,[62] proponents of the all-volunteer system are more numerous and among them, General J. Lacaze, a former Army chief of staff, is one of its staunchest partisans.[63] It is true that the Persian Gulf conflict, regarded by many as typical of the future form of war waging, demonstrated, in the French case, how the conscript model could jeopardize a massive external deployment.

It is not the primary purpose of this study to speculate about the future of conscription, even less to declare it finished and discuss alternatives. Unless the international environment becomes massively pacified, it is probable that an armed force relying on a form of military service, undoubtedly refashioned, will remain in place in France. It is sure that the reconfiguration of the global threat system, which seems to assume a south-south dimension with a possible shift on the north-south axis, is susceptible to the production of crises which an all-volunteer would handle more adequately. However, the harmonization of east-west relations, the formation of democratic regimes as successors to communism, and the stabilization of the European theater remain problematic, indicating that predictions of a "warless society" are quite premature. In this context, which implies heavier military engagements, a mixed military organization with a military service remains valid in France. This being said, the military service cannot be maintained as it once was. If it must operate in a spirit of equality and universality, the only means to justify it, it will have to be greatly reorganized. Among the reforms possible, the multiplication of short alternative civilian services, in addition to military service in a strict sense, is the most logical.[64] In such circumstances, then, the service of conscientious objectors would become a form of service as any other, perceived as such by its beneficiaries as well as the rest of the society.

7

The Federal Republic of Germany: Conscientious Objection as Social Welfare

JÜRGEN KUHLMANN
EKKEHARD LIPPERT

The right to conscientious objection is more unequivocally specified in the Constitution of the Federal Republic of Germany than in any other country in the world. Article 4 of the Basic Law of 1949 states: "No one shall be forced to do war service with arms against his conscience." This fundamental right became operative in 1956 with the formation of the Bundeswehr and the introduction of male conscription. Subsequent judicial and administrative rulings have made the right of conscientious objection equally applicable to both peacetime military service and war service.

In German constitutional law the right to object to military service for reasons of conscience takes priority over the principle of compulsory military service. This right extends to the service member already in uniform as well as to the potential draftee. From a legal standpoint, a person's conscience is considered to be "an inner moral conviction of what is right and wrong and the resulting obligation to act or not act in a certain way.... "[1] Selective conscientious objection, however, is not allowed under German law. A German CO must, in theory if not in actuality, be against the use of all armed force.

There is virtually no precedent for the contemporary legitimacy of conscientious objection in German history.[2] Certain exemptions, later withdrawn, were granted to Mennonite communities in the kingdom of Prussia of 1780. During World War I those few men who refused to do active duty for reasons of conscience were either declared to be of unsound mind and ordered to undergo psychiatric treatment, or accused of incitement to disaffection in the armed forces, and sentenced accordingly. With the reinstatement of compulsory military service in the so-called Third Reich, conscientious objectors were initially imprisoned. After 1938, and particularly after the beginning of World War II, conscientious objection was punishable by death. During this period, conscientious objectors, notably Jehovah's Witnesses, were sent to concentration camps and executed.

The Standing of the CO in the Federal Republic

In terms of the "new conscientious objection," the key point is that secular grounds are on an equal basis with religious ones to establish the bona fides of conscientious objection in Germany. This has been true since the founding of the Federal Republic shortly after World War II. "The decision made for reasons of conscience can be based on religious conviction, ethical or humanitarian views, or ideological-pacifist reasons. Rational and intellectual consideration or political opinions alone are not sufficient, but they can become intensive enough so as to affect a decision for reasons of conscience."[3] Interestingly enough, the term "conscientious objector" per se is not used in Germany. The exact word is *Wehrdienstverweigerer* or "defense service refuser."

Early on, Germany set up a system of alternative civilian service for recognized conscientious objectors. This form of service was initially referred to as *Ziviler Ersatzdienst* or "alternative civilian service." Since 1973, the official term has been *Zivildienst* or "civilian service." The shift in terminology reflects the growing equivalency of civilian and military service in the Federal Republic. Significantly, Germany allows no non-combatant military service. All conscientious objectors must perform their service outside of the armed forces. Thus, *Zivildienst* has become the hallmark of the institutionalization of conscientious objection the Germany.

Up to 1984 every person seeking conscientious objection status had to establish his credibility to the satisfaction of an examining board. This oral inquest was a grueling event for the conscientious objection applicant. Persons granted objector status would perform *Zivildienst* for the same duration as that of a drafted soldier, usually two years during this period. Exempted from military conscription, in addition to those who failed entrance standards, were young men who took part in civil defense or disaster control work, who volunteered for overseas development work, who were members of the border police, or who were enrolled in theology schools.

Nineteen eighty-four was a watershed year in conscientious objection. Three changes of consequence occurred in that year. One was the distancing of *Zivildienst* from military service by shifting administrative responsibility from the Ministry of Defense to the Ministry for Youth, Family Affairs, Women and Health. Second, the term of civilian service was set at one-third longer than that of military service, the rationale being that military service was more onerous and had reserve obligations following active duty.[4] Thus from 1984 to 1990, the civilian server performed twenty months of duty compared to fifteen months for the conscript.

The most far-reaching of the 1984 changes was the easing of procedures for recognition of conscientious objection. Under the new format, the Federal Office of Civilian Service merely checks written applications to see that they correspond with the legal requirements pertaining to completeness and credibility. Only COs already in the military are required to undergo an oral examination. The applications includes a life history and a personal statement of one's motives for seeking conscientious objection status. The Office of Civilian Service is not allowed to conduct follow-up investigations of CO applicants. For all practical purposes, the applicant's written documents are the sole source on which decisions to grant CO status are made.

In the 1970s approximately half of all CO applicants were recognized. By the late 1980s the figure was close to 99 percent.[5] In other words, recognition of conscientious objection had become largely pro forma. An applicant's willingness to perform *Zivildienst* became the de facto criterion of CO credibility. In reality, no one is forced to do military service in Germany despite the existence of military conscription.

Up through the mid–1960s, the number of applications for conscientious objector status was fairly low, rarely rising above 4,000 a year. Although data are not definitive, we can fairly safely assume that a large number of these early COs were religiously motivated. Starting in the late 1960s, however, with the rise of a so-called extra-parliamentary opposition to German defense policies as well as widespread revulsion toward the Vietnam War, the number of applications increased dramatically, reaching 35,000 in 1973.

Since then, with the exception of several "interruptions" caused by domestic policy, the upward trend has continued. By the late 1980s the number of applications for conscientious objection was approaching 80,000 annually. The steady upward trend derived in large part from the increasingly critical discussion of security policy. Ultimately, the rise in conscientious objection indicated the weakening basis of legitimation of military defense among the cohort of young men liable for military service.[6] What has to be stressed is that the rapidly increasing applicants was correlated with a growing percentage of recognitions of conscientious objection claims by the authorities. By the end of the 1980s approximately one of every four potential draftees was declaring conscientious objection and selecting *Zivildienst* over military service. Following German reunification, the number of COs doubled and reached an unprecedented 151,000 in 1991. Put in another way, about half of potential draftees were conscientious objectors.

We must make mention of "absolutists," conscientious objectors who reject any cooperation with the state system.[7] According to German law, complete objection is liable to prosecution since the objector evades both civilian and military service. It is difficult to obtain statistics on the number of absolutists. The Federal Office for Civilian Service registers only persons objecting to *Zivildienst;* the Ministry of Defense only those objecting to the military call-up. Only the criminal proceedings, which often are in various states of appeal, give us some inkling of this phenomenon. In 1986 the Federal Office for Civilian Service passed 126 cases on to the state prosecutor, most which seem to have involved Jehovah's Witnesses. We estimate that at the upper limits, there are no more than 2,000 potential absolutists each year.

Zivildienst: Underpaid Social Work

The German Federal Constitutional Court has ruled that rendering civilian service is the "completion of compulsory military service with other means and without arms."[8] This is to say that conscripts in Germany have the right *not* to bear arms. The fact that the Bundeswehr does not allow conscripts to complete their military service within the armed forces without arms is what makes *Zivildienst* legally necessary. The purpose of *Zivildienst* is to ensure equity in the draft. From a constitutional and legal standpoint, commitment to social welfare is a derivative and subordinate goal of *Zivildienst*.

We will argue, however, that the true consequence of conscientious objection in the Federal Republic has become the social work aspect of *Zivildienst*. Conscientious objectors undertaking civilian service must perform tasks that serve the public well-being. To put it more plainly, *Zivildienst* has become underpaid social work.

At the start of 1989 there were 19,479 recognized civilian service work places. Civilian service sponsors, with a few exceptions, do not fall under the purview of the state; rather they are operated by non-governmental organizations. The charitable services of the Protestant and Catholic churches, the German Red Cross, and the German Non-Sectarian Welfare Organization together engaged about 60 percent of all conscientious objectors serving in 1989. Local agencies accounted for most of the rest. By law, no *Zivildienst* sponsor can have an official political goal of its own.[9] However, the organization Greenpeace gained recognition in 1988 following a long dispute that was eventually settled by the courts.

At the start of the 1990s *Zivildienst* sponsors offered close to 100,000 service slots of which virtually all were filled. Conscientious objectors were primarily called up to work in the fields of nursing and social welfare (61 percent), handicrafts (12 percent), ambulance and rescue services (9 percent), and individual care for seriously disabled persons (6 percent). Remarkably, this large enterprise required only 670 full-time employees in the Office of Civilian Service.

The function of the conscientious objector in *Zivildienst* can be described, in a slightly overdrawn manner, as temporary replacements for service gaps in a market-oriented society. Conscientious objectors are employed in positions where private provisions for assistance in distress are not or will not be applied. These types of situations arise, for example, when the elderly, sick, or disabled are no longer attended to by their families and are entrusted to the care of voluntary or governmental welfare agencies. Conscientious objectors doing civilian service attend to people who live at the edge of prosperous society, despite the tightly woven social net in Germany.

Conscientious objectors doing civilian service are the indispensable junior staff for voluntary welfare organizations. In many cases, it would no longer be possible to afford professional staff in place of conscientious objectors. Estimates are that conscientious objectors account for about 10 percent of the total number of junior staff members in voluntary welfare organizations. Also germane, conscientious objectors are characterized as dutiful and hardworking staff who are well accepted by their supervisors.

Experience has shown that the social function assumed by conscientious objectors would only be performed inadequately, if at all, if they were based on the
workings of the free market, even a social market as in Germany. Whenever the
material profit from the service remains negligble or when the the service cannot
be financed by the affected marginal groups, the obvious and less expensive solution
is for the state to obtain social work in the form of services of the common good
through conscription.

In the future *Zivildienst* will gain new sociopolitical significance for two reasons.
First, as the population ages, there will be a greater demand for care of elderly
people. Second, the state will be increasingly strained to find funds to provide for
public health and social services. In this connection, voices demanding an obligatory
social service role for young women may become more insistent.[10]

Since 1971 the number of positions available in *Zivildienst* has doubled every
five years. By the end of the 1980s there were more than twelve times as many
places available as there were twenty years earlier. Is this increase merely a reaction
to a growing demand caused by an increasing number of conscientious objectors?
Or is something else happening? According to official guidelines, the state denies
recognition of any *Zivildienst* position "if it can be proved that they replaced a
former place of employment or would prevent establishing a new place of employment."[11] In other words, the CO is not to displace a regular worker. In reality,
however, the argument that no suitable applicants were found for an advertised
position is usually enough to retain the status of state recognition.

In effect, however, this policy conceals the question whether civilian service
sponsors exploit conscientious objectors as cheap labor. Conscientious objectors
receive, like conscripts doing military service, their pay from the state. In 1991
this amounted to approximately six dollars a day. *Zivildienst* sponsors may provide
housing, food, and work clothes. If not, civilian servers will receive additional
stipends for these expenses, a kind of equivalent for the fact they are not eating at
the mess hall or living in the barracks.

We do not have unequivocal facts that could provide a conclusive answer to
how much is being saved by using a conscientious objector in place of an employed
worker in a social service role. But the evidence is quite clear that the costs to
utilize a conscientious objector are much less than those required to hire a regular
civilian employee to do the same work.[12] It is relevant to note here that some social
relief organizations, which did not exist earlier because they would have been too
expensive to operate, have been created within the framework of *Zivildienst,* notably
mobile services and individual care for seriously disabled persons.

What we do know is that two empirical studies on costs of personnel in voluntary
welfare and religious assistance organizations have come up with very similar
results.[13] Both studies, independent of each other, concluded that, on the average,
each conscientious objector earned a "net surplus" of approximately $22,000 for
the sponsoring organization. Much of this surplus value seems to have been chan-
neled into the central organization of the sponsoring agency.

It appears that the sponsoring agencies of *Zivildienst* recognize that there is
some element of economic exploitation of conscientious objectors. Even if such a
view is rarely stated publically, it is not refuted either. The pointed statement of

the representatives of the Lutheran Church is on the mark: "Civilian service participants are cheap labor for the social sector . . . They can be employed anywhere without having to observe the inhibitory restrictions of labor laws . . . Civilian service participants can be employed very quickly to handle any activities that have become unattractive and for which employees cannot be found any longer."[14]

Social Profile of Conscientious Objectors

The basic right of conscientious objection has been sarcastically referred to as the "basic right of secondary-school graduates." At the same time the Bundeswehr has been jocular labeled an "army of workers and farmers." Both characterizations have more than a grain of truth.

In Germany possessors of the *Abitur,* the elite secondary school graduates, have traditionally made up the future business and professional classes. Empirical data support the characterization of COs as disproportionately coming from the upper classes. In the early 1970s the proportion of secondary-school graduates made up 50 percent of conscientious objectors applicants compared to 15 to 20 percent of the conscript age group. Indeed, this may understate the higher class background among recognized conscientious objectors. One study concluded that "the only distinction between recognized objectors and applicants is the significantly higher level of education, higher intelligence, and superior eloquence" of the former group.[15] Data from the 1980s seems to indicate that the class bias of conscientious objectors has changed little in recent decades.[16]

Studies of the personality traits of conscientious objectors present more or less consistent findings. A 1981 study described "the typical conscientious objector" as one with some political alienation, who rejects military principles of order, who is dissatisfed with his school, and who has a more than average consumption of alcohol and drugs.[17] A 1986 study characterized conscientious objectors as "distinctly rejecting the state's law and order authorities, [having] a disposition toward unconventional forms of protest (in part accepting violence), and a high degree of alienation from German defense policy."[18] Another study concluded that the decision to be a conscientious objector is "the combined product of a crisis and alienation from the system as well as the structure of their moral consciousness."[19]

A significant finding that supports the secularization theme of this volume are the reasons given for objection to military service by conscientious objectors. Fifty-eight percent objected for nonreligious reasons, 18 percent gave religious grounds, 13 percent cited personal reasons, and 10 percent offered political arguments. Put in another way, fewer than one in five conscientious objectors gave traditional religious reasons for their decisions. The secularization of conscience seems far along among conscientious objectors in contemporary Germany society.

Attitudes toward Conscientious Objection

The overriding finding from survey data is a pronounced and growing appreciation of conscientious objection and civilian service in the German public at large. At one level the growing acceptance of *Zivildienst* correlates with a growing skepticism of the value of military service. But we think there is more to it than that. We hold that the liberalization of procedures to become a conscientious objector and the resultant increase in the number of civilian servers has affected the very fabric of German society. This in turn has led to the growing visibility and appreciation of *Zivildienst* by the German public.

For many years conscientious objection was considered deviant behavior in Germany. This was especially the case a generation ago, and especially so among older people who viewed conscientious objectors as draft dodgers. Among young men aged sixteen to twenty-four conscientious objection, however, has consistently had a more positive image.[20] This has become particularly true in recent years. By 1988 among young people the image of a conscientious objector was higher than that of a young man who had decided to volunteer for military service. *Abitur* holders in particular ascribed higher status to civilian servers. A conservative information service remarked: "If this trend continues it is foreseeable that the conscript who joins the Bundeswehr will be the exception: a reversal of the legal situation, which declares the conscientious objector as the exception."[21]

To keep matters in perspective, however, we must stress that service in the Bundeswehr also receives an ongoing positive rating.[22] We appear to be entering an era in which both military servers and conscientious objectors are gradually attaining a similarly high level of approval. The castigation of the conscientious objector as a draft dodger no longer finds much of an echo in the general public. This reflects the public's understanding that both conscripts and conscientious objectors have a basic right confirmed in the emerging civic culture as well as in the German constitution.

The issue of the duty equivalency of military and civilian service is one that cannot be easily resolved. On the one side, there are those who note that the conscientious objector has a more normal 40-hour work week than the conscript, that he is relatively unsupervised off duty, and that he will not be in harm's way in the event of hostilities. On the other side, supporters of *Zivildienst* hold that the CO typically serves a longer tour, that much of his work is emotionally draining, and that his work is of more social value than that of the soldier, much more so in the contemporary Europe of the post–Cold War era.

After the Cold War

During the 1980s planners of military personnel were worried about the demographic trough of the 1990s and the impending difficulties to maintain manpower levels in the Bundeswehr. The disintegration of the Warsaw Pact and the Soviet Union changed all of that. Instead of increasing the term of military conscription, as had been proposed, the term was reduced from fifteen to twelve months in 1990. Accordingly, *Zivildienst* would entail fifteen months of service. Despite this reduction in the term of service, agitation to make civilian and military service congruent will probably accelerate.

Germany played an insignificant military role in the war in the Persian Gulf.

Only eighteen planes and their support personnel were sent to Turkey to protect that country from possible Iraqi attack. Yet, sixty men in air force support units that were to take part in the deployment declared they would seek objector status. Overall, the number of German soldiers and reservists applying for conscientious objection status quadrupled in January 1991 compared to the same period a year earlier. That feature of the ''new conscientious objection'' applying to service members already in uniform was quite evident in post–Cold War Germany.

An even more fundamental question in the Federal Republic of Germany is the future of conscription. The end of the Cold War and the reunification of Germany brings the conscripted army itself into question. Ironically enough, Germany society may miss its conscientious objectors more than its drafted soldiers. The civilian servers have become an inexpensive part of a delivery system of social services for which there is no readily available replacement.

8

Denmark: The Vanguard of Conscientious Objection

HENNING SØRENSEN

In Europe, the Scandinavian countries historically have been in the vanguard in recognizing the right of conscientious objection and, in most cases, in liberalizing provisions for COs, including alternative service. Among these advanced countries, Denmark has been a leader of this movement toward liberalizing and secularizing conscientious objection.

Universal compulsory military service for males was first introduced in Denmark by the Danish Constitution of 1849, and remains in force to the present day. (Before that time, only the rural population had been conscripted, as needed.) Initially, however, conscription was not implemented universally. Although the urban population was now included in the program, ministers, teachers, and members of certain other occupations were exempted. In addition, between 1849 and 1867, it was legal for other persons to purchase exemption from the draft.[1]

Although no provision was made for COs, some persons asserted religious scruples against bearing arms. The earliest case of conscientious objection recorded by the Danish authorities occurred in 1884, and it involved religious objection to military service.[2] The objectors reportedly were not treated too harshly; express provision was not made for them.[3]

Beginning around the turn of the century, a number of socialists and anarchists refused military service on political grounds; they were treated as military defaulters. Their protests intensified during World War I, which they opposed as a "capitalist's war." In that conflict Denmark remained a legally neutral, if well armed, nation. Increasingly between 1914 and 1917, the Danish Socialist party and a significant number of socialists (called "consistent antimilitarists") protested against the war and against compulsory military service. Unlike the small number of religious objectors, the socialists posed a political problem because of their numbers. The result was explicit recognition of conscientious objection by the Danish government.[4]

In 1917 the Danish Parliament passed an alternative service law that recognized conscientious objection (although in order to qualify, objection had to be based on more than "antimilitarism"). It also provided for alternative public service work for COs.[5] Article I of this law stated: "The Minister of Defense may exempt from military service persons who present valid evidence that their conscience forbids them such service. Such persons should be employed in civil duties for the State."

With the passage of the 1917 law, the Danish Parliament became the first government in *continental* Europe to recognize the right of conscientious objection (Britain had recognized it in its conscription act of 1916). Conscientious objector status was based on religious or ethical pacifism. In both cases, it was required that the CO be opposed to all wars or killing of human beings and to any use of violence, even in self-defense. Neither selective objection nor politically based objection was legally acceptable.

The application procedure for COs remained basically the same from 1917 to 1968. Each applicant had to explain the nature of his objection either in writing or orally before his local "Revising Council," and had to supply documentary evidence and two character witnesses. The local police then questioned the applicant and his witnesses to verify his beliefs and sincerity; this procedure suggests the degree to which COs were suspect. Next, after its own inquiries and deliberation, the Revising Council sent its opinion about the applicant's sincerity and its recommendations to the Ministry of War, which made the final decision about the individual's CO status.

Jurisdiction over COs was shifted in 1933 from the Ministry of War to the Ministry of the Interior. Even under the Ministry of War, however, the COs were not subject to the military code of discipline. Instead, in the early period, they were subject to disciplinary punishment determined by the chief of the work camp. There was no appeal from that decision, just as there was no appeal by the military conscript from disciplinary decisions made by commanding officers. As a result of the 1933 shift in jurisdiction, alternative servers were subject to a senior works foreman, with the possibility of appealing to the Ministry of Interior, under a civilian work law. In 1975 an elaborate appellate procedure was established, in which complaints were routed first to the Disciplinary Committee and then to the Appeal Committee, whose decision was final.

Civilian Alternative Service

In the original program, authorities chose by lottery the numbers of conscripts required for induction, including the COs. The COs who were called could serve in noncombatant roles in the military if they chose to do so, but serving soldiers were not entitled to apply for transfer to civilian alternative service. Initially those approved COs who did not wish to serve as military noncombatants were assigned to alternative civilian service at the same pay and length of service (twenty months) as conscripted soldiers. Most of the COs in the World War I period were assigned to forestry work in camps at Gribskov and Kompedal-Plantage, where they worked under a camp commandant. One of the camps closed down in 1920; the other contained only six COs by 1922.[6]

From 1917 to 1962 COs were required to serve in governmental agencies. Most were put to work in the so-called Civil Service in conservation projects in the state forests. During this period, despite their opposition, COs were counted in the numbers of the Total Defense system of Denmark. In 1962, however, the minister of the interior made an administrative decision that the COs could serve in other kinds of work in the public interest, such as in welfare institutions, kindergartens, public libraries, and other cultural institutions. Beginning in 1970 overseas voluntary service was permitted. In 1983 COs were allowed to work for peace and environmental organizations. In 1986 the government stopped employing COs in the Civil Service; as a result, they have now been fully removed from the Total Defense system.

Today, conscientious objectors in Denmark are allowed to work in governmental or nongovernmental organizations as long as they are nonprofit bodies. The categories include social work, peace organizations, environmental agencies, and cultural work. The latter, which includes work at libraries, museums, broadcasting stations, and the like, is most often requested by the COs.[7]

The CO and alternative service regulations have continued in Denmark since 1917, even during the German occupation of the country during World War II. The provisions for length of service have been changed several times, however. In May 1933 an amendment reduced the term of military or civilian alternative service from twenty to fifteen months. Other changes followed, but COs and military draftees continued to serve equal terms until April 1952, when the period of alternative civilian service was increased to twenty-four months. The discrepancy between the length of military and civilian service continued into the 1960s, when the former served fourteen to sixteen months and the COs served twenty-two months. In 1986, after several reductions, civilian service was cut to nine months, the same as the term for draftees serving in the military. The 1986 law stated that the burdens of service for the military draftee and the CO civilian server should be equal. Thus the Danish government formally abandoned the practice of requiring COs to serve longer terms than military conscripts.

Until the late 1960s the government continued to ask applicants to demonstrate that they were opposed to violence under any condition. They were not recognized as COs if they accepted the use of violence to protect themselves or their families, or if they agreed to defend the nation but rejected, for example, the deployment of Danish troops in NATO. Nor did the government recognize "nuclear pacifists," who refused to serve in the military because of the potential use of nuclear weapons.

Among the most active of the CO support groups in Denmark has been the Aldrig Mere Krig (AMK), an affiliate of the War Resisters International organization, whose headquarters are in London. In 1963 the Danish government appointed a commission to review CO provisions. Representatives of AMK were included as members of the commission, and they encouraged its recommendations for liberalization, as did other pacifist organizations, such as the Danish branches of the Fellowship of Reconciliation and the Women's International League for Peace and

Freedom. By the mid–1960s, partially as a result of this effort, more than half of the alternative servers were working outside the CO camps for organizations for disabled children and the elderly or for Mellemfolkeligt Samvirke, a Danish group that sends young volunteers to perform relief work or participate in community development programs in developing countries.

Liberalization in the Late 1960s

With its tolerant government and its strong, vocal CO movement, Denmark took the lead in the secularization of conscience and the liberalization of CO provisions that began in Europe and America in the late 1960s. Most of these changes, however, were introduced through administrative decisions rather than legislation, thus avoiding a public debate on the subject in Parliament.

In 1968 a three-party coalition government allowed political, private, even selective objectors to qualify as conscientious objectors. This historic change in the acceptable bases for recognizing conscientious objection was due largely to the influence of the pacifist-oriented Radical Left (RV) party. As the price of participation by the Radical Left party, the two other parties in the governing coalition had to accept political COs as well as selective and discretionary conscientious objection. Through an administrative decision, the executive branch of the coalition government decided that COs no longer would be required to explain the reasons for their request for nonmilitary service, even if they were already serving in the military.

Thus since 1968 CO status has been automatically granted to anyone who requests it. In effect, young men may become COs merely by signing and submitting a CO application to the government. An appropriate form can even be obtained from one of the CO organizations, such as the Association of Conscientious Objectors. Because the applicant's beliefs and sincerity are no longer an issue, the government also has abandoned the practice of interviewing the applicant and his character witnesses.[8]

With that change, the CO's right to perform civilian alternative service was also more firmly established. This was a true alternative service in governmental or nongovernment organizations, rather than in the so-called Civil Service, in which COs had been included in forestry work gangs and counted as part of the Total Defense system. Moreover, liberal administrative decisions in the 1970s and 1980s reduced the length of civilian alternative service so that now—as noted above— the term is the same as that for draftees performing military service. Furthermore, administrators have expanded the number of places where the alternative servers may work. These now include schools, libraries, and other governmental agencies, as well as nonprofit private institutions, such as hospitals, nursing homes, child care centers, and the facilities of peace and environmental organizations. Largely as a result of efforts by the Danish peace organizations, a Voluntary Service Overseas (VSO) program has been established, in which, after 1970, COs could serve abroad for twenty-four months. Few COs applied for such a long term, however.

Denmark has also recognized the right of soldiers and other members of the armed services to become COs while serving in the military. Indeed, one can be credited for the number of days already served in uniform. In 1952 the medical corps was issued arms, which narrowed the COs' choice of noncombatant military service. Since that time, the number of noncombatant military COs has declined.

Today a Danish conscript can serve in any one of four different capacities: in the military, as a CO alternative server, in the Voluntary Service Overseas, or in the Civil Service. If he does not chose any of these options but refuses to cooperate in any manner, he will be sentenced to jail as an absolutist for the period of his declared national service, between one and twelve months.

Since the introduction of the conscription law, a comparatively few COs—the absolutists—have declined to cooperate in any way with conscripting authorities, refusing either military or civilian alternative service. Initially they were treated as military defaulters. Later the penalty for total noncooperation was changed to imprisonment for a term equal to that of alternative service.

In recent years the majority of young men who have taken the absolutist position have been Jehovah's Witnesses. In an attempt to keep the system functioning smoothly, Danish authorities automatically register conscripts declaring themselves Jehovah's Witnesses for the Civil Service rather than for the armed forces. Furthermore, the Jehovah's Witnesses are given shorter terms of alternative service (one to six months) than the average conscript, who generally serves nine months. If a Jehovah's Witness still refuses to cooperate, the court usually sentences him to jail for the number of months he was assigned to perform alternative service. In practice, however, the Jehovah's Witnesses are released after serving only half their jail sentences, and their names are then deleted from the official conscription lists.[9]

Thus the management of the CO system has been civilianized and liberalized, as exemplified by the many changes noted above: equal terms of service for the military and for civil conscripts, the weakened influence of the Ministry of Defense, the abandonment of questioning of CO claimants by police officers, the provision of several options of service for the COs, and the attempt made to accommodate even the absolutist COs, the Jehovah's Witnesses.

Indeed, within the armed forces and among some other Danes, there is a feeling that the COs in Denmark are treated more favorably and have a much lighter burden than the conscripts who enter the military. In 1972 an armed forces study group stated explicitly that the equalization of the burden between COs and conscripts had gone too far in favor of the COs.[10] For example, because there are 526 civilian stationing posts—far more than there are military bases—it is much easier for COs than for military conscripts to be stationed closer to their homes.[11] This study group calculated that 16 percent of the draftees in the army, 30 percent in the air force, and 50 percent in the navy were stationed outside their home counties in Denmark; the percentage for COs was much lower. In addition, the number of accumulated working hours for all nine months of service is 2,714 hours for the CO and 3,256 hours for the military conscript. As for work schedules, the CO generally works an eight-hour day shift, whereas the draftee may be called upon to work night or day. Furthermore, the draftee is not paid overtime, as is the CO civilian server; both receive the same regular monthly salaries of Dkr. 10.000 (the equivalent of $1,600).[12]

In the early 1970s with the liberalization of the CO provisions and with dramatic increases in the numbers of COs, three public opinion surveys were taken on the subject in Denmark; these were the only such polls in Denmark up to that time. The first survey, a Gallup poll taken in 1971, showed that 51 percent of respondents accepted the idea of exemption from military service for reasons of conscience (37 percent opposed this idea and 12 percent had no opinion). The second survey, also taken in that year, emphasized that the number of COs had increased drastically and asked whether that development should be prevented. Fifty-one percent of the respondents thought it should; 32 percent thought it should not. Taken together, these surveys suggested that a majority of the Danish population in the early 1970s agreed with the liberal policy towards COs, but a majority also wanted a solution to a practical problem faced by the armed forces.[13]

The third poll, conducted in 1972, asked about acceptable motives for COs. A slight majority (52 percent) held that religious reasons were acceptable as the basis for avoiding military conscription; 24 percent opposed this view. Pacifist reasons were accepted by 35 percent and opposed by 35 percent. Political reasons were accepted by only 19 percent and rejected by 52 percent.[14] Those who rejected all three reasons, and thus opposed conscientious objection as a whole, generally were older than thirty years of age and had less education than the other respondents. More important, although the poll showed that a majority opposed political motives for COs, the Danish government (largely through administrative actions in the executive branch) already had expanded the basis for conscientious objection to include political beliefs.

In 1990 the Danish public was polled once again on the issue of conscientious objection. The results of this Gallup poll showed a significant increase in liberal attitudes. Instead of the bare majority (51 percent) who accepted the idea of conscientious objection in 1971, two-thirds (66 percent) accepted it now. In response to a second question, which asked whether the drastic increase in the number of COs should be prevented, although 51 percent in 1971 considered this a problem that needed to be resolved, only 33 percent in 1990 thought the government should act to prevent the increased numbers of COs. Clearly the public's attitude has become liberal towards conscientious objectors in Denmark in the past twenty years.

Growing Numbers of COs in Denmark in the 1970s

Conscientious objectors were not numerous in Denmark between 1917 and 1945, although it is difficult to calculate the precise numbers because the government did not keep figures for that period. Consequently the data are based mainly on the records kept by the Danish branch of the War Resisters League and by the CO Association. These figures, however, are considered fairly accurate, even if it is sometimes difficult to determine what was measured—the number of persons requesting CO status and service, or the number who actually performed CO service in a given year. Between 1917 and 1931, it appears that about three hundred COs actually served. The numbers of COs rose from fifty-nine in 1931 to more than five hundred in 1935; thereafter they dropped until they reached a low point of about one hundred in 1943.[15]

TABLE 8.1   Absolute and Relative Number of COs Each Year,
1945–1989

Year	Total number of conscripts	Number of COs	Percentage
1943–1964	—	39–505	0–2
1965	27,500	490	2
1966	33,700	540	2
1967	33,600	672	2
1968	31,900	1,107	4
1969	28,500	1,766	6
1970	27,100	2,456	9
1971	28,200	4,200	15
1972	35,000	4,489	13
1973	22,600	3,987	18
1974	22,400	4,161	19
1975	29,700	3,136	11
1976	39,500	2,255	6
1977	39,200	814	2
1978	31,300	763	2
1979	31,600	909	3
1980	23,200	816	4
1981	31,000	606	2
1982	31,800	466	1
1983	33,400	366	1
1984	34,000	319	1
1985	34,600	218	1
1986	32,200	232	1
1987	30,000	355	1
1988	30,400	484	3
1989	29,700	590	4

In 1945 the Danish government began to record the number of registered COs. These figures show that the numbers of COs in particular periods seem to correlate with economic, military, and cultural developments. As displayed in Table 8.1, the Danish armed forces contained between thirty thousand and forty thousand conscripts a year between 1945 and 1989. The number of serving COs averaged about 2 percent of that force, between four hundred and six hundred persons. Yet between 1968 and 1976 the numbers of serving COs increased to more than a thousand each year, and indeed to more than four thousand (19 percent) in the early 1970s. Since that time it has fallen dramatically.[16]

The drastic increases that began in 1968 may be explained by the youth revolt in most Western countries during the time when the Vietnam War was unpopular and when the military was drawing much criticism. Earlier international events also appear to have caused sudden increases in the numbers of COs in Denmark: with the Korean War and the arming of NATO in 1950–1953, the number of COs leapt from 132 in 1949 to 505 in 1952 before falling to 262 in 1953.

There is some correlation between numbers of COs and economic conditions. Increases in the number of COs in the 1960s coincided with a period of major prosperity in Denmark between 1960 and 1972. Similarly, the number of COs decreased in the recession period from 1973 through 1985. On the other hand, the rather weak economic situation between 1945 and 1960 was characterized by a rather stable number of COs, about one hundred to two hundred a year. Perhaps in periods of economic recession, young men feel less secure and are less willing to challenge the dominant values of society.

Other factors are involved as well. One is demographic; the overall figure is influenced by the need for conscripts as defined by the armed forces. Fitness criteria may change in accordance with the demands for military personnel. Another factor is the political-bureaucratic desire of governmental authorities to minimize the CO problem. For example, a large percentage of the registered COs, particularly from the beginning of the 1970s, never received a call to serve.

Because in the 1980s a sizable surplus of young men was available for the armed forces, the liberal conscientious objector system in Denmark did not create a numerical shortage of soldiers. The qualitative situation is more difficult to evaluate, however. On the one hand, the armed forces have lost some of the better-educated and more intelligent young men, who are now serving as COs instead of as soldiers. This fact, combined with the perception that COs serve under better conditions, may have weakened the general will to defend the country. On the other hand, company and battery commanders feel "a certain degree of satisfaction" that their military units do not contain COs, who might be "troublemakers."[17]

Conclusion

In regard to the three-stage paradigm of the evolving relationship between COs and the state, the Danish experience suggests that in some cases a two-stage evolution may have taken place. Ethical secular and religious criteria were recognized at about the same time rather than sequentially. This recognition occurred in the World War I era; probably it was influenced by the nation's neutralism and the political strength in Denmark of the socialists and other so-called "consistent antimilitarists." In the late 1960s, prodded by the Radical Left (RV) party, the Danish government recognized even politically-motivated secular COs and went even farther than most other countries in accepting selective objection to particular wars. Because the Danish system no longer asks for a CO's motive, any young man can avoid military service for any reason simply by deciding to register as a CO and perform civilian alternative service. In its permissiveness toward COs, the Danish government may have alienated many persons in its armed forces, but it also placed itself in the vanguard of the liberalization and secularization of conscientious objection in the Western world.

9

Norway: Toward Full Freedom of Choice?

NILS PETTER GLEDITSCH
NILS IVAR AGØY

Although most of the Scandinavian countries have been in the vanguard of the liberalization of conscientious objection, their individual traditions and sociopolitical conditions have created national variations. Norway, for example, has a strong tradition of egalitarian conscription dating back to the eleventh century and reinforced by the modern constitution of 1814, when the nation gained its independence from Denmark. National service remains compulsory in Norway: all men between the ages of eighteen and forty-four are eligible for conscription for twelve months' service in the army or fifteen months in the navy or air force. The military, however, has been challenged by a strong peace movement in modern times. In the aftermath of World War I, the Norwegian government recognized religious and secular conscientious objectors and offered them the option of performing alternative civilian service. The number of COs has grown dramatically, especially since the late 1960s, but several issues concerning conscientious objection in Norway remain unresolved.

Conscription has ancient roots in Norwegian history. As early as the eleventh century, after the unification of the kingdom under Harold Fairhair and his descendants, the *Gulating* code prescribed that all men, freeborn or thrall, were to meet at a specified place in the event of an attack on the realm. This system fell into disuse during the late middle ages. Norway came under the domination of Denmark in the late fourteenth century, and military matters were handled mostly by professional soldiers in the pay of the Danish monarch, with the occasional use of armed peasantry. In 1628, however, a Norwegian national army was formed by King Christian IV; it was based on conscription of the peasants, who were led by a professional officer corps. In a land of small farms, every four (later, two) full-sized farms were required to provide a soldier for the army; sailors were drafted from the coastal population. This system lasted with only minor changes until Norway gained independence from Denmark in 1814.[1]

The new, liberal constitution of 1814 stated, "Every citizen of the State is in general equally bound to defend his native country . . . without any regard to birth or fortune." This egalitarian principle was established against strong opposition from groups that still wanted to limit conscription to the farming population.[2] Consequently it was not applied fully for many years. The urban population was exempt from conscription until 1854, and the population of northern Norway until 1897. In addition, conscripted young men could escape personal service in a number of ways, especially through the purchase of a substitute.[3] These escape routes were eliminated in the 1870s and 1880s. Since then conscription has been general, except that until 1910 and again from 1926 to 1935, a proportion of the conscripts were excused from military service by lot. In addition, when Norway was occupied by the Germans during World War II, military conscription was suspended, although Norwegian citizens in Allied territory were called up, and the Germans in occupied Norway tried with varying degrees of success to draft Norwegian men into semi-military work brigades.

Conscientious objection is a comparatively modern phenomenon in Norway. The medieval laws did not allow any objection; any man who failed to appear for muster was declared a criminal. During the period of Danish domination there were no provisions for objectors, and it is known that some soldiers were punished for becoming objectors on religious grounds. The first conscientious objector in the modern sense appeared in 1815. Like all other objectors from then until the 1880s, he was a Quaker.[4] The government suggested exempting the pacifist Quakers, but the *Storting,* the Norwegian parliament, refused to adopt such a proposal. Instead, the early objectors were punished with fines, lashings, or imprisonment (sometimes repeated imprisonments). These actions caused some young men to emigrate. Beginning in the 1880s, they also caused a small but vociferous group in the peace movement to demand the legalization of objection on grounds of conscience.

Around the turn of the century, the peace movement pressed repeatedly for exemption for conscientious objectors.[5] Although five such bills were rejected between 1896 and 1903, conscientious objection had been added to the national debate and the public agenda. Party because of public indignation over the imprisonment of "sincere young men," authorities avoided additional jailings. In 1900 the government offered to allow COs to serve without arms in the military. When this did not prove effective, the commanding general of the army in 1902 declared in effect that sincere religious objectors would not be prosecuted.

At the same time, beginning in the first decade of the twentieth century, nonreligious objectors to military service started to appear.[6] These were mainly socialists. The new Military Penal Code of 1902 had not been designed to deal with the objector problem, and unintentionally, it forced the courts to treat such political objectors more strictly than in the past. Therefore, even as the religious COs went free, the nonreligious objectors were faced with prison sentences. From 1909 onward, the government introduced several bills that attempted to resolve the issue;

partly because of irreconcilable differences among the groups involved, however, the achievement of a satisfactory settlement was delayed until after World War I.[7]

In the wake of the war, in which Norway remained neutral, the number of objectors increased dramatically (to 460, or 2.5 percent of the conscripts recruited in 1921), and the parliament finally accepted a broad, liberal proposal for conscientious objection and alternative service. The Labor Party, which had gained increasing political strength based on support from industrial workers, small farmers, and fishermen, agitated successfully for legal provisions for political objectors. Consequently, in March 1922, Parliament adopted an amendment to the Military Penal Code (Paragraph 35, Section 5), which stated: "Refusal on the part of a conscript is not punishable if based on serious religious conviction or on other serious grounds of conscience." Pacifism was not strictly required, but COs had to be sincerely opposed to any kind of military service, including noncombatant military service.

On the same day in 1922, the parliament also adopted the Civilian Conscript Workers' Law, which provided alternative civilian service for COs. From 1922 to 1965 the period of such service was one-and-one-half times the initial length of service of draftees in the infantry. In 1965 it was reduced to the term of military service plus four months, which amounts to sixteen months, the current requirement. Otherwise the alternative-service men had the same rights as military draftees in regard to pay, allowances for clothing and dependents, and other provisions. They remained entirely under civilian control, however, within a supervising agency in the Ministry of Justice. This law was implemented by royal decree on June 1, 1923. Until the late 1950s, a significant proportion of the alternative civilian service was carried out in work camps; it included road building, forestry, and agriculture.

The 1922 law liberalizing conscientious objection had been unclear about strictly "political" objectors, and subsequent court decisions had varied.[8] In 1925, Parliament further amended the Military Penal Code and declared in effect that a draftee could not be punished for refusing military service if he did so because "military service of any kind is contrary to his serious conviction." That formula is still the main criterion today.[9] With the passage of the 1925 amendment, authorities wanted to open the way for exemption to those who objected on the basis of an "obviously serious and personal conviction—be it religious, political, or otherwise." Nevertheless, legal scholars have debated whether the 1925 law intended to justify what today is called "political objection,"[10] and this legal battle is reflected in a struggle that continues today. Although applications for CO status can include political as well as ethical and religious reasons, applications may be rejected (and have been rejected by some courts) if they are based on purely political motives.

During the 1950s and 1960s the Norwegian government considered various proposals for new CO legislation. During this period, there was a marked increase in the number of objectors, particularly political objectors. In 1951 the number of COs peaked at 1,371, which represented 7 percent of the men drafted that year. Beginning in the early 1950s, a growing number of COs also expressed dissatisfaction with the nature of their alternative service; they wanted to contribute directly to meaningful peacebuilding and socially relevant work. A number refused to continue their work and went to prison for this cause; among them was noted peace researcher Johan Galtung, who served six months in jail in 1954–1955. The Ministry of Justice did little to accommodate the COs.

In 1953 the government appointed a public committee to evaluate existing arrangements for COs. The 1955 report of the committee (*Rode-utvalget*) recommended changing "serious conviction" to "religious or moral conviction," and requiring COs to oppose "under any circumstances use of weapons against human beings" instead of merely opposing military service of any kind.[11] It also sought to limit the number of CO appeals, which were burdening the judicial system, and to use the COs for defense-related purposes, such as unarmed service in the military or participation in civil defense. This government-backed report generated considerable criticism. The peace movement created an alternative committee and produced a counter-report.[12]

On March 19, 1965, after much debate, Parliament passed a new law for COs. Reforms had been proposed by the Labor government then in power. The new legislation—an Act for Exemption from Military Service for Conscientious Objectors—went into effect by royal decree on June 3, 1966. After completing their service, COs might be recalled for refresher courses in civil defense in a manner corresponding to the reserve exercises of military conscripts.

The criterion for exemption as a CO was broadened under the 1965 law to include objection to "military service of any kind without entering into conflict with [one's] serious conviction." The important thing was the objector's position—that he would not perform any kind of military service—rather than his reasons. The debate in Parliament showed that the legislators had no intention of condoning strictly "political" or "selective" objection. Men who would not serve in the Norwegian armed forces under existing conditions, but who might be willing to do so under other circumstances, were not granted CO status.

Under the new arrangement, the Ministry of Justice continued to make the initial decisions on CO applications from new draftees. (CO applications by those already in the military were processed instead through the Ministry of Defense to the Chief Police Officer and then to the Ministry of Justice for final decision.) A civilian conscript who was denied CO status by the agency was asked to pledge his willingness to perform military service. If he declined to do so, the state automatically took the matter to court, though as a civil, not a criminal, case. If the conscript lost the case and still did not agree to serve, he was charged and convicted for criminal violation of the Military Penal Code. If he won the case, he was assigned to alternative civilian service.

In the 1960s the government shifted the assignment of alternative-service COs from the traditional work camps in forestry and agriculture to the health and social services sector, which needed additional workers. Two-thirds of the COs were employed in that sector in 1969, and 60 to 70 percent in 1989. Trade unions periodically protested the practice of employing COs in jobs that had a permanent character. Furthermore, in periods of high unemployment, it was increasingly difficult to justify the use of COs in health and social services, which are publicly funded.

Between 1965 and 1970, the total CO rate grew from 1 percent to 4 percent of the annual number of conscripts. The number of ''selective'' or ''political'' objectors increased during this period. At the same time, public opposition in Norway to membership in NATO was increasing, particularly as a result of dissent against actions by other NATO members. These included the U.S. role in the Vietnam War, the military coup in Greece, and the colonial wars of Portugal in Africa. The courts faced considerable difficulty in weighing ''serious conviction'' against opposition to ''military service of any kind.'' Consequently both the courts and the Ministry of Justice have tended in recent years to broaden the criteria so that they generally accept as COs so-called ''nuclear pacifists,'' who are opposed to the use of weapons of mass destruction but not necessarily to war in general. These individuals must be sufficiently clear about their inability to serve in the Norwegian armed forces at the present or in the foreseeable future.

The Liberal Conservative government, which replaced the Labor government in 1965, wanted to set stricter rules for civilian alternative service. The Justice Ministry followed a restrictive line and rejected several potential employers of COs. Imprisoned COs, particularly those who had refused to perform civil defense and those who actively sought to have peace organizations of United Nations bodies recognized as alternative service received media attention and much public support. Only a handful of ''peace-relevant'' employers have been approved; a number of COs have gone to prison because they would not perform the assigned alternative service, which they considered meaningless or defense-related. In January 1990, in line with recent demands from the COs, the Ministry of Justice announced that environmental protection would become a priority area for alternative civilian service.[13]

The 1965 statute, which remains the basic law regarding conscientious objection, has caused much dissent. Each year about a dozen objectors, mostly absolutists who refuse to perform alternative service, have been sentenced by the Norwegian courts to serve in a camp or in prison. The great majority of these have been Jehovah's Witnesses. Some of the Norwegian courts have imprisoned strictly ''political'' objectors who would be willing to perform alternative service. This practice has attracted the attention of Amnesty International, which in 1972 began to urge Norway to change it. Norway also has been on Amnesty International's list of countries with ''prisoners of conscience,'' a considerable political embarrassment to a country that prides itself on its record regarding human rights.[14] In its most recent report (1992), Amnesty called for the release of three political objectors.[15]

A new public committee on conscription was appointed by the government in 1974. By then the number of objectors had reached unprecedented levels (2,675 COs, or 8.5 percent of the recruits conscripted that year). In addition, recurrent controversies arose over the content and the goal of the alternative service program. In its 1979 report, the committee split into military and civilian factions on all the major issues.[16] The military faction (the majority, led by the committee chair) recommended retaining the 1965 criterion for conscientious objection and suggested that all COs be required to serve under the Directorate of Civilian Preparedness. The civilian faction urged that the criterion for COs be expanded to include objection to "service in the military defense without entering into conflict with [one's] serious conviction," thus more clearly allowing objection on "political" grounds. The civilian minority also recommended allowing alternative service outside civil defense. The non-Socialist coalition government, which took office in 1981, largely accepted the majority report, although it recommended transferring only some of the COs to civil defense.[17] Faced by strong opposition from the COs, many of whom regarded civil defense as an extension of the armed forces, the authorities compromised, and only those objectors who agree are used in the civil defense service.

The annual CO rate has remained between 6 and 9 percent. As part of its program for the 1985–1989 period, the Labor Party was committed to work to legalize "political" objection. Both the military establishment and the civilian prodefense community, however, warned strongly that such a reform might sound the death knell for the principle of conscription, and the issue remained controversial even within the Labor Party. Consequently, when Labor formed a new government in 1986, it dragged its feet on the issue and finally put a watered-down proposal before the Parliament in 1989.[18] In return for a modest liberalization of the basis for objection (which did not entail any change in the wording of the law), the government suggested restrictions on the nature of alternative service. The parliamentary committee deliberations were not finished before the 1989 elections. The elections resulted in the formation of another non-Socialist coalition government, which withdrew the proposal. Thus the 1965 statute, as modified by several Supreme Court decisions, remained in force.

On June 13, 1990, Parliament adopted a new law that formally extended the right of conscientious objection to "nuclear pacifists"—that is, those who refuse to perform military service because of their opposition to nuclear weapons. The law went into effect in January 1991, but its precise meaning remains unclear. It appears to exempt only those who object entirely to nuclear weapons, including their very existence (as in the policy of nuclear deterrence). It is possible that those individuals who object only to the specific use of nuclear weapons, as envisioned in NATO defense policy, may not qualify for CO exemption. The issue may not be clarified until the first cases reach the Supreme Court of Norway, a process requiring several years.[19]

The Rate of Conscientious Objection

In absolute numbers and in the proportion of COs to conscripts, there have been six periods in modern Norwegian history when the numbers have risen rapidly (see Figure 9–1).[20] The first two occurred just before and just after the turn of the century, with peaks in 1898 and 1908. A third (and larger) wave started during World War I and increased until 1921. A fourth period immediately preceded World War II. The fifth began early in the Cold War in the late 1940s, and peaked with a new all-time high in absolute numbers in the early 1950s. The sixth and most drastic increase occurred in the late 1960s and early 1970s. From that time on,

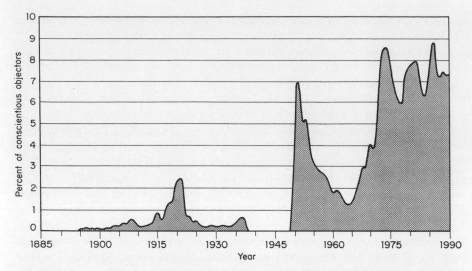

FIGURE 9-1. The relative number of conscientious objectors in Norway, 1885–1990. The curve shows the number of men applying for alternative service as percentage of the cohort called up for military service in that year. The numerator is the number of objectors regardless of whether their applications for CO status were granted and regardless of how many later returned to the military. Recruitment statistics are not available for the periods 1938-40 and 1947-50. There are no CO figures for the period of the German occupation of Norway (1940–1945) and the following two years. *Sources:* Nils Ivar Agøy, *"Kampen mot vernetvangen": Militærnekterspørsmålet i Norge 1885–1992*, Graduate thesis in history, University of Oslo, 1987, 19, 134; *Rode-utvalget: Utkast til lov om fritakelse for vepnet militær tjeneste av overbevisningsgrunner*, Ministry of Justice, Oslo, 1955, 64; Om militær verneplikt og sivil tjenesteplikt, *Stortingsmelding* no. 27, Ministry of Justice, Oslo, 1989, 13; Information from the Conscription Service, *Generalkrigskommissariatet, January 1990 and November 1991.*

with some ups and downs, the absolute and relative numbers of conscientious objectors have remained high.[21]

The government and the military view conscientious objection as a form of "loss" from the military population. Two other sources currently account for a greater "loss" than conscientious objection: transfers to civil defense (9 percent) and medical exemptions (12 percent).[22] Even though conscientious objection was always a fairly marginal activity in terms of numbers, the peak rate of 8.8 percent in 1986 and the example of neighboring Denmark, where 15 percent of the cohort in 1971 was transferred to alternative service, led to considerable concern about the future of the conscript army. In Norway the authorities reject a significant proportion of the applications for CO status. The rejection rate peaked at 19 percent in the most recent five-year period, 1985–1989. According to officials at the Ministry of Justice, the overwhelming majority (80 to 90 percent) of those rejected were turned down because the ministry did not find the applicants' personal convictions

TABLE 9.1   Religious Grounds for Conscientious Objection, 1955–1989

Year	ca. 1950	1955	1962	1972	1983	1989
Percentage	72	54	62	31	21	14
(*n*)	(182)	(62)	(115)	(546)	(543)	(170)

Sources: (1950) Based on Gleditsch and Agøy study in 1990 of a 10 percent sample of successful applications filed by the CO administration at Dillingøy: (1955) Johan Galtung, *Hva mener sivilarbeiderne? En undersøkelse på Havnås leir for vernepliktige sivilarbeidere* (What are the Opinions of the Conscientious Objectors? A Survey of Havnås Camp) (Oslo: University of Oslo, Department of Sociology, *Stensilserie*, 1957); (1962) An unpublished study by Richard Edvarson, cited in Sverre Røed Larsen, "Conscientious Objection in Norway: A Study of a Protest Group" (Graduate thesis in sociology, University of Oslo, 1973); (1972) Sverre Røed Larsen's own study, ibid.; (1983) CO Secretariat, *Sivilarbeidermes syn. En motmelding til: Stortingsmelding 70 "Om Verreplikt"* (The View of the COs: A Counter-Report to "On Conscription," *Stortingsmelding* 70 [1983–1984] (Oslo: Central Secretariat of the COs, 1984); (1989) Franz Hendriksen, Dan Rande, Erik Pettersen, and Kim Sander, *Who Knows? Statistical Study of the Spring 1989 Class [of COs]* (Farstad: Forskolen for sivile tjenestepliktige, 1989).

to have the necessary "firmness and strength." Only 10 to 20 percent were rejected because the basis of their conscientious objection lay outside the scope of the law.[23]

Among those who initially are refused CO status, a small minority persist and eventually are brought before the courts. Since 1972 more than four hundred CO cases have been tried in the courts, including sixteen that reached the Supreme Court. The judiciary has found it difficult to interpret the 1965 law; more than half of the COs (53 percent of the recorded cases) prevailed in the courts. Among those who lost, about half yielded to military service when called up again.[24] Others refused again, and then were convicted under the Military Penal Code. Currently they are sentenced to three to four months in jail. Theoretically a CO can be sentenced an indefinite number of times for repeated offenses, but since the 1910s no one seems to have been jailed more than twice for this offense. Since about 1914, administrative practice has been to suspend part of the second verdict and to deprive the offender of his "right to defend" the country. The number of COs in jail is a very small proportion of the CO population, but, as mentioned above, the incarceration of these "prisoners of conscience" is a continuing political embarrassment.

The Secularization of Conscientious Objection

In recent years, there has been a pattern of increasing secularization in the motivation of COs in Norway. In the late nineteenth century, when conscientious objection first became a public issue in the country, most of the objectors gave religious reasons for their stance. One recent study concluded that between 1885 and 1902, religious motives were mentioned explicitly by thirty of the forty-four objectors (only two were known to have nonreligious motives). In the first two decades of the twentieth century, religious objectors composed between 60 and 90 percent of the objectors each year.[25]

In the early Cold War period, studies of COs in service show that religious grounds declined but still were the primary motivation, at least as formulated explicitly by the successful objectors (see Table 9.1). In the 1970s and 1980s, however, the traditional pattern was reversed: religious objectors became a clear minority, dropping to 31 percent in 1972 and 14 percent in 1989.

The secularization of conscientious objection, as shown in Table 9.1, is part of the secularization of Norwegian society. Norway is a highly homogeneous country with respect to religion (as well as language, ethnicity, and culture); in 1980, 88 percent of respondents reported that they belonged to the (Lutheran) state church.[26] This figure represented a steady decline from the postwar level of 96 percent. The Norwegian Humanist and Ethical Union, founded in 1956, has shown a major increase in membership from about a thousand in 1970 to approximately forty thousand in 1990.[27] In part this growth has been due to state financial support, introduced in 1981, for religious and philosophical communities outside the state church.

As far as religious conscripts are concerned, groups outside the Church of Norway are overrepresented among the conscientious objectors. The state church is, of course, a part of the establishment in many ways, and as such tends to support the armed forces. At the same time, in recent years the church has tended toward a liberal position on the extension of the basis for conscientious objection.

Among those Norwegians who belong to other religious communities, most are Protestants of some sort. Because conscientious objection, statistically speaking, is a relatively marginal phenomenon, it can be influenced by religious minorities; for a long time the CO community was influenced heavily by Pentecostals, an evangelical group. The origin of the Pentecostals' pacifism is unclear, being rooted in the group's culture rather than in any theology; this aspect, however, may be weakening as the Pentecostals become more integrated into mainstream society.[28] Some religious COs in Norway belong to "Smith's Friends," a particular Norwegian group,[29] and some are Baptists or Methodists.

The CO community always has consisted of people of widely different backgrounds and attitudes. In the first two decades of the twentieth century, the majority of the COs appear to have been from the working class.[30] In the 1920s and 1930s, the CO community included a disproportionate number of students. Among its ranks were a number of nonreligious, left-wing socialists who opposed what they called "capitalist wars." After the Labor Party's strike against the military in 1923–1924— a strike that resulted in the jailing of many Labor Party leaders, including the two who later served as prime ministers from 1945 to 1965—the Labor movement continued its opposition for more than a decade to what it considered class-oriented armed forces. Middle-class "bourgeois pacifism" also grew during the interwar period. The first Norwegian branch of the War Resisters' International (WRI) was organized in 1925, and a more durable WRI body, *Folkereisning Mot Krig*, was established in 1937. Many of the Norwegian members signed the WRI's pledge against war on the basis of a pacifism that included a mixture of religious and humanistic motivations.

In the 1950s and early 1960s, when a large proportion of COs served in work camps, the CO community there was polarized, mainly but not entirely, between religious and nonreligious COs. Johan Galtung found three major categories among the COs in the camp he studied.[31] One consisted largely of Pentecostals and members of similar religious organizations; these COs were strongly religious and only weakly political. Galtung found that this group received a high degree of support from family and friends, and was not much interested in CO activism or nonviolence as a means of defense. The second group of COs was highly political and either nonreligious or at most weakly religious. They received much less support from family and friends, and a large majority favored CO activism and nonviolent defense. Together these two groups composed 63 percent of the COs. The third category comprised a group that Galtung characterized as both strongly religious and strongly political.

Differences within the CO community have not disappeared entirely since Galtung's study in the 1950s, but a report from the CO Secretariat concluded in 1984 that the image of polarization no longer applied.[32] Larger differences might have been found if the Pentecostals had been separated from the others in the attitudinal study. The decrease in polarization has occurred partly because the CO rate has dropped among Pentecostals, but mostly because the Pentecostals have been swamped by large numbers of more worldly minded COs.

There is not much systematic evidence for any clear relationship between secularization and changing social background of the COs. Tonstad's study shows that in the early 1970s COs were clearly overrepresented at higher levels of education, although at each level they make up only a minority of the cohort.[33] Nonreligious COs probably have somewhat higher levels of education than the average religious CO.

Causes of Changes in the Rate of Conscientious Objection

The rate of conscientious objection is determined by a number of factors. To sort these out conclusively, we need better data than are currently available, but some tentative explanations are possible. Part of the recent political debate about the liberalization of the law regarding conscientious objection is rooted in the deep fear that such liberalization, which offers greater freedom of choice than in the past, will lead to higher rates of objection, which may endanger the entire system of conscription. The available data, however, provide no evidence for such an effect. The first CO law of 1922 was followed by a sharp decrease in objection. The 1965 law—hardly a liberalization—was followed by an increase that was due largely to other factors. The sharp increase in CO rates in the early 1970s was not due to any liberalization of the law.

In fact, the reverse seems to be more pertinent: Major increases in the rate of conscientious objection lead to legal changes.[34] At the turn of the century and in the World War I era, mounting numbers of COs led to civilian political pressure for legislation. This pressure led in turn to the administrative reform of 1902 and subsequently to the legislation of 1922.[35] In the 1950s and the 1970s the effect was the opposite: strongly increasing rates of conscientious objection led to pressure from the military for restrictive reforms. The efforts by the military failed, but the proposed changes in the law were seriously retrogressive. In the 1980s the continuing embarrassment of jailing "political objectors" led to an attempt to liberalize the law.

Political movements come and go, and political changes are particularly strong and rapid among the young. The dramatically rising CO rate in the late 1960s and early 1970s may be explained at least partially by the radical youth rebellion of the period, including such diverse phenomena as hippies, student radicals, Marxist revolutionaries, and political terrorists. Such an explanation, however, does not explain why conscientious objection did not decrease in the more conservative 1980s. In fact, the "conservative" periods of the early 1960s and the 1980s were periods of peak antinuclear activity, generating the strongest peace movements in many Western countries since the 1930s.[36] This fact might account for the high CO rate in the early 1980s but not for the peaks in the early 1950s or the early 1970s. Nor did the decline in the peace movement in the late 1980s seem to result in any reduction of COs.

Conscientious objection rates have probably been influenced by international crises.[37] Conscientious objector rates increased before and during the two world wars, the Korean War, and the Vietnam War. It is too simplistic to say that the threat of danger causes more young men to avoid military service through conscientious objection. The most significant increases in the CO rate occurred during the Vietnam War, which posed no physical danger to Norwegians. A more plausible intervening variable between international crises and increases in the CO rate is domestic militarization. An examination of Norwegian military expenditure shows six periods of rapidly rising military expenditure: the late 1890s, the era of World War I, the late 1930s, the early 1950s, the late 1960s and early 1970s, and the early 1980s.[38] These coincide with periods of increasing conscientious objection.[39] Rising military expenditures bring national security issues into the domestic environment. They raise issues of priority and sharpen public awareness, particularly among the ages eligible for conscription.

A "ratchet effect" seems to operate for CO rates similar to that for military expenditure. Although rates decrease after a peak, they do not necessarily return to the previous level. Indeed, the long-term trend in conscientious objection is clearly upward. In the case of COs, this effect may be interpreted as the result of transmission between friends and from parents to children. The greater the number of COs, the less the stigma on conscientious objection then and later.

Conscientious objection in Norway has been rising over the past hundred years. To a significant degree this can be seen as a result of transmission or inheritance. International crises (mediated by domestic militarization) have driven up the rates, but the evaporation of crisis does not necessarily bring them down again. The improvement of alternative civilian service—the shift from isolated work camps to integration into health care and social services—also may have stimulated conscientious objection since the mid–1960s. Legal changes do not seem to have a very clear effect. Rather, they are themselves influenced by the increasing rates of conscientious objection. Among the most dramatic aspects of the evolution of conscientious objection, particularly in the past thirty years, has been its increasing secularization. Nonreligious conscientious objection has been firmly established in law and administrative practice for seventy years. Whether purely political and selective objection qualifies an applicant for CO status is still an unresolved political and legal controversy in Norway.

The Future of Conscientious Objection in Norway

The end of the Cold War led a number of European countries in 1990–1991 to begin cutting military expenditures and reducing the size of their armed forces. In Norway even the parties on the Right became willing to consider reductions. In the 1980s there had been more than enough recruits, but reduced age-cohorts were projected because of dwindling birth rates. If the threat had continued, there might have been increasing pressure to introduce female conscription, but in the absence of the need for additional soldiers, female conscription seems unlikely in the foreseeable future.

Will conscription itself survive? With its roots in the Norwegian constitution and in the country's democratic tradition, it probably has support from a wider community than the military itself. The ideology behind conscription, however, may be undermined by a withering of the threat, by consequent increased avoidance of military service through medical and other exemptions and through absenteeism, and by efforts to save money on military expenditure by reducing the number of men called up and shortening their term of service.

What will be the future of conscientious objection and of alternative civilian service? With the decline of international tensions and the blurring images of the enemy, military service may become less meaningful, and more people may refuse to serve. This development may make conscientious objection even more respectable. To what extent will the alternative work of the COs be socially meaningful?

Since the 1950s, the peace movement and the CO community in Norway have been trying to mobilize support for an "extended concept of defense." This concept encompasses a program of nonmilitary civilian resistance to the threat of enemy invasion and occupation, as well as various international peacekeeping and peacemaking efforts, such as increased developmental assistance. To fit such an extended concept of defense, the CO community has advocated an extended concept of national service.[40] Although public debate about the extended concept of defense has subsided since the 1970s, the idea is still alive in the peace movement; with the end of the Cold War, the more traditional opponents might become more interested because it offers new, largely nonviolent tasks for the military.[41]

Conscientious objectors in alternative service have become increasingly important to Norwegian society. Originally they were used mainly in forestry and agriculture, but increasing mechanization reduced their usefulness in those sectors of the economy. At the same time, health and social services expanded rapidly, and there was a need for additional labor in those areas. The growth of the elderly population already has placed major strains on the delivery of these services, and all indicators point to a deepening of the crisis in the future. It will be extremely difficult to overcome this crisis in health care and social services with professional help only. Thus one of the "traditional" tasks of alternative civilian service is assuming an urgency that might be viewed as comparable to national security. In another area of social concern, it has been argued that the threat to the environment is a major threat to the nation, and that conscientious objectors should be organized to work collectively for environmental protection, perhaps in conjunction with a program of nonmilitary civilian defense.[42]

A wider concept of national service, one that encompasses the tradition of the citizen-soldier as well as local, national, and international civic programs, has been advocated in the United States by Charles C. Moskos and others.[43] There is a strong case for re-evaluating conscription in Norway from the same perspective. Several tasks might be defined as equivalent, with wide latitude of choice on the basis of qualifications and individual preferences. The service, but not its form, would be compulsory. There would still be an opportunity for conscientious objection to military service, but the positive aspects of seeking other forms of service would be important. Conscripts who were not conscientious objectors to military service might give even higher priority to tasks such as environmental protection or international developmental assistance.

As many countries previously caught up in the East-West conflict begin to see the possibility of reducing their peacetime military expenditures, conversion is added to the political agenda. The discussion of national service suggests that conscription—an institution originally developed for a very specific purpose—may be converted to fit a much broader range of needs. Conscientious objection has helped to bring about that situation, but may itself become much less relevant in the process.

10

South Africa: From Laager to Anti-Apartheid

ANNETTE SEEGERS

Beyond the legal demise of apartheid, the future of South Africa remains unknown. However, with its polarized racial situation and its divided white minority, South Africa has traditionally had a particular problem with compulsory military service and conscientious objection. South Africa's experience with conscientious objection can best be understood by dividing its history into four periods.[1] The first starts with the years between the creation of the Union of South Africa—in 1910—and 1961, when the Republic of South Africa left the British Commonwealth and assumed for the first time sole responsibility for its own defense. The second period, from 1960 to 1983, represents the first policy towards conscientious objectors by the newly independent South African military. In the third period, from 1983 to 1990, a new policy is introduced: alternative service for COs. The final period, from 1990 on, heralding the dismantling of apartheid, portends a new era for COs as well as for all of South Africa.

Establishment of the Union of South Africa

Following the establishment of the Union of South Africa in 1910, combining the former Afrikaner (Boer) republics with the two British colonies, the government adopted the Union Defense Act 13 of 1912. It provided for the creation of a military force eventually known as the South African Defense Force (SADF). The law declared that all male citizens between the ages of 17 and 65 were liable for military service in time of war, and that in peacetime young men were subject to up to three months' military training annually during a four-year period, usually after their twenty-first

127

birthday. Although the vast majority of the population was black, only whites were subject to this law; in effect South Africa inaugurated an all-white military system. Further, young men had to take military training and service only if volunteer numbers fell short of requirements (generally 50 percent of those liable for training in any given year).[2]

The act of 1912 also provided exemptions on educational, personal, and professional grounds, except when volunteer numbers were insufficient. In addition exemption was allowed for conscientious objection, defined "objectively" as stemming from membership of certain pacifist, religious denominations. Section 82(2) of the act stated: A person who *bona fide* belongs and adheres to "a recognized religious denomination, by the tenets whereof its members may not participate in war," may be granted exemption from serving "in any combatant capacity in time of war," but may be required to "serve in a non-combatant capacity." Failure to report for duty could result in a fine and a prison term of up to five years. Legislators clearly were unwilling to grant COs full exemption from military service—only from bearing arms and participating in combatant duty.

The state did not conscript for military service between 1912 and 1960. Even during the two world wars, the South African military was a volunteer force. The pacifist churches in South Africa were small, limited to a minuscule group of Quakers and to slightly larger groups of Jehovah's Witnesses and Seventh-Day Adventists.[3] Pacifist views were overshadowed in white South Africa by strong cultural-political traditions emphasizing service to the state, the relative unimportance of individuals and their conscience, and the high esteem for authoritarian institutions.[4]

To understand the issue of conscientious objection before 1960 one must also consider an important qualification made to military service. Because of objections to service in those wars seen as beneficial to the British Empire, mainly among Afrikaners of Dutch and German descent,[5] the legislators of 1912 adopted a provision that service in wars beyond South Africa's borders required an individual soldier's consent. As late as 1976 this requirement remained legally binding.

Provision for Conscientious Objection

The Defense Act of 1957, which replaced the 1912 act, stated that the South African Defense Force's small permanent component would be supplemented by conscripted national servicemen, a reserve force (called the Citizen Force), and territorially based commandos. Those eligible for service were male citizens between eighteen and thirty-five. As before, conscription would be applied to whites only. For national service, a ballot system was devised to select white males who were at least eighteen years old. Some provisions were made to postpone service, for example, for economic hardship, student deferment, and certain occupational exemptions. Those were narrowly applied by special Exemption Boards appointed by the Ministry of Labor, and their decisions were considered final.[6]

The 1957 Defense Act, which was implemented in 1960, provided for conscientious objection. Again, COs had to be members of recognized religious denominations that forbade combatant duties; their sole relief was in performing noncombatant duties in a military organization. Refusal of service could meet with a fine or up to eighteen months' imprisonment.

Realizing that many white males would now be forced to serve in the military because of conscription, members of peace churches and especially Jehovah's Witnesses challenged the policy. Those CO draftees who continued to protest in the SADF were, by all accounts, treated harshly (for example, continual three-month periods in a detention center and solitary confinement).[7] By 1972 the situation for Jehovah's Witnesses had improved only marginally. Total actual time spent in detention was reduced to a maximum of twelve months; nonmilitary clothing was provided for those who refused to wear a military uniform; and coerced participation in military drill was abandoned.[8]

Following republican independence in 1961, the Republic of South Africa increased its military demands on white males. In 1964 the size of the national servicemen's component was increased to 16,500, and in 1967 national service was universally applied to all males between seventeen and thirty-five. The length of national service was extended in 1972 to one year, with a subsequent five years of attendance at encampments for nineteen days. In 1977 national service was lengthened to two years, with another eight years of various military duties (including service in the annual "camps"). An important change was that the Defense Act clause that had required soldiers' individual consent before employment beyond South Africa's borders was dropped in 1976, and South African troops were used against guerrilla forces in Namibia (then South-West Africa) and in the former Portuguese colonies of Angola and Mozambique.

Several religious and secular organizations debated military service,[9] but resistance to service beyond the peace churches was slow to emerge. The beginning of other groups' opposition is commonly traced to two incidents in the mid-seventies.

In 1974 Roman Catholic Archbishop Denis Hurley of Durban issued a statement that to defend white South African society by force of arms was to defend apartheid, and that to defend apartheid was to defend an unjust cause. He emphasized that it was impermissible for Christians to fight an unjust war.[10] Archbishop Hurley's use of just-war doctrine subsequently found support in a resolution of the South African Council of Churches (SACC). Although not issuing a specific call for conscientious objection, the resolution urged church members to reconsider their position both in society and the military, and it commended church members who were conscientious objectors.[11]

The moral grounds for the Council of Churches' position were varied. By invoking the just-war doctrine, the position raised the issue of when the use of violence was justified. But there also was the question of whether South African society (including its government) was a just society on the grounds of more general principles of "justice and peace." The heart of the matter was not war itself—with its attendant moral and lawful dilemmas—but rather whether the military was the instrument for perpetuating an unjust society.

Despite the churches' path-breaking action in 1974, momentum was slow. All the parliamentary political parties criticized the Council of Churches' resolution, as did almost all the major "white" newpapers.[12] The state responded by adding a clause to the Defense Act, setting a fine of 6,000 South African rand (equal to $3,000 at 1987 U.S. rates of exchange) or six years' imprisonment for individuals encouraging citizens to refuse military service.

Consequently, the movement for conscientious objection retreated somewhat; but beginning in the mid-seventies, events changed its context. Starting in 1972, the South African Defense Force expanded its presence in Namibia; in 1981 it intervened for extended periods in Angola, which obtained independence from Portugal in 1974 and was the base for guerrillas of the South-West African People's Organization (SWAPO). In South Africa itself, riots by blacks in 1976 and 1977— in which hundreds were killed—saw the first major expressions since the early 1960s of violent protest by the disenfranchised.

By the late 1970s objection to military service had increased and assumed various forms. Unofficial figures, for example, suggest that in 1975–1978 3,500 men failed to report for military duty.[13] Some young men said they could not take up arms against liberation organizations and black fellow citizens; others opposed the use of the military to defend apartheid in South Africa.[14] Apartheid, not war, was the issue.[15]

Although a small number of COs from other churches appeared, the Jehovah's Witnesses continued to compose the largest single group of objectors. Those who refused to serve in the military were imprisoned. Support for the COs initially came mainly from individual churches and parishes, but in 1978 an umbrella organization, the Conscientious Objectors Support Group, was founded. A loose alliance of supporting bodies, COSG focused primarily on providing interpersonal community support for those COs who faced hardship because of their principles.[16] A secondary aim was to increase public awareness of such dissent through a newsletter, *Objector*, and through public meetings.

One by one, the major religious denominations came to support conscientious objection. In 1977 the Bishops' Conference's call for the right to object on the ground of conscience was endorsed by the Church of the Province of South Africa, the United Congregational Church, the Methodist Church, and the Roman Catholic Church. Later the Baptist Union of South Africa, which had strongly condemned the Council of Churches' resolution in 1974, also recognized the right of conscientious objection and called for alternative service for such objectors.

Conspicuous by their absence were the Afrikaans churches, or *susterkerke*, which both supported apartheid and condemned conscientious objection. The largest denomination, the Nederduitse Gereformeerde Kerk, declared pacifism to be "unchristian," and asserted that individuals did not have the right to challenge the state on the grounds of religious theory or just-war doctrine. Its reasoning was that the South African state was an entity created by God and thus objection to it was unfounded.[17]

How did the South African state respond to the challenge presented by the quickened pace of conscientious objection? By all accounts the number of objectors remained small, particularly in proportion to the number of men conscripted. In 1982 only 263 COs were serving sentences in military detention barracks.[18] Yet the government felt enough pressure to appoint a commission of inquiry that year to investigate the issue. The Naude Commission defined conscientious objection narrowly and in traditional terms and accepted as COs only those who were pacifists from recognized churches and who were opposed to all wars. The following year, the commission's definition became law in the Defense Amendment Act of 1983.

Alternative Service for COs

The 1983 act was the first defense measure in South Africa to authorize alternative service for recognized religious COs. It provided two categories: noncombatant "alternative" service for objectors who would serve in a military organization but who refused, for example, to wear a uniform or carry or use weapons; and service other than in the military, such as hospital work, which entailed a length of service amounting to one-and-one-half times that of military duty. Since military service was for four years, alternative service was for six years. For those who had completed some portion of service, the length of alternative duty was reduced accordingly.

Who was to decide the sincerity and fate of the objectors? The Defense Act of 1983 created a Board for Religious Objection (BRO), whose members would be appointed by the minister of manpower in consultation with the minister of defense. The board's composition consisted of a chairman (to be a sitting or retired judge from the Supreme Court of South Africa), three theologians (each representing a different denomination),[19] and two members of the South African Defense Force (one of whom would be a chaplain). A quorum consisted of the chairman and three members, one of whom had to be the chaplain.

What were the criteria for certifying a young man as a conscientious objector? What was the required substance of the applicant's claim? The 1983 law specified only that the young man put in writing the "grounds upon which the application is based," indicating "books of revelation and the articles of faith upon which the religious convictions of the applicant are based." In effect, this definition replaced the older "objective" requirement—membership in a peace church—with a more "subjective" test: the determination of a deeply held, religiously based, pacifist belief. Secular grounds for conscientious objection were excluded.

The BRO did not have the legal authority to determine whether or not a particular view was religious. That authority rested solely with the South African courts. In practice, however, the board developed certain criteria to assess the beliefs of CO applicants. It favored applicants who belonged to a recognized religious denomination whose doctrines prohibited members from participating in war. Most important was evidence that the applicant indeed subscribed to those beliefs.[20] In emphasizing "belief," the board said it had to be theistically religious.[21] "It need not be a Christian religion," a judge explained. "It need not be a belief in one God. It can be a belief in a multiplicity of gods, *as long as it is a belief in a Supreme Being or Beings of a divine nature whose precepts have to be obeyed*" (emphasis added).[22]

The board's interpretation of a legitimate religious basis was challenged in 1986, when it rejected the application of a follower of Theravada Buddhism. Exemption had been denied on grounds that the applicant did not believe in a "Supreme Being or Beings of a divine nature whose precepts have to be obeyed.'' The applicant had indeed stated that ''if someone asked me is there a God, I would say I do not know.''[23] However, upon appeal, a provincial court reversed this ruling in favor of the applicant. The court declared that the legislators in 1983 could not have meant to exclude nontheistic religious denominations from the category ''religion,'' because the South African Constitution in 1983 recognized freedom of religion. Since the applicant could show ''books of revelation and articles of faith'' to support his claim, he should be classified as a religious objector.[24]

It is possible that the Board for Religious Objection may be able to broaden the definition of conscientious objection to include secular grounds. There were secularly grounded objectors in the 1980s, but they did not apply to the board.[25] In other cases the results were punitive.[26] In 1989, however, Douglas Banks formulated his objection in secular terms of ''moral conscience'' and took his case to the Supreme Court of South Africa. As of this writing the court has not delivered judgment, and it is not clear whether the criteria for COs will be further liberalized.

While the creation of alternative service in 1983 was generally applauded, some argued that lawmakers created the CO program for partisan and punitive reasons. According to liberal critics, the system was partisan because it allowed military men to dominate the board, and it sought to split churches and other groups supporting conscientious objection. Critics point to the length of civilian alternative service (one-and-one-half times that of total military duty) and the often menial positions at poor rates of pay. Obviously, the government wished the conditions of alternative service to act as a deterrent.[27] Nevertheless, many men applied for such service. According to the minister of manpower and the current BRO chairman, 1,890 conscripts applied to the board for CO status between 1984 and 1989. In 1989 alone, 286 national servicemen applied for religious objector status; of these 167 were Jehovah's Witnesses.[28]

In the 1980s conscientious objection became politically intertwined with resistance to war and apartheid. In 1983, with the establishment of the End Conscription Campaign (ECC), an organization was created solely devoted to opposition to conscription in the service of apartheid. According to the ECC, conscription was used to defend and implement the policies of apartheid, to maintain South Africa's illegal occupation of Namibia, and to wage war on the frontline states, Angola and Mozambique. Conscription, it was argued, both violated the fundamental right of freedom of conscience and contributed to an acceptance of political and social militarization.[29]

The ECC was even more successful than its founders had anticipated. The government, describing the campaign as a ''radical'' organization cooperating with South Africa's enemies, began a campaign of harassment against it. In spring 1986, following widespread violence, the government of President P. W. Botha declared a nationwide state of emergency—delegating almost unlimited power to the security forces.

In 1989 End Conscription Campaign sought a court injunction against the South African Defense Force to prevent the SADF from harrassing the organization. The Cape Supreme Court found in favor of the ECC.[30] However, because of the nationwide state of emergency in 1986, the government made it illegal for anyone to make "a statement which contains anything which is calculated to have the effect or is likely to have the effect of inciting the public or any person or category of persons to discredit or undermine the system of compulsory military service."[31] Similar prohibitions followed, and in 1988 the government formally "banned" the ECC from engaging in any activity other than its own internal affairs. As a result ECC membership dwindled, and the remaining members became embroiled in debates over the proper course of action.

Despite the government's apparent success against the ECC, the trials of COs in the 1980s revealed that the military was being forced to cope with "war resistance" from within.[32] The SADF developed a policy of tacit compromise. Upon receiving complaints or refusals by conscripts or training "campers" to perform certain kinds of military service, the SADF would "informally accommodate" such objections. Often this accommodation was accompanied by various forms of humiliation, such as to being made to stand outside offices in full view of other troops. Eventually, objecting conscripts would be assigned to staff offices or be posted to main bases rather than being forced to patrol the black townships. (The extent of this accommodation and the members involved are unknown.)

Dismantling Apartheid

Conscientious objection in South Africa entered a new phase on February 2, 1990. The new government of President F. W. de Klerk—moving toward a dismantling of apartheid and having ended South Africa's wars against its neighbors—announced that national service would be reduced to one year's duty, prison terms of objectors would be cut by half, and the ban on the ECC would be lifted.[33]

In the future, conscientious objection thus will take place in a drastically altered political context: The psychology underlying the issue and indeed the very nature of the conflict situation in South Africa have changed dramatically. The major churches are now even more critical of the state's demands on its citizens. The principle of conscientious objection is widely recognized. The scope of religious objection has been broadened: Alternative service possibilities exist.

Although it is tempting to be optimistic about the future prospects of conscientious objection in South Africa, caution demands the observation that the South African state does not easily reduce its demands on its citizens. Those who object to military service on grounds of conscience will continue to face a long, hard struggle.

Conclusion

Conscientious objection in South Africa has since 1910 been an issue best understood within the context of divisions within the white minority of this predominantly nonwhite nation. Conscription applied only to whites. For fifty years, under primarily British rule, dissent from compulsory military service came primarily from Afrikaners, many of whom opposed being compelled to fight in wars they viewed as beneficial to the British Empire. After Nationalist party governments furthered apartheid in South Africa in the 1950s and withdrew from the British Commonwealth in 1961, such anti-British opposition to conscription ended. It was replaced by conscientious objection, which became in political practice, closely linked with internal dissent against apartheid and its wars, an opposition that came primarily from the non-Afrikaner white conscripts and their supporters.

When the newly independent Republic of South Africa was introduced in the 1960s, a small number of conscientious objectors appeared, the majority of them Jehovah's Witnesses. Objection was grounded in their refusal to fight for the state and in the universal pacifism of peace churches. The state, which progressively increased military obligations, initially responded with highly punitive actions. Jehovah's Witnesses were, and indeed remain numerically, the majority of COs in South Africa. By 1983, however, growing support for conscientious objection among various mainline religious denominations led the state to recognize and broaden the criteria for conscientious objection from institutional to functional religious grounds, and to create options for alternative service.

Since South Africa is currently undergoing a major political transition, it is impossible to forecast a definitive conclusion regarding conscientious objection. For the moment, the state has contracted its demands of military service. Accordingly, the requirements of alternative service have also been contracted. Yet a hard-won, albeit limited, precedent stands: An individual's religious objection to military service ought to be and is recognized as inviolate terrain. Secular objection, although not yet officially recognized by the government, has already produced informal accommodation within the military.

11

Switzerland: Questioning the Citizen Soldier

KARL W. HALTINER

Switzerland is the only Western democracy that as yet offers no official civilian alternative service for conscientious objectors. Indeed, conscientious objection is legally still a crime in Switzerland.

Widely known for its long-standing tradition of democracy, Switzerland, a confederation composed of twenty-six cantons, each of which has considerable local autonomy, is less well known for its tradition of universal conscription in the militia. For centuries all male Swiss citizens have been trained to defend the democratic community, a role seen as bestowing their rights of citizenship. Because of the political and social importance of this militia principle, the symbolic functions of a citizen army developed comparatively early.

Symbolic functions of the citizen army include the role of the military as the "school of the nation": the symbol of civil honor and national identity. The degree of military participation has determined the degree of civil integration and closeness to the social and political core of Swiss society. Because of this close link between the civic and military tradition, the issue of conscientious objection has long defied resolution in Switzerland.

The peculiarities of the Swiss political and military system help to explain the dilemma that conscientious objection poses to the country. Article 18 of the federal Constitution of 1848 (revised in 1874, and in force today) states: "Every Swiss is liable for military service." Article 49, which grants religious freedom and freedom of conscience, states: "Religious beliefs do not relieve anyone of his duty as a citizen."

Obviously the Constitution values the citizens' duties higher than their freedom of conscience. Swiss authorities agree that Article 18 does not allow exemption

135

from universal conscription on principle, including conscientious objection. Every male Swiss either undergoes periodic military service over a thirty year period or, if unable to serve for medical reasons, pays a "substitution tax" for each year of service missed. To refuse the draft or subsequent summons, for any reason whatever, means prosecution, with prison sentences of up to three years. This equality—a phenomenon that has sometimes been called "military socialism"—makes the problem posed by conscientious objection highly significant. The democratic principle of tolerance for different opinions conflicts with the democratic principle that all citizens are equal before the law.

Switzerland relies on a militia system rather than a standing army.* Article 13 of the Constitution forbids the federation to keep standing troops. After undergoing basic training of seventeen weeks at age twenty, each draftee must perform another thirty-two weeks of military service in refresher courses over the next thirty years. During these three decades of his life, he remains a regular member of the militia, which includes home maintenance of personal equipment, a rifle, and ammunition, and participation in compulsory target practice. Except for a small corps of professional instructors, officers and non-commissioned officers (NCOs) have the same militia status as troops; they enter as regular militia recruits. Advancement to higher rank follows recruit training and, subsequently, graduation from appropriate training schools.

The law provides for compulsory service, if necessary, to secure sufficient numbers of officers and NCOs. Therefore, militiamen never know upon entering the army whether they will have to serve more than the minimum duty. This peculiarity of the system makes it even more difficult to find an alternative civilian service for COs that will be at all equitable with the varying lengths of compulsory military service that draftees face.

Even though the phenomenon of conscientious objection has changed somewhat, as has public opinion and policy toward it, COs are still prosecuted by military courts. Since judges have tried to elicit the reasons for objection, it is possible to trace primary motives for more than a century. The Swiss data strongly support the thesis that conscientious objection in highly industrialized, modern societies has become increasingly secularized.

Changing Motives of COs, 1848 to the Present

Conscientious objection has evolved in three stages in Switzerland (see Figure 11–1). The phenomenon of refusing military service in any form first occurred in Switzerland four centuries ago, following the Reformation. In the sixteenth century members of radical evangelical movements, especially the early Baptist groups, such as Anabaptists and Mennonites, refused to serve in the military, often failing to appear at the mandatory drafts. Later, as documented in 1780, they expressed a willingness to build dams on the rivers instead of performing military service,

*For the Swiss, the militia, although not a standing army, is considered a regular army.

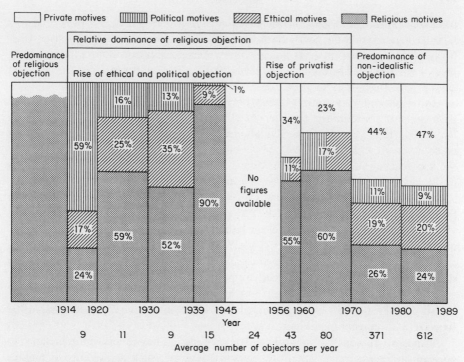

FIGURE 11-1. Changing motives of military objectors in Switzerland, 1900–1989. *Source:* Chief military attorney of Switzerland (Berne).

but authorities refused to accept this.[1] Many of these early Baptists, therefore, emigrated to lands where religious objection to bearing arms was tolerated.

Unification of independent cantons into the modern federal state of Switzerland in 1848 did not effect any change in the tradition of universal military obligation. The principle stating that every male Swiss citizen was required to perform military service was established in the new federal Constitution.

Few individuals refused to perform military service from 1848 to 1900. Probably not more than five persons a year were convicted on such a charge, most of them Jehovah's Witnesses or other sects.

With the spread of socialist and Marxist ideas, political objection to military service gained in Switzerland early in the twentieth century. Calling the bourgeois state and its army repressive instruments of the capitalist class, socialists rejected military service on behalf of the state. They were not pacifists, however. Many of them supported revolutionary violence to further the class struggle.

Troops were often used against strikers between 1900 to 1932; this and the growth of socialism produced an increase in the number of political objectors. Many went to jail for refusing to serve (there were seventeen such convictions in 1902 alone). Swiss socialists' opposition to conscription grew during World War I and the postwar period. Although Switzerland has remained neutral in that and every other war since 1815, it nevertheless increased its defenses during wartime, and increased call-ups contributed to increased objection. In 1917, thirty-seven objectors were sentenced, and the Swiss Socialist party, which rejected such defense measures, decided to support COs financially. Under such circumstances political objectors outnumbered religious ones, from 1917 to 1922 and again during the Great Depression, from 1929 to 1936.

In 1936 faced with an overt fascist threat in Europe, the Swiss Socialists resumed their support for military defense. Accordingly, political objection declined. In World War II 90 percent of the COs who refused military service did so for religious reasons. Between 1914 and 1945, about eight to ten persons a year (a peak of forty-six was reached in 1940) were convicted of refusing military service.[2] The militia grew from 450,000 in 1914 to 630,000 in 1939.[3]

The number of COs and others refusing to bear arms significantly increased in Switzerland after 1945. For two decades after World War II, the number of convictions averaged around forty a year, while the army consisted of more than 800,000 militiamen. The main reasons for conscientious objection were still religious, but a new kind of motive gained relevance. Whereas previously the motives had been mainly idealistic (religious, ethical, or political), during the 1950s and 1960s a significant percentage of COs said, for the first time, that their motives were privatistic. In 1956–1959 these amounted to 34 percent of the COs; in 1960–1969 they were 23 percent (see Figure 11.1).

Privatistic reasons lacked an idealistic character. They involved a reluctance to perform military service largely for personal reasons, such as inability or unwillingness to integrate into the military hierarchy or refusal to do the required career service, for example, as officers or NCOs. Whether a new phenomenon or not, statistically speaking, privatism as a basis for conscientious objection clearly became significant only after the Second World War.

As in other Western countries, the number of military objectors rose sharply in Switzerland in the late 1960s. Applications for permission to perform military service with noncombatant units also increased significantly. At the same time the character of conscientious objection changed. Privatistic motives became dominant after 1970 (see Figure 11.1). Religious motives, which were predominant in the nineteenth century and only somewhat less so until the late 1960s, are now of minor importance, representing the attitudes of less than one-quarter of the COs. Religious motives were gradually supplemented from 1914 to 1966 by ethical-moral and political (mainly socialist) motives, and from 1967 to the present by largely non-religious, non-idealist, privatistic motives. Thus, the long-term trend in Switzerland clearly indicates a secularization of the motives for conscientious objection to military service.

Despite the increasing numbers of COs since the late sixties, the total number of objectors remains quite small compared to the strength of the army, which has been around 625,000 since 1971. Among entering recruits, COs have never exceeded 1 percent of the total even in years in which the number of those refusing to do military service was high. In addition to the manifest forms of conscientious objection, however, latent forms of avoiding military service have also increased since the late 1960s. The number of those using false medical reasons as a pretext has clearly grown in the last few years. The dropout quota in recruit schools soared to 14 percent in the 1980s from 1 percent or 2 percent in the 1950s. Similarly, the percentage of soldiers convicted of leaving their post, going absent without leave, or being insubordinate has also grown steadily. The past twenty years have seen a growing disengagement from military matters in Switzerland.

COs and the State

The attitude adopted by governmental authorities and political elites concerning COs has evolved in three stages: pre–World War I; 1914 to 1950; and 1950 to the present.

The first stage—prior to the First World War—is characterized by the fact that universal military obligation was consistently imposed. Before 1900 COs were so isolated they bothered neither authorities nor the public. In the mid–1800s, before the federal state was founded, some cantons refused to accept any objectors; others made exceptions for religious minorities, particularly for members of historic peace churches who were willing to pay a fine or supply a substitute.

The federal Constitution of 1848, revised in 1871 and in force today, put forward a national standard: conscription of all male Swiss (except the medically unfit, who paid a substitution levy). The military penal code of 1851 made no mention of conscientious objection. In practice, such behavior was regarded as "insubordination," "leaving the post," or "desertion." And, as the law made no distinction between times of war and times of peace, such offenders were severely punished. In addition to being sentenced to prison, objectors often were deprived of their right to vote.

Objectors were not necessarily discharged from the army.[4] Instead, after serving a jail sentence, an objector generally received another summons to military service; if he still refused, he was sentenced again. It was not uncommon for objectors to be sentenced several times (such recidivism amounted to 37 percent of all such convictions between 1914 and 1926).[5] In Switzerland objectors to military service, including COs, are still tried by military, not civilian courts.[6]

The second stage, from around 1914 to 1950, began with the issue of the Marxist cases in World War I, which caused civil authorities and public opinion to face the problem of increased and political military objection. The military suggested that objectors who had served one jail sentence should be allowed to perform some kind of alternative service instead of being returned to prison.[7] In parliament, the first attempt to introduce an alternative to military service on the basis of freedom of choice was made by the socialists.[8] In 1923, after some difficulty, socialists and pacifists collected forty thousand signatures for a petition asking that COs be allowed to perform alternative civilian service that would last one-third longer than regular military duty.[9]

The 1923 petition and subsequent similar ones in the 1930s were rejected by the federal parliament. The government, military authorities, and a majority in parliament feared that alternative civilian service would weaken the militia and might also set a precedent for the dissolution of universal military obligation.[10]

Most legal experts have said for years that alternative civilian service would be feasible in Switzerland only with a change in the federal Constitution obtained through a plebiscite. However, until the mid-twentieth century neither the political elite nor a sizable segment of the public was willing to accommodate such a change. Political and military authorities alike consistently refused all proposals for alternative civilian service or, indeed, for any improvement in the status of COs. This reflected not only the intent of the Constitution but probably also the view of the majority of the population.

Nevertheless, extensive public debate of conscientious objection in the World War I era had produced some changes, particularly in the way the military dealt with COs. In the 1927 revision of the military penal code, specific penalties were provided for military objection, which was distinguished from desertion, missing military service, and insubordination. Article 81 of the amended code states that whoever refuses a draft notice in peacetime can be sentenced to up to three years in prison. In wartime, the sentence can be increased. Until some changes were made in 1950 and 1967 there was no distinction between motives for objection on the basis of Article 81, which meant that all objectors—whether their motives were religious, ethical, political, or private—faced the same sentence.

Before 1950, however, informal practices were developed to cope with the increasing pressure of conscientious objection; these are still applied. Although even today no one is legally entitled by statute to perform noncombatant service, it was and still is possible for persons refusing to bear arms to perform their military service—without weapons—in the medical corps or the air raid protection corps. Others can also ask for a reassignment to those units for the same reasons.

Persons who wanted an exemption for conscientious reasons were often sent to a psychiatrist for assessment. If declared medically handicapped, they were exempted from military service. This procedure was confirmed in 1966.[11]

In the third stage, from the 1950s to the present, the political elite, and increasingly the public as well, have concluded that it is against the democratic ideals of religious freedom and tolerance to treat COs as common criminals. But Article 18, which until 1992 categorically excluded any legal alternative to military service, remained a major obstacle. In two plebiscites, in 1977 and 1983, a majority of voters rejected constitutional amendments to authorize alternative civilian service. Instead, some amelioration was achieved through the federal parliament, which responded to an increasing number of petitions.[12]

In 1950 Switzerland started to differentiate between religious and other objectors to military service. Those who refuse on strong religious grounds could serve their prison sentence in a state of ''half-detention'' (residing in prison but working during the day in an institution for the common welfare—primarily in medical care, forestry, or road building). Further, religious objectors no longer lost their civil rights. In 1967 the federal government expanded these provisions to apply also to objectors whose claim was based on ethical reasons. All other military objectors continued to be sentenced to full detention in prison, and most are also discharged dishonorably from the army. In practice, prison sentences now usually run between seven and ten months. The half-detention system, used since 1950, came close to a kind of alternative service but retained a criminal stigma. Semi-detention had the status of a jail sentence; it was registered in police records.

A dramatic increase in the number of objectors in the late 1960s—in 1965 about one hundred objected to any military service, and three hundred took up noncombatant duties—led to the first direct popular attempts to revise the Constitution's military provision through an initiative.[13]

Early in 1972, a number of high school teachers launched the "Münchensteiner Initiative," which sought to introduce alternative civilian service for COs whose position was based on nonprivatistic reasons. The term of service granted after scrutiny of conscience would be the same as the sum of the militia service rejected. Although the federal parliament accepted the initiative, it decided, in formulating the proposed amendment, to allow alternative civilian service only for religious and ethical COs; other motives, including political ones, would not qualify. In 1977, this amendment was rejected in a public vote 62 percent to 38 percent.

Prior to the vote on the Münchensteiner Initiative, another initiative committee was formed by groups wanting a more far-reaching solution. They proposed—in a precisely worded amendment to Article 18—alternative civilian service, without regard for motive, for any CO prepared to work one and one-half times the duration of regular military duty in an alternative venture. Such ventures included "the propagation of peace," "the abolishment of the causes of violence," "the improvement of human life conditions," and "the strengthening of international solidarity." In 1982, the majority of the parliament refused to identify itself with this amendment. The legislators declared that universal conscription would thereby be reduced to simply a choice between military and "peace" service.[14] Subsequently, the measure was rejected in 1983 by a majority of those voting in the plebiscite.

Since the two initiatives were rejected, and the amendment to introduce a civilian service had clearly failed, a more limited reform was adopted. After submission of a parliamentary petition in 1984, the government in 1987 introduced a bill to "decriminalize real objectors for conscientious reasons."[15] The measure was approved by a majority of the voters in a referendum in June 1991. Under this new law, military objection still remains punishable, but there is a modicum of liberalization. Objectors who are judged by divisional military tribunals to be motivated by religious or "fundamental ethical values" and are likely to suffer "a severe conflict of conscience" can, under the 1991 law, be given lighter prison sentences than other objectors. In addition, the new law permits the military courts to sentence religious or ethical COs to perform a kind of collective labor service—generally in reforestation work or medical care. This service lasts for a period up to one and one-half times longer than the rejected military service, but is not to exceed two years. After such service, objectors can have their criminal conviction for refusing armed service expunged from police records.

The 1991 reform did not meet the expectations of CO organizations because it only improved objectors' position on a de jure rather than a de facto basis. In 1990, 581 persons claiming to be COs were sentenced to prison terms of up to 10 months.[16] Under the new law, conscientious objectors whose motives are seen as political or personal are still imprisoned, but in practice that imprisonment lasts six months at most. Furthermore they still have to prove to a military tribunal that they are acting out of severe religious and ethical conflicts.[17]

But the referendum of June 1991 had indicated a clear change of mind toward conscientious objectors among the Swiss people. By this shift in opinion the Federal parliament was encouraged in December 1991 to make a new attempt to change Article 18 of the Constitution. To the famous phrase "Every Swiss is liable for military service" an amendment was to be added stating that "The law will provide for the organization of civilian service." On May 17, 1992 a majority of 82.5 percent of the Swiss who voted (a 39 percent turnout) accepted this amendment.[18] Thus the way to exempt conscientious objectors legally from military service is now open in principle. But it will not be easy to find a concrete service model that meets both the interest of those who want to maintain an equal sharing of the burden in defense matters and those who plead for a liberal solution. Both groups still have the opportunity to ask for a referendum on the forthcoming implementation statute by collecting fifty thousand signatures. Even though Switzerland has declared its willingness to find a legal solution for COs, it still remains among those nations without alternative civilian service.

In keeping with the "decriminalization" of 1991, the refusal to bear arms is already treated differently; it is now legally regulated. However, only those able to substantiate religious or fundamental ethical motivation to military tribunals are exempted from bearing arms. In the latter case, the ministry of defense, at the request of a civilian appeal committee, makes the final decision.

Changing Public Values and COs

The dramatic increase in the number of military objectors in Switzerland since the end of the 1960s—reaching nearly four hundred and six hundred annually in the 1970s and 1980s, respectively—cannot be due only to the initial and unsuccessful governmental attempts in that period to decriminalize religious and ethically motivated objection. Rather, the increase in COs occurred simultaneously with increases in other Western democracies from 1965 to 1970. The number of Swiss objectors continued to rise despite the fact that, in national plebiscites, Swiss voters twice rejected constitutional amendments to legalize alternative civilian service.

The most probable explanation for the increase in both COs and privatistic (nonidealistic) motives among them is that a value change began to take root in the Western democracies after 1945, which accelerated in the late 1960s. The rapid structural alterations in society in the postwar period—notably growing urbanization, mobility, improved living standards, expanded information networks, and higher educational levels—were accompanied by erosion of the traditional value system.

Empirical studies have indicated numerous value changes in Switzerland in the postwar period.[19] Among these, values of social conformity (obedience, order, social prestige) generally have tended to lose relevance in favor of those of individuality (self-fulfillment, independence), privacy, and equality (democratization, participation, equal opportunity). The rise of conscientious objection and especially the change in motives for COs can be seen as one indicator of this process of individualization. The growing relevance of individual values has undermined the authority of traditional conveyors of values, such as the family, the church, the

school, and the army. Tolerance for "deviant behavior" (including conscientious
objection) has become more and more acceptable.

These changing values have strongly altered Switzerland's national security
policy and the legitimation of its army. The Swiss population's confidence in the
capacity of a small, neutral nation to defend itself in a modern war, especially
nuclear war, actually declined during the 1980s. This declining credibility caused
more and more pacifists and military objectors to question the meaning as well as
the purpose of the army. So did the end of the Cold War. Many young people no
longer hide their sympathies for conscientious objectors. A growing number would
be willing to undertake some nonmilitary work for the community that would have
social use and meaning.

The militia army has lost its former central position as a key symbol of Swiss
national identity, as an ideal of civil participation, and as a place for a rite of
passage into manhood. The army today is increasingly considered a necessary evil,
solely for defense. In 1976, 49 percent of adults agreed that the army had a central
role in Swiss society; that number sank to 41 percent in 1983 and to 36 percent in
1989. During the same period, the percentage of those who agreed with the necessity
of maintaining a Swiss army declined from 86 percent in 1970 to 61 percent in
1991.[20] (In a November 1989 plebiscite, a constitutional initiative to abolish the
Swiss army received 36 percent of the votes.) This erosion of traditional legitimation
is an example of what Max Weber called *Entzauberung* (desymbolization), and it
shows a trend toward desanctification of the army in Swiss society.

As values of individuality and privacy have increased in significance, integration
of conscripts into the army has become more difficult. Due to a growing value gap
between the Swiss military and the civilian social system, the positive incentives
for citizens to commit themselves to the army are declining.[21] Escapism is increasing
across broad socioeconomic range. There is also a growing tolerance toward criticism of the army and toward acceptance of military objectors. Thus COs not only
face much less social stigmatization in Swiss society, but they can also increasingly
count on respect shown for their attitude. Whereas in 1976 only 64 percent of the
Swiss population would tolerate propaganda for military objection and against the
militia army, in 1983 and 1989, the figures grew to 75 percent and 87 percent,
respectively. Surveys show that, since 1976, more than 80 percent of the population
has agreed with the idea of allowing alternative civilian service.[22]

Why then were the two proposed constitutional amendments to legalize alternative service for COs so massively rejected in 1977 and 1983? The answer must
be that universal conscription in Switzerland has always served both to make maximum use of the military potential and to reinforce the democratic ideal of sharing
the military burden equally among the male population. In a 1983 survey, just
before the second plebiscite, although 58 percent of Swiss respondents listed respect
for individual conscience higher than the principle of universal conscription, three-
quarters of them also considered military service an obligation of citizenship. Only
16 percent were ready to abolish conscription. Thus, among the Swiss population
there seems to be a conflict between accepting alternative civilian service (out of
respect for the individual's conscience) and holding on to the ideal of a shared
military burden among *all* citizens. The principle of tolerance competes with those

of equality and justice. Alternative service for COs can only be successfully introduced through a plebiscite if citizens are convinced that the burden of civilian
service is not lighter than that for the required military service. This was not the
case in 1977 and 1983. The adoption of the 1992 referendum may indicate a major
change, but agreement on a specific program of alternative service may take quite
some time.

Conclusion

Switzerland is still the only democratic country in Europe today that offers no
official program of alternative service for COs: So far there is only the choice
between non-combatant military service or a court-imposed prison term. In the latter
case, the objector goes either to jail or to a kind of collective labor service (which
is also considered a legal punishment). This reflects an old tradition in Switzerland,
a basic disapproval of escape from military service. In the Swiss democracy, the
citizens have been granted a direct voice for centuries, yet their rights are linked
to their duty as citizens to defend their rights and their nation by force if necessary.
Conscientious objectors, therefore, have traditionally been considered state-
objectors. This rejection of COs has softened only gradually in the course of the
twentieth century.

As long as the phenomenon of conscientious objection remained quantitatively
unimportant (that is, limited to a few members of peace churches and Jehovah's
Witnesses), it was not a major issue. When socialist, class-based objection suddenly
arose around the time of the First World War, the general negative attitude of public
opinion toward military objection hardened. The state prosecuted the political objectors while simultaneously trying to ease the problem by allowing the growing
numbers of ethical and religious objectors to perform non-combatant service.

This distinction between so-called "good" and "bad" conscientious objectors
was made very early on, and it continues to survive. Any liberalization of the
treatment of COs began with the religious objectors first, and only later, if at all,
was it applied to political or privatist objectors.

In the late sixties, the number of persons who refused to do military service
grew comparatively rapidly due in large part to an ever-growing individualization
and a decreasing conformity in modern Western society. At the same time religious
and ethical motives were overshadowed mainly by individual, privatistic motives.

Beginning in the 1980s both the political elite and the public have shown an
increasing understanding for the COs, who are still a small minority compared to
the size of the Swiss army. This growing tolerance has come at a time when the
militia-army has lost its former position as a national symbol of integration and as
the "school of the nation." The secularization of conscientious objection in Switzerland reflects a major trend in this modern democratic society.

Even though a majority of the Swiss voters agreed in May 1992 to amend the
Constitution to permit civilian alternative service, the militia system and general

conscription are still important principles in Switzerland. A civilian service that favors conscientious objectors over the soldiers has little chance of being accepted politically. Nevertheless, the Swiss people will probably soon have to vote in yet another referendum to obtain a specific program with a just solution for the small but growing minority of Swiss citizens who refuse military service.

12

Israel: Conscientious Objection in a Democracy under Siege

YORAM PERI

The Palestinian uprising in the Israeli-occupied territories that began in December 1987 poses challenges of an unprecedented nature and difficulty for Israeli society. One of those challenges comes in the form of a conscientious objection to perform military service. Yet the intifada has not appreciably affected the high public support for the army in Israel. In 1987 slightly less than 90 percent of Israelis declared themselves as having faith in the army; they ranked it the most trustworthy of Israeli national institutions. (In comparison, the courts of law won the trust of 80 percent of the public; the political parties, only 30 percent.) Three years after the outbreak of the intifada, the Israel Defense Forces (IDF) continued to head the list of the most trusted institutions. In fact, its support had risen: in 1990 over 90 percent of the public declared themselves to have faith in the army.

At the same time, however, some one hundred officers and noncommissioned soldiers have been tried and jailed for refusing to perform military service in the West Bank and Gaza Strip. In addition to them, several thousands are in a gray area of refusal. These latter are not put on trial, and therefore no report about them goes to the higher military authorities or the public.

Many questions need to be explored. How can this contradiction between growing popular support for the army and an increase in conscientious objection be explained? What does refusing military service mean in Israel? Is unwillingness to fight against the intifada a continuation of the type of refusal that first surfaced during the Lebanese war in 1982? Or is this a new phenomenon, different from its predecessors? How do the authorities respond to it? And does refusal signal a change in civil-military relations in Israel?

The Early Period: 1948–1967

The nature of the Zionist movement, and the policies it pursued from its inception a hundred years ago until statehood was achieved in 1948, made it very unconducive to conscientious objection. The Jewish people, after having been dispersed throughout the world for two millennia, initiated a return to their ancient homeland to found a modern state. This "national liberation" effort acquired a strong centralized, collectivist character—a state of mind that then dominated the Jewish community of prestate Palestine under the British mandate (1917–1948); and it continued to influence Israeli society even after establishment of the state. It was the source of a highly organized polity, which in turn created the authority of national institutions in a society still lacking national sovereignty.

In addition, Zionist ideology called for the shaping of a new society distinct from that which had characterized the *galut* (the Jewish exile). This meant that Jews would no longer be powerless and dependent on the goodwill of others. They were to become a nation capable of determining its own future. All this would be made possible by military strength.[1] Although the mainstream rejected those factions of the Zionist movement that championed power for its own sake (to the point where their ideology became militaristic), the realpolitik of the moderates kept them from belittling the importance of military might. This attempt to find a middle ground between the need for power and its adoration was expressed in a description of Yitzach Sadeh, one of the founding fathers of the Israeli military: "He loved the rifle, but hated the war."

The conditions of an entire nation mobilized in the effort to establish a strong, independent nation-state are incompatible with the growth of a tradition of refusal. In fact, against such a background, conscientious objection is perceived to be antithetical to the prevailing value system. To recoil from the use of power becomes a form of disassociation from the collective effort.

This situation has not changed in the second half of the century, after the founding of the state. Israel's actual establishment was bound up with a long and costly war (in which 1 percent of the Jewish population of six hundred thousand was killed). After the War of Independence, the new state failed to gain legitimacy in the region, both in the eyes of the neighboring Arab states and the Palestinians. The Arabs collectively did not recognize the state of Israel, and they refused even to recognize its right to exist. Destroying Israel through armed struggle became an Arab national goal. The subsequent reality for Israel has been the omnipresence of war in its national life. Over the course of forty-two years the IDF has participated in seven wars of varying types—from one-front wars to wars on all fronts against a coalition of four national armies. The conflicts have varied in duration from one hundred hours (the Sinai Campaign of 1956) to a little less than two years (the War of Independence, from December 1947 until June 1949) to longer than two years (the ongoing intifada, which began in December 1987).

Even in periods between wars there was no peace, save for the single exception of Israel's relations with Egypt since 1979. During these times a condition reigned that was defined variously as "neither war nor peace," "less than war," "beleaguered war," or "latent war." In truth hostile actions against Israel never ceased, neither along its borders nor inside its territory. To put it another way, Israel's "natural" state of existence is one of permanent war.

Being a democracy under siege—a small society in constant conflict with a much larger external enemy—reinforced those same factors that had prevailed during the pre-state era: the collectivist pressures pushing toward consensus, solidarity, and conformity. The situation also made the army, "which was what stood between survival and death," no less than an exalted national institution, widely respected and even beloved.[2] In addition, a citizen's army was needed to equalize the huge gap in the balance of forces between Israel and the Arab states. In the wake of the War of Independence, proposals to create a standing army were rejected; instead, it was decided to build the IDF around a large reserve force. The professional army would constitute its backbone, and the conscripted forces were to be the school in which almost every Israeli trains for a military role.[3]

This is how Israeli society became a nation in arms. As Yigal Yadin, Israel's second chief of staff and later deputy prime minister, put it in what became a well-known phrase: "Israelis are soldiers on an eleven-month leave out of each year." Unlike in other Western democracies, the boundary between the army and the civil society in Israel is not fixed; rather, it is fragmented.[4] The military has an expanding role in society. Further, the military and the civilian sectors intrude upon each other. There is a civilianization of the military and a militarization of society, but not in a hawkish sense.[5]

Taking this background into consideration, one understands why it was so difficult for a pacifist movement to grow and develop during the first twenty years of Israel's existence. Save for a few exceptions, the question of civil disobedience was never raised. The country's security doctrine, which crystallized in the late 1950s, also contributed to this situation. Based on the concept of "wars of no choice," the doctrine meant that the use of military power and the decision to go to war were anchored in the definition of a "just war," that is, one perceived to be in self-defense, waged as a last resort. The Christian theological underpinnings of the concept do not, of course, apply.

The principle of a citizen's army, or a nation in arms, was given legal basis in 1948 in the Law for the Israel Defense Forces, which established conscription. It included several qualifications. Complete exemption is granted to married women, pregnant women, and mothers. In contrast to these automatic exemptions, there are also discretionary exemptions. In other words, the law established an administrative function by which the minister of defense is authorized to grant exemption from military service under certain conditions, without an explicit right to exemption having been established in the law. On this basis three sectors of the Israeli population are exempted from conscription.

The first group consists of the Arab citizens of Israel. According to the Israeli Proclamation of Independence, Arabs were to be full and equal citizens of the state of Israel. It was assumed, however, that it would be impossible to draft Arabs into the army. Although the Arabs constitute one-fifth of the population and have a political affiliation to the state, their national affiliation is Arab. Obviously the conscription of Arabs into the army was perceived as a grave threat to national security and was thus unthinkable. At the same time, in the desire to make military service a universal value and to avoid the appearance of discrimination on the basis of nationality, this exemption was not included in the general law, but was made an administrative decision of the minister of defense. In contrast to Moslem and Christian Arabs, other minorities do serve in the armed forces: Bedouins, only by volunteering; and the Druze, who are drafted.

A second group enjoying exemption are religious Jews. However, the basis for this exemption is very different from that common to Christian societies. In negotiations over the status of the army in the new state held with David Ben-Gurion, the leader of the Mapai or Labor party (then the dominant political party in Israel), representatives of the religious parties requested that yeshiva (religious seminary) students be excused from conscription.

This request was not justified in terms of pacifism, nor was it born of antimilitary sentiments or of a refusal to learn a military profession. Rather, it was a matter of "preventing neglect of the Torah." According to a Jewish tradition of several hundred years, if a young man desires to dedicate his life to religious study, the community must allow him to do so. It is said that "more than the Jews kept the Sabbath, the Sabbath kept the Jews." The Jewish people's survival through hundreds of years of *galut* was possible only because they closely observed the strictures of their religion.

The secular national leadership's positive response to this request stemmed from the its desire to find some kind of expression for the special standing of the yeshiva and the Jewish values it symbolized in a post-Holocaust world—a world where the yeshivoth of Europe had been decimated. This arrangement was also a part of a wider agreement on issues of state and religion between Mapai and the religious parties that was designed to pave the way for political cooperation. In a wider context, the agreement was to be a part of the consociational arrangements that would prevent a Kulturkampf between the religious and secular publics in the young state. The request was granted and draft exemptions were granted to yeshiva.

Religious tradition was also the basis for exempting a third group in Israeli society, religious women. Section 30 (4) of the Military Service Law of 1959 states: "a woman . . . for whom reasons of conscience, or reasons of religious consciousness [later changed to "religious family life"], prevent her from serving in the armed forces, shall be exempt from such service." Here, too, the reasoning was neither pacifist nor antimilitary. Religious tradition does not permit daughters either to stray from their father's authority or to live in a sexually mixed society. Military service would directly violate both these proscriptions, thus contradicting the traditional religious way of life. The same desire to avoid religious-secular tensions that led the secular authorities to grant exemptions to yeshiva students also convinced them to exempt religious women. It is noteworthy that, in regard to women, Israeli law provides for exemptions based on reasons of conscience; this is not an acceptable criterion for men. The exemptions granted to women for reasons of conscience are general, complete, and not selective.

The minister of defense's wide-ranging authority in granting exemptions from military service allowed it to respond to the few cases of conscientious objection on pacifist grounds that did arise.[6] The first known instance of refusal to serve in the armed forces came in 1954 only five years after the end of the War of Independence and the passage of the Law of Military Service. To the public, Amnon Zichroni was no conscientious objector but rather a draft evader. He was supported by a prestigious group of writers and intellectuals, however, among them Hugo Bergman and Martin Buber, who saw Zichroni's refusal as a means of combating the growing etatist tendencies in the new country. But their request for an exemption for Zichroni went unanswered. The minister of defense, Pinchas Lavon, insisted on trying Zichroni, who was eventually imprisoned. A small organization called the ''International Movement of Conscientious Objectors'' was established in Israel that same year, but failed to achieve any widespread recognition of acceptance.

There were a few cases of conscientious objection during the ensuing years, but the army kept these out of the public eye. They included pacifists, Jehovah's Witnesses, those willing to be drafted but not wear a uniform, and others who refused to carry a gun. In some instances the army granted requests for exemption; in others, the authorities were less accommodating. Pressure was used to convince the individual to retreat from his stance. If this failed the army was prepared to release the CO from service by declaring him unfit on psychological or sociological grounds. The possibility of having such a stigma recorded forever on one's personal documents was, and still is, an efficacious means of discouraging potential objectors. It is common for Israeli employers to request that a job applicant present a certificate of discharge from the army. Whenever the individual went public with his refusal, the authorities did not hesitate to bring him to trial.

1967: Occupied Territories and Selective Objection

The Six-Day War in June 1967 marked the beginning of a new chapter in conscientious objection in the state. A consensus exists in Israel that the Six-Day War was a just war. As such, no instances of refusal are known to have occurred during the course of the fighting. Three years later, however, after Israel had begun to tighten its hold over the territories conquered in the war, a new pattern of noncompliance emerged: selective refusal, that is, refusal to serve in the occupied territories.

Two types of rejection occurred in this period: moral refusal, giving vent to the individual's inner ''cry of conscience''; and political refusal, with the intent to influence government policy.[7] Neither type signified a change in the basic perception that the 1967 war was just. There was, however, a definite attitudinal change toward continued Israeli control of the captured territories. Those who refused on moral grounds claimed they were incapable of serving in an army of occupation. In contrast, political objectors were concerned that government policies were not bringing peace any closer; refusal to serve in the territories translated into a form of pressure on the government to change those policies.

The first cases of refusal to be publicized came after the Six-Day War and were of the political variety. They were not actual refusals, however, but only declarations of intent. In 1970 a group of high school students sent a letter to then Prime Minister Golda Meir in which they announced that, once inducted into the army, they intended to refuse to serve in the territories because they did not believe the prime minister's policies were directed to achieving peace. (The immediate motivation for their protest was Meir's refusal to allow Nachum Goldman, president of the World Jewish Congress, to meet with Egyptian President Nasser in Cairo.) Over the next several years similar letters were written. Among them was one in 1978, signed by one hundred students declaring that, in the event of war, they would refuse to defend the Jewish settlements in the occupied territories.

The Yom Kippur War (1973) gave birth to waves of extraparliamentary protest against the government; declamatory refusal was a part of this phenomenon. This time, however, reserve soldiers were protesting—both officers and noncommissioned soldiers. Upon returning from the war, they announced they would not participate in another one if the political situation in the country did not change.

In this period (1967–1982) there were also several instances of actual refusal. Giora Neuman's refusal in 1970–1971 was total, although he was no pacifist. Neuman was one of four high school students—members of a Trotskyite organization—who announced their unwillingness to join an "occupation army." Neuman's three comrades were exempted from conscription for psychological reasons, but Neuman spent eight months in prison. In the end he arrived at an understanding with the army: He would work in a hospital with both military and civilian patients during his term of service.

In a second case Gadi Algazi was willing to enter the army but on condition he could serve within the borders of the state of Israel, and not in the occupied territories. Algazi was a member of a group of twenty-seven who sent a letter to Minister of Defense Ezer Weizman in 1980 stipulating their intention to refuse to serve in the territories because of "opposition to the occupation and suppression of the Palestinian people." Algazi was tried and spent close to a year in prison. He was released when he agreed to serve in the occupied territories. In one of those twists of history, Algazi would be decorated for his actions during his army service.

Like the pre–1967 phenomenon of total refusal, refusal to serve in the territories, either declamatory or actual, met with harsh public criticism. The perception of refusal as being principally a political act led to widespread hostility toward military refusers and enabled the civilian authorities to mount an indoctrination campaign aimed at youth. In contrast, military authorities dealt with the specific incidents quietly, case by case, as they had before 1967. At times, the IDF would exempt someone from conscription on grounds of unsuitability; and sometimes, the army informally agreed to exempt soldiers from service in the territories by stationing them within the borders of Israel.

This case-by-case effort to resolve the issue of refusal through various ways without raising public awareness continued for years; it corresponded to the generally informal character of the IDF as well as the modus operandi of the Israeli civil service. This was the antithesis of de Gaulle's famous statement (made during deliberations over the possible legalization of conscientious objection in France), "I will accept conscientious objection, but not conscientious objectors." In Israel, objectors were tolerable; objection was the problem.

In the Gadi Algazi case of 1980 the army's flexible policy, however, met with strong criticism from the Supreme Court. Algazi had asked the army to consider his request for selective exemption, and that it respond as it had in the past (that is, to excuse Algazi from serving in the territories). He considered the army's rejection of his petition to be a case of illegal discrimination; after serving three consecutive one-month prison sentences, he turned to the Supreme Court.

The IDF was unable to deny the petitioner's claims. Instead, the army's counsel explained: "Army authorities had given refusers a guarantee that they would be stationed according to their wishes, within the borders of Israel, as long as refusal was an isolated phenomenon. Now policy has changed. What had once been sporadic instances of refusal with which the IDF was prepared to live, has changed in character and become an organized protest whose aim is to turn the IDF—the national army, necessarily disengaged from any political or ideological arguments—into the battleground for a kind of confrontation which the army cannot be associated with."[8]

The Court rejected Algazi's request for an injunction requiring the minister of defense not to station him in the territories. At the same time, however, the Court criticized the IDF for not publicizing its new rules and regulations and warned the authorities not to differentiate between soldiers with similar records. The deputy president of the Supreme Court, Justice Haim Cohn, wrote: "Because this matter is not enacted in the laws governing the army, but is an army order, functioning as only an internal army guideline . . . we must make note of the change in army policy: we must assume that since that decision was made, the general rule of not granting an exemption from service in the territories to a soldier for reasons of conscience is permanent and consistent."[9]

Lebanon: Conscientious Objection during Time of War

In the Lebanese war, which began in June 1982 and ended with the withdrawal of the IDF from Lebanon three years later, Israel was faced with a new brand of conscientious objection: objection during time of war. This was impelled by the special nature of this war, which was different from any of its predecessors.[10] It was the first time since the Israeli security doctrine had been formulated in the 1950s that the IDF went to war without a national consensus. Prime Minister Menachem Begin defined the war in Lebanon as a "war of choice." Thus, it also negated the tradition of fighting only just wars, that is "wars of no choice."

In addition, the war in Lebanon was waged in areas of dense civilian population. Issues of just use of arms now became increasingly important, and troubling, for the IDF soldier. These dilemmas found dramatic expression in the case of Col. Eli Geva, a highly decorated officer and commander of an armored brigade. Geva opposed the occupation of Beirut not only on professional grounds, but because of the high risk it would entail for both his troops and the civilian population. If such a mission were to be ordered, Geva made clear, he would request that the chief of staff of the army relieve him of his command; he would remain with his unit as a tank driver. Geva, for whom everyone had predicted a brilliant future in the IDF, brought his case before the minister of defense and even the prime minister. Ultimately, he was discharged from the army by the chief of staff, an action that became a controversial political affair in its own right.[11]

In contrast to the conscientious objection common to the years 1967–1982—a selective refusal to serve that was largely declamatory—the war in Lebanon gave birth to the type of refusal most feared by professional armies: that occurring during time of war. The extent of this phenomenon was also unprecedented. Beginning in September 1982, when the IDF spokesman first announced the trial and imprisonment of three soldiers for refusal to join their units in Lebanon, an average of three additional soldiers were tried each month. May 1983 marked a record month: twenty-seven trials. All in all, 143 soldiers and officers, the majority reservists, were tried during the course of the conflict. Throughout the war the IDF attempted to downplay the significance of these events. However, in 1986, Lt. Gen. Moshe Levi, approaching the end of his tenure as chief of staff, admitted that refusals to serve in Lebanon, particularly after the battles ended, had played a role in Minister of Defense Moshe Arens's decision to begin a withdrawal of the IDF from Lebanon.

A number of organized groups advocated civil disobedience during this period. This, too, was unprecedented. They included "Mothers Against Silence." But most notable was an organization of the refusers themselves called *Yesh Gvul* ("There's a Limit"). In less than a year *Yesh Gvul* collected 1,470 signatures of reservists, among them officers, expressing approval for *Yesh Gvul*'s program.[12] A study made of the selective refusers during the Lebanese war also uncovered those who acted out of moral, rather than political, motives.[13] Nevertheless, it was the political refusals that most disturbed and provoked the public. The fact that several of the central figures in *Yesh Gvul* had belonged to extreme radical-left political organizations only reinforced the group's negative image. It did not even gain the support of the left-wing political parties or dovish organization such such as "Peace Now." In fact, these groups made every effort to dissociate themselves from *Yesh Gvul* and its ideology.

In light of the new nature of refusal, both in quality and quantity, the defense establishment could not continue its traditional policy of a case-by-case response. Those who declared their refusal were tried, and 143 were sentenced to prison terms of varying lengths. In addition to this official response, a less formal reaction by the authorities dealt with a phenomenon called the "gray area of refusal." In hundreds of cases, reservists—non-commissioned soldiers and officers alike—expressed their unwillingness to serve in Lebanon and were released from duty by their immediate commanders. Alternative service arrangements were made within the unit itself, such as postponement of reserve duty to a future date (when the unit would not be sent to Lebanon), an assignment within Israel, or a release for medical, family, or work reasons, and so on. The informality and even intimacy that characterize relations between officers and noncommissioned men in the IDF make this kind of response possible, without any reports on the matter being sent to the higher levels of the army.

Intifada: The Beginning of Legitimation

The latest chapter in the history of refusal in Israel began in December 1987 with the outbreak of the intifada—the Palestinian uprising in the West Bank and Gaza Strip. For the first time in its history, the IDF faced a popular uprising and found itself fighting against unarmed civilians, including women and children. This confrontation provoked doubts among large segments of the Israeli public as to the actual justification of such a "war." The prevailing view of the military and political leadership in Israel, accepted by a large majority of the public, contends that the intifada is a continuation of the age-old war of the Arabs against Israel; it is simply being waged by different means. In contrast, other Israelis sense a new and fundamental element in the intifada, one not present in previous wars: a legitimate struggle by the Palestinians to liberate themselves from the iniquities of Israeli occupation. Do the rules of jus ad bellum pertain to this war against the Palestinians?

The intifada presented the IDF with a series of difficult professional and moral dilemmas: how to respond physically to the uprising, what weapons to use, and under what circumstances to introduce live ammunition. What other means of battle (for example, rubber bullets, plastic bullets, clubs) are legitimate for use against insurgents who are not defined as "combatants" but who are also more than "disturbers of the peace"? What means can be used against children under the age of criminal responsibility who break the law? In general, Israel had to define the limits of power in a war against subversion. Since December 1987 Israeli society has been deeply troubled by these questions.

Opposition to the war against the intifada triggered a spread of refusal to serve in the West Bank and Gaza, unprecedented in both number and character. After two years the total number of those tried and imprisoned was more than one hundred. The overwhelming majority of these refusers have been reservists, including one with a captain's rank. But several conscripts have also refused. And in contrast to the war in Lebanon, when refusals were made after the soldier had already spent time at the front, now they were refusing even before being sent to fight the intifada.

In addition to the 102 officers and noncommissioned men who have been tried and imprisoned, a much larger number of refusers prefer not to declare publicly their intentions, thus avoiding trial. Instead, they reach an agreement within their units, in greater numbers than those who did so during the war in Lebanon. According to varying estimates, approximately ten cases of this "gray refusal" occur for every CO who actually goes to trial. The phenomenon of hidden refusal has grown and must also be accounted for. It is unclear how many should be defined as war refusers or COs; some simply want to avoid military service altogether. In the war against the intifada, reserve units were called up for periods of two months or more in the years 1988–1989. This caused a high degree of evasion through the means available to reservists: trips taken abroad during periods of reserve duty or release for family, medical, or work reasons, and so on. The total number of those who evade service in such ways is impossible to calculate, but it ranges from one thousand to several thousand.

An even more significant change appears in the social background of the conscientious objectors. They come from the elite of society: One-quarter are kibbutzniks, one-quarter are officers, and a disproportionate number are university graduates. Today's refusers do not belong to those sections of Israeli society that have traditionally been estranged from the army. The opposite is true: They represent groups whose contribution to the state's military security has traditionally been high.

The political background of the conscientious objectors has also changed. This group now comprises those who are apolitical as well as those from the "legitimate" parts of the political left. What's more, organizations of the nonradical left have expressed either their support for or, at least, an "understanding" of the refusal to fight against the intifada. Even though their overall numbers are not large, the shift in attitude is significant. Public opinion surveys have also uncovered considerable support for refusal. A survey of high school students' attitudes to military service found that 53 percent justify, to one extent or another, refusal to serve in the territories.[14] A mock public trial was held in June 1989 at the University of Tel Aviv on the subject of service in the territories and participation in the war against the intifada. Two-thirds of the audience supported exempting an officer from his duty to serve. The stigma of refusal, at least in the context of the intifada, has begun to weaken.

Why then, despite these developments, has the change been only slight? There are two reasons. First, the majority of the public continues to accept the view of the military-political elite that the intifada is a continuation of the Arab war against Israel by different means. This explains not only the increase in support for the IDF noted at the outset of this chapter, but also the popular demand to adopt harsh measures against the Palestinians. This attitude prevails especially among social groups with lower levels of education or income, or who have a Sephardic or religious background.[15]

Second, refusal to fight against the intifada has become a subject of debate at a time when public opinion, and especially that of the "talking classes" in Israel, is concerned about a weakening of the rule of law. These fears are provoked by activities of the radical right. In the late 1970s and into the 1990s various ultra-nationalist groups have made their opposition to a withdrawal from the territories abundantly clear, even if both the government and the Knesset were to agree to mandate such a withdrawal. In spring 1982, during the final stages of the Israeli withdrawal from Sinai, as stipulated in the Camp David Accords, their position took an active rather than theoretical expression for the first time. Settlers and their supporters physically resisted the IDF during the evacuation of the city of Yamit.

On November 4, 1985, the regional council of Judaea, Samaria, and Gaza (which represents the Jewish settlements in the occupied territories) passed a motion stating that, in the event of a decision to return the territories, the law should be disobeyed. "Any government in Israel which would carry out any of the above actions (a return of, or an initiative to return, the territories) we will regard as an illegal government."[16] Soon afterward a Jewish terrorist underground, which had been active against Arab targets in the territories, was uncovered. The claim that obedience to the law has its limits, and that even in a democratic state there are matters about which an individual has the right to act according to his or her conscience—even if doing so violates the law of the land—is a stance taken mostly by the jingoist right. In light of a possible weakening of the rule of law, the left has found it difficult to encourage refusal to serve on the grounds of conscientious objection.[17] It can be assumed that, under different circumstances, the left would express greater support for conscientious refusal to serve in the military.

The change in the nature of refusal since the intifada has provoked a change in military policy. The general staff initially made substantial efforts to downplay the significance of refusal. It argued that refusal was a marginal social phenomenon. The army at first continued to be flexible in cases of undeclared refusal, solving the problem within the framework of the soldiers' own units. But with declared refusal, a hard line policy of trials and prison terms came to be adopted. In certain cases the refuser is sent consecutive call-ups for reserve duty, which means that, upon release from prison, if the refuser maintains his position, he is immediately tried and jailed again.

A change in IDF policy was initiated, however, when Rami Hason was sentenced in April 1989 to fifty-six days in prison after having already served five previous sentences. In August the head of the IDF manpower branch recommended that regional commanders imprison first-time refusers to terms of fourteen days, and second-timers to a shorter sentence. After a third refusal the soldier would be transferred out of his unit and reassigned to a post somewhere in Israel. And it was recommended that officers be immediately transferred out of their units. The IDF does not consider the new policy to be a capitulation to pressure; rather, it insists that transfers are punishment and, thus, an appropriate deterrent.[18]

Conclusion

The relative increase in conscientious objection, as a consequence of the intifada and a weakening of the stigma traditionally attached to such actions, testifies that refusal is no longer an exceptional phenomenon: It is a new development in civil-military relations in Israel. Significantly, the opposition to military service by Israeli conscientious objectors has always been couched in secular terms, moral or political, rather than a convoluted harking back to a Judaic tradition of absolute pacifism.

Also important is that most of the intifada refusers come from reserve units, not from the professional officer corps or from among conscripts. These reserve units consist of a wide cross section of civil society and reflect the unprecedented fissures it is experiencing over the both the justice (or injustice) of the war against the intifada and the means used to fight it. Reservists are displaying other signs of change: a reduced level of motivation, volunteerism, and internal cohesion. As it is, the collectivist character of Israeli civil society—sacrifice for the public good— has weakened over recent years, replaced with a growing ethos of individualism. This trend is particularly evident among the country's youth.

It is unlikely that in the foreseeable future any further changes will be made in the army's attitude and policy toward conscientious objection, either the general or selective type. Military service ceases to be a symbol of citizenship only in modern nation-states that no longer fight wars, or where the likelihood of conflict is remote. Israel still lives in a reality of permanent war. Disassociation from the army means disassociation from the state, the embodiment of the very collective that continues to be threatened by external military forces. Such actions are antithetical to the Israeli civil religion. As long as Israelis feel that the war is not over—and the intifada has only strengthened this feeling—it is inconceivable that non-service in the military will gain legitimacy.

An expression of the willingness of the Israeli public to mobilize itself for national goals is found in the very words of the draft notice sent to sixteen-year-olds. This is the notification that requires youngsters to register with the draft board, in anticipation of their conscription at the age of eighteen: "Those eligible for the draft are called by the law to do their duty—but they volunteer to do it." When a government is able to present a legal obligation as if it were an act of volunteerism, it cannot be expected that exemption from that service could ever be considered a civil right.

13

The German Democratic Republic: Dissidence That Prevailed

WILFRIED VON BREDOW

The political system and the social structure of the German Democratic Republic (GDR) is literally history. The unification of the GDR with the Federal Republic of Germany in 1990 brought a final end to the old Soviet-socialist regime. This chapter on conscientious objection in the GDR is therefore of necessity a retrospective one.

It is difficult to trace the development of conscientious objection in the GDR because of the sparse sources available. Under the old regime conscientious objection was regarded as hostile behavior by the communist party and its allies. There are no official statistics or open debates and no empirical research; only silence "from above" and the courageous, but of course often repressed, attempts of those who tried to bring conscientious objection into the political arena. All this changed in the fall of 1989.

The Leap into a "Civil Society"

Looking back, it seems both logical and bizarre that during the 1980s the old regime tried to intensify militaristic nationalism. The GDR directed a broadly instrumented campaign against the "class enemy" both within the country and in the other German state. Vladimir Tismaneanu puts it like this:

> The role of the Nationale Volksarmee has become so prominent that it is no exaggeration to describe the GDR as a militaristic society. To be sure, the SED [*Sozialistische Einheitspartei Deutschlands* or Socialist Unity Party, that is, communist party] retains political control over all sectors of the East German system,

including the military. But the SED has itself internalized militaristic views and values and imposed them on the whole society. In addition, one cannot overlook the militaristic tendencies shown by the introduction of mandatory military education in schools and universities; the government's adamant opposition to conscientious objection; and the open celebration of militaristic traditions including those associated with Prussian Junkerdom.[1]

These observations were made during the first half of 1989! And they were, indeed, mostly correct (with the exception, perhaps, of Tismaneanu's hint of the celebration of Prussian militaristic traditions, another interesting subject).[2] Some months later, the quasi-totalitarian control of the SED collapsed. The militaristic "reforms" did not work—not because they were too little or too late, but because they went too far in the wrong direction. The GDR entered the status of a genuine civil society in November 1989. One of the spectacular changes was a complete revision of the regulations concerning conscientious objection.

Again, it is both logical and bizarre that conscientious objection was removed from deep, dark limbo to a breathtaking liberalism in the final months of the GDR. The decree of February 2, 1990 states that every conscript (including active and reserve soldiers) has the right to conscientious objection on religious or ethical grounds. Conscientious objectors are bound to perform a civic service. Military service already performed will be deducted from the length of the civic service. Both military and civic service are equally termed for twelve months.

Conscientious objectors must make their intent and reasons known in writing. The statement should also contain ideas or rather suggestions about a possible workplace as a civilian alternative server. Those who also object to civic service (total conscientious objectors—*Totalverweigerer*) will receive an official rebuke or pay a fine, but they need not fear detention.

In truth, this very liberal regulation was not an expression of strength and self-confidence on the part of the interim government. On the contrary, it was a rather hasty response to the ongoing decline of the state's authority. By mid–1989 the Nationale Volksarmee, (NVA) with approximately 173,000 soldiers, was already a military organization with dramatically decreased size and internal cohesion. Strikes and collective expressions of discontent had been observed over the recent past. In March 1990, the minister of defense, Hoffmann, had talked publicly about a merger of the two German states' military forces in the event of Germany's reunification.[3] The new CO regulations were, of course, to be transitory and made moot when unification led to the adoption of the statutes of conscientious objection of the Federal Republic of Germany.

General Conscription in the GDR

The Nationale Volksarmee has been a conscription army since 1962. Prerequisite to introducing general conscription was the construction of the Berlin Wall (August 1961) and the completion of the inner German border. After 1961 it was practically impossible for East Germans to leave the country unless permission was granted by the government.

The constitutional base of the general conscription in the GDR were Articles 7 and 23 of the Constitution. Article 23 reads (in the version dated October 10, 1974): "Every citizen has the duty to serve and contribute to the defense of the German Democratic Republic in accordance to its laws." A special Defense Law (enacted October 13, 1978) states in its third paragraph:

> (1) The citizens of the German Democratic Republic serve in the Nationale Volksarmee or the Grenztruppen der Deutschen Demokratischen Republic (Border Defense Forces of the GDR) as a consequence of their constitutional right and their honorable duty to protect peace and the socialist fatherland and its achievements on the base of the relevant laws and other judicial regulations . . . (3) The state and its organs, the institutions for the direction of the economy, the Kombinate, companies, institutions, co-operatives and social organizations are obligated to raise the readiness and the capacity of all citizens for the military protection of socialism. They are obligated to prepare all necessary steps for this purpose.

The law concerning military service (*Wehrdienstgesetz*) includes details for preparing for military service (in schools and universities) and for managing conscription. In peacetime men only are drafted. Women may, however, become professional soldiers in the Nationale Volksarmee. The general purpose of conscription in the GDR is expressed in paragraph 23 of the *Wehrdienstgesetz:*

> The superiors have the duty to constantly confirm the leading role of the the SED and to educate their subordinates in such a way that their loyalty and devotion to the working class and its Marxist-Leninist party, their love for their socialist fatherland, their ties with the people of the German Democratic Republic and their positive attitude towards proletarian internationalism are permanently deepened and strengthened.

Conscription in the GDR (up to November 1989) had to be understood as an important element of a centralized process to form an ideologically standardized society, in turn led by the SED. Political dissent, deviations from the norms and values of the leading party could not be included. Military service in such a society was regarded as a means of "human standardization." With this premise, conscientious objection had no legitimate place in such a society.

Conscientious Objectors: The Improbable Minority

Even if conscientious objection had no legitimate place in the GDR regime, its social existence was undeniable. To cope with this "contradiction," the National Defense Council issued a "Decree on the Formation of Construction Units in the area of the Ministry of National Defense" in September 1964.[4] Service in the construction units substitutes for military service.[5] It is performed without weapons but does require a special uniform, and soldiers in such units are led by military personnel. Duties entail: (1) collaboration in the construction of roads and other traffic lines;

(2) improvement of defense and other military installations; (3) removal of maneuver damages; and (4) emergency help in the event of catastrophes.

Those who serve in construction units are called *Bausoldaten* (construction soldiers). This service is possible for conscripts who object to military service on religious or similar grounds. No formal examination of those reasons is introduced (which means, likewise, there is no formal right to serve as a construction soldier). Construction soldiers take a solemn promise (not an oath) "to serve faithfully and for all time the German Democratic Republic, my fatherland, and to use all my strength for the increase of its preparedness of defense."

Before this decree was issued, during the period between 1962 and 1964, the GDR tried to market the slogan "Where socialism and peace are in power, there is no place for pacifism." This campaign, however, was a failure. It is not possible to estimate the number of conscientious objectors during this time period. Bernd Eisenfeld, one of the best informed students of conscientious objection in the GDR and a construction soldier himself in the GDR prior to leaving the country, hints at the existence of some cases of exemption from military service before 1964.[6]

Motives for the Formation of Construction Units

The East German media naturally did not report the existence of the construction-unit decree, wanting to prevent an increase in the potential for conscientious objection. It is therefore a little difficult to reconstruct the motives that prodded the government into action. But in general terms, we may distinguish three different motives:

> 1. *Pragmatism.* During the mid-sixties a need arose for military installations, especially for new airfields, and to improve existing ones. Construction soldiers seemed to be a cheap and available labor force.
> 2. *Legitimation.* The GDR leadership regarded the sixties as the decade to form the genuine "socialist association of humans" (*Sozialistische Menschengemeinschaft*), and it seemed imprudent to commence this new stage of socialism with a mounting opposition.
> 3. *Education.* Establishing special units for COs can be interpreted as an attempt to control and, perhaps, even change the deviant behavior of a small, but potentially dangerous, minority.

Estimates of Conscientious Objectors

Official figures on the number of conscientious objectors are not available. It is possible, however, to put together personal experiences of former East German conscientious objectors, speculations, generalizations, and some indirect information about East German dissidents. Eisenfeld collected some quantitative information about the construction units, and my remarks here are again based on his research. From November 1964 to the end of 1977 the construction units changed their composition every eighteen months. The cohorts were sometimes larger, sometimes smaller. The first cohort (November 1964–April 1966) comprised 220 conscientious objectors altogether, at four different places. The next five cohorts (until fall 1976) had about 250 conscientious objectors each, and the following two cohorts were again 220 each. Approximately 2,100 conscientious objectors had performed their service in the Nationale Volksarmee as construction soldiers by the end of the 1970s.[7] As best as can be surmised, the numbers dramatically increased during the 1980s: approximately 600 construction soldiers were drafted in 1980, about 800 in 1981, and 1,000 in 1983.[8]

Some number of conscientious objectors, however, for various reasons were simply not drafted. One group in this category of COs was comprised of "total conscientious objectors," for example, members of some Christian sects, who refused to serve in the construction units. Eisenfeld speculates that there were some two hundred COs a year were not being drafted. This means that by the end of the 1970s, all in all, perhaps nine thousand to ten thousand young men had undergone the ordeal of questioning the right of the state to force them to handle weapons in defense of socialism.

Along with the development of conscientious objection to military service during the eighties, another form of objection manifested itself—the result of two governmental actions. In 1978 the GDR made military instruction (*Wehrunterricht*) mandatory in schools, and the Military Defense Law of 1982 declared that in a general mobilization, women also would be conscripted and should be prepared for this possibility in peacetime.

Many women protested openly against integration into the military system. Mandatory military instruction in schools was also the object of numerous protests and petitions. After negotiations between the Protestant churches and the SED, it was conceded that "male youngsters who object to service with a weapon in the camps and the education of the Gesellschaft für Sport and Technik (Association for Sport and Technology) may alternatively take part in camp education for civil defense or the education in Red Cross activities for girls."[9]

Motives and Social Profile of Conscientious Objectors

Again the researcher faces difficulties. No empirical study of conscientious objectors in the GDR is available. Thus it is necessary to rely on personal witnesses and some attempts at generalization. And again the research of Eisenfeld offers the bulk of the limited (and perhaps distorted) information available.

During the 1960s and 1970s, 90 percent of the conscientious objectors were active members of a Christian denomination. Of these, only 15 percent were Catholic. These figures, confirmed by many personal accounts, illustrate the absolutely dominant role of the Protestant churches in all matters of spiritual and political opposition in the GDR. During the 1980s this Christian orientation received a new dynamic from the peace movement and pacifism. In East Germany the peace movement reflected a special inconsistency. Both the government and the communist party alike always reiterated their peace-loving nature. Any dissenting opinion about the origins of international conflicts and the road toward peace in the nuclear age was automatically regarded as a form of political betrayal. The self-perception of a large majority of conscientious objectors during the 1960s and 1970s may be summarized as follows: a courageous confession, based on Christian or other ethical values, and the determination to maintain one's personal integrity even if this entails a considerable setback of career expectations; the demonstration of a "new morale," of the strength of the concept of nonviolence in politics and of its potentially positive implications for society; and the existence of a peaceful attitude that tends to overcome conflicts and hostility by means of solidarity and compassion.

Although the familiar problems concerning the collection of data surface again, some data are available. Eisenfeld indicates the following social composition of the construction units from the mid-sixties to the mid-seventies: workers 44 percent, artisans 30 percent, university students 12 percent, church employees 8 percent, white-collar employees 4 percent, and farmers 2 percent. Since the 1970s no drastic changes in this picture seems to have emerged. The dominant proportion of workers and artisans is surprising in light of the fact that the bulk of COs in the Federal Republic (and most other Western European countries) come from middle-class backgrounds with advanced educations. Put in another way, the lower level of the secularization of conscience in the GDR led to a lower socioeconomic status of conscientious objectors than in the West.

The main reason for this atypical social composition of the conscientious objectors in the GDR can probably be found in its special system of sanctions and rewards. Young men who opted for conscientious objection had to be aware of the possibility of severe discriminations later in life. Although duty as a construction soldier was legally equivalent to military service, the state could always eliminate COs when admission to a university or attractive jobs were at stake.[10] In a political system in which the leading party and a vast bureaucracy have their hands in nearly every important decision, the mechanisms of discrimination work quite successfully.

The Role of the Churches and the Peace Movement

From 1949 to 1989 the GDR was a society in which various Christian denominations, chiefly the Protestant churches, not only were concerned with pastoral duties, but were also confronted with protecting political dissidents and opponents of the regime. This latter function, though certainly a noble one, was not sought by the churches; the structure of the regime and its political culture forced the churches into this role. Protestantism, comparable to Catholicism in Poland, has deep roots in the northeastern regions of Germany. The attitude of the GDR leaders toward the churches was highly ambivalent: On the one hand they would have preferred to rid themselves of these institutions, which Karl Marx had severely criticized; on the other hand, the churches were an undeniable necessity, indispensable for handling reluctant and "politically unwilling" citizens. The regime needed the churches and so put little pressure on them in order to use them as mediators in the event of internal difficulties.

The Protestant churches—most of them organized in the Evangelische Kirche in Deutschland and, after the partition of this body during the late sixties, in the Evangelische Kirche in der Deutschen Demokratischen Republic (both Lutheran)—had broken with the traditional, state-centered political past. After the catastrophe of the Third Reich, they had begun to reformulate their relationship with nonspiritual authorities. Part of this complicated process was an upgrading of the esteem in which pacifism and conscientious objection was held. This attitude was naturally praised by the GDR leaders when the churches opposed the West German rearmament during the early 1950s. Ten years later, the same attitude was less valued, since it concerned itself then with the Nationale Volksarmee.

The Protestant bishops in the GDR have always been advocates of generous and liberal regulations for conscientious objectors. Protestant pastors have organized groups of construction soldiers. One such group met in November of 1974 and held a seminar in Leipzig on "Conscientious Objection in the GDR—Ten Years After." The results of this seminar became the basis for an official paper of the Evangelische Kirche in the GDR entitled, "Tendencies in the Development of the Problems of Construction Soldiers."[11] During the 1980s the Protestant churches became the protecting framework for the activities of a nongovernmental, even antigovernmental, peace movement. It was more than just a secondary response to the activities of the Western peace movement, though it was strongly influenced by what went on elsewhere. The basic religiosity of the East German CO movement set it somewhat apart from similar movements in Western countries.

The peace movement in the GDR had to come to terms with the propaganda of both the leading party and the state, which tried to "sell" the Soviet alliance and socialism as the "truest and biggest peace movement in the world." The authorities tried to portray opponents to their propaganda as wrong, ridiculous, or insane. This propaganda was occasionally attuned to popular sentiment, but it remained, on the whole, hypocritical in the minds of those who remembered—among other things— that the Nationale Volksarmee took part in the occupation of Czechoslovakia in 1968. Two small incidents further illustrate the growing difficulties of the regime.

The "Initiative Sozialer Friedensdienst": Spring 1981

The construction soldiers have always been discontented with their work. Starting in 1964 there were proposals to change the nonmilitary service into a proper civic service. One of these proposals was distributed to a small segment in May 1981 by three employees of the Protestant church of Saxony. Readers of the resolution, which was addressed to the Volksarmmer—the East German Parliament—were asked to back it with their signatures. The resolution's content was the text of a new and improved law for conscientious objectors. The government was asked to create a Social Peace Service whose length was to be twenty-four months (as opposed to eighteen months of military service). Conscientious objectors would perform their civic service in such crucial social areas as social and physical care in homes for children, the elderly, and the disabled, providing services in hospitals, drug counseling, social work in rehabilitation clinics, general social services in the community, and ecology (as a potential field). The longer time span was supposed to convey the dedication of conscientious objectors.

Although unsuccessful, the Social Peace Service initiative (*Initiative Sozialer Friedensdienst*) generated considerable interest among young Christians in the GDR. The SED countered with strong reproaches against signers of the appeal; even covert threats seem to have been issued. Nonetheless, despite the opposition of both the

SED and the government, there were reported cases where construction soldiers were able to work as "social peace workers" after 1981.[12]

"Swords to Plowshares"

The slogan "Swords to Plowshares," with its accompanying emblem, was very popular among Christian members of the peace movements in East and West. In the GDR, it seemed to be a revival of the old biblical quest for peace and, at the same time, a reminder of the traditional socialist quest for peace. The emblem depicts the statue that was presented to the United Nations by the Soviet Union. At first glance the use of this emblem in a socialist country seems nonprovocative. In 1981, however, the GDR government reacted nervously and tried to repress both slogan and emblem, publicly urging those who had sewed the badge on their shirts and jackets to remove it. In schools teachers urged their students to do likewise. The SED's youth organization even launched a political campaign against the slogan in the spring of 1982. The slogan was officially forbidden in March 1982. The churches tried to play the conflict down, but the most important consequence of the campaign was the further growth of the distance between the regime and the young generation.[13]

Conclusion: Conscientious Objection and Legitimation

The history of general conscription and conscientious objection in the GDR between 1962 and 1989 must be interpreted as a permanent struggle between the regime's demand for comprehensive availability from its citizens and a small, but growing, proportion of the population that did not accept such demands. It is also the history of a failure: The regime was unable to attain legitimacy in the eyes of its people. For the greater part of the period the phenomenon of conscientious objection remained in the shadow of other political conflicts. Conscientious objectors were a small, marginal group lacking a common perspective. Not only powerless, they faced the risk of dropping out of the everyday life of East Germany.

This constellation changed at the end of the 1970s. The security policy of the Warsaw Pact gradually lost its credibility. The distinction made by the GDR leaders between a "good" peace movement in the East and a "bad" peace movement in the West was unconvincing. Certainly both intensification of internal repression and attempts at militarization during the early 1980s proved to be a crucial political mistake. From then on the opposition groups in the GDR came closer together and gradually lost their "loyalist" approach in their criticisms of the government. Whether an earlier drive toward reforms in the regime,—that is, a development tuned in with Gorbachev—could have stopped the decay of the GDR is debatable— probably not.

Looking back, it is noteworthy to mention that the history of conscientious objection in the GDR was indeed an East German history, and up to the 1980s it was little related to the more secular CO movement in West Germany. But again, all this is history. The future will see a united Germany within a vastly different international framework. It may well be that this Germany will want to continue the conscription system. My hypothesis, however, is that general conscription can be ''saved'' only if military service becomes one type of public service among other forms of non-military service. Then conscientious objection will be considered quite ''normal'' behavior without facing discrimination or carrying ideological baggage.

14

Socialist Countries of Eastern Europe: The Old Orders Crumble

ANTON BEBLER

This chapter deals with the phenomena of conscientious objection in states that called themselves "socialist" and that were ruled by communist parties. The focus is on the socialist countries of Eastern Europe during the period of communist rule, but the chapter concludes with some brief observations on the postcommunist era.[1]

Even before the communist era social conditions worked against the acceptance of conscientious objection in Eastern Europe. Most of the states in this region had long-standing traditions of conscription. Excepting a few interludes between the two world wars, the countries of Eastern Europe had low levels of political tolerance, weak political parties, and scarely independent judiciaries. The strength of pacifist denominations, moreover, was much lower than in most Western countries. In brief, and with some oversimplification, the societal context of Eastern Europe has been inhospitable to the recognition of conscientious objection. These conditions became even more pronounced during the later socialist era.

The Stalinist Mode and COs

The predominant mode of dealing with conscientious objection in socialist states fits quite well with the more general phenomena of "Stalinism." The Stalinist pattern starts in the Soviet Union of the early 1930s. The mode was one of harsh suppression of radical conscientious objectors coupled with occasional arbitrary allowance of non-combatant service for partial objectors. With rare exceptions, the existence of conscientious objection was never officially acknowledged, much less publically discussed, and factual data on conscientious objection were not available. The Stalinist mode of dealing with conscientious objection later spread to other socialist states, either by imposition from the Red Army or by imitation of the Soviet model. In broad strokes this state of affairs characterized the socialist states of Eastern Europe through the mid–1980s.

The close fit between the Stalinist way of handling conscientious objection and communist-style socialism is supported by some evidence. In spite of appreciable differences between the socialist states, similar military systems developed: a universal military obligation for males (some also had limited obligations for women) coupled with a strong Marxist ideology of international proletarian solidarity. The similarity in the terms used to describe military service and military duty is striking: "highest" (Bulgaria, Czechoslovakia), "holy" (Soviet Union, Hungary, Romania), "holiest" (Poland), and "honorable" (East Germany). Refusal to participate in "just defense of the fatherland" was tantamount to betrayal and a criminal act. The potential military confrontation with "imperalism" precluded any official acceptance of alternative civilian service.

The Stalinist manner of dealing with conscientious objection conformed with other features of authoritarian communist systems, such as the de facto elimination of political competition, the suppression of opposition, harsh policies toward religious and cultural pluralism, and widespread violations of human rights. It is significant that in two quite different multinational states, the Soviet Union and Yugoslavia, the criminalization of conscientious objection occurred more or less simultaneously with the abolition of territorial militias, the banning of minority languages in the military, and a policy of cultural assimilation aimed at creating the "new socialist man." In the Soviet Union these developments took place in the 1930s, in Yugoslavia during the postwar era of the 1940s.

Communism as distinguished from Stalinism, however, does not necessarily mean repression of conscientious objection. There have been periods of outright legal protection, or tolerance, or, at least, benign neglect of objectors. No better example exists than in the mother country of communism itself, the Soviet Union. On January 23, 1918, the founder of Soviet Russia, V. I. Ulyanov-Lenin, signed the first decrees that allowed religious objectors to substitute an unspecified citizen service for military service. On January 4, 1919, the Soviet state decreed that all religiously motivated objectors were exempt from military conscription. A year later, a judicial procedure for implementing this right was established. In point of fact, the Leninist Soviet Union was not only much more tolerant of conscientious objection than the preceding tsarist regime, but even more advanced than that of most contemporary Western countries.[2]

The Soviet toleration of conscientious objection ended de facto with the consolidation of Stalinism in the 1930s. But it was not until 1939 that conscientious objection was legally abolished on the spurious grounds that no individual had sought such status. As late as 1990 the criminal codes of the Soviet Union mandated harsh punishments for "evasion" of military call-ups, registration, training, and the like.

The prototypical conscientious objection cases in the Soviet Union and the other socialist states of Eastern Europe involved hard-core religious objectors: Old Believer Russian Orthodox, Pentecostals, Nazarenes, Tolstoyans, Adventists, and, above all, Jehovah's Witnesses. The very large growth in the number of COs that began in the early 1980s reflected a shift in motives, with non-religious objectors coming to the forefront in both visibility and numbers.

Erosion of the Stalinist Mode

The Stalinist mode of handling conscientious objection began to ameliorate in the mid–1960s. The first socialist state to recognize the possibility of conscientious objection was the German Democratic Republic. This process is described in detail by Wilfried von Bredow in chapter 13. Suffice it to say here that the first chink in the armor of Stalinism was the East German creation of unarmed military construction units in 1964 in which conscientious objectors could serve. The German Democratic Republic, of course, was the socialist state most permeable to Western standards of conscientious objection, notably those coming from the Federal Republic of Germany. It appears that a similar use of construction battalions began in Czechoslovakia in the late 1960s. By 1972 unarmed construction units had also come into being in the Soviet Union. These *stoybat* served not only as a repository for conscientious objectors, but also as a place to send suspected dissidents and offspring of "bourgeois" families who might be deemed enemies of the state.

Another procedure for administratively eliminating the problem of conscientious objection was to remove COs from the conscription rolls by classifying them as mentally deranged persons. Needless to add, those exempted in this fashion subsequently suffered discrimination in job placement, admission to higher education, and the like.

A particular type of exemption from military service found in some socialist countries deserves mention. Workers performing physically demanding jobs with acute labor shortages could be excused from conscription. In Bulgaria, for example, exemptions were given to workers in iron and steel plants, ship-building, and mining. A similar treatment had been accorded Polish coal miners. Whether or not any conscientious objectors took advantage of these occupational exemptions is unknown. Of course, under Stalinism, numerous exemptions and deferments existed for occupational groups of critical importance to the military-industrial complex, as well as a certain amount of de facto exemption for university students.

The clear trend over time was for secular objectors to supersede religious objectors. Political opposition in Eastern European states typically had highly critical attitudes toward the military policies of their respective governments and the Soviet presence on their soil. These oppositional activities generated several dozen known cases of politically motivated refusals to serve. Intellectuals, students, and some self-employed members of the middle strata have been the most active in the secular opposition groups. With the notable exception of the Evangelical Church of the German Democratic Republic, and the partial exception of some priests in the Catholic Church in Poland and Hungary, the established churches of Eastern Europe generally maintained a critical attitude toward conscientious objectors, a position stemming from "just war" doctrines and a generalized belief in loyalty to the state.

Advocacy of the legalization of conscientious objection and the introduction of alternative service among Eastern European dissidents clearly was influenced by practices in the West, especially those in the Federal Republic of Germany, the Netherlands, Austria, and the Scandinavian countries. The socialist regimes, on the other hand, stressed ideological dogmatism, nationalist and xenophobic resistance toward foreign influences, to discredit the dissidents and the pacifists among them.

Still, several regimes found it prudent to make some concessions quietly. In 1977 Hungary followed East Germany by allowing members of peace sects to do unarmed service in military units. The Hungarian state did not allow such conditions to apply to either Catholic or nonreligious objectors. It also would not accommodate itself to the absolutist demands of the Jehovah's Witnesses. In 1980 Poland quietly introduced civilian service without weapons in civil defense, fire-fighter units, and in humanitarian jobs in hospitals and social services. The objectors served without military uniforms and without pay. Both the religious and nonreligious could avail themselves of this form of alternative service, as could the physically unfit.

The political opposition in several Eastern European states espoused the cause of conscientious objection as a matter of principle. Thus, when the representatives of the Charter 77 of Czechoslovakia and Solidarity of Poland met at the Polish-Czechoslovak border on the nineteenth annversary of the Soviet-led invasion of Czechoslovakia, their joint statement included a demand for the right to perform alternative civilian service. A particular kind of pacifist dissidence developed around the resistance to mandatory military instruction in secondary schools and in universities. The political opposition used the known cases of persecution of (mostly religious) objectors to highlight the regimes' repressive natures. For their part, however, the radical pacifist groups did not actively cooperate with political opposition groups, preferring instead to plead their cases quietly with the regimes.

It is somewhat of an irony that it was when Poland was still in the hands of a military regime that it became the first communist government to introduce alternative civilian service for both religious and secular ("moral") conscientious objectors. Much of the criticism of the existing military system revolved around a sentence in the conscript's oath "to safeguard peace relentlessly in the fraternal alliance with the Soviet Army and other allied armies." Prodded by the draft resistance organization Freedom and Peace, Gen. Woljciech Jaruzelski began to take steps to ease up on conscientious objectors. A Rubicon was crossed in July 1988, when Poland officially allowed young men to perform a three-year alternative service in lieu of a two-year military draft requirement.[3] A university student, after graduation, could perform a two-year civilian service instead of a one-year military service.

The Polish system, however, was by no means modeled after the North Atlantic pattern. Determination of conscience was handled through boards operating under the aegis of the military/police. Objectors, who received free room and board but no compensation, performed unpleasant menial jobs in hospitals and social welfare institutions. In the first three months of the new law, 764 persons claimed the status of conscientious objector, of which 480 were granted. Secular objectors outnumbered religious objectors by about two to one. In 1989 the number of objectors was about 1,500, only about one percent of the total number called to serve in the armed forces. General public support of conscription in Poland meant there were few takers of the newly legalized conscientious objection.

Following a reformist revolt within the communist party in 1988, Hungary adopted the most liberal policies toward conscientious objectors of any of the Eastern socialist countries. In January 1989, in its effort to "enter Europe," Hungary introduced a clause on alternative civilian service in its constitution. Shortly thereafter, parliament passed the necessary legislation specifically adhering to the basic recommendations of the United Nations Commission on Human Rights, that is, the universal right to conscientious objection, alternative civilian service, an end to imprisonment, and impartial review boards. At the time of enabling legislation, the Hungarian civilian alternative service was ten months longer than the normal two-year conscription period.

The Hungarian case is also interesting in that figures were released on the number and background of the conscientious objectors who were in prison in 1988, the last year of the old order: 148 Jehovah's Witnesses, 6 Roman Catholics, 1 Nazarene, 1 Seventh-Day Adventist, and 4 who objected on nonreligious grounds. These numbers give us a rare insight into the social composition of absolutist COs in an authoritarian socialist state.

Yugoslavia

From the 1940s until well after Marshal Tito's death in 1980, the Yugoslav system of dealing with conscientious objectors followed the typical Stalinist pattern. This was somewhat anomalous inasmuch as Yugoslav society had been considerably liberalized in comparison with other Eastern European socialist states. Refusal to serve in the military (including refusal to receive a call-up notice, refusal to report, refusal to accept arms, and so forth) was punishable under a variety of criminal codes. Objectors to conscription were subjected to the military judiciary, a situation that greatly reduced rights for independent counsel, open trial, and effective appeal.

Convicted objectors usually received sentences of three years, although the maximum penalty could be as long as ten years. The catch was that multiple sentences could be served up to thirty years of age. The object of this system was manifestly to deter objection. The intended cruelty of the system was highlighted by the case of Ivan Cecko, a Jehovah's Witness, who was sentenced four times for a total of twelve years for the same offense.

The number of convicted conscientious objectors sentenced by Yugoslav military courts averaged about ten persons a year after the early 1970s.[4] Amnesty International reported at least twenty imprisoned COs in 1989.[5] Of course, some COs were simply classified as "unfit" by local induction boards and thus effectively dropped from the call-up rolls. Still, the Yugoslav manner of dealing with conscientious objection was quite regressive.

Starting in the mid–1980s, this inhumane system came under public criticism in the process of liberalizaton and de-Titoization of the one-party political system.

The most prominent opponents of the harsh treatment of COs were found in Slovenia, long the most Western and liberal republic of Yugoslavia. The demand to legalize conscientious objection and to introduce alternative civilian service was adopted by the official youth organization in Slovenia in the summer of 1986. A call for a public debate on the issue was supported by a federal youth congress. The resolution was thwarted, however, by a pro-military lobby within the Yugoslav Union of Socialist Youth.

At the forefront of the efforts to prevent a public debate on conscientious objection was Milan Daljevic, a retired three-star general, who used—or better, abused—his new civilian position as a leader in the Socialist Alliance. Daljevic argued that legalization of conscientious objection would introduce inequality among Yugoslav citizens and would be incompatible with the defensive doctrine of Yugoslavia, and claimed that only a very small minority among the Yugoslavs favored liberalization of objection to military service.[6] Daljevic was seconded by other proponents of the status quo who asserted that it was unethical for objectors to be defended without contributing to the country's defense, that the separation of church and state precluded recognition of religious objectors, that one's religious beliefs could interfere with a citizen's obligations, and so forth. Underlying all these arguments was the fear of the Yugoslav military that even a small concession to the objectors would lead to a floodtide of refusals, and thereby undermine the federal army.

The effort to recognize conscientious objection seemed to be going nowhere when the issue suddenly resurfaced with no prior public airing. In February 1989, a persistent minority on the Praesidium of Yugoslavia (a collective presidency and the commander-in-chief) persuaded enough other members to override the conservative opposition and introduce a form of legal conscientious objection. The action of the Praesdium seems to have been moved by both a genuine concern over Ivan Cecko's plight and the need to burnish Yugoslavia's image in the West. In any event, the Praesidium proposed that the federal parliament amend the military conscription law. The amendment passed despite some opposition from members of parliament from Serbia and Montenegro, the republics with disproportionate numbers among the Yugoslav professional military. Deputies from the more developed republics of Croatia and Slovenia almost universally voted for the amendment.

The April 1989 legislation allowed for conscientious objection on a very restricted basis. Only religious grounds were acceptable. Objectors would serve in noncombatant, nonarmed roles, but must be in military uniform. Such objectors, moreover, would serve twice as long as regular conscripts. There was no alternative civilian service, but military commanders had the power to grant or withhold the status of conscientious objection. No provision for appeal existed outside the military framework. Clearly, these CO provisions fell far short of standards set up by the United Nations Human Rights Commission and the Conference on Security and Cooperation in Europe.

With the impending breakup of Yugoslavia, events began to take a different turn. Slovenia, the most politically liberal republic, passed a constitutional amendment in October 1990 that went far ahead of the Yugoslav strictures. Civilian alternative service was established for both religious and secular objectors with a term the same length as military service. Civilian commissions for processing applicants were set up. Essentially, Slovenia set up a CO system paralleling that of the more advanced Western countries.

As civil war broke out in Yugoslavia in 1991, the actual turn of events was hard to predict. But by 1992 it was evident that desertions and draft dodging were severe even in the Serbian heartland of the old Yugoslavia. Although much of this avoidance of military service was undoubtedly motivated by self-interest, the issue of conscientious objection will continue to grow in Yugoslavia and its successor states.

Since the Revolutions of 1989

Following the momentous events of 1989 in Eastern Europe, the situation of conscientious objectors changed dramatically. With the dissolution of the German Democratic Republic in October 1990, the West German system of dealing with conscientious objection was extended to the five new *länder* in the Federal Republic of Germany. On March 5, 1990, the Czechoslovak parliament legalized conscientious objection on both religious and secular grounds and provided for alternative service. Poland partially legalized objection for both traditional peace sects and nonreligious objectors. Bulgaria allowed for some forms of nonarmed military service in uniform for religious objectors. Only Romania and Albania, as of 1991, maintained the old Stalinist model of handling conscientious objection, though even in these states, one could safely predict that there would be shifts in a liberal direction with some form of legal conscientious objection, most likely as part of comprehensive military reforms.

Developments in the former Soviet Union are of particular significance. Prior to the termination of that state, draft resistance had become so endemic that the very basis of the Soviet military was threatened. One knowledgeable source in Moscow stated that in 1989 there were four hundred thousand refusers for military service in the Soviet Union, but that only two or three thousand of these could be considered either religious or philosophical objectors.[7] Both popular opinion and local authorities in the Baltic and Caucasus republics supported avoidance of service in the Soviet military. In 1990 Lithuania, Estonia, and Latvia had developed programs of alternative service for those wishing to avoid military service. In the case of Latvia, the new alternative service was open to all draftees, not just to conscientious objectors.

What must be stressed, however, is that almost all of the draft avoidance in the last days of the Soviet Union was typically based on opposition to serving in a Soviet military rather than toward military service per se. Where the Red Army was once the ultimate embodiment of the Soviet socialist state, by 1990 it had become a reflector of the divisions and tensions tearing the Soviet Union apart. How the revived nationalisms of the new republics would deal with conscientious objection was yet to be determined.

The Union of Sovereign States, the first and short-lived successor entity to the

Soviet Union, contained a provision for conscientious objection in its draft law of August 15, 1991. The draft law allowed for alternative service with a longer time commitment than conscripted service. Both moral as well as conventionally religious reasons would be acceptable for objector status. In the Commonwealth of Independent States that came into being in late 1991, provisions for conscientious objection were held in abeyance pending a more comprehensive military reform. In the event of an independent Russian military, the likely outcome would be a conscientious objection system somewhat resembling that of the other ex-socialist states. A move toward a completely professional military in Russia would defuse most of the agitation centering around conscientious objection.

Toward the Future

How do these developments in socialist and ex-socialist states correspond with the secularization thesis and stages of conscientious objection presented in this volume? In brief, the evidence from Eastern Europe generally supports the thesis, but with the major modification that all three stages have been greatly telescoped in the contemporary period. Typically, the early socialist states started with a brief era of tolerance for religious conscientious objection but then regressed into a Stalinst mode of repression. The late Stalinst mode allowed some forms of de facto recognition of strongly religious COs by allowing performance of unarmed military service. With the implosion of the communist states in 1989, the more economically developed ex-socialist states rapidly implemented policies that corresponded in basic respects with the status of COs in the advanced countries of Northwestern Europe.

To conclude, policies toward conscientious objection will show some diversity in the former communist countries. But the direction will be toward the more liberal end of the spectrum. Indeed, by the early 1990s, the more developed of the ex-socialist states—notably, Poland, Hungary, the Czech and Slovak republics, Slovenia, and the Baltic states—were implementing more humane policies toward conscientious objection than those of the Mediterranean countries of NATO. Regarding conscientious objection, at least, some ex-socialist stages had leapfrogged over the longer-standing democracies on the southern rim of Europe.

PART IV

THE SECULARIZATION
OF CONSCIENCE
RECONSIDERED

15

Legal Aspects of Conscientious Objection: A Comparative Analysis

MICHAEL F. NOONE, JR.

In Shakespeare's *The Life of Henry V* one of the private soldiers waiting to do battle at Agincourt muses on the morality of Henry's mission: "But if the cause be not good, the King himself hath a heavy reckoning to make, when all those legs and arms and heads, chopped off in a battle, shall join together at the latter day [of judgment], and cry all, 'We died at such a place'.... Now, if these men do not die well, it will be a black matter for the King that led them to it." The king, in disguise, responds at length, asserting, "Every subject's duty is the King's, but every subject's soul is his own."[1]

In this statement, the sovereign attempted—as many sovereign governments still do—to create two mutually exclusive categories: the realm of action, which the state is free to regulate; and the realm of conscience, which, in most democratic societies, the state is expected to avoid. The categories are attractive, but false: By regulating or demanding action, the state creates conflicts of conscience, and it is within this zone of conflict that the law attempts to accommodate—if not to reconcile—these conflicting demands.

A survey of current governmental practices regarding the treatment of conscientious objectors should recognize three fundamental aspects of that treatment that otherwise might be overlooked. First, conscientious objection is a Western concept, derived from eighteenth-century religious beliefs, and is a response to the practice of conscription. These considerations shape the legal structures that have been erected to protect the conscientious objector. In describing these structures, this essay examines the law in two aspects: law as a product, a series of rules or principles, produced primarily by legislatures; and law as a process, the means of enforcing those rules and principles, produced primarily by judges and other functionaries of the state. Most legal scholarship has focused on the law of conscientious objection as a product; very little has been written about the ways in which it has been applied.

Second, because of the historical origins of the issue posed by conscientious objectors, the focus has been primarily on the absolute objector—the pacifist, traditionally motivated by religious belief—who refuses to serve when called as a conscript. The civilian absolute objector, however, represents only one type of objector, because two sets of variables are involved in classifying the CO: his status (civilian or soldier) and his objection (absolute or selective). The absolute civilian objector raises rather clear-cut problems for the law as product: Should he be protected from conscription? Under what circumstances? Should alternative service be required? He also raises problems for the law as process: Who should hear his claim? What procedures should be followed? Most legal thought has been devoted to legislation concerning the civilian absolute objector. Very little scholarly consideration has been given to the legal rules regarding the serviceman or servicewoman who later concludes that he or she no longer can serve in good conscience and seeks release as an absolute objector. Although few in number, these individuals would seem to warrant some legal protection given that the law routinely recognizes that a person's moral judgments may change.

Third, in recent years selective conscientious objection has come to be recognized as a significant problem. Michel Martin's essay in this volume describes the consequences when France sought to use conscripts in Algeria between 1954 and 1962. Yoram Peri describes the Israeli experience in Lebanon and in the *intifada*. Selective objectors may object to a particular war (such as that of France in Algeria or the United States in Vietnam), to a particular military operation (as in the Israeli incursion deep into Lebanon, or the massive U.S. deployment and war in the Persian Gulf in the winter of 1990–1991), or to the use of a particular weapon (such as nuclear devices). Legislators may be willing to pass laws to protect the person who believes that God or his conscience has told him not to kill anyone; it is much more problematic to protect the person who claims the right to decide whom, how, and when he will kill.

This problem becomes even more acute when the selective objector is in uniform. Although one may be tempted to say that soldiers, once committed to the military, have an obligation to obey all lawful orders, certainly the law could distinguish appropriately between refusals based on cowardice and those grounded in morality. Very little has been written about the selective conscientious objector, and most of this writing has concerned legislation about civilian selective COs. The problem posed to the administrative system by military selective conscientious objectors is much more difficult. How can a soldier who claims that a particular act of war violates his conscience receive fair and dispassionate treatment from a military system designed to enforce discipline, one that implicitly accepts the morality of the act to which he objects?

In the preceding paragraphs I have suggested certain fundamental legal distinctions that must be made in discussing conscientious objection: law as product or process, absolute or selective objection, and military or civilian objection. Before attempting to summarize how various legal systems have approached these distinctions, I will suggest that the military/civilian dichotomy conceals categories that may be important in particular systems. How, for example, is a reservist to be treated? As a civilian claiming protection from involuntary recall to active service on moral grounds, whether selective or absolute, or as a soldier seeking release from active duty on the same grounds? The court apparatus is parallel in most legal systems: courts-martial for soldiers, civil trials for civilians. Should the conscientious objector be able to call on the civilian system for protection, whatever his or her status?

This legal dimension of conscientious objection is more complex than might be thought. The above categories will help clarify the situation as I describe the ways in which various governments have dealt with conscientious objectors. In this project, I have relied primarily on governmental reports, particularly those made to the United Nations in the early 1980s[2] and those submitted to the International Society for Military Law and the Law of War in response to a 1987 survey.[3] I have attempted to supplement this material, but the governmental reports did not always use the categories I use here. Therefore my summary is impressionistic even while it conveys an understanding of how the law has been structured to respond to conscientious objection. The survey confirms the thesis of this book: Within the past twenty-five years, the law as a product has come to recognize secular grounds for conscientious objection. In my judgment, this development has created profound problems for the legal process. This chapter focuses on those Western European systems that have treated the conscientious objector most generously.

Numerically, however, most nation-states do not legally recognize conscientious objection as grounds for being excused from military service. The United Nations' report listed seventy-four countries in the 1980s with conscription and only sixty without a draft.[4] Of the seventy-four nations that practiced conscription, only twenty-six (slightly more than one-third) recognized conscientious objection.

Constitutional Bases for Exemption from Military Service

A state's constitution delineates the rights and duties of citizens in relation to the central government. In several countries, such as Brazil, Switzerland, and Italy, the obligation to perform military service is part of the constitution. Therefore any legal protection for conscientious objectors would have to be included in the constitution, either directly or by judicial interpretation.[5] No constitution explicitly authorizes selective objection, but several recognize conscientious objection. The constitutions of some other countries, such as the Federal Republic of Germany (FRG), provide that no person may be compelled against his conscience to render military service involving the use of arms. Although these countries may rely on conscription, the constitutional protection biases the legal process in favor of recognizing claims of conscience.

In other countries, such as the United States, neither the duty of military service nor the right of conscientious objection is mentioned in the national constitution.

In such cases the national legislature is relatively free to set the terms and conditions of both service and exemption. The lawmakers, however, may be constrained by the judiciary, which, in the United States, for example, has the right to overturn laws that violate fundamental norms. In view of these differences among nations, humanitarian efforts (such as the recent moves by the Council of Europe's Committee of Ministers to "harmonize" national laws relating to conscientious objection)[6] will have to overcome deeply rooted national traditions reflected in diverse individual constitutions. Guatemala's firm response to the United Nations survey may be representative of those countries that refuse to make any provision for conscientious objection.[7]

Statutory Structures to Protect Conscientious Objectors

The following discussion is a summary of the main features of legislation (law as product) in nations that recognize conscientious objection, whether or not recognition is based on a constitutional mandate. I make some reference, however, to problems of administration (law as process), both as a consideration in preparing regulations and as reflected in judicial decisions. The statutes surveyed have two common characteristics. First, they are intended to protect only civilians (not uniformed members of the armed forces), and they are drafted to apply only to conscripts, not to volunteers. The second characteristic should be emphasized because of its consequence: Several nations, such as the United States, have elaborate statutory systems designed to deal with the conscientious conscript but have not had to implement them for several years because they have relied solely on volunteer forces. Any attempt to treat such CO systems as useful models must acknowledge that they were designed for wartime mobilization, not for peacetime conscription, and have not been tested recently. In the latter years of the Vietnam War, the administration of the U.S. laws regarding alternative service broke down completely,[8] although the system for excusing COs from the draft continued to function.[9]

Because conscientious objection originally arose as a problem posed by dissident religious groups, those countries which accorded legal protection to COs did so by requiring that they be acknowledged members of a recognized religious sect that professed pacifism as a fundamental tenet. Many individuals, however, did not meet this criterion. As religious belief in the West loses its traditional importance, legislators have attempted to liberalize the definition in order to permit others to claim the same protection, whether they are members of a nonpacifist sect or are even wholly irreligious. France's recent statement is representative: The National Service Code[10] simply gives young men who object to military service "*pour des motifs de conscience*" the right to choose alternative civilian service.

Although such liberalized definitions bear some resemblance to traditional provisions for conscientious objection, they often cause difficult, if not insuperable, problems for the administrative process. How is sincerity to be determined? Should it be presumed? Is the government obliged to prove that the applicant is insincere,[11] or is the applicant to prove his sincerity?[12] In the latter case, the law must provide for a personal hearing because the determination no longer will be based largely on a straightforward letter from an objector's pastor (as was the case under the traditional definition), but now will depend on a careful assessment by administrators of facts peculiar to the individual's claim. Democratic legal systems seek to limit the unfettered exercise of bureaucratic discretion particularly when a decision affects a citizen's liberty. Therefore national service laws in democracies typically provide for appeal from adverse decisions. As the definition of a CO becomes more vague, the criteria for successful appeal become more problematic.

A few nations, of which South Africa is a recent example, provide for religiously based conscientious objection but do not limit the claim to traditional pacifist sects (see Annette Seegers's chapter in this book). These nations can expect the same "process" problems as those confronted by states that apply a purely secular standard. The next section, "Establishing Eligibility," examines these process problems in greater detail.

The timing of the claim of conscientious objection is not important if the exemption pertains only to members of traditionally pacifist churches. Government officials responsible for conscription and military personnel planning can estimate fairly well the number of such traditional pacifists that can be expected in each age cohort, and church members know that they will be excused. In a broader definition of conscientious objection, however, a high degree of uncertainty exists for both the objector and the government. A nontraditional objector, once his views have crystallized, seeks early recognition (that is, before he has received his draft notice) for several reasons. If his claim is denied, he will have time to appeal without facing the threat of imminent induction. Moreover, if his appeal is successful, he can tell others that his views have been validated.

The bureaucrat, on the contrary, seeks to postpone recognition until after the potential objector has been brought into the conscription process. The official fears that an exemption, once granted, rarely will be surrendered voluntarily, even if the objector's views change as a result of age or experience. Early exemption allows opponents of military service to assemble the numbers more easily and to use them to influence the political process. The bureaucrat can hope that the conscripted objector will be disqualified on other grounds, such as health or marital status, so that the government's projected conscription figures (and the public's perception that most eligible young men serve willingly) will be unaffected by these so-called "hidden objectors." National service laws typically reflect the concerns of the bureaucrat, not those of the objector. In Austria, for example, the objector has only two weeks from the date he receives his call-up order to assert his claim. After this deadline, he may not assert a claim until after completing his military service.

In most nations a conscript's application for conscientious objector status is typically treated as falling within the executive function, and, more specifically, as a matter for the department concerned with the armed forces. Even those countries that have established independent agencies to handle conscription, such as the United States, rely heavily on military manpower planners and other uniformed personnel to accomplish their tasks. Such an assignment of responsibility has important consequences because the objector's application will be evaluated by an agency whose primary obligation is to fill military quotas, not to excuse individuals from service. Traditionally, national legislatures were disinclined to establish truly independent

TABLE 15.1   Outcomes of Applications for Conscientious Objector Status,
West Germany

Year	1984	1985	1986	1987
Number of Applications	43,875	53,907	58,693	62,817
Status granted	51,223	60,842	56,281	51,817
Status denied	9,642	9,082	8,016	5,537
Convictions after denial	16	19	34	—

Note: Decisions exceeded requests because of a backlog from prior years.

agencies, and instead made the legal presumption that military authorities would protect the rights of the genuine COs. In recent years, however, most European states have joined the United States in placing responsibility for the exemption decision on some agency other than the department responsible for the military.

Establishing Eligibility: National Practices

Not surprisingly, there is a broad spectrum of governmental attitudes towards the testing of the applicant's sincerity. At one extreme are the liberal approaches of the Italian[13] and West German governments. For example, the Basic Law of the Federal Republic of Germany (as pointed out by Kuhlmann and Lippert in their chapter in this book) provides that no one may be compelled against his conscience to render military service involving the use of arms. The law would thus permit the conscription of conscientious objectors to serve in noncombatant roles, but a claim of conscientious objection, if sustained, would relieve the applicant of all military obligations. A principled objection to military service is the only requirement: The applicant's motives, whether religious, political, or philosophical, are irrelevant. Written applications are submitted to an office in the Ministry of Youth, Family Affairs, Women, and Health, and decisions are made without a personal hearing. As in many European countries, the application in Germany must be accompanied by a police certificate of good conduct. It is not clear why such certification is required—whether the law assumes that applicants with police records are less likely to be sincere conscientious objectors, or whether applicants with police records may be ineligible for conscription on those grounds.

In each year in the 1980s approximately 10 percent of young West German males sought conscientious objector status (see Table 15.1). West German students freely admit that successful applications for conscientious objector status are circulated, copied verbatim by many other applicants, submitted by those applicants, and approved by authorities.[14]

Those countries that expect a CO applicant to establish his credentials differ greatly in their approach. These differences may be at the lexical level. In Switzerland, for example, the Federal Military Department proposed that a CO must offer evidence that rendered it likely (*"Si l'auteur rend vraisemblable . . ."*) that he could not reconcile the demands of conscience with the obligations of military service. In contrast, the Swiss Society of Officers proposed that a CO be obliged to prove (*"demontrer"*) that he is suffering from a severe conflict of conscience and that ethical and psychological considerations should be disregarded as too vague to guarantee justice.[15] Such distinctions are important. Judges and bureaucrats are used to working with such semantic distinctions, and the language of the rules must be taken seriously.

Administrative procedures for asserting a CO claim vary, although within a relatively limited range. In Belgium applicants must make their request in writing (there is a special procedure for illiterate applicants), describe their motives precisely, and supply the names of individuals who can attest to the sincerity of those motives.* The minister of the interior acknowledges the application, places the applicant on a "provisionally accepted" list, then assembles relevant information from judicial or community authorities. Within two months, the file is transferred to the president of the Council of Conscientious Objectors. Then the applicant is invited to appear at a hearing, at which he may be accompanied by legal counsel. The Council sessions and its decisions are public. Decisions must be made within two months of the hearing, and can be appealed to a *Court de Cassation*.

The entire Belgian structure is biased in favor of the applicant. The Ministry of Interior, not of War, is the responsible agency. The Council of COs has no other purpose than to hear claims, is part of a civilian ministry, and must act on the case within a very short time (thus limiting the government's opportunities to challenge the application).

In extending the law to protect social or political motivations, the Belgian legislature attempted to distinguish between objections related to the fundamental institutions of society (these were not acceptable) and objections related to the processes—such as war—by which the institutions carried out their functions. This distinction, which was offered by the Roman Catholic Pax Christi group, proved difficult to apply.[16] Because Belgium is one of the few countries that recognizes selective conscientious objection,[17] it is not surprising that the liberal Belgian system seems to be designed to grant conscientious objector status on demand.

Norway's constitution (cited in the chapter by Gleditsch and Agøy in this book) provides that it is the duty of all male citizens to serve the nation, but it permits exemption from military service on the basis of conscience. Although the grounds must be sincere, they need not be religious; but they must be universally pacifistic. Like the U.S. Supreme Court, Norway's highest tribunal has ruled that selective conscientious objection is not an acceptable basis for a CO exemption. Norwegian courts, however, have granted conscientious objector status to individuals who admit that they would be willing to use deadly force in self-defense. Judicial review is permitted after an application is rejected.

The statistics suggest the operation of a rather benign system in Norway (see Table 15.2).

France's Law of July 8, 1963 permitted candidates for conscription to seek

*The provisions for conscientious objection were still in operation in Belgium in the late summer of 1992, but the Belgian government was seriously considering a bill to terminate compulsory military service there in 1994. (Telephone interview by the editors with the military attaché at the Belgian Embassy, Washington, D.C., August 7, 1992.)

TABLE 15.2 Outcomes of Applications for Conscientious Objector Status, Norway

Year	1984	1985	1986
Number of applications	2070	2096	2497
Status granted	1376	2096	2497
Status denied	262	416	268
Convictions after denial	—	11	14

Note: Decisions exceeded requests because of an accumulation of cases from prior years.

exemption based on philosophical or religious convictions or opposition to the personal use of weapons. The law was amended in 1985 to recognize any motive based on conscience, whether religious or secular. After the law was liberalized, twenty-five hundred requests were made; more than 95 percent of these were approved.[18] The high rate of approval may be due in part to the fact that the defense minister has no express power of investigation, although he is responsible for determining status. That official cannot launch an inquiry or summon applicants for an interview. Furthermore, refusals to grant CO status may be challenged in court. A computer search revealed four cases decided between 1985 and 1987 by the French Council of State's section on litigation: Three were in favor of the government and one was in partial support of the CO applicant.[19]

In Austria, conscientious objection and alternative service have been recognized since 1975. Applications are submitted to the Alternative Service Commission, an organ of the Federal Ministry of the Interior, which accords the claimant the right to a nonpublic hearing. He may be accompanied by counsel. The Commission includes representatives nominated by youth, business, and labor organizations. The military is not represented. Rejected applicants (but apparently not the government) may appeal adverse decisions to an upper chamber of the Commission; ultimately they may appeal to the Constitutional Court, if a constitutional issue is involved. Between 1981 and 1985 CO applications averaged four thousand annually. Austria, however, did not report to the United Nations on the actions taken on the applications.

The Dutch constitution provides for exemption from military service because of conscientious objection. The Military Service Act of 1978, which implements the provision, states merely that the objection must be universal and must relate to the use of means of force. During parliamentary debate on the bill, the minister of defense stated that the objection need not be religiously based. The Dutch response to the 1987 questionnaire from the International Society for Military Law and the Law of War carefully distinguished other kinds of moral objections that, in themselves, would not qualify an applicant as a CO, for example, the refusal to surrender one's personal autonomy to military discipline or to wear a uniform. (These attitudes, however, might reflect a more fundamental objection, which would qualify.) Unlike most countries, the Netherlands recognizes selective conscientious objection, including objections connected with the political purpose of the proposed use of armed force.[20]

In the Netherlands CO applications are submitted to the minister of defense, who refers them to a committee, which holds a hearing. If recognition is denied, the claimant can appeal to the Administrative Disputes Division of the Council of

TABLE 15.3   Outcomes of Applications for Conscientious Objector Status, The Netherlands

Year	1984	1985	1986	1987
Number of applications	2733	2968	2803	—
Status granted*	2079	2321	2216	—
Status denied*	285	175	163	—
Convictions after denial	—	10	9	11

*Includes requests made in prior years.

State. At least one case—which held that recognition, once granted, could not be withdrawn—has been decided by the State Council's Judicial Division. The percentage of favorable actions in the Netherlands is quite high (see Table 15.3).

In summary, the great majority of Western European conscripts who claim conscientious objector status from military service are granted exemptions, usually without the need for a personal hearing. This finding suggests that the phrasing of the CO's claim generally determines the outcome. Thus the applicant with superior writing skills (or access to someone who has those skills) can expect to fare better than a less articulate individual. In practice, such a process effectively excuses any well-educated conscript who is willing to write an appropriate description of motives. When a military system has more potential manpower than it needs, the government may conclude that articulate opponents can be excused without any loss of political credibility or efficiency (as long as they do not become too numerous). Current Western European military systems were *not* designed to maximize the nation's wartime mobilization potential, but rather to meet peacetime requirements for conscription or (at most) the wartime necessities envisioned for a short and limited war.[21]

If, however, the military system is designed not for peacetime conscription but for major wartime mobilization, a process designed to excuse those who can prepare a more convincing CO form is manifestly unjust. Personal hearings should be required, even though they would still be biased in favor of the more articulate.[22] Although educational levels in many areas of the world have increased in the past seventy-five years, it is useful to recall that in World War I, 90 percent of the conscientious objectors who appeared before British tribunals had only an elementary school education.[23] The goddess of justice is often portrayed as blind—presumably to distinctions of class, wealth, or education—but any system of personal hearings that depends on the applicant's verbal ability to rationalize his behavior will discriminate in favor of the advantaged.

Israel, which does not recognize conscientious objectors other than Orthodox Jews, offers a possible model in its treatment of recalcitrant reservists. Many such reservists refused, for example, to participate in operations north of the "Green Line" in Lebanon on the grounds that the invasion was immoral. The decision about their sincerity and treatment was left to the individual who knew them best—their commander. Israeli practice is discussed more fully in the chapter by Yoram Peri in this book; it suggests that any determination based on sincerity of belief should be made at the lowest practicable level of government, and then only after a thorough evaluation of the individual's character and behavior. Because such a decision is based largely on intangibles, it is not susceptible to judicial review. Potential miscarriages of justice cannot be avoided, but they can be mitigated by devising fairly moderate sanctions.

Alternative Service

Any society that permits its conscripted soldiers to face wartime death or peacetime inconvenience, but that is willing to excuse conscientious objectors, will demand that the persons excused perform some duties in lieu of military service.[24] All systems that allow COs to avoid military duty make some provision for alternative service. They vary as to whether alternative service will include noncombatant service in the armed forces, and, if so, whether the option will be determined by the state or by the CO.

Traditional conscription programs in the World Wars—insofar as they recognized conscientious objectors—assumed that most objectors (religiously motivated pacifists) would be willing to serve in a role that did not require them to use weapons. Peacetime conscription systems that permit secular (that is, ethical, social, philosophical, or cultural) COs can expect that many of their objections will concern the use of armed force in any fashion, and therefore that many of the COs will reject any duty related to the military (even in the medical corps, for example). In this regard, a rather clear distinction can be made between the treatment of the problem by Western European nations (NATO and France) and by members of what was the Warsaw Pact until 1990. As I will discuss in a subsequent section, "Countries Undergoing Fundamental Change," East European Countries in the Warsaw Pact insisted that objectors perform noncombatant military service, whereas the West has been more generous in allowing civilian alternative service.

In both the rules and the ways in which they are administered, variations exist even within the West. Who should administer the alternative service system? In Norway, it is the Ministry of Justice. In West Germany, it is the Federal Office of Civilian Service, which is part of the ministry responsible for determining conscientious objector status. What sort of alternative service is acceptable? In Norway and Austria, it may be performed under the auspices of government-approved social, religious, or humanitarian organizations, public or private. Austria requires that alternative service be rendered outside the armed forces, whereas Belgium assigns men to unarmed military service or to civilian service. Civilian service may be performed in unarmed civilian disaster units, or in public health organizations assisting the aged or the mentally or physically handicapped, or it may involve social or cultural tasks. Places of employment must be approved by the Belgian Minister for Employment and Social Service. The Federal Republic of Germany simply requires social service for the common good, performed under the supervision of an employer approved by the Federal Office of Civilian Service.

Should the term of alternative service equal or exceed that expected of conscripts? The term of service in Belgium depends on the task assigned. It is half again as long as military service in the case of assignment to civil defense or public health, and doubled for an assignment to cultural or social work. The Federal

Republic of Germany requires all COs to serve one-third longer than conscripts. Austria requires the same term of service from conscripts as from objectors.

Should the conditions of alternative service attempt to emulate those of conscripts? Unfortunately, neither the United Nations report nor the responses gathered by the International Society considered this topic. Wartime alternative service traditionally has been designed to match the inconvenience and discomfort—although not the threat of death or mutilation—that the soldier might face. There is no indication that peacetime alternative service attempts to duplicate the conditions suffered by the typical conscript. Distinctive clothing is not required. Some nations insist that service be performed at a place other than the applicant's native region, and some limit the amount of compensation that may be received to that which a conscript earns. Certainly no effort is made to duplicate the disciplinary code of the military, although most legal systems have sanctions that mimic or duplicate those portions of the typical military code relating to absence from the place of duty.

What sanctions should be imposed for failure to perform or complete alternative service? Who should impose them? In the Federal Republic of Germany, sanctions are imposed by the civil courts according to penal regulations similar to those applicable to individuals in the armed forces. Revocation of CO status is possible after a hearing, but only if it is determined that the condition that warranted granting CO status no longer exists. In such a case, the objector would be subject to a fine or imprisonment if he refused to serve in the active force. In France, the National Service Code requires employers of objectors to report absenteeism and other work violations. Sanctions include loss of accrued leave (vacation time), but they may be imposed only after the offender has been informed of the suspected offense.[25] In Norway, if a CO refuses to perform alternative service, authorities seek a court order requiring service at a specified location. The objector will be confined for a period of time if that order is disobeyed, but the confinement is not treated as imprisonment.

Should exempted objectors be subject to any civil restrictions? In Belgium they are prohibited, until they reach the age of forty-five, from holding any position that may require them to bear arms or to participate in the sale or manufacture of arms or ammunition. More typical, however, is the Federal Republic of Germany, which imposes no civil restrictions.

Sanctions for Those Refusing Any Service

All national service codes surveyed contain provisions for criminal punishment, fines, or imprisonment.[26] These provisions, which also reflect law as a product, provide that the punishment be imposed either after a civil trial or, rarely, by the military courts. The code provisions, however phrased, raise two fundamental questions. First, should conviction be treated like any other criminal conviction? Or should it be treated specially because an act of refusal based on conscience deserves special consideration, even though the refusal was rejected?[27] Second, should conviction bar any subsequent efforts to conscript the young man or should he remain subject to conscription? Israel, which does not officially excuse conscientious objectors, deems them still liable; in one sample, 10 percent of the objectors had been punished more than once.[28] Those countries that bar such succ ::%s:SATURN:%s:desks:ns may do so on legal grounds (for example, that the national service code bars the conscription of such individuals) or on practical grounds. The statistics on conviction supplied by the countries responding to the 1987 questionnaire suggest that multiple convictions are not imposed in Western Europe, and that many refusers are not prosecuted at all.

The Special Case of the Jehovah's Witnesses

Although this sect is comparatively small, it creates unique legal problems because of its beliefs and its fervor. Countries that granted exemptions to religious pacifists did so on the premise that such pacifists oppose all wars. Jehovah's Witnesses, however, assert that they will fight on God's behalf, but not on behalf of any government. Nor will they agree to perform alternative service, because such service would breach their covenant with God to preach the imminent end of the world. The structure of their church also raises questions about eligibility when members claim that they are all ministers of religion and therefore are all entitled (in those states that exempt clergymen)[29] to recognition on those grounds.

Although treatment of this intransigent group varies slightly from country to country in terms of process, the legal status of Jehovah's Witnesses remains constant because no country has been willing to single them out for special statutory protection.[30] Therefore it has remained for the bureaucrats to decide whether the individual Jehovah's Witness should be punished for his refusal to accede to the wishes of the state. Any national service system intended to produce military manpower in wartime could not permit such exceptional treatment; the treatment of obdurate Jehovah's Witnesses by democratic societies in both world wars included prosecution and imprisonment. No court or legislature could have defied public opinion by granting them absolute protection.

Countries Undergoing Fundamental Change

As noted earlier, the Soviet Union and the Eastern European nations all relied on conscription to serve their military needs when they belonged to the Warsaw Pact. The Soviet Union made no provision for conscientious objection; Eastern European countries have made some exceptions. Recent news reports, however, suggest a slow transition to models more representative of Western Europe. In Poland, for example, the "Freedom and Peace Movement," at its national convention in June 1988, proposed a change in the Mandatory Draft Act to permit alternative service for those who objected to military service on religious, moral, or philosophical grounds. Previously a decree of the Polish Council of Ministers had permitted substitute service, but only for reasons of ill health. The reform movement also challenged the policy by which all decisions regarding alternative service were made by military officials. The new Polish government acceded to their requests.[31] Like Poland, Hungary and the German Democratic Republic (East Germany) had limited programs that permitted conscientious objectors to serve in unarmed military construction units, but Hungary limited such permissions to Jehovah's Witnesses.[32] On March 1, 1989, Hungary announced the release of all seventy persons jailed for refusing military service.[33] The easing of tensions between Eastern and Western Europe probably means that conscientious objectors in most Eastern European countries will be treated more favorably and that conscription laws there will be liberalized, if not eliminated.

Similarly, the South African government appears to be in the process of relaxing its system for handling conscientious objection.[34] Some liberalization begin in 1983, when the South African law was changed to permit noncombatant or even alternative civilian service for religiously motivated objectors. The exemption was not limited to members of the traditional peace churches; by court decision, it was held also to encompass Theravada Buddhism, which does not acknowledge a supreme being.[35] Secular pacifists and selective objectors remain unrecognized. The process for recognizing objection is under the control of a military board,[36] while alternative service is controlled by the Ministry of Manpower. A news report of February 1, 1990, announced that the Pretoria government had halved (to three years) the sentence imposed on conscientious objectors;[37] this reduction may represent a major step in liberalizing the legal system in South Africa.[38]

The Military Conscientious Objector

Although the legal protection afforded civilian conscientious objectors has been a matter of concern in many countries, the plight of the military objector has received very little attention. This lack of attention is surprising because the problem posed by military conscientious objection can arise in any nation that relies on military forces, whether active or reserve.

Austria, Belgium, France, Italy, and the Netherlands represent one extreme in regard to military COs. Although they are liberal in their treatment of conscripts, they responded to the United Nations survey by stating that they would accept no requests from serving soldiers. The United Kingdom reported the existence of administrative arrangements for the separation of military objectors; the Council of Europe reported on the 1979 release of a British captain who claimed conscientious objector status. Norway and Sweden reported that it was possible for a serving soldier to be released for reasons of conscience. The Federal Republic of Germany also accepts CO applications from uniformed members of the armed forces and from reservists. In Germany, in such a case, a panel is convened by the minister of defense, and the applicant must appear in person at the hearing. Panels involving reservists include two members designated by local political authorities.

Comprehensive information regarding the U.S. process for handling uniformed COs, which is found in Department of Defense Directive 1300.6, suggests the issues that must be considered by any system designed to deal with this problem.[39] What classes of military personnel should be covered? Members of the active force and members of the reserve forces subject to activation? Retired members of the forces who may be subject to recall in times of grave national emergency? Officer candidates? What grounds should warrant favorable treatment? Only grounds that would excuse conscripts (namely, total pacifism)? Or should requests based on selective conscientious objection (to the use of certain weapons, for example) be accepted?[40] What time limits should be imposed on such requests? Should requests based on an imminent assignment to a position of danger (such as the military operations in Panama or, more recently, the Persian Gulf) be distinguished from requests based on an imminent assignment involving a morally objectionable weapon (such as the strategic nuclear missile force)?

What should be the legal consequences of a pending application? Many of those countries that grant conscientious objector status defer a conscript's call to active duty until the completion of action on his request for exemption. Should a pending military application affect access to classified information or to sensitive weapons systems? Should it affect a pending reassignment or promotion? Receipt of special pay or entitlement? Authority to command subordinates? Should it affect the obligation to comply with military orders?[41]

Should applications by uniformed COs be acted upon by the military, or by some other agency that has no direct interest (as in the case of most western European conscripts)? If military authorities are to be given responsibility (as is the case in every country to my knowledge), at what level of authority in the hierarchy should the final decision be made? On the one hand, those who know the applicant best (that is, those in command of his unit) would seem best qualified to evaluate his sincerity.[42] On the other, officials may decide that such decisions are so controversial that they should be made by a centralized authority with more experience. In the U.S. system, all discharges for conscientious objection must be approved at the highest level of command, although other classes of discharge for administrative reasons (including persistent minor misconduct) have been delegated to subordinate units.

What factors should be considered relevant in deciding whether the technically valid reasons of military COs are sincere? In the United States, the individual's prior disciplinary record is considered to have some probative value. It is assumed that soldiers with unblemished records are more liable to be sincere than those who have been involved in disciplinary incidents or who have been less than satisfactory in performing their duties. Is that assumption appropriate? The U.S. system also requires the uniformed objector to establish his sincerity by offering persuasive reasons for his refusal to serve. It may be true that the heart may have reasons which reason cannot know, but legal systems and philosophers[43] give primacy to the reasoned and articulate objector, thus confusing clarity of expression with sincerity.

What role, if any, should religious or medical officials play in evaluating the objector's reasoning? The U.S. military relies on a chaplain's evaluation of the sincerity of the religiously motivated objector. In doing so, the military risks confusing orthodoxy with sincerity.[44] U.S. military regulations also provide for a psychiatric evaluation for uniformed COs; this provision suggests either that the authorities assume that the soldier who expresses moral qualms about continuing military service is mentally unstable or that psychiatrists are particularly well qualified to evaluate the objector's sincerity. Both assumptions are questionable.

What should be the legal consequences of a rejected application for a uniformed CO? Should the application be treated as a nullity, and the objector retained in the service and subjected to punishment for disobedience of orders? This is the position taken by the U.S. military.[45] Should the objector be separated in any case? If he is separated, how should his service be characterized by the military authorities? While awaiting separation should he remain subject to punishment for offenses relating to the status he sought (for example, refusal to wear a uniform)? Should the treatment of his case be affected by such factors as the extent of the government's investment in his training (for example, for pilots) or by his existing service obligation? During the Vietnam War a disproportionate number of medical school graduates, who had received government subsidy for their education in return for a commitment to serve in the military for a specified number of years, developed qualms of conscience between the date they completed training and the date when they were to be called to active duty. Probably the sincerity of such a subsidized physician's claim would be tested more rigorously than that of an unsubsidized conscript, although the fact of payment has no logical relation to the question of sincerity.

What should be the legal consequences of an application by a uniformed CO that is accepted? If the applicant had been punished for an offense relating to his objection, should that punishment be expunged? Whether he is separated or transferred to noncombatant status (an option in the U.S. military), should the characterization of his service (as satisfactory or unsatisfactory) while he was awaiting a decision be affected by the fact that his application was granted? Should the government's treatment of his claim be influenced by such factors as the government's investment in his training or an existing service obligation? In the Vietnam War, the U.S. government was unsuccessful when it attempted to recoup the cost of military academy education from graduates who subsequently sought and were granted discharge as conscientious objectors.[46]

Finally, what role, if any, should nonmilitary judicial authorities play in reviewing the government's denial of status to military objectors? The same role that the court system plays when the objector is civilian? One can argue that the interests of the state are implicated in quite a different fashion when the individual seeking recourse is already a member of the armed forces. Despite its strong bias toward judicial review of government action, the United States has failed to develop a coherent, principled approach to this issue.*

These questions suggest some of the problems raised by the uniformed conscientious objector. In nations that consider such claims, the number of such objectors is so small that presumably each case is treated ad hoc. The only data available are from the U.S. response to the 1987 questionnaire by the International

---

*As a result of the controversial handling of CO claims put forward by some American uniformed personnel during the Persian Gulf War of 1990–1991, a bill that addressed some of these issues, H.R. 5060, "The Military Conscientious Objector Act of 1992," was introduced in the U.S. House of Representatives on May 5, 1992 (see chapter 2 in this volume). (Eds.)

Society for Military Law and the Law of War supplemented by statistics supplied by the Department of Defense. In order to put that data (which reflects discharges, not applications) in perspective, I have listed the total number of individuals in each branch of the service at the time the discharges were granted (see Table 15.4).

Because the United States currently relies on an all-volunteer force and has been influenced less strongly than Europe by value changes affecting attitudes toward military service,[47] its experience with uniformed COs may not be capable of extrapolation for other countries. The absence of news reports or scholarly comment[48] may indicate that peacetime in-service conscientious objectors are so rare that most armed forces have not encountered the need to develop special laws on this matter.

International Law and Conscientious Objection

Although national law addresses the problem posed by the conscientious objector—primarily the civilian objector to military service—national regulations may be affected by norms developed by the international community. In regard to conscientious objection, those norms have yet to be stabilized. Not all authorities agree, for example, that conscientious objection is a human right, as some human rights and pacifist organizations have argued. Two important European court decisions have addressed the subject, however, at least in the context of the European Community. The European Commission of Human Rights reviews all individual applications that claim violations of the European Convention on Human Rights and Fundamental Freedoms. In 1985 it concluded that a Swedish law exempting Jehovah's Witnesses but denying CO status to other objectors was valid because membership in an organized religion was a legitimate means for determining sincerity of belief.[49]

The European Court of Human Rights, to which appeals from the Commission may be taken, made an important ruling in 1984 in the case of *de Jong, Baljet, and van den Brink* v. *The Netherlands*.[50] That decision involved three conscripts who had been convicted after refusing military service on the grounds of conscientious objection. Baljet and de Jong were members of a battalion alerted for peacekeeping duties in Lebanon. While their application for release from active duty as COs was pending, they refused to participate in a military exercise. Van den Brink had refused to seek exemption as a conscientious objector. After being drafted forcibly, he was tried for insubordination. The Court concluded that there had been a violation of Article 5 of the European Human Rights Convention, which requires individuals charged with an offense to be brought promptly before a judicial officer. The Court, however, rejected Baljet's and de Jong's argument that they had been discriminated against because they were members of a unit selected for service that might involve combat. Both decisions affirmed the right of national governments to regulate the lives of service members; they also can serve as precedents for future appeals that conscientious objector status indeed is protected under the European Human Rights Convention.

TABLE 15.4   Outcomes of Applications for Conscientious Objector Status among
Members of U.S. Armed Forces

Year	Branch of service	Strength	CO discharges	Noncombat status granted
1985	Air Force	603,898	37	4
	Army	780,648	63	15
	Marines	198,241	22	5
	Navy	568,781	41	5
	TOTAL	2,151,568	163	29
1986	Air Force	605,800	32	2
	Army	770,904	73	19
	Marines	196,273	22	1
	Navy	570,973	16	3
	TOTAL	2,143,950	143	25
1987	Air Force	606,800	38	2
	Army	774,104	44	2
	Marines	199,600	12	0
	Navy	583,800	22	3
	TOTAL	2,164,304	116	7
1988	Air Force	606,300	25	Not available
	Army	776,440	13	"
	Marines	198,200	11	"
	Navy	585,000	38	"
	TOTAL	2,165,940	87	"
1989	Air Force	579,200	37	"
	Army	766,500	22	"
	Marines	195,300	11	"
	Navy	583,900	43	"
	TOTAL	2,124,900	113	"
1990	Air Force	571,000	20	"
	Army	761,100	7	"
	Marines	195,300	22	"
	Navy	590,500	37	"
	TOTAL	2,117,900	86	"
1991	Air Force	517,400	32	"
	Army	731,700	44	"
	Marines	195,700	13	"
	Navy	584,800	42	"
	TOTAL	2,029,600	131	"

Sources: Strength figures pertain to active duty personnel and are drawn from the annual publication *The Military
Balance;* CO figures for 1985–1987 are from U.S. response to the 1987 questionnaire by the International Society for
Military Law and the Law of War; CO figures for 1988–1991 are from Department of Defense personal communication
to the author, April 1992.

Conclusion

Any effort to reduce the lessons learned from this comparative survey to a standard model for the legal treatment of conscientious objectors could be criticized quite properly for failing to recognize national traditions and circumstances. Yet before a government evaluates or establishes a legal apparatus intended to protect drafted civilians who are conscientious objectors to military service, one fundamental question must be answered: Why does the state have conscription? If the government concludes that a direct and immediate threat to national security is present, then the law will make little or no provision for conscientious objectors. Such is the case in Israel, Cuba, South Africa, and those countries where conscription is linked directly to any situation viewed as a national emergency.

In Western Europe, as the perceived threat to national security has become more remote in recent years, conscripts' legal rights have been expanded until it has become relatively easy in most of those countries to avoid involuntary military service. Exemption *laws* were drafted to assure parents and conscripts that only exceptional cases would be excused, but the actual *process* is usually biased towards granting exemption to any objector willing to "play the game" by appropriately completing the requisite forms. Switzerland has proved to be an exception to the general rule because of its unique national tradition of armed neutrality and the previously revered position of its militia army raised through universal male conscription, but the situation there may be changing.

In those non-Western nations that rely on conscription, a contrary model appears: Few provide for conscientious objectors. That fact is understandable in the case of nations facing an external security threat. In the others, it is possible that relatively universal conscription is intended to discipline or acculturate young men who otherwise might threaten internal security. Moreover, many of these non-European countries rely on traditions that emphasize communal obligations rather than individual rights.

Finally, those countries that do not have conscription but rely on all-volunteer armed forces rarely provide "standby" rules to protect conscientious objectors. The United States is the exceptional case, and may make such CO provisions largely for domestic reasons—that is, as a gesture toward religious sensibilities and as evidence of its resolve and ability to mobilize if the need arises.

Whereas the laws protecting the right of conscientious objection for Western European conscripts are moderately stringent as written (law as product) and relatively lax as applied (law as process), a different pattern emerges in regard to the in-service objector. The person in uniform may receive some formal protection in the few countries that recognize that their conscripts may change their minds after entering service. The Netherlands is representative of this minority. More typically, no special legal provisions apply once a person is in uniform, and decisions regarding the soldier's future are usually made ad hoc after authorities evaluate the sincerity of his or her claim.

Once again, the seriousness of the threat facing the nation and considerations of morale and discipline will affect the final disposition of the cases of in-service objectors, whether by court-martial or by separation. Although my research cannot confirm this point, I suspect that non-NATO countries generally are more severe in their treatment of in-service objectors. This disparity may be eliminated as the members of NATO and of the former Warsaw Pact look more to the Conference on Security and Cooperation in Europe (CSCE) as the forum for resolving their differences. Since 1975 the more broadly based CSCE has monitored compliance with the Helsinki Accords, and efforts have been made to include conscientious objection among the Accord's guarantees.[51] State practice, if not the law, may lead to more generous treatment of all European conscientious objectors.

The future is not bright for legal protection of conscientious objectors in the non-Western world. The United Nations Commission on Human Rights continues to press for recognition of conscientious objection, the evaluation of objectors' claims by independent bodies, and provision for alternative service.[52] Yet even in those states that implement the United Nations' proposals, legal problems of statute law and administrative process will persist throughout the evolution of the right of conscientious objection, problems enlarged by the growing secularization of conscience.

16

Conclusion: The Secularization of Conscience Reconsidered

CHARLES C. MOSKOS
JOHN WHITECLAY CHAMBERS II

The "new" conscientious objection, by definition, must imply significant departure from previous usage. Otherwise "new" is just another misapplication of an overworked adjective. This book would offer a useful perspective on the study of conscientious objection even if the only new dimension were a dispassionate and comparative approach to the topic. It has done that and much more: This multinational study of conscientious objection in the West demonstrates the recent and unprecedented reshaping of conscientious objection and its relationship to the armed forces, the state, and to society. The new dimensions—the augmenting, indeed, near supplanting, of the old religious and communal grounds for objection by a new secular and often privatized base; the proliferation of COs in uniform; and the recognition and acceptance of these trends by the state—warrant the appellation the "new" conscientious objection.

Secularization of conscience and modern individualism have been the driving forces in the exponential rise of this resistance to military service. Although the speed and consistency of this increase vary from one country to another, the general direction is clear. The center of gravity of conscientious objection has moved from the traditional peace churches to the more inclusive mainstream religious denominations to an ever-widening group for whom objection to military service is based solely upon humanistic or private motives. This new conscientious objection operates not only among civilian draftees resisting conscription, but also has spread to members of uniformed services raised entirely by voluntary enlistment without resort to conscription.

In comparative terms, religious motivation has diminished dramatically in importance. In those Northern and Western European countries where current data are available, religious objectors make up only a small minority of the total number of COs. The percentages are remarkably similar even among different nations: 15 percent in the Netherlands, 18 percent in Germany, 14 percent in Norway. The upsurge in secular conscientious objection in these countries is a harbinger of future developments. It has been duplicated already in post–Cold War Eastern Europe and is likely to be replicated next in the nations of Southern Europe. By far the largest part of this extraordinary increase in conscientious objection in recent decades has been due to the growth of modern individualism and the secularization of conscience, and their corresponding, if grudging, acceptance by the state as a basis for conscientious objection.

The Stages of Conscientious Objection

A complex and controversial subject such as conscientious objection obviously presents a dilemma to those who wish to study its evolving relationship to the state. The greater the reliance on a conceptual scheme, the greater the simplification required. Conversely, the greater the incorporation of exceptions and detail, the greater the danger of obscuring the points central to the subject itself. The authors of the essays in this volume were invited to prepare factual case studies that would test the hypothesized sequence of the evolution of conscientious objection to military service and its relationship to the state.[1]

The conceptual scheme, as explained in the first chapter, consists of three stages. In Stage 1, generally in early modern Western society, official recognition of conscientious objection is granted but is usually limited to traditional peace sects. Accommodation is restricted primarily to noncombatant military service. In Stage 2, which characterizes many modern Western societies, authorities recognize a broader religious criterion for conscientious objection, and allow some forms of alternative civilian service. In Stage 3, typifying postmodern Western society, the new conscientious objection emerges and is recognized by the state: Secular motives are accepted along with (in some countries) selective objection to particular wars and discretionary objection to nuclear weapons. In Stage 3 the definition of recognized COs is liberalized and civilian alternative service is fully legitimized as the functional equivalent of military service. The new conscientious objection of Stage 3 is qualitatively and quantitatively different from that of the earlier stages: The total number of COs expands dramatically, especially because of the secular objectors, and nonreligious conscientious objection is recognized among military personnel on active duty as well as among potential civilian draftees.

The comparative analysis provided in this volume clearly supports the "secularization of conscience" thesis and generally upholds the three-stage evolution and liberalization of the relationship between COs and the state. The evidence, however, requires certain comments on variations in the original conceptual scheme. These variations can be grouped into three categories: the timing of the stages, the sequence of the stages, and the possibility of bypassing some of the stages.

The first observation is that the various trends associated with the secularization of conscientious objection and its acceptance by the government do not occur uniformly in every country. Different countries can be characterized as more liberal on different aspects of the subject. The United States was the first to allow some right of conscientious objection at the national level; this took place in the mid-nineteenth century during the Civil War. Yet the formal recognition of conscientious objection, together with provision for rudimentary alternative civilian duties, had occurred in several English colonies in America as early as the seventeenth century, long before the establishment of the republic. Britain in 1916 was the first European nation to grant official recognition to COs while at war. The Netherlands in 1923 was the first to accept selective conscientious objection and the first European nation to establish civilian alternative service.[2] In the late 1950s, the Federal Republic of Germany was the first country to move toward a massive alternative civilian service program for conscientious objectors. By the 1980s Denmark became the first country in which alternative service was made less onerous than peacetime military service.

France set up a de jure system of conscientious objection in 1983, but obstacles in the political culture have worked to restrict its implementation. The issue of conscientious objection in the former German Democratic Republic (East Germany) is particularly notable because COs there became the nucleus of a revolutionary yet nonviolent movement that ultimately overthrew the regime. In South Africa, the situation of conscientious objectors is still evolving but seems to be on a fairly predictable track of secularization and liberalization. Switzerland continues to be an anomaly, an otherwise advanced European democracy that only in 1992 began to take the first steps to allow for conscientious objectors outside military service.[3]

The second comment on the unifying concept of the book represents a partial factual modification to the three-stage scheme of secularization. Even in Scandinavian countries, where nonreligious objection was furthest advanced, secular criteria for conscientious objection followed closely after the de facto recognition of religious motives. This development surely was influenced by the fact that all of these nations were neutral in World War I. It also may have reflected the widespread prevalance of "antimilitaristic" sentiments among socialist and radical pacifist groups and their influence in those multiparty states.[4] These developments foreshadowed the secularization of conscience that occurred later in other countries. In no society, however, has the state ever recognized secular grounds before religious motives as the basis for accepting conscientious objection and exempting COs from combatant military service.

A third observation is in the realm of conjecture. By the early 1990s the former socialist countries of Eastern Europe were moving rapidly toward the North Atlantic model.[5] Certain ex-communist countries have leapt from Stage 1 to Stage 3, completely bypassing Stage 2. This development was especially notable in the "Western" countries of Eastern Europe—Poland, Hungary, the Czech and Slovak Republics, Slovenia, and Croatia. In fact, in 1991 these countries were more liberal in their standards of conscientious objection than the NATO countries of Mediterranean Europe. How other Eastern European countries will fare remains to be determined. A reasonable surmise, however, is that unless clashes of ethnic nationalisms lead to increased use of conscripted military forces, these areas too will eventually accept more liberal standards of conscientious objection as they seek to emulate the civic culture of the West.

Modernization, Individuation, and Secularization

If there is an underlying theme in theories of change in contemporary Western societies, it is captured in the word *modernization* and in associated terms such as *rationalization, bureaucratization,* and *liberalization.*[6] From this perspective, the secularization of conscientious objection documented in this volume is a particular manifestation of a larger and more general development. As suggested above, this trend is not presented here as a unilinear conception of history as inevitable modernization, with an insistence that societies evolve through similar stages and eventually arrive at some universal configuration. Rather, the editors assert that meaningful generalizations can be made about a particular social phenomenon—in this case, the secularization of motives among conscientious objectors to military service and its recognition by the state—as it occurs in a relatively narrow spectrum of societies, namely Western industrialized democracies with strong Christian traditions.

Part of the dramatic increase in the numbers of secular conscientious objectors and in their recognition by the state is related to the emergence of the modern Western concept of the individual. Indeed in *The Republic of Choice,* Lawrence M. Friedman writes of a glorification of a person's free, open choice and a right to develop and be oneself—in effect, to choose oneself and one's life.[7] Transmitted particularly by the mass media and the consumer culture, this new individualism has spread in the past several decades in varying degrees throughout the West and has become incorporated increasingly into the culture and into political, legal, and other institutions.[8]

Traditionally, the concept of a "right" was balanced with that of a "duty"; theoretically, the creation of rights implied the creation of duties.[9] In modern Western law and politics, however, the trend has been the expansion of citizens' rights and entitlements without concomitant increases in their duties. In fact, the sense of obligation to the national community appears to have diminished considerably. In the United States, this trend has sparked a significant debate about the need for a new emphasis on responsibilities and civic duty.[10]

Religion, another traditionally binding force associated with responsibilities and duties, also has been affected by the forces of modernization and individualization. The new emphasis upon individual freedom of choice and self-fulfillment has contributed, particularly in pluralistic countries such as the United States, to the erosion of religious ties imposed by others, such as those inherited from one's parents, or simply followed out of habit or tradition.[11] More prominent in twentieth-century Western culture, at least until the past decade, have been the linkage of modernization with a focus on scientific, rational thought, and the de-emphasis of intense religious experience and non-rational systems of belief—in short, an emphasis on secularization.[12]

To what degree have the churches themselves helped to promote the secularization of conscientious objection? Certainly mainstream churches reflect the contemporary cultural struggle between the forces of institutional tradition and those of modernist liberation. The liberal mainstream churches were influenced profoundly by a theological eclecticism that drew from various sub-theologies: liberation theology, feminist theology, black theology, and eco-theology, to name the most prominent. Most of these sub-theologies addressed particular grievances, but all borrowed heavily from secular movements. More arguably, justification by ascribed faith gave way to justification by self-articulated humanism, which itself was replaced by justification by deed. This development paralleled the shifting rationales for conscientious objection—the deed, in this case, being alternative civilian service. As a result, the liberal mainstream churches tended to support blanket conscientious objection, whether secular or religious.

Even though most of the anti-establishment movements of the 1960s were deeply secular in origin, they exerted a strong influence on mainline churches, especially on the liberal clergy and hierarchy. Suspicion and opposition spread to include not only war, military buildups, and nuclear weapons, but also the institution of the military itself. The intensity may have been new, but the sentiment was rooted in attitudes developed early in the twentieth century. Even before World War I, liberal Protestant churches in the United States, Britain, the British Commonwealth, Scandinavia, and (to a lesser degree) other parts of Europe were influenced by leaders of an expanded peace movement, progressive reformers, social democrats, and other internationalists who advocated the limitation or elimination of the use of armed forces to settle international disputes. This peace advocacy, which was particularly strong in the first and the third decades of the twentieth century, anticipated the eventual openness of mainline liberal religious establishments in the West to conscientious objection in any form.[13]

One can argue that the liberal churches of the West have moved in recent years from regarding themselves as the definers of conscience to a position of partnership with secular supporters of conscientious objection. The growing acceptance of all forms and bases of conscientious objection—found today in liberal Protestant denominations, the Roman Catholic Church, and Reform Judaism—is influenced more strongly by secular pacifism, including nuclear pacifism, than by the traditional Christian peace sects.[14] This is not to say that the liberal clergy have abandoned the moral high ground on the issue of conscientious objection; rather, they have accepted enlarged definitions of conscience and have welcomed others to join them.

At a 1989 interdenominational international conference on conscientious objection (the first such conference ever held), keynote speaker H. Lamar Gibble characterized the World Council of Churches as seeming to "legitimate conscientious objection more from a secular human rights perspective than from the Judaeo/Christian imperative, 'Thou shall not kill.' "[15] Gibble, a member of the Church of the Brethren, a historic peace church, also stated that "conscientious objection to military service was increasingly reduced to an individual state of distress and *the foundation of the New Testament was disregarded.*"[16]

Many contending and overlapping influences played a role in the emergence of the new conscientious objection. In addition to the secular influences in the religious establishments of the West, attitudes and events of the 1960s produced both idealistic dissent and disenchantment with dominant institutions. Also influential was the increased international emphasis on human rights that emerged in the 1970s. Thermonuclear weapons, the nuclear arms race, and the threat of global destruction generated an anti-nuclear pacifism that not only cleared the way for a proliferation of conscientious objectors, religious or secular, in or out of uniform, but also affected segments of society largely untouched in the past by pacifism, such as portions of the scientific and business communities and the American bishops of the Roman Catholic Church.

Many people, of course, object to military service for reasons having no connection with religious beliefs, secular humanism, or even the purposes for which armed forces might be used. One cannot discount trends in the contemporary culture particularly emphasized in the 1970s and 1980s: self-centered privatism, the "me generation," and the impact of materialism and satisfaction of individual wants. Many persons simply do not want their lives interrupted by service in the military. They view military service as a waste of time, a burdensome duty, or, in the event of war, too dangerous. Self-interest always has been present among some of those seeking to avoid military service. Even in countries with conscription, there are often many avenues for avoidance of military service, including various medical, mental, dependency, occupational, or student deferments or exemptions. In regard to conscientious objection, however, we would argue that such personal sentiments are much more likely to be couched in terms of formal conscientious objection when secular motives are routinely accepted than under the more stringent religious tests of old.

Whatever its causes, the multifaceted trend toward secularization has moved conscientious objection from a relatively marginal phenomenon to one directly affecting the raising of armies. Today no general study of armed forces and society in Western democracies can be made without taking into account the new conscientious objection. The skyrocketing number of conscientious objectors and draft avoiders in the United States during the Vietnam War helped bring conscription to an end in 1973. Even in the brief war in the Persian Gulf in 1991, conscientious objection became a public issue and a concern at the highest levels of command in the American military. In most of Western Europe, conscientious objection has become an indelible part of civil-military relations. Since the late 1960s the rate of conscientious objection has increased at least tenfold in Germany, Austria, the Netherlands, Denmark, Sweden, and Norway. A similar dramatic upward curve may be expected in the southern rim of Western Europe and in the former communist countries of Eastern Europe.

The significance of the new conscientious objection, however, lies not only in the quantitative increase but also in the qualitative differences from the old conscientious objection. The introduction of secular criteria for recognition as a CO marked the end of the period when the typical CO was a rural (or an occasionally urban) young man with comparatively little education, who probably belonged to a minor pacifistic or apocalyptical religious denomination. Presentation of secular grounds for recognition as a CO, certainly before the procedure becomes routinized, necessarily relies on assertions that are well-articulated and involve relatively sophisticated moral and ethical positions. These are precisely the grounds expressed most effectively by well-educated and well-off youths.

The change in the grounds for conscientious objection has enabled young people who are not members of historic peace sects to become COs. Simply put, increased numbers of middle- and upper-class youths have qualified as COs. The secularization of conscientious objection and the performance of alternative service by more educated youths thus accompanies a downward trend in the class background of entering recruits in countries with conscription as well as in those with solely volunteer armies. This trend, especially in the ground forces, is creating armies whose ranks are composed increasingly and disproportionately of working-class people.

The fact that secular COs are likely to come from higher social levels than do most of the traditional religious objectors has caused some concern in the Northern European countries where conscientious objection is most widespread. Even when the quantities of draftees are sufficient (no sure thing in itself), the escape of a significant percentage of upper-status youths raises important questions about equity and about the quality of the recruits whom conscription brings into the military. Of course, many young men from the higher social strata were able to avoid military service without recourse to conscientious objection. Rather, they sought relief from the military through exemptions based on health, mental state, student status, professional employment, and the like.

The growing social gap between generally higher-status draft avoiders and lower-status draftees is duplicated in class terms in many all-volunteer armed forces. In societies with all-volunteer forces or with conscripted forces where conscientious objection is widespread, young men from more affluent and more highly educated classes are much less likely to serve in the military than young men who are less affluent and less well educated.[17] In effect, in both volunteer and modern conscript forces, only those draftable men who want to serve in the military actually do so.

The changing social composition of the rank and file in the armed forces both affects and reflects politics and culture. Conscientious objectors are no longer a marginal social group. Increasingly they come from the same strata as the cultural and political elites, or at least from the middle and upper classes to which these elites respond.

For some time, Nils Petter Gleditsch of Norway and others have argued that the loosening of standards for conscientious objection and the creation of alternative options for military service come *after* significant increases in the numbers of conscientious objectors, not before. Liberalization results from popular pressures. Certainly it is true that authorities have responded in part to popular pressure in liberalizing CO provisions. Yet it is also apparent that the state's accommodation is due to the upward shift in the social composition of conscientious objection and consequently to the increased political influence and activity of the COs.

Conscientious objectors and their supporters no longer keep a self-imposed distance from the centers of power that characterized the typical isolated rural peace sect. They have become engaged in politics as an issue-oriented pressure group, as typified by the Central Committee for Conscientious Objectors, the War Resisters League, and the National Interreligious Service Board for Conscientious Objectors. A broad coalition of groups, particularly since the 1960s, has pressed for liberalization and secularization of the standards for conscientious objection. The historic peace churches, pacifist and antiwar groups, and CO support groups have been joined by mainstream religious bodies and civil liberties agencies and, most recently, by international human rights agencies such as Amnesty International and the Commission on Human Rights of the United Nations.

In the evolution of the relationship between conscientious objectors and the state, despite national differences, the first official recognition of CO status generally comes from the legislative branch. That recognition, however, is generally very narrow in scope. Any liberalization that follows in modern democracies usually comes from the judiciary, if the nation in question permits its courts such authority. Otherwise, in the process of widening the criteria for objection, the executive branch is the governmental agent of liberalization. Indeed, the legislatures in contemporary democratic states are typically the most reluctant branch of government to liberalize provisions for conscientious objection.

This pattern is consistent with what we know about popular attitudes towards conscientious objection. Public opinion surveys show much greater acceptance of religiously motivated COs than of secular COs. On such an emotionally charged issue as allowing some young men to avoid compulsory military service, particularly in time of war or other emergency, elected legislative bodies are often much more responsive to the popular will than are nonelected judges or administrators. Legislatures find it difficult to act in matters where the voters may be bitterly divided— as when the CO issue pits veteran and patriotic organizations and the military against pacifists, civil liberties advocates, CO supporters, and many religious bodies. Being more distant from direct public control, the courts in such countries as the United States, Australia, and South Africa have been among the most active governmental agencies recently in broadening the rights of conscientious objectors.

In countries with conscription and alternative service, where public opinion survey data on the subject are available (primarily in Western Europe), the data suggest that the general public there holds the draftee who accepts military service in higher regard than the conscientious objector who performs alternative civilian service. The significant exception is Germany, where public opinion surveys show a growing acceptance of the view that civilian alternative service is the civic equivalent of military service. Germany's *Zivildienst* (civilian service) program, of course, is by far the most extensive system of alternative service in the world. The German case suggests that at least in some cultures the general public evaluates youth service not so much in terms of whether it is military or civilian, but whether that service is important.

Anomalous cases are democratic countries where the right of conscientious objection either does not exist or is severely circumscribed. In Switzerland although changes were in the offing by 1992, conscientious objectors must serve in noncombatant assignments in the military or receive prison sentences. Limited forms of alternative service exist in Spain and Italy, and may become available in Greece. Portugal, the Mediterranean exception, has allowed conscientious objectors since

1976, an outcome of the end of dictatorship there and of widespread resistance to Portugal's colonial wars in Africa. In Israel, "gray COs," soldiers who will not serve in certain assignments, for whatever reason, often are allowed to avoid those assignments through behind-the-scenes negotiations at the local unit level.

Such an informal, pragmatic response to conscientious objection by uniformed personnel is echoed in the experience of the All-Volunteer-Armed Force in the United States. During the Persian Gulf War of 1991, a number of soldiers, probably a thousand or more, asserted their conscientious objection to being deployed for Operations Desert Shield and Desert Storm. Most of these individuals apparently were mobilized reservists. Despite a few highly publicized cases, the U.S. Army did not court-martial all or even most of those men and women in uniform who suddenly declared themselves to be COs. The majority of cases were handled quietly at the local unit level, mostly through transfers, waivers for nondeployment made on grounds other than conscience, or simply release from service. Conversely, the U.S. Marine Corps sought to maintain its discipline and its fighting image by a marked intolerance of conscientious objectors in its ranks. The Marines' leaders took a firm stand against any such accommodation, and in the glare of considerable publicity court-martialed and incarcerated some fifty Marine COs.[18]

The most direct challenge to the state, as well as to our concept of the new conscientious objection, is presented by the absolutists. These objectors, mainly religious, refuse to cooperate in any way with the conscription system or the military. Absolutists reject both noncombatant military service and civilian alternative service. Jehovah's Witnesses, the largest group of absolutists, are primarily from working-class backgrounds and remain outside the mainstream of their countries' religious, cultural, and political life.[19] They are not pacifists; they are willing to fight for the Lord at Armageddon but not for temporal powers here and now. In totalitarian states under Hitler and Stalin, Jehovah's Witnesses who refused to serve in the armed forces were physically abused, placed in concentration camps, and sometimes executed. Yet their steadfastness led to the first accommodation to COs by communist regimes. Jehovah's Witnesses and other absolutists were coerced into unarmed construction battalions, such as the *stoybat* in Russia and the *Bausoldaten* in the former German Democratic Republic (East Germany).

The treatment of Jehovah's Witnesses in contemporary democracies can be viewed as an index of the liberalization of conscientious objection in those countries and also as a measure of the tolerance of a country's civic culture. In the United States and Britain, Jehovah's Witness COs almost always were jailed in World War I, and they made up the large majority of incarcerated objectors in World War II. In the early 1990s, even in the more modern Mediterranean democracies, Jehovah's Witnesses who refused military service were put in prison. Often they were subjected to multiple jeopardy by being sentenced repeatedly for failure to accept induction orders. In Northern and Western Europe, a different treatment has emerged. There, Jehovah's Witnesses receive de facto exemption from compulsory military service on ersatz psychiatric grounds or they are excused by authorities who simply do not enforce the law but instead dismiss them, in essence, as a small, marginal, and extreme group.

Formal acceptance of the right of conscientious objection and of alternative civilian service has become a hallmark of most liberal Western parliamentary democracies. The movement for such recognition was projected onto the international stage in 1987, when the United Nations' Human Rights Commission adopted a resolution specifically urging universal recognition of the right of conscientious objection. Virtually every Western nation voted in favor; the Soviet Union abstained; adamantly opposed were Iran, Iraq, and the People's Republic of China.[20] In short, developments toward the expansion and legitimation of conscientious objection were most evident in Western democracies.

In an earlier era, in much of the world, a mass conscript army based on universal military training and service was regarded in many countries as a sign of an advanced nation-state, particularly when such a national force replaced the hired professional armies of the monarchies. Today higher standing in the international community is more likely to be acknowledged by the recognition of conscientious objection and the provision of alternative civilian service for COs. Nations that abuse human rights, such as by denying and persecuting conscientious objectors, lack such standing. In October 1989, for example, the European Parliament adopted a resolution calling for "the right to be granted to all conscripts to refuse military service, whether armed or unarmed, on grounds of conscience" and urging that "a declaration setting out the individual's motives should suffice in order to obtain the status of conscientious objector." The Parliament also urged that the right to civilian alternative service for COs be recognized in the European Convention for the Protection of Human Rights and Fundamental Freedoms.[21] In 1990 a similar standard was proposed by the thirty-five–nation Conference on Security and Cooperation in Europe (CSCE).[22] Advanced thinking in the West has led people to regard conscientious objection to military service as an international human right.[23]

Some words of caution are in order. We do not put forward the secularization thesis in a deterministic manner. It is not necessarily true that societies become less religious as they grow more technologically advanced and more bureaucratically complex. Social scientists did not predict the recent recent rise of Christian evangelism, Islamic fundamentalism, or Jewish orthodoxy. It could be argued plausibly that the forces of skepticism may be waning.[24] If the thesis of this book is correct, however, such an ebbing of secularism almost certainly would be accompanied by a decrease in conscientious objection—unless, of course, the new religiosity contained a strong element of the pacifism normally associated with the traditional peace sects.

Will conscientious objection expand into areas where it is presently weak or nonexistent—that is, just about everywhere outside North America and Europe—and where it is not recognized by the state? Such proliferation most likely would occur only with the rise of secularization and democracy in those areas. It is unlikely that a revival of Christianity in Latin America or its spread in Africa and Asia, problematic in itself, will lead to the emergence of conscientious objection and its recognition there. Indeed, the fastest-growing Christian denominations in these regions are fundamentalist in theology, conservative in politics, and nonpacifist in principle. Even less likely is a turn toward pacifism in the non-Christian religions indigenous to those areas. Rather, the fate of conscientious objection elsewhere in the world seems to depend largely upon the spread of secularization and liberal democracy outside the North Atlantic region.[25]

Whither Conscience and Service?

The dramatic increase in the secularization of conscientious objection leaves us with a paradox. The new conscientious objection seems to offer two possible scenarios for the future. From one perspective, expansion and liberalization of conscientious objection can be viewed as part of the erosion of the ideal of the citizen-soldier, based on the citizen's obligation to perform military service when called upon, a hallmark of most Western democracies (and nondemocracies) for two centuries or more. From another perspective, however, the increase in conscientious objection and in liberal programs of alternative service can be regarded as part of the rise of the civilian server, an expansion of citizenship duties beyond the framework of the military into broader areas of national and community service.

In regard to the first alternative scenario—the decline of the mass conscript army—although it is presumptuous to speak of "the end of history," the end of the Cold War means that a momentous change has occurred in the dominant perception of threat and in the international security environment. Although the future will not be free of conflict, we are witnessing the dawn of an era of greatly reduced military forces in Europe and the United States. It is likely that many of the continental nations of Europe will replace their drafted standing armies with professional all-volunteer forces, as has taken place already in Britain and the United States, or will move to a system that combines a drafted reserve force with a small professional military.

The political forces pushing for an end to conscription are formidable, if sometimes contradictory. They include CO and peace organizations, many religious groups, radicals who viscerally dislike any military establishment, libertarian conservatives who prefer a military recruited on marketplace principles, government administrators looking for budget cuts, policy proponents who seek to transfer military spending to social programs, ethnic minorities who oppose being conscripted into larger state armies, young people imbued with the individualism and materialism prevalent in Western youth culture, and even some military leaders who prefer to deal with a well-paid, well-trained professional force rather than with an army filled with sullen draftees.

To be sure, conscientious objection will not disappear even in an era of professional military forces. The Persian Gulf War is only the most recent demonstration that resistance to military service occurs even in an all-volunteer armed force, especially in the presence of major public disagreement about the necessity or the morality of the military action. The secularization of conscience also has contributed to the rise of the conscientious objector in uniform, whether draftee or volunteer. Even so, increasing the reliance on a volunteer professional military will lessen the impact of conscientious objection.

The second alternative scenario—the expansion of the concept of citizen service—appears less likely, at least at first glance, than the continued decline of responsibilities to the larger community. Yet there are some indications of a possible trend toward civic service, even though it is in bits and pieces. In Germany, the tens of thousands of young men who now perform civilian alternative service instead of serving in the military have become an integral part of the delivery of social services in that country. Indeed, with the end of the Cold War and the possible demise of conscription, concern in Germany may focus more on the loss of conscientious objectors performing civilian work than on the loss of draftees and the reduction in the size of the army. Indeed, the extraordinary proliferation of alternative civilian servers in Germany poses an unanticipated question. If conscription ends because there is no need for a mass army with the end of the Cold War, who will perform the vital social services now being undertaken by COs avoiding military service?

In its European heartland, civilian alternative service, the de facto criterion of conscientious objection, will likely cross new frontiers, both figuratively and literally. Almost surely, we can expect an end to time differentials between civilian and military service. In addition, peace work will likely be accepted as legitimate alternative service in certain countries in the not too distant future. Concomitant with the maturing of the European Community, we may anticipate COs being allowed to perform their alternative service outside the CO's home country.

In the United States, the debate on national youth service continues—indeed grows—despite the end of conscription.[26] The idea of civic service programs for young people began in the early twentieth century with William James's famous formulation of a "moral equivalent of war."[27] The Civilian Conservation Corps (ccc), the Peace Corps, and Volunteers in Service to America (vista) were federal programs that proved tremendously popular. Since the 1970s state and local voluntary youth service programs have burgeoned. In 1990 a National and Community Service Act was signed into federal law to establish pilot programs for civilian youth service. Some of the most important precedents in the United States were the alternative programs developed for conscientious objectors.

In 1993, President-elect Bill Clinton advocated a voluntary national service program for youth, the first time the issue had ever been raised at the presidential level.[28] It is noteworthy that, while a Rhodes Scholar, Clinton showed interest in taking part in a "community action project" in lieu of military service. These sentiments were expressed in a letter Clinton wrote during the Vietnam War explaining his dropping out of the Reserve Officers Training Corps at the University of Arkansas.[29] The 1969 letter itself became a topic of controversy during the campaign. Unremarked upon by almost all commentators, but highly significant for our purposes, the young Clinton placed his wish for alternative service specifically in the context of selective conscientious objection.

An important philosophical question is whether military and civilian alternative service are close together or poles apart. Of course they are both. They are far apart in that the soldier and the conscientious objector have diametrically opposed moralities concerning the use of lethal force. But they are close together in that in a democracy both the draftee who serves in the military and the conscientious objector who performs civilian alternative service are viewed increasingly as fulfilling a civic duty.

The secularization and liberalization of conscientious objection raises an intriguing possibility. With the termination of the Cold War, what used to be considered alternative service may become the primary service. The old widespread military obligations of citizens may be supplanted by new, broader forms of civilian service. In the end, the citizen server may replace the citizen soldier.

APPENDIX A

Australia

Hugh Smith

Australia was the first country in the world to enact continuing national legislation protecting the rights of conscientious objectors. Australia's first Defense Act in 1903 granted total exemption from military service to those who could demonstrate a conscientious objection to bearing arms.

Since that time Australia has fought in a number of wars and has operated four schemes of compulsory military training. Issues relating to conscientious objection have risen under each of these schemes, but the broad pattern has been to expand the rights of the objector. That Australia has fought most of its wars with volunteer forces, however, means that it has avoided many of the difficulties surrounding conscientious objection.

In 1911 Australia introduced compulsory part-time military training for males, the first English-speaking nation to do so in peacetime. The relevant legislation granted exemption from combat duties to those "who are forbidden by the doctrines of their religion to bear arms," but went on to state that such objectors should be assigned non-combatant duties "so far as practicable." The training scheme operated with some contention (only part of it concerning conscientious objection) from 1911 to 1929, being interrupted by World War I and severely curtailed after 1921.

Australia fought World War I without any form of conscription—the only belligerent to do so. Attempts by the government to introduce compulsory military service through referendums failed. Thus, the government avoided confrontation with potential conscripts who were opposed to the war on other than religious grounds.

In 1939 the government announced a new compulsory military training scheme. Trainees would be required to fight in defense of Australia and its overseas territories such as Papua, but not farther away. Combat in Europe, Africa, and the Far East was left to volunteers until 1943, when conscripts were made liable for service in a defined area of the Southwest Pacific.

The legislation relating to conscientious objection now took on added importance. As early as 1910 the definition of conscientious objection had been widened to refer simply to "conscientious beliefs." The Defense Act of 1939 spelled out clearly that the term applied "whether the beliefs are or are not of a religious character." This resolved the problems faced by secular pacifists and by objectors who belonged to other than sectarian peace churches. Thus, a major expansion of the grounds for conscientious objection had occurred with little public controversy.

During World War II out of more than 250,000 conscripts, some 2,791 sought exemption on grounds of conscience. Of these, 636 were found not to be genuine, 1,076 were directed to noncombat duties in the military, and 1,014 (all but 41 of whom performed specified civilian work) were exempted from military service.

The National Service scheme of 1951–1959 involved full-time military training, but not overseas service. Military operations during this period in Korea, Malaya, and Borneo were conducted by volunteer forces. Issues of conscientious objection were muted.

Australia's participation in the Vietnam War created the most serious difficulties. A selective, full-time military service scheme was introduced in 1964 with the clear intent that conscripts would be required to serve in overseas combat. This was a major departure from the Australian tradition of only volunteers fighting wars distant from Australia. Again, conscientious objector status was granted on either religious or secular grounds.

During the Vietnam era some 50,000 young men were called up, of whom 1,012 applied for conscientious objection status. Seventy-two percent were granted total exemption, 14 percent were exempted from combat duty only, and 137 individuals were refused exemption of any kind. These proportions were about the same as those of World War II. Even though the number of draft resisters was small, their political significance was great. Their detention in military prisons (until 1968) and the obvious sincerity of some of them aroused a measure of public sympathy. The detained COs became focal points of opposition to the war. Australia's involvement in the Vietnam War came to an end in 1972 and the National Service scheme was terminated by the Labor government elected that same year.

From 1965 onward claims for conscientious objection exemption were heard by magistrate courts and on occasion appeals reached the High Court. In the process certain issues were clarified: the depth and sincerity of conscientious beliefs, the compelling nature of an individual's conviction, the need for at least some measure of reason and logic in the beliefs concerned, the problem of advice given to those claiming exemption, the matter of claims for exemption by those already serving in the armed forces, among others.

The most difficult issue revolved around those conscientious objectors who opposed a particular war (specifically the Vietnam War) without being across-the-board pacifists. The reasons given included lack of a just cause and the manner in which hostilities were conducted. The High Court, while recognizing that an individual might have a conscientious objection to fighting in a particular war, rejected arguments that the existing legislation could be interpreted to cover selective conscientious objection. Attempts by the opposition Labor Party to amend the law to permit selective objection proved futile. In the public debate the government argued that conscientious objection to particular wars amounted simply to political opposition and was liable to abuse by "shirkers" and "draft dodgers."

After 1972 military service and conscientious objection remained off the political agenda for some years. In 1983, however, shortly after the election of the Hawke Labor government, a bill was introduced to incorporate selective conscientious objection in the National Service legislation. Though inoperative, such legislation would form the basis of any future military service scheme. The intent of the proposal was to initiate discussion in an atmosphere of calm prior to any acutal conflict. The grounds for exemption included the justness or otherwise of the war or campaign, the use of particular weapons, and the manner in which hostilities might be conducted.

The proposal was referred to a bipartisan committee of the parliament, which held hearings and issued its report in 1985. The conclusion was to recommend exemption from military service for any person "whose conscientious beliefs do not allow the person to participate in a particular war, or in particular war-like operations." Australia, the committee argued, should expand the rights of conscientious objectors even to the point of involving defense of the homeland.

In 1986 the government announced its acceptance of the main principles of the parliamentary committee. The government, however, did not follow up with proposed legislation. It appeared to be having second thoughts on allowing citizens to seek exemption from service in a particular war, especially given the strong opposition of the Defense Force, which stressed the practical difficulties of the principle of selective conscientious objection.

Nor was the government encouraged by an incident following the 1990 decision to send three naval ships to the Persian Gulf during the war there. One seaman went AWOL prior to sailing and made contact with an antiwar senator. Amid considerable publicity, the sailor voiced his political objection to the military buildup and criticized the motives of Australian and American leaders. The sailor's action, however, received little support from the general public and he was duly court-martialed.

It seemed unlikely that any government would enact provisions for selective conscientious objection. Nevertheless, in May 1991 the minister of defense announced that the government intended to introduce legislation to permit claims for exemption from particular wars or military operations. A year later, however, the legislation was indefinitely tabled. For the time being at least, Australia is not destined to be at the forefront of another expansion of the rights of conscientious objectors.

APPENDIX B

Bulgaria

Stephan E. Nikolov

"A woman who has not given birth is not a woman; a man who has not been a soldier is not a man." So goes a popular Bulgarian proverb. The general acceptance of military service in Bulgaria goes back a long way. Indeed, the Bulgarian army predates the Bulgarian state. A continental system of military conscription was adopted in 1878 shortly after Bulgaria obtained autonomy from the Ottoman Empire. Bulgaria became an independent state in 1908 and during the Balkan Wars of 1912 mass conscription was effectively imposed on the male youth population. In broad respects, this pattern of high military legitimacy has continued through the two world wars, the interwar period, the communist era, and into the present.

Following the communist takeover in 1946, the Bulgarian military was thoroughly Sovietized. No right of conscientious objection was allowed. As in other communist systems, the conscription was tempered, or perhaps better, corrupted, by privileged youths who were able to obtain more pleasant assignments and shorter terms of obligation. Even under the Stalinist regimes of Georgi Dimitrov and Tidor Zhikov, however the armed forces were among the most respected institutions in Bulgarian society. The generally high regard the military enjoys in Bulgaria continued into the post-Zhikov era that started in 1990. Public opinion surveys in 1991 showed that by far the most popular political personality to be Dobri Djurnov, an army general and minister of defense. There are, of course, class and regional differences. Support of the military system is highest in the lower social strata and in rural areas, and weakest among urban higher classes.

About 85 percent of the Bulgarian population is nominally Eastern Orthodox. The Bulgarian Orthodox Church, however, has never had as strong a grip on the populace as the national Orthodox churches have had in Serbia, Greece, Romania, Ukraine, and Russia. Only a fraction of the nominal membership are practising Orthodox. In any event, the Bulgarian Orthodox Church has no pacifist element.

On the contrary, Orthodox priests lead prayers for victory in battles, serve as chaplains in the military, and bless soldiers to fufill their duty to the Fatherland. Indeed, the church hierarchy is likely to define any delinquency from military service as a sin.

The population is about 10 percent Muslim (precise figures are in dispute), of whom about half are ethnic Turks and half Pomaks, ethnic Bulgarians whose ancestors converted to Islam. In general, the Muslims are viewed as a potential "fifth-column" by the military command. Muslim-minority soldiers are not allowed into the military academy and the officer corps is heavily imbued with anti-Turk and anti-Muslim sentiments. A crude attempt in the mid–1980s to give Bulgarian names to the Muslims caused a major upheaval in Bulgaria and subsequently caused many to seek refuge in Turkey. An unusual wave of military defections occurred during the late 1980s among ethnic Turkish soldiers who insisted on leaving for Turkey with their families. We have no data on these numbers, and this is a chapter that will have to be written by historians at a later time.

In practice, the state excludes Muslims from normal military service. Recruits from Muslim backgrounds (and others suspected of being unreliable) are assigned to construction battalions, *stroitelni voiski,* units very much like the Russian *stoybat* and the East German *Bausoldaten*. Non-Muslims suspected of political unreliability may also end up in the *stroitelni voiski*. (It is a historical irony that Tidor Zhikov was placed in one of these units in the thirties for his antiregime activities as a communist). These units are used for heavy labor and are either unarmed or trained with outdated, one-shot rifles.

Less than one-half of 1 percent of the Bulgarian population has a religious affiliation other than Bulgarian Orthodox or Islamic. Yet even the small number of Jehovah's Witnesses, Seventh-Day Adventists, and Pentecostals cause trouble for the system. During the first decades of the Bulgarian communist state, such individuals, especially Jehovah's Witnesses, were constantly surveilled by the security agency and persecuted as "American agents." Members of pacifist sects dared not resist conscription openly, but once in the service they sought to avoid carrying arms.

In the 1950s and 1960s radical religious objectors were punished by military courts and transferred to disciplinary regiments, where they were forced to do hard and often senseless work, such as carrying heavy stones from one place to another and then back again. By the 1970s an informal policy developed of assigning Jehovah's Witnesses the most menial and dirty work in a regular battalion, and effectively letting them avoid actual military training. It must be stressed that the numbers of these religious sectarians was always quite small.

Once the "velvet revolution" of the East Europe reached Bulgaria in 1990, military personnel policies began to change somewhat. Decree Number 126, passed in 1990, formally disbanded communist party control of the military, though the practical effects of this decree seemed to have been minor, at least during its first two years. Opposition leaders in the democratically elected parliament advocated a reduction in both military manpower and the length of military conscription. For the first time, there was even some discussion of moving toward a professional military. Yet, in reality, military reform was a low priority in postcommunist Bulgaria. Economic collapse dominated the public agenda.

As of early 1992 there was no serious discussion of genuine recognition of conscientious objection in Bulgaria. If such an event does come to pass, it is likely that Bulgaria will leap over the conventional stages of conscientious objection noted in the West. Secular and religious objection, that is, will be granted at the same time, if any conscientious objection is to be granted at all.

APPENDIX C

Greece

Dimitrios Smokovitis

Greece has had some form of military conscription since the early twentieth century. The country has fought in numerous wars in this century: the Balkan Wars, World War I, World War II, and a civil war in the late 1940s. Even in contemporary times, Greece has reasons to fear hostilities from its neighbors to the east and north. Thus, the principle of obligatory military service has strong roots in Greek history that are further strengthened by the country's geopolitical vulnerability.

Conscientious objection as an issue has only surfaced in Greece in recent years. Excepting monks and clergy of "recognized religions," all Greek males between the ages of eighteen and forty are liable for military service. Exemptions are granted only for physical and mental reasons. The numbers exempted on these grounds are small compared to other West European nations. Prior to 1977 there were absolutely no provisions for conscientious objection.

The only historically visible group of COs have been Jehovah's Witnesses, a sect comprising a fraction of 1 percent of the Greek population. A person refusing his military call-up could be sentenced to a maximum of five years in prison. To compound matters, multiple sentences were meted out to some objectors. That is, upon release from prison, an objector would be called up again and then sentenced once more for refusal to accept conscription. In this harsh manner, some Jehovah's Witnesses served sentences of ten, fifteen, or even twenty years. Although precise figures are not readily available, an informed estimate is that between three hundred and six hundred Jehovah's Witnesses were in jail at any one time in the period before 1977.

As amended in 1977, Law 731/77 allowed those objecting to military service on religious grounds to perform unarmed military service for four and a half years—double the term of the typical draftee. No provision was allowed for alternative service outside the military. Some number of Jehovah's Witnesses have taken this noncombatant option, but many have not. Those COs who can be transferred from military prisons to an agricultural prison are credited for two days off their sentences for each day's farm labor. As of 1992, almost all imprisoned COs, some four hundred, were still Jehovah's Witnesses.

The issue of conscientious objection took a more dramatic turn with the case of Michael Maragarakis. A young art teacher, Maragarakis refused to report for military service in December 1986. The significance of Maragarakis's action was that he based his objection to military service on nonreligious pacifist grounds. He offered to perform alternative civilian service, but refused to perform unarmed service in the military. After some media attention, Maragarakis was sentenced by a military court to four years in prison.

In February 1988, Maragarakis conducted the first of what would be several hunger strikes. These gained widespread attention both within Greece and in Western Europe. The government made some efforts to negotiate by promising to introduce legislation to allow for civilian alternative service. This had not come to pass as of 1992. Another ten or so secular conscientious objectors have appeared on the Greek scene following Maragarakis. After his release from prison, Maragarakis traveled widely in Europe, bringing further attention to the situation of the conscientious objection in Greece.

In 1988 the conscription law was modified again. Under the new terms nonreligious as well as religious reasons are acceptable for conscientious objector status. The CO must still enter the military to perform unarmed service. No civilian alternative service is allowed. The option of unarmed military service is still punitive in that the term of service remains twice that of the military conscript. In practice, informal means to handle conscientious objectors have developed within the Greek armed forces. Many COs are assigned work in military hospitals, where they effectively avoid handling weapons.

Another case that received international attention was that of Daniel Kokkalis, a Jehovah's Witness who claimed military exemption on the basis of being a religious minister of his denomination. The Athens Military Court decided that the Jehovah's Witnesses were not a "known religion," and therefore Kokkalis could not be exempted. Some thirty-one months into his sentence, Kokkalis was able to appeal to the Council of State, the highest administrative court in Greece. In October 1990 the court found for the defendant. Kokkalis was not released from prison, however, because the Council of State is technically not empowered to revoke penal decisions.

The situation in the early 1990s is as follows. Public opinion generally is not supportive of conscientious objection. Politicians seem to be of the opinion that a pro-CO position is not a vote getter. Yet there are undeniable pressures to conform to more accepted Western patterns of conscientious objection. In particular, resolutions of the Council of Europe, the European Parliament, and the Conference on Security and Cooperation in Europe have an effect on the political elite in Greece.

The future will most likely find some adjustments with Greece moving closer to Western European models. Some form of civilian alternative service is probable, with efforts to make it more commensurate in time with that of military conscription. Such an option might be particularly attractive to university youth.

Although the trend toward a more liberalized approach to conscientious objection will continue, Greece will probably remain for some years the European democracy with the most restrictive pattern of conscientious objection. The reality of Greece's strategic vulnerability will continue to constrain options for conscientious objection.

APPENDIX D

Italy

Marina Nuciari

Article 52 of the Italian Constitution enacted in 1945 states that "the defense of the Country is a sacred duty of the citizen" and "military service is compulsory within the limits and ways established by the law." In its original formulation, there was no provision for conscientious objection of any sort. But the constitution permitted subsequent legislation to define how the military obligation could be fulfilled and modified in light of societal changes.

Legislation passed in 1950 allowed for the possibility of service in unarmed military roles. A 1966 law extended the exemption from direct military service to young men who had performed a civilian service in a developing country. The effects of this law were practically nil, however, as only a maximum of one hundred permissions per year could be granted.

Watershed legislation passed in 1972 brought major changes in the state's treatment of conscientious objection. The 1972 law recognized the right to object to military service for those "who declare to be against in every circumstance a personal use of arms for conscience reasons, pertaining to a general conception of life based on deep religious or philosophical or moral beliefs." Thus, both religious and secular, but not political, motives became grounds for conscientious objection in Italy.

The 1972 law also stipulated that recognized objectors could perform alternative civilian service. Such service was to be for a period eight months longer than the regular conscripted military service: twenty months instead of twelve months. The civilian service could be performed within the areas of social services, civil protection, education, and environmental work. In case of war, objectors could be assigned to nonarmed service, even if this might involve possible physical risk. In a precedent-making decision, the Constitutional Court in July 1989 ruled that the length of the alternative civilian service and military service would be the same.

Prior to 1972 the number of COs was negligible and almost entirely limited to Jehovah's Witnesses, a marginal group in Italian society. Most of these sectarian objectors were imprisoned, though undoubtedly some took the unarmed military option available during the 1950s and 1960s.

Since 1972 the number of conscientious objector applications has risen dramatically: two hundred in 1973, one thousand in 1977, four thousand in 1980, six thousand in 1988, and close to fourteen thousand in 1989. The sharp increase in 1989 reflects the court decision to equalize the time commitment of both civilian and military service. Virtually all applications are accepted, though there is some question as to whether the Italian system is creating enough civilian service positions to meet the increased number of conscientious objectors.

Available data show that conscientious objectors tend to be better educated, come from higher socioeconomic backgrounds, and are more likely to be Northerners than are non-COs. A discernible trend toward a somewhat greater class spread is evident in the most recent years.

We also have survey data on the important question of the motives of the conscientious objectors. The reasons given were: philosophical or humanitarian, 38 percent; religious, 32 percent; military avoidance, 14 percent; political, 14 percent; and other, 2 percent. Inasmuch as military avoidance and political reasons are precluded as a legitimate basis for conscientious objection, we can only surmise that the COs presented more acceptable philosophical or religious grounds in their applications.

The secularization of conscience thesis is clearly supported in the Italian case. But the phenomenon needs a closer examination as well. As Guido Sertorio has suggested, what we are witnessing is not so much a growth in "active pacifism," as a kind of "passive pacifism." This is the view that military service is a waste of time for the individual because war is impractical or even impossible. When an equitable choice is given between civilian and military service, civilian service will be in the ascendancy. Italy may be on the verge of a boom in alternative civilian service through the mechanism of conscientious objection.

APPENDIX E

The Netherlands

J. G. van de Vijver

With a long tradition of political freedom and religious liberty, the Dutch government has recognized conscientious objection for a considerable period. But the Netherlands has pursued a relatively moderate policy in the twentieth century, and the issue continues to present some political problems.

Early History

As early as the sixteenth century, Dutch rulers tolerated refusal by non-resistant religious pacifists to perform military service. The Mennonites of Middleburg received such exemption in 1577. In 1834 a small communitarian pacifist sect of *Nieuwlichters* (''New Lighters'') persuaded the House of Orange to allow conscripted members, who were primarily from the poorer class and could not afford to hire substitutes, to perform noncombatant duties when conscripted.

The issue of modern conscientious objection in Holland began to emerge in 1898, when the old system of periodic conscription that permitted draftees to purchase substitutes was replaced by a new continuous system of conscription that held all conscripts to personal military service. Soon an ''antimilitarist'' movement developed. Composed mainly of left-wing socialists and anarchists, its members began to urge and sometimes practice draft refusal as part of their campaign to abolish war. In the same period, Dutch Tolstoyans, calling themselves Christian Anarchists, advocated draft refusal as well as total nonviolence. Some twenty cases of draft refusal by socialist or Tolstoyan objectors were reported between 1896 and 1914, with almost all of the men receiving sentences of about six months in prison. During World War I, about five hundred persons refused to serve when neutral Holland mobilized its armed forces. Most of these objectors were socialists and political or religious anarchists.

Conscientious objection was first officially recognized by the Dutch government in 1917 as a result of increasing numbers of draft refusers, the promulgation of a manifesto initiated by progressive clergy, and a desire by the government to avoid persecution of religious minorities. On November 9, 1917, the minister of war issued an army order allowing religious objectors who were opposed to killing human beings under any circumstances the right to appeal for official recognition as conscientious objectors after they were drafted into the army. The minister of war appointed a secret advisory commission, which examined claimants on their sincerity. Recognized COs were required to serve in the military, indeed to accept voluntarily an extra year of service, but they were assigned to noncombatant duties. There was no provision for civilian alternative service. Of the several hundred objectors, only about 140 applied for noncombatant service, and of these only about a dozen were accorded recognition.

Sympathy for sincere objectors grew in the wake of World War I, and, in 1922, the Constitution was modified to authorize statutory exemption for conscripts or those already in the military who had "serious conscientious objections." As a result of much public pressure, particularly galvanized by sympathy for one imprisoned CO who maintained a long hunger strike, the parliament in July 1923 adopted the Law on Refusal of Military Service (*Dienstweigeringswet*). This statute, which went into effect on June 1, 1924, expanded the recognition of conscientious objectors to those who on moral or religious (though not political) grounds were opposed to killing human beings in any circumstances. Dominated by religious parties, the government held COs to a strict interpretation of the biblical commandment "Thou shalt not kill."

The 1924 law offered the first alternative civilian service in the Netherlands. Once again COs were allowed to serve an extra six months in noncombatant military service. But now they were given a choice of performing alternative civilian service that would last a year longer than the military service of regular conscripts. Refusal to cooperate with these provisions was a criminal offense warranting a sentence of up to one year in prison. This remained the basic law regarding conscientious objection until 1964 (except for the period of German occupation, 1940–1945, when the military service law was in abeyance).

Conscription for overseas service increased the problem of conscientious objection. Article 35 of the Constitution had preserved the right of the citizen to be free from compulsory military service overseas. However, during World War II the exiled government in London claimed jurisdiction over Dutch subjects living in areas under allied control, and it revoked Article 35 in order to be free to send its forces overseas. With the liberation of the Netherlands in early 1945, the government reinstituted the Military Service Act to reestablish control of the Dutch colonial empire in Southeast Asia. Thousands of Dutch conscripts, including the small number of complete pacifists, evaded or refused service or deserted in protest, and the government in 1946 repealed the short-lived provision for compulsory overseas military service.

Modern Liberalization and Secularization

Since the mid–1960s there have been two major liberalizations of the CO provisions in the Netherlands, and these accepted a secular basis for conscientious objection. In 1964, after more than a dozen years in which changes were under consideration, the parliament adopted a Law on Conscientious Objection to Military Service (*Wet Gewetensbezwaren Militaire Dienst*), which in essence recognized sincere secular as well as religious objection. The law widened acceptable dissent from opposition to "the killing of fellow human beings" to religious or moral convictions that prohibited the objector "from taking part in any act of war." Thus, COs no longer had to oppose any taking of human life, even in individual self-defense; they had instead only to oppose military violence, albeit all, not selective, military violence and war. In the parliamentary debates of 1962 that led to the 1964 act, theological issues had virtually disappeared from the discussion, replaced in the majority view by concerns of balancing the secular interests of the individual with those of society.

Subsequently, in the late 1960s and early 1970s, the Dutch government came under pressure for further liberalization of its CO policies, largely because of the more widespread introduction of nuclear weapons by the NATO forces. An Inter-church Peace Council proposed making the legal definition simply "insurmountable conscientious objections to personally performing military service." A number of Dutch Reformed churches appealed for amendments to recognize conscientious objection against the use of nuclear weapons and other weapons of mass destruction. The movement was supported by other groups, including the *Verening Dienstweig-eraars*, a trade union established in 1972 for persons who refused to perform their military service. The issue came to a head in 1974, triggered particularly by the case of a principled young objector, who, opposed to NATO's nuclear war policy, had failed to qualify under existing law and was sentenced to twenty-one months in prison. A number of Christian pacifists formed a group, "Church and Peace," to work for and with conscientious objectors. The state secretary of defense, a socialist, visited the young draft refuser in prison, and the progressive cabinet supported amending the military service law.

A new statute, which went into effect in 1978, broadened acceptance of conscientious objection to include sincere opposition to guarding or employing nuclear weapons or any other aspect of military force to which an individual had serious conscientious objections. In the wording of the new law, such objection was defined as "insurmountable conscientious objection to personally performing military service in connection with the use of *means of force* [by] . . . the Dutch armed forces" (emphasis added). Implementation of the law made it clear that conscientious objections no longer needed to stem from religious or moral sources. Indeed, any reference to religion was taken out of the statute, which accepted sincere politically motivated objection as well as selective objection, such as to the use of nuclear weapons.

The continuing debate on this issue in the Netherlands involves how to determine the sincerity of COs and what to do with absolutists (or "total objectors") who refuse any cooperation with the conscription system. Currently, once a young man is drafted and files a claim as a CO, an investigating committee and an appointed psychiatrist question him and his family, neighbors, and others to determine the sincerity of his beliefs and the consistency of his behavior. Since 1964 those whose claim is rejected have been permitted to appeal to an administrative judge (rather than a military agency). But some Dutch legal scholars and others have advocated abolishing this process and, as in the Federal Republic of Germany, allowing a claimant's acceptance of a longer term of alternative civilian service to be the implicit validation of his sincerity.

As for absolutists, in the 1980s a dozen or so annually were sentenced to a year in prison for refusing any cooperation with the conscription system. From 1987 to 1992 the government considered a bill that would enable civilian criminal judges to *sentence* such absolutists to alternative service. However, this bill was withdrawn in 1992 because the number of new absolutist cases had declined to only one or two a year and military criminal law was changed to improve the handling of such cases.

The Changing Nature of Objection

The Dutch pattern resembles that of most other countries in Northwestern Europe. There has been a dramatic increase in the number of COs since the late 1960s. The annual number of COs recognized in the Netherlands grew from some 200 a year in the 1950s and early 1960s to 700 a year in the late 1960s. In the early 1970s, it soared to 2,000 or 3,000 a year, where it has remained ever since. In 1989, for example, 2,900 persons were granted CO status out of a conscript class of 45,000 which in turn was drawn from some 120,000 young men liable for the draft. The religious basis for the beliefs of those seeking to become COs has become relatively less important as draft refusers have reflected the secularizing trend that has characterized this phenomenon in the West. Of the 2,705 persons who filed claims for CO status in 1988, for example, only 406 mentioned that they were religious.

In contrast, among the absolutists who refuse to perform either military or civilian alternative service, the majority are religious. A few are Mennonites, but most are Jehovah's Witnesses. Constituting approximately 150 objectors a year, the Jehovah's Witnesses in Holland, as elsewhere, refuse to apply for CO status or to recognize the authority of the conscription system. Viewing the Witnesses as a small, isolated, and recalcitrant religious group, the government has, since 1974, granted them annual deferments, amounting to an exemption. Other absolutists, some political, some religious, and numbering about ten annually through the 1980s, were sentenced by military judges to a year in prison, which in practice has meant about nine months' incarceration.

The End of Noncombatant Military Service

In 1978, the Dutch government terminated the provision that had allowed COs to agree to non-combatant service in the military. Instead, the legislators made civilian alternative service the only option for recognized COs. The option of noncombatant military service (or what in Holland was called "partial conscientious objection") had had a long history in the Netherlands, as in most other countries that recognized conscientious objectors. From 1917 to 1924, this was the only form of objection recognized in the Netherlands, and such COs were kept in the military for an extra year. Under the 1924 law, which also recognized civilian alternative service, the "partial COs" who agreed to noncombatant military duty served half a year longer than other conscripts, but six months less than alternative civilian servers. In 1964 the terms of service between the partial COs and the regular conscripts had been equalized.

The Dutch government's 1978 decision to eliminate the option of noncombatant military service for COs was due to several factors. One was that in the 1970s only about 6 percent of the COs choose that option. More important, there was a dramatic increase in the number of conscripts opposed to having any relationship with nuclear weapons, and there was considerable public support for that position (53 percent in 1980). Faced with growing numbers of anti-nuclear COs, the military decided that it could not have two categories of servicepeople, those who would and those who would not carry out all tasks assigned to them, including the guarding of nuclear weapons. Thus the Dutch ended noncombatant military service for COs, and also accepted opposition to nuclear warfare as a basis for refusal to perform military service. At the same time, the government accepted the fact that service people already in uniform could become conscientious objectors. Such objectors in the military would be shifted to alternative civilian service.

Civilian Alternative Service

The duration of alternative civilian service in the Netherlands has always been longer than that of military service, from an extra year under the 1924 law to an extra half-year under the 1964 law. Under the present law, it is one-quarter longer than that of military service. In 1992 it is sixteen months, compared to twelve months of military service for a regular conscript.

From 1924 to 1938 COs performed their alternative service "according to their abilities" in government agencies, such as the Forestry Commission, Inland Revenue, Central Statistical Office, and electrical generating plants. In the 1930s high civilian unemployment combined with public protests that the alternative service was too easy led the government to direct COs to more strenuous and less competitive work, such as in forestry, agriculture, and psychiatric hospitals. Since 1953 alternative service has been broadened to include care for the elderly, disabled, and the ill, as well as work in organizations or institutions engaged in welfare, education, cultural activities environmental preservation, Third World assistance, and work for peace. In 1973 two recognized COs refused their civilian service because it was directed by the Ministry of Defense. When they were supported by numerous groups, the government in 1975 shifted responsibility for supervising alternative service to the Ministry for Social Affairs and Employment.

Conclusion

The Netherlands, like much of the West, has moved from acceptance of only religious objectors to recognition of conscientious objection on any sincerely held basis, secular or religious. Indeed, the majority of COs at present are admittedly not religiously motivated. The Dutch parliament has eliminated noncombatant military service for COs, and the government directs all recognized COs into civilian alternative service. Although there is considerable acceptance of conscientious objectors, especially antinuclear objectors, the Netherlands takes a stricter position than Denmark or the Federal Republic of Germany in regard to proof of the sincerity of COs and to the burden imposed on those who choose civilian alternative service.

Notes

1.
The Secularization of Conscience

1. See the article in this volume by Jürgen Kulhmann and Ekkehard Lippert on the Federal Republic of Germany. See also Craig R. Whitney, "Cold War Past, Germans Ask Why Army Is Still Necessary," *New York Times,* 23 June 1992, Al, which gives figures on skyrocketing CO rates in post–Cold War Germany; R. McCartney, "West German Conscientious Objectors Now Legion," *Washington Post,* 11 Oct. 1988, A12, A14; Joe Gray Taylor, Jr., "The *Bundeswehr* and German Society," *Parameters: Journal of the U.S. Army War College* 13 (September 1983): 68–76. The situation in Germany was exacerbated during the Persian Gulf War when in January 1991 alone, 7,000 German Army reservists applied for conscientious objector status (more than applied during all of 1990) to avoid possible service in the Middle East. See Stephen Kinzler, "Gulf War Sets Off Crisis for Germans," *New York Times,* 17, Feb. 1991. Marc Fisher, "More Germans File as Objectors," *Washington Post,* 6, Feb. 1991, A23, reported that in January 23,197 soldiers and reservists in the German Army had claimed conscientious objector status.

2. See the articles in this volume by Anton Bebler on Eastern Europe, Wilfried von Bredow on East Germany, Karl Haltiner on Switzerland, Annette Seegers on South Africa, and Yoram Peri on Israel. The most recent published survey is Amnesty International, *Conscientious Objection to Military Service* (London: Amnesty International, 1991), a 55-page pamphlet published in January 1991 (AI Index POL 31/01/91). A sampling of material from CO and draft resistance organizations in various countries is contained in an annual bulletin produced by the European Bureau for Conscientious Objection, Brussels, Belgium, and DFG-VK, Bonn, Germany; the latest edition is *The Right to Refuse to Kill* (March 1991).

3. Resolution adopted on June 29, 1990 at the Meeting of the Conference on the Human Dimension of the Conference on Security and Cooperation in Europe (CSCE), Copenhagen, Denmark.

4. In 1972, for every hundred young Americans inducted into the armed forces, 131 were exempted as conscientious objectors. U.S. Selective Service System, *Semiannual Report of the Director of Selective Service for the period January 1 to June 30, 1973* (Washington, D.C.: Government Printing Office, 1973), 55; see also chapter 2 in this volume by John Whiteclay Chambers II on the United States.

5. Figures vary widely, particularly because many of the CO claims were handled at the local unit level and did not reach the top levels of each military service in Washington. Among the CO organizations, the National Interreligious Service Board for Conscientious Objectors (NISBCO) in Washington, D.C., concluded that even though their cases were not widely reported, as many as fifteen hundred to two thousand military members had applied for discharge as COs. See "Military COs' Catch–22 Continues," NISBCO, *The Reporter for Conscience' Sake* 48 (May 1991): 1. For additional information on this subject, see the essay on the United States in this volume by John Whiteclay Chambers II. For press accounts, see David Gonzalez, "Some in Military Now Resist Combat," *New York Times,* 26, Nov. 1990, A7; Katherine Bishop, "Turning against the Military Life They Once Chose," ibid., 14, Jan. 1991, A5, A12; Marc Fisher, "The Army's Conscientious Question," *Washington Post,* 9, Feb. 1991, D1. The Defense Department reported that between August 1990 and September 1991, some 567 military personnel filed for CO status. Of those, 270 were approved and 203 were denied. Nearly one hundred refused to report to their units and faced charges. Karen M. Thomas, "For Military Objectors, No Easy Way Out," *Chicago Tribune,* 8, Mar. 1992, A6.

6. More than seventy-five servicemen and -women claiming conscientious objector status had been incarcerated primarily at the Marine facility at Camp Lejeune, N. C., but a few had been held at Army bases at Fort Lewis, Wash., and Fort Sill, Okla. See Michael Marsh, "Mistreated COs Prompt Movement for Change," War Resisters League, *The Non-violent Activist* 9 (March 1992): 13–14; Peter Applebome, "Epilogue to the Gulf War: 25 Marines Face Prison," *New York Times,* 3, May 1991, A14; David Stoler, "Lejeune COs Face Courts-Martial," *CCCO News Notes* 43 (Spring 1991): 1. With a change of Marine commandants, many of the Marine COs held in the brig at Camp Lejeune were released on six months clemency review, while others had their sentences reduced from thirty to fifteen months. See "Most COs Released from Prison at Camp Lejeune," NISBCO, *The Reporter for Conscience' Sake* 48 (October–November 1991): 7. As of February 1992, the Marine Corps had convicted under court-martial forty-six COs of whom fourteen were active duty personnel and twenty-two reservists. USMC, personal communication to the editors of this volume, February 1992.

7. Three cities in California—San Francisco, Berkeley, and Oakland—adopted ordinances in January 1991 declaring sanctuary for COs; CCCO-Western Region, with headquarters in San Francisco, *The Objector: Journal of Draft and Military Information* 11 (January–February 1991): 5. In addition, a number of churches in Atlanta, Boston, New York City, the San Francisco Bay Area, and Seattle offered sanctuary to military personnel refusing deployment to the Persian Gulf. Laurie Goodstein, "Churches Give Resisters Shelter from War's Storm," *Washington Post,* 27, Feb. 1991, A3.

8. There have, however, been studies of pacifism or draft resistance in certain wars or particular countries that include information on conscientious objectors. For an indispensable historical treatment of sectarian and non-sectarian pacifists up to World War I, see three books by Peter Brock, *Freedom from Violence: Sectarian Nonresistance from the Middle Ages to the Great War* (Toronto: University of Toronto Press, 1991); *Freedom from War: Nonsectarian Pacifism, 1814–1914* (Toronto: University of Toronto Press, 1991); and *Pacifism in the United States: From the Colonial Era to the First World War* (Princeton: Princeton University Press, 1968). Other studies include Charles Chatfield, *The American Peace Movement: Ideals and Political Activism* (New York: Twayne, 1992); Charles DeBenedetti with Charles Chatfield, *An American Ordeal: The Antiwar Movement of the Vietnam Era* (Syracuse, N.Y.: Syracuse University Press, 1990); Patricia McNeal, *Harder than War: Catholic Peacemaking in Twentieth-Century America* (New Brunswick, N.J.: Rutgers University Press, 1992); David Cortright and Max Watts, *Left Face: Soldier Unions*

and Resistance Movements in Modern Armies (Westport, Conn.: Greenwood Press, 1991); Cynthia Eller, *Conscientious Objectors and the Second World War: Moral and Religious Arguments in Support of Pacifism* (New York: Praeger, 1991); Lawrence M. Baskir and William A. Strauss, *Chance and Circumstance: The Draft, the War, and the Vietnam Generation* (New York: Knopf, 1978); Stephen M. Kohn, *Jailed for Peace: The History of American Draft Law Violators, 1958–1985* (New York: Praeger, 1986); Sandi E. Cooper, *Patriotic Pacifism: Waging War in Europe, 1815–1914* (New York: Oxford University Press, 1991); Caroline Moorehead, *Troublesome People: Enemies of War, 1916–1986* (London: Hamish Hamilton, 1986); Richard Taylor and Nigel Young, eds., *Campaigns for Peace: British Peace Movements in the Twentieth Century* (Manchester: Manchester University Press, 1987); Nigel Young, "War Resistance, State and Society," in *War, State and Society,* ed. Martin Shaw (London: Macmillan, 1984); Martin Ceadel, *Pacifism in Britain, 1914–1945: The Defining of a Faith* (Oxford: Oxford University Press, 1980); Lawrence S. Wittner, *Rebels against War: The American Peace Movement, 1933–1983* (Philadelphia: Temple University Press, 1984); David S. Surrey, *Choice of Conscience: The Vietnam Era Military and Draft Resisters in Canada* (New York: Praeger, 1982); Rachel Barber, *Conscience, Government and War: Conscientious Objection in Great Britain, 1939–1945* (London: Routledge & Kegan Paul, 1982); Charles DeBenedetti, *The Peace Reform in American History* (Bloomington: Indiana University Press, 1980); Michael Ferber and Staughton Lynd, *The Resistance* (Boston: Beacon Press, 1971); Willard Gaylin, *In the Service of Their Country: War Resisters in Prison* (New York: Viking Press, 1970); John Rae, *Conscience and Politics: The British Government and Conscientious Objectors to Military Service, 1916–1919* (Oxford: Oxford University Press, 1970); Mulford Q. Sibley and Philip E. Jacob, *Conscription of Conscience: The American State and the Conscientious Objector, 1940–1947* (Ithaca: Cornell University Press, 1952); Edward Needles Wright, *Conscientious Objectors in the Civil War* (Philadelphia: University of Pennsylvania Press, 1931); and Norman Thomas, *The Conscientious Objector in America* (New York: B. W. Huebsch, 1923). Lillian Schlissel, ed., *Conscience in America: A Documentary History of Conscientious Objection in America, 1757–1967* (New York: E. P. Dutton, 1968), is a useful collection of documents.

Official accounts include U.S. Selective Service System, *Conscientious Objection,* Special Monograph no. 11, 2 vols. (Washington, D.C.: Government Printing Office, 1950); Walter Guest Kellogg, *The Conscientious Objector* (New York: Boni and Liveright, 1919; reprint, New York: Garland Publishing, 1972).

Notable for being one of the few treatments of conscientious objection from a military sociology standpoint as well as for its insights is Gwyn Martin Edmonds, *Armed Services and Society* (Leicester: Leicester University Press, 1988), 136–147. A study of the social psychology of conscientious objection based on interviews with Israeli COs 1982 to 1985 is Ruth Linn, *Not Shooting and Not Crying: Psychological Inquiry into Moral Disobedience* (Westport, Conn.: Greenwood Press, 1989).

9. Existing comparative literature is confined to compilations of statutes, incidence of conscientious objection, and public opinion survey data. See François Godet, "L'Objection de Conscience," *Revue de droit militaire et de droit de la guerre* 29 (1990): 13, reports on conscientious objection in twelve nations compiled in 1987 by the International Society for Military Law and the Law of War, Brussels, Belgium; Asbjorn Eide and Chama Mubanga-Chipoya, eds., *Conscientious Objection to Military Service; A United Nations Report Prepared in Pursuance of Resolutions 14 (XXXIV) and 1982/30* of the UNESCO Commission on Human Rights, Subcommission on Prevention of Discrimination and Protection of Minorities, *United Nations Document E.CN.4/Sub.2/1983/30* (New York: United Nations, 1988); and Devi Prasad and Tony Smythe, eds., *Conscription: A World Survey: Compulsory Military Service and Resistance to It* (London: War Resisters International, 1968). For CO provisions,

see the listing in Amnesty International, *Conscientious Objection to Military Service*, App.; for the means of raising armies, see the annual surveys, of which the most recent is *The Military Balance, 1990–91* (London: International Institute for Strategic Studies, 1990), which shows eighty countries that rely on some form of military conscription. One early attempt at comparative analysis was Edward R. Cain, "Conscientious Objection in France, Britain, and the United States," *Comparative Politics* 2 (January 1970): 275–308.

10. For the literature on selective conscientious objection, see Michael F. Noone, Jr., ed., *Selective Conscientious Objection: Accommodating Conscience and Security* (Boulder, Colo.: Westview Press, 1989); and Ralph Potter, "Conscientious Objection to Particular Wars," in *Religion and the Public Order,* ed. Donald A. Giannella (Ithaca, N.Y.: Cornell University Press, 1974), 44–94; Kent Greenwalt, "All or Nothing at All: The Defeat of Selective Conscientious Objection," in *The Supreme Court Review,* ed. Philip B. Kurland (Chicago: University of Chicago Press, 1971), 31–94; James Finn, ed., *A Conflict of Loyalties: The Case for Selective Conscientious Objection* (New York: Pegasus, 1968). On discretionary objection and the issues raised by nuclear weapons, see, for example, Mary Eileen E. McGrath, "Nuclear Weapons: A Crisis of Conscience," *Military Law Review* 107 (Winter 1985): 191–253; and James L. Carney, "Is it Ever Moral to Push the Button?" *Parameters: Journal of the U.S. Army War College* 18 (March 1988): 73–87.

11. Bonni McKeown, *The Peaceful Patriot* (Capon Springs, W.Va.: Peaceful Patriot Press, 1987), the story of Thomas Bennett, medic in B Company, 1st regiment, 14th Infantry Division, who was killed on Chu Pa Mountain in Vietnam in February 1969 and received posthumously the Congressional Medal of Honor.

12. This is not a hypothetical case; see George Lardner, Jr., "Draft Dodging Rises Dramatically in Soviet Union," *Washington Post,* 3, Mar. 1991, A23.

13. Charles Eric Lincoln, *The Black Muslims in America,* rev. ed. (Boston: Beacon, 1973), 205–6. On refusal by Black Muslim service people to deploy in the Persian Gulf, see "Navy Orders Trial for 2," *Boston Globe,* 30 Mar., 1991, 6; "Amidst Controversy over Military Treatment of Muslims: Charges against Sailors Dropped," *Reporter for Conscience' Sake* 48 (April 1991): 7; El Hajj Mauri' Saalakhan, "The U.S. Military and [Muslim] Prisoners of Conscience," Ibid. 48 (August 1991): 5. Of the forty-six Marine COs court-martialed during the Persian Gulf War, twenty-four were black, and two of these were Black Muslims. USMC personal communication to the editors, February 1992. For more on this issue, see the essay in this volume by John H. Stanfield II.

14. Amnesty International, *Conscientious Objection to Military Service,* 2.

15. A general overview of concepts of nonviolence in the major religious traditions may be found in John Ferguson, *War and Peace in the World's Religions* (New York: Oxford University Press, 1978).

16. David S. Ruegg, "Ahimsa and Vegetarianism in the History of Buddhism," in *Buddhist Studies in Honour of Walpola Rahula,* ed. Somaratna Balasooriya et al. (London, 1980); and Padmanabh S. Jaini, *The Jaina Path of Purification* (Berkeley: University of California Press, 1979). For the Gandhian approach, see Joan Bondurant, *Conquest of Violence: The Gandhian Philosophy of Conflict* (Princeton: Princeton University Press, 1958).

17. On Islam, see James Turner Johnson and John Kelsay, eds., *Cross, Crescent, and Sword: The Justification and Limitation of War in Western and Islamic Tradition* (Westport, Conn.: Greenwood Press, 1990); Majid Khadduri, *War and Peace in the Law of Islam* (Baltimore: The Johns Hopkins University Press, 1955); Eric Schroeder, *Muhammad's People* (Portland, Maine, 1955); and H. A. R. Gibb and J. H. Kramers, *Shorter Encyclopedia of Islam* (Ithaca, N. Y.: Cornell University Press, 1953), 89, 230.

18. During the Vietnam War, the Boston rabbinical court, one of the most liberal of the Orthodox Judaic courts in the United States, struggled to work the Jewish legal tradition

regarding military service and war into something resembling pacifism and conscientious objection. See, for example, Everett E. Gendler, "War and the Jewish Tradition," in *A Conflict of Loyalties: The Case for Selective Conscientious Objection,* ed. James Finn (New York: Pegasus, 1968), 78–102; Julius Kravetz, "Some Cautionary Remarks," Central Conference of American Rabbis, *CCAR Journal* 15 (January 1968): 78–79. In regard to nonviolence and the Jewish tradition, see D. Martin Dakin, *Peace and Brotherhood in the Old Testament* (London, 1956); Nathum N. Glatzer, "The Concept of Peace in Classical Judaism," in his *Essays in Jewish Thought* (University, Ala.: University of Alabama Press, 1978); and André Neher, "Rabbinic Adumbrations of Non-Violence," in *Rationalism, Judaism, and Universalism,* ed. Raphael Loewe (London, 1966).

19. The standard work is Roland H. Bainton, *Christian Attitudes toward War and Peace: A Historical Survey and Critical Re-evaluation* (Nashville, Tenn.: Abingdon Press, 1960); see also Paul Ramsey, *War and the Christian Conscience* (Durham, N.C.: Duke University Press, 1961); John Courtney Murray, *Morality and Modern War* (New York: Council on Religion and International Affairs, 1959); Geoffrey Nuttal, *Christian Pacifism in History* (Oxford: Oxford University Press, 1958); and the discussion of nonviolence in the field of Christian ethics in James F. Childress, *Moral Responsibility in Conflicts* (Baton Rouge, La.: Louisiana State University Press, 1982). Ronald G. Musto, *The Catholic Peace Tradition* (Maryknoll, N.Y.: Orbis Books, 1986) examines the Roman Catholic experience, as does, in a broader context, Gordon C. Zahn, *War Conscience and Dissent* (New York: Hawthorne Books, 1967). Of course, there is also a literature within Christianity endorsing armed force when necessary against evil; the modern classic is Reinhold Niebuhr, *Moral Man and Immoral Society: A Study of Ethics and Politics* (New York: Macmillan, 1932); for a recent defense within the U.S. military, see Donald L. Davidson, "Modern War and the Christian Conscience," *Military Chaplain's Review* (May 1990): 35–42. See also the citations to the "just war" doctrine in n. 21.

20. Maximilian was later canonized. See Herbert Musurillo, ed., *The Acts of the Christian Martyrs* (Oxford: Oxford University Press, 1972), 244–48; Brock, *Freedom from Violence,* 6; and, more generally, J. Helgeland, R. J. Daly, and J. P. Burns, *Christians and the Military: The Early Experience* (Philadelphia: Fortress Press, 1985).

21. On "just war" doctrine, see James Turner Johnson, *Can Modern War Be Just?* (New Haven, Conn.: Yale University Press, 1984); and *Just War Tradition and the Restraint of War: A Moral and Historical Inquiry* (Princeton: Princeton University Press, 1981); Michael Walzer, *Just and Unjust Wars, A Moral Argument with Historical Illustrations* (New York: Basic Books, 1977); Frederick H. Russell, *The Just War in the Middle Ages* (Cambridge: Cambridge University Press, 1975). See also the National Council of Catholic Bishops, *The Challenge of Peace: God's Promise and Our Response, A Pastoral Letter on War and Peace* (Washington, D.C.: United States Catholic Conference, 1983); and the debate it engendered, including Robert Markus, "Saint Augustine's Views on the 'Just War,' " *Studies in Church History* 20 (1983): 1–13; and Charles J. Reid, Jr., ed., *Peace in a Nuclear Age: The Bishops' Pastoral Letter in Perspective* (Washington, D.C.: The Catholic University of America Press, 1986). On the application of just-war theory to the Persian Gulf War, see David Decosse, ed., *But Was It Just? Reflections on the Morality of the Persian Gulf War* (Garden City, N.Y.: Doubleday, 1992).

22. Strictly speaking, the Orthodox Church theology does not accept "just war." Rather, all war is evil, but sometimes a lesser evil must be chosen to resist a greater evil. For a clear exposition of this view see Alexander F. Webster, "The Pacifist Option: An Eastern Orthodox Moral Perspective on War in the Nuclear Age" (Ph.D. diss., University of Pittsburgh, 1988). See also Lawrence Uzzell, "Rumors of Wars in the NCC," *American Orthodoxy* 1 (Fall 1991): 7–9. For a contrary view, see Stanley S. Harakas, "No 'Rumors of

Wars' in the Greek Fathers,'' ibid. 1 (Winter 1992): 8–9, who holds that there can be no just war in Christian Orthodoxy. This is a shift from Harakas's earlier view of the legitimacy of just war. See his "The Morality of War," in *Orthodox Synthesis,* ed. Joseph J. Allen (Crestwood, N.Y.: Vladimir's Seminary Press, 1981), 67–96.

23. For a fuller treatment of early sectarian pacifism in Christianity, see Brock, *Freedom from Violence,* 1–120. Even before the Reformation, the Waldenses in the twelfth century in Southern France and Northern Italy were the first significant group of sectarian pacifists; however, the nonviolence of Waldensianism had waned by the sixteenth century. The rebirth of nonresistance occurred in Zurich in the 1520s with the emergence of the Brethren, who later spread into Northern and Eastern Europe, subsequently joined in their nonresistant pacifism by the Anabaptists, who were also part of the Radical Reformation. Among the various groups were sects of Brethren as well as Hutterites and Mennonites.

24. James M. Stayer, *Anabaptists and the Sword,* 2nd ed. (Lawrence, Kans.: Coronado Press, 1976); and George H. Williams, *The Radical Reformation* (Philadelphia: Westminster Press, 1962); see also the excellent summary in Brock, *Pacifism in the United States,* 3–8. A different emphasis is contained in Norman Cohn, *The Pursuit of the Millennium: Revolutionary Millenarians and Mystical Anarchists of the Middle Ages,* rev. and expanded ed. (New York: Oxford University Press, 1970), 250–80.

25. Cornelius J. Dyck, ed., *An Introduction to Mennonite History: A Popular History of the Anabaptists and the Mennonites* (Scottdale, Pa.: Herald Press, 1981).

26. Richard K. MacMaster, *Land, Piety, Peoplehood: The Establishment of Mennonite Communities in America, 1683–1790,* vol. 1 of *The Mennonite Experience in America* (Scottdale, Pa.: Herald Press, 1985); see also Wilbur J. Bender, "Pacifism among the Mennonites, Amish Mennonites and Schwenkfelders of Pennsylvania to 1783," *Mennonite Quarterly Review* 1 (July 1927): 29–32.

27. Theron F. Schlabach, *Peace, Faith, Nation: Mennonites and Amish in Nineteenth-Century America,* in *The Mennonite Experience in America* (Scottdale, Pa.: Herald Press, 1988), 2:230–94.

28. Rufus D. Bowman, *The Church of the Brethren and War, 1708–1941* (Elgin, Ill.: Brethren Publishing House, 1944); see also Brock, *Pacifism in the United States,* 159–92.

29. Hugh Barbour and J. William Frost, *The Quakers* (New York: Greenwood Press, 1988); Peter Brock, *The Quaker Peace Testimony, 1660–1914* (Syracuse, N.Y.: Syracuse University Press, 1991); and *Pacifism in the United States,* 21–158.

30. William Kaplan, *State and Salvation: The Jehovah's Witnesses and Their Fight for Civil Rights* (Toronto: University of Toronto Press, 1989), 3–13, 190–223; see also Herbert Hewitt Stroup, *The Jehovah's Witnesses* (1945; reprint New York: Russell and Russell, 1967,); Barbara Grizzuti Harrison, *Visions of Glory: A History and a Memoir of Jehovah's Witnesses* (New York: Simon & Schuster, 1978); and the *1975 Yearbook of Jehovah's Witnesses* (Brooklyn, N.Y.: Watch Tower Bible and Tract Society, 1974), 94–116, 205–10.

31. Gary Land, ed., *Adventism in America: A History* (Grand Rapids, Mich.: Eerdmans, 1985); Richard W. Schwarz, *Light Bearers to the Remnant* (Mountain View, Calif., 1979); Don F. Neufeld, ed., *Seventh-Day Adventist Encyclopedia* (Washington, D.C.: 1976); and the comprehensive, M. Ellsworth Olsen, *History of the Origin and Progress of Seventh-Day Adventists* (Washington, D.C., 1925). Only 12 percent of the 6.2 million Adventists today live in North America; Ari L. Goldman, "Foreign Influence Gains in the Adventist Church," *New York Times,* 17 July 1990, A16.

32. See the essay in this volume by John Whiteclay Chambers II.

33. *Whitaker's Almanac, 1899,* 400, "a conscientious objector to [compulsory] vaccination can escape all penalties." Quoted in "Objector," *Oxford English Dictionary,* 2d

ed., 29 vols. (Oxford Clarendon Press, 1989), 10:645; for further usage of the term, see also "Conscientious Objector," ibid., 3:755. Although the 1890s and World War I saw the first widespread use of the term, Peter Brock has traced the term "conscientious objection" to military service or war to 1846, when it was mentioned several times by pacifists, antimilitarists, and political radicals in their relatively short-lived campaign against compulsory militia service and recruitment for the British Army. See Brock, *Freedom from War,* 319, n. 47.

34. Apart from the nonresistant religious sects, there were in Europe and America in the nineteenth century numbers of liberal pacifists from the middle and upper classes who were followers of Leo Tolstoy or who were members of the proliferating nonsectarian peace societies. Until the early twentieth century, conscription systems generally permitted a conscript to hire a substitute or pay a commutation fee, provisions that enabled the upper- and much of the middle-class to escape service. Such provisions were eliminated at the turn of the century, and governments then generally refused to recognize the conscientious objections of men who were not members of historic pacifist sects. On the peace movements and the Tolstoyans, see Brock, *Freedom from War;* and Sandi E. Cooper, *Patriotic Pacifism.*

35. Although socialist traditions were antimilitaristic, they were not, strictly speaking, pacifistic. Socialists opposed standing professional armies as instruments of capitalist rule, but in several of the continental European nations, the socialists supported militia systems of citizen-soldiers precisely as antimilitarist measures. See David B. Ralston, *The Army of the Republic: The Place of the Military in the Political Evolution of France, 1871–1914* (Cambridge, Mass.: Harvard University Press, 1967), 131–32, 314, 348–55; and George J. Neimanis, "Militia vs. the Standing Army in the History of Economic Thought from Adam Smith to Friedrich Engels," *Military Affairs* 44 (February 1980): 31–33. See also the essays in Charles Chatfield and Peter van den Dungen, eds., *Peace Movements and Political Cultures* (Knoxville, Tenn.: University of Tennessee Press, 1988); and John R. Gillis, ed., *The Militarization of the Western World* (New Brunswick, N.J.: Rutgers University Press, 1989).

36. See Charles Chatfield, *For Peace and Justice: Pacifism in America, 1914–1941* (Knoxville, Tenn.: University of Tennessee Press, 1971); Peter Brock, *Pacifism in the United States,* and also *Twentieth-Century Pacifism* (New York: Van Nostrand Reinhold, 1970); Martin Caedel, *Pacifism in Britain, 1914–1945* (Oxford: Oxford University Press, 1980); Richard Taylor and Nigel Young, eds., *Campaigns for Peace.*

37. Prasad and Smythe, eds., *Conscription: A World Survey,* 130–35.

38. Barber, *Conscience, Government and War;* Sibley and Jacob, *Conscription of Conscience,* 354–55, and passim.

39. *U.S.* v. *Seeger* 380 U.S. 163 (1965); quotation at 165.

40. *Welsh* v. *U.S.,* 398 U.S. 340 (1970).

41. Selective objection was rejected by the Supreme Court in *Gillette* v. *U.S.,* 401 U.S. 437 (1971).

42. Prasad and Smythe, eds., *Conscription a World Survey,* 49–53; see also the essay in this volume on the Federal Republic of Germany by Jürgen Kulhmann and Ekkehard Lippert.

43. See the article in this volume by Anton Bebler on the former socialist countries of Eastern Europe.

44. It is difficult to obtain precise and comparable information about CO provisions for every country with conscription, as attested by the leading compendiums, including Amnesty International, *Conscientious Objection to Military Service;* the United Nations report by Eide and Mubanga-Chipoya, *Conscientious Objection to Military Service;* Prasad and Smythe, eds., *Conscription: A World Survey;* and the annual report by the International Institute for Strategic Studies, *The Military Balance.* Nevertheless, it appears that there are few exceptions

to the generalization that non-European countries with conscription do not recognize conscientious objection. Among the exceptions, which seem to be Brazil, Guyana, Suriname, Uruguay, and Zambia, some recognize conscientious objection in their constitutions but have neither adopted statutory provisions nor effectively implemented that recognition. In addition, as Annette Seegers shows in her essay in this volume, South Africa recognizes conscientious objection but only on narrowly-defined religious grounds; and, as Yoram Peri indicates in his essay, although Israel does not officially recognize conscientious objection, exemptions are in practice granted for religious, family, or other reasons, including unsuitability for reasons of conscience.

45. On the rise of the culture of "rights" in the United States in recent years, see especially Lawrence M. Friedman, *The Republic of Choice: Law, Authority, and Culture* (Cambridge, Mass.: Harvard University Press, 1990).

2.
Conscientious Objectors and the American State from Colonial Times to the Present

1. Statutory exemption to compulsory militia service was granted by colonial legislatures in British North America to religious pacifists such as the Quakers, who insisted upon it as a legal right. This provision is related more directly to modern statutory exemptions for COs than was the European Mennonites' earlier release from military service by German princes upon the payment of a fee. The European experience was a premodern example of protection; it was personal exemption of feudal subjects through deferential payment to their prince, rather than a statutory exemption based upon the rights of subjects or citizens. (This essay does not deal with pacifist Native Americans, such as the Hopi, because the tradition of pacifism and conscientious objection in the United States derives from the European and colonial American experience, not from that of the Indians.)

2. The definition of pacifism used in this study is opposition to war or participation in war that is based on a higher principle than personal expediency, political interests, or sympathy for the enemy cause. This is a variant of a definition put forward by Gordon C. Zahn, "A Descriptive Study of the Sociological Backgrounds of Conscientious Objectors in Civilian Public Service during World War II" (Ph.D. diss., Catholic University of America, 1953), 10, and modified slightly by Cynthia Eller, *Conscientious Objectors and the Second World War: Moral and Religious Arguments in Support of Pacifism* (New York: Praeger, 1991), 6.

3. Surprisingly, there is no detailed scholarly account of the full history of conscientious objection in America. Historical aspects of conscientious objection have received scholarly attention in articles and a few monographs, including Edward Needles Wright, *Conscientious Objectors in the Civil War* (Philadelphia: University of Pennsylvania Press, 1931); Mulford Q. Sibley and Philip E. Jacob, *Conscription of Conscience: The American State and the Conscientious Objector, 1940–1947* (Ithaca: Cornell University Press, 1952); and the valuable collection of documents edited by Lillian Schlissel, *Conscience in America: A Documentary History of Conscientious Objection in America, 1757–1967* (New York: E. P. Dutton, 1968). COs have been included as one aspect in studies of pacifism and draft resistance, such as Charles DeBenedetti, *The Peace Reform in American History* (Bloomington: Indiana University Press, 1980); Peter Brock, *Pacifism in the United States: From the Colonial Era to the First World War* (Princeton: Princeton University Press, 1968); Lawrence S. Wittner, *Rebels against War: The American Peace Movement, 1933–1983*

(Philadelphia: Temple University Press, 1984); and Stephen M. Kohn, *Jailed for Peace: The History of American Draft Law Violators, 1658–1985* (New York: Praeger, 1986).

4. John Whiteclay Chambers II, *To Raise an Army: The Draft Comes to Modern America* (New York: The Free Press, 1987).

5. Much of the following historical account of the evolution of American military institutions is drawn from my earlier study, Chambers, *To Raise an Army*, 1–71 and passim. For the colonial period, see also Douglas E. Leach, *Arms for Empire: A Military History of the British Colonies in North America, 1607–1763* (New York: Macmillan, 1973), 290–98.

6. Peter Brock, *The Quaker Peace Testimony, 1660–1914* (Syracuse, N.Y.: Syracuse University Press, 1991).

7. Richard K. MacMaster, *Land, Piety, Peoplehood: The Establishment of Mennonite Communities in America, 1683–1790,* vol. 1 of *The Mennonite Experience in America* (Scottdale, Pa.: Herald Press, 1985). The first Mennonites to come to America came from Holland and settled in New York in 1663; they were scattered after the British conquest of the Dutch colony. The first permanent settlement in America by this sect was started in Pennsylvania by German Mennonites in 1683.

8. Rufus D. Bowman, *The Church of the Brethren and War, 1708–1941* (Elgin, Ill.: Brethren Publishing House, 1944). Brethren, known as Dunkers, began to arrive in America in the 1720s, settling especially in Pennsylvania and Virginia. Mennonites and Brethren cooperated closely in America although they came from somewhat different traditions. (Mennonites derived from the Anabaptist radical wing of the Reformation that began in the sixteenth century. Brethren stemmed from German Pietism, which began in the eighteenth century. However, the Brethren later adopted adult baptism and entered the Anabaptist tradition.)

9. Joseph Besse, *A Collection of the Sufferings of the People called Quakers for the Testimony of a Good Conscience,* 2 vols. (London, 1753), 2: 378–82.

10. For such sentiments, see Guy F. Hershberger, "A Newly Discovered Mennonite Petition of 1755," *Mennonite Historical Quarterly* 33 (April 1959): 143–51.

11. On this religious diversity, see Jon Butler, *Awash in a Sea of Faith: Christianizing the American People* (Cambridge, Mass.: Harvard University Press, 1990). The tension between the secular humanist and the orthodox and evangelical values is examined in John M. Murrin, "Religion and Politics in America from the First Settlements to the Civil War," in *Religion and American Politics: From the Colonial Period to the 1980s,* ed. Mark A. Noll (New York: Oxford University Press, 1990), 19–43.

12. The early statutes on compulsory militia training and service as well as on various exemptions, including those for conscientious objectors, are listed and often reprinted (many in fascimile) in U.S. Selective Service System, Special Monograph no. 1, *Backgrounds of Selective Service,* 2 vols. (Washington, D.C.: Government Printing Office, 1947). Puritan Massachusetts, which previously had sought to drive Quakers out of the colony, was forced by King Charles II in 1665 to grant them religious freedom. For the Massachusetts statute of October 11, 1665 exempting Quakers from militia service, see ibid., vol. 2, part 6: 76. For a much more direct and lasting exemption for Quaker COs in Massachusetts, see the specific "Act to Exempt the People Called Quakers from the Penalty of the Law for Non-Attendance on Military Musters," Dec. 31, 1757/58, ibid., 49. The Rhode Island statute of 1673 is reprinted at ibid., vol. 2, part 12:13, 16.

13. The Charter of Liberties of 1701 (technically the Fourth Frame of Government of the colony of Pennsylvania) explicitly stated that the principle of liberty of conscience was to remain "inviolably for ever." The statute is printed in Commonwealth of Pennsylvania, *Colonial Records [of Pennsylvania, 1683–1790],* 16 vols. (Philadelphia: J. Severns and Co., 1851–1853), 2:56–60.

14. Hermann Wellenreuther, "The Political Dilemma of the Quakers in Pennsylvania, 1681–1748," *Pennsylvania Magazine of History and Biography* 94 (April 1970): 135–72.

15. Rhode Island statute of August 13, 1673, in John Russell Bartlett, ed., *Records of the Colony of Rhode Island and Providence Plantations in New England,* 10 vols. (Providence, R.I.: A. C. Greene & Brothers, State Printers, 1856–1865), 2:498–99. On colonial Rhode Island and Quaker pacifists in general, see Brock, *Pacifism in the United States,* 37–45; and Sydney V. James, *Colonial Rhode Island: A History* (New York: Scribner's, 1975), 151–2, 216–25.

16. MacMaster, *Land, Piety, Peoplehood,* 229–48.

17. Many Quaker politicians of that period were apparently more flexible on the defense issue than has been traditionally believed. See Jack D. Marietta, *The Reformation of American Quakerism, 1748–1783* (Philadelphia: University of Pennsylvania Press, 1984), 131–86.

18. Col. George Washington to Gov. Robert Dinwiddie, August 4, 1756, in *The Writings of George Washington,* ed. John C. Fitzpatrick, 39 vols. (Washington, D.C.: Government Printing Office, 1931–1938), 1:420. See also Peter Brock, "Colonel Washington and the Quaker Conscientious Objectors," *Quaker History* 53 (Spring 1964): 12–26.

19. MacMaster, *Land, Piety, Peoplehood,* 248.

20. See Richard K. MacMaster, "Neither Whig nor Tory: The Peace Churches in the American Revolution," *Fides et Historia* 9 (Spring 1977): 8–24; Wallace Brown, "Loyalists and Non-Participants," in *The American Revolution: A Heritage of Change,* ed. John Parker and Carol Urness (Minneapolis, Minn.: Association of the James Ford Bell Library, 1975), 126–27.

21. Delaware (1776 Declaration of Rights, sect. 40); Pennsylvania (1776 Declaration of Rights, sect. 8); New York (1777 Constitution, sect. 40); New Hampshire (1784 Constitution, sect. 8).

22. Arthur J. Merkeel, *The Relation of the Quakers to the American Revolution* (Washington, D.C.: University Press of America, 1979), 326; Marietta, *Reformation of American Quakerism,* 233–35. Less reliable is William C. Kashatus III, *Conflict of Conviction: A Reappraisal of Quaker Involvement in the American Revolution* (Lanham, Md.: University Press of America, 1990).

23. Quoted in Brock, *Pacifism in The United States,* 240.

24. MacMaster, *Land, Piety, Peoplehood,* 254, 256.

25. Statute of July 18, 1775, printed in *Journal of the Continental Congress,* 2: 189; see also George Washington to Pennsylvania Council of Safety, January 19, 1777, and January 29, 1777, *Writings of George Washington,* ed. Fitzpatrick, 7: 35, 79.

26. Analysis of the framers' attitude towards the draft remains controversial; for a dispassionate, insightful historical analysis, see Charles A. Lofgren, "Compulsory Military Service under the Constitution: The Original Understanding," *William and Mary Quarterly* 3d ser., 38 (January 1976): 61–88.

27. North Carolina, Virginia, Rhode Island, and Pennsylvania in *Debates in the Several State Conventions on the Adoption of the Federal Constitution,* ed. Jonathan Elliot, 4 vols. (Philadelphia: J. B. Lippincott, 1896), 1:334–35; 2:531; 3:657–59; and 4:243–44. For a list of twelve early state constitutions that recognized the right of freedom of conscience, see Harrop A. Freeman, "A Remonstrance for Conscience," *University of Pennsylvania Law Review* 106 (April 1958): 809 n. 8.

28. For the 1789 debate over Madison's CO amendment, see U.S. Congress, *Annals of Congress: The Debates and Proceedings in the Congress of the United States, 1789–1824,* 42 vols. (Washington, D.C.: Gales and Seaton, 1834), 1st Congress, 1st sess., 1:431–34, 451, 749–51, 766–67; see also Richard W. Renner, "Conscientious Objection and the Federal Government, 1787–1792," *Military Affairs,* 38 (December 1974): 142. The CO

provision was part of the proposed Bill of Rights from the beginning. In the 1980s, archivists discovered a first draft of the Bill of Rights written in July 1789 by Rep. Roger Sherman of Connecticut, which included a provision protecting "the rights of Conscience in matters of religion" and, in the militia clause, ensuring that "military Service shall not be required of persons religiously scrupulous of bearing arms." Unsigned, undated draft (on which Madison had noted "by Mr. Sherman July 1789"), vol. 11, James Madison Papers, Library of Congress.

For an inferential argument that Madison and other defenders of the CO amendment assumed that, despite the Senate elimination of a number of specific amendments, the right of religious conscientious objection would be protected by the first amendment guaranteeing freedom of religion and the ninth amendment guaranteeing the sanctity of those nonenumerated rights retained by the people, see Maj. David M. Brahms, USMC, "They Step to a Different Drummer: A Critical Analysis of the Current Department of Defense Position Vis-A-Vis In-Service Conscientious Objectors," *Military Law Review* 47 (January 1970): 6–11.

Subsequently, the federal militia act of May 8, 1792, which remained the basic national militia law for more than one hundred years, offered indirect protection for COs by exempting from military duty "all persons who now are or may hereafter be exempted by the laws of the respective states."

29. For the classic statement, which became highly influential in the twentieth century, see Henry D. Thoreau, "Civil Disobedience," *A Yankee in Canada, with Anti-Slavery and Reform Papers* (Boston: Ticknor and Fields, 1866), 123–51.

30. The standard work on the subject, Wright, *Conscientious Objectors in the Civil War,* has been supplemented by more recent scholarship, including Theron F. Schlabach, *Peace, Faith, Nation: Mennonites and Amish in Nineteenth-Century America,* in *The Mennonite Experience in America* (Scottdale, Pa.: Herald Press, 1988), 2:141–200; Bowman, *Church of the Brethren;* Brock, *Pacifism in the United States,* 689–866; James W. Geary, *We Need Men: The Union Draft in the Civil War* (DeKalb, Ill.: Northern Illinois University Press, 1991), 36–37, 56, 63, 109–10, 162–63; and David Martin Osher, "Soldier Citizens for a Disciplined Nation: Civil War Conscription and the Development of the Modern American State," (Ph.D. diss., Columbia University, 1992).

31. Virginia gave COs the choice of noncombatant militia service or payment of five hundred dollars and a 2 percent tax on their property; North Carolina offered them the option of paying a hundred-dollar exemption fee or performing alternative service in hospitals or salt mills.

32. Samuel Horst, *Mennonites in the Confederacy: A Study in Civil War Pacifism* (Scottdale, Pa.: Herald Press, 1967), 89–95; John Whiteclay Chambers II and David M. Osher, "Introduction" to the reprint edition of Fernando G. Cartland, *Southern Heroes, or the Friends in Wartime* (1895) and Ethan Foster, *The Conscript Quakers* (1883), reprinted together (New York: Garland Publishing Inc., 1972).

33. On Lincoln, see his famous letter to Eliza P. Gurney, September 4, 1864, reprinted in *The Collected Works of Abraham Lincoln,* ed. Roy P. Basler, 8 vols. (New Brunswick, N.J.: Rutgers University Press, 1953), 8:535–36; Wright, *Conscientious Objectors in the Civil War,* 121–31. Lincoln had Quaker great-grandparents from Pennsylvania and Virginia on his grandfather's side, and the president said on several occasions that he was of Quaker descent. See Daniel Bassuk, *Abraham Lincoln and the Quakers,* Pendle Hill Pamphlet 273 (Wallingford, Pa.: Pendle Hill Publications, 1987), 5–6, 27–28.

34. Gen. Thomas J. Jackson, quoted in David H. Zigler, *A History of the Brethren in Virginia* (Elgin, Ill.: Brethren Publishing House, 1908), 98.

35. Chambers, *To Raise an Army,* 206–19; Charles Chatfield, *For Peace and Justice: Pacifism in America, 1914–1941* (Knoxville, Tenn.: University of Tennessee Press, 1971), 42–87.

36. C. Roland Marchand, *The American Peace Movement and Social Reform, 1898–1918* (Princeton: Princeton University Press, 1972); Horace C. Peterson and Gilbert C. Fite, *Opponents of War, 1917–1918* (Madison, Wis.: University of Wisconsin Press, 1957). On opposition to the war by the majority of American socialists, see Milton Cantor, "The Radical Confrontation with Foreign Policy: War and Revolution, 1914–1920," in *Dissent: Explorations in the History of American Radicalism,* ed. Alfred F. Young (DeKalb, Ill.: Northern Illinois University Press, 1968), 215–49.

37. Chambers, *To Raise an Army,* 73–204. The administration rejected the proposal of the "preparedness" movement for a permanent policy of universal military training and service.

38. U.S. Congress, House Committee on Military Affairs, *Hearings on the Selective Service Act . . . April 14 and 27, 1917,* 65th Cong., 1st sess. (Washington, D.C.: Government Printing Office, 1917), 9.

39. Ibid., 85; see also Baker to Woodrow Wilson, July 18, 1918, quoted in *Congressional Record,* 65th Cong., 3d sess., February 12, 1919, 3237.

40. Section 4 of the Selective Service Act of May 18, 1917, *Public Law No. 12, 65th Cong., 1st sess.* (Washington, D.C., 1917); see also U.S. Secretary of War, *Statement concerning the Treatment of Conscientious Objectors in the Army* (Washington, D.C.: Government Printing Office, 1919).

41. Woodrow Wilson to John Nevin Sayre, reply of May 1, 1917 of Sayre to Wilson, April 27, 1917, reprinted in *The Papers of Woodrow Wilson,* ed. Arthur S. Link, et al., 69 vols. (Princeton, N.J.: Princeton University Press, 1966–1993), 42; 159–60, 179.

42. Chambers, *To Raise an Army,* 216–17; the best statistical source is the report by Frederick Keppel in Secretary of War, *Statement concerning . . . Conscientious Objectors,* 17–25.

43. The U.S. government did not maintain a separate list of COs who died in military prisons, only statistics covering all inmate deaths. The number of COs who died in military prisons, most from pneumonia or other ailments connected with their harsh treatment (as well as, in the case of one man, Ernest Gellert, suicide), is compiled here from the names listed in "C.O.s Who Died in Military Prisons," typed list, American Civil Liberties Union (ACLU) Files, 1918, 71:67; clippings, 87–97; news release, n.d., Federated Press Service, 122:69 (these sources differ over whether there were thirteen or fifteen deaths); all in ACLU Papers, Princeton University Library, Princeton, N.J.; Kohn, *Jailed for Peace,* 42, n.17, lists 17 names. The quotation is from Leonard Wood to Jacob Greenberg, October 21, 1918, ACLU Files, 96:17.

44. Mark A. May, "The Psychological Examinations of C.O.'s," *American Journal of Psychiatry* 31 (April 1920): 154–61. For the Russellites (Jehovah's Witnesses) in World War I, see A. T. Rogerson, *Millions Now Living Will Never Die* (London: Constable, 1969), 196; and *1975 Yearbook of Jehovah's Witnesses* (Brooklyn, N.Y.: Watch Tower Bible and Tract Society, 1974), 94–98, 101–11.

45. May, "Psychological Examinations," 160–61; but see also Chatfield, *For Peace and Justice,* chaps. 1–2.

46. Secretary of War, *Statement concerning . . . Conscientious Objectors,* 17–19, 25. For opposing views on the government's policy, see Walter Guest Kellogg, *The Conscientious Objector* (New York: Boni and Liveright, 1919; reprint with introduction by John Whiteclay Chambers II, New York: Garland Publishing Inc., 1972); and Norman Thomas, *The Conscientious Objector in America* (New York: B. W. Huebsch, 1923). The best-known memoirs by absolutists are Ernest L. Meyer, *Hey! Yellowbacks! The War Diary of a Conscientious Objector* (New York: John Day Co., 1930) and Kenneth I. Brown, ed., *Character "Bad": The Story of a Conscientious Objector as Told in the Letters of Harold Studley Gray* (New York: Harper and Row, 1934).

47. See James C. Juhnke, *Vision, Doctrine, War: Mennonite Identity and Organization in America, 1890–1930,* in *The Mennonite Experience in America* (Scottdale, Pa.: Herald Press, 1989), 3:239–40.

48. Paul L. Murphy, *World War I and the Origin of Civil Liberties in the United States* (New York: W. W. Norton, 1979), but see also David M. Rabban, "The First Amendment in Its Forgotten Years [1890–1917]," *Yale Law Journal* 90 (January 1981): 514–96.

49. Harlan Fiske Stone, "The Conscientious Objector," *Columbia University Quarterly* 21 (October 1919): 253–71. Nevertheless, during a wave of nationalistic sentiment in the interwar period, the U.S. government forbade American citizenship to pacifist immigrants, including a Hungarian woman and a Canadian minister, who refused to swear that they would bear arms in defense of the United States: *U.S.* v. *Schwimmer,* 279 U.S. 644 (1929) and *U.S.* v. *Macintosh,* 283 U.S. 605 (1931).

50. A Gallup Poll conducted in January 1940, after the 1939 invasion of Poland and the outbreak of the Second World War, but before the spring 1940 German invasion of France and the Low Countries, asked what should be done with COs if the United States went to war. Among the respondents 37 percent favored noncombatant military service for COs, and 13 percent thought COs should be completely exempted from military service. However, 24 percent wanted the military to force COs to fight, and 9 percent recommended that they be imprisoned or even executed. Some 16 percent did not express an opinion. Hadley Cantril, *Public Opinion, 1935–1946* (Princeton: Princeton University Press, 1951), 135.

51. The phrase is that of L. William Yolton, executive director of the National Interreligious Service Board for Conscientious Objectors (NISBCO), Washington, D.C.; telephone interview with the author, January 18, 1990. For the evolution of the CO clause in the 1940 draft law, see E. Raymond Wilson, "Evolution of the Conscientious Objector Provisions in the 1940 Conscription Bill," *Quaker History* 64 (Spring 1975): 3–15; John M. Glenn, "Secular Conscientious Objection in the United States: The Selective Service Act of 1940," *Peace and Change* 9 (Spring 1983): 55–71; and J. Garry Clifford and Samuel R. Spencer, Jr., *The First Peacetime Draft [1940]* (Lawrence, Kans.: University Press of Kansas, 1986), 126–29, 221–23.

52. Chatfield, *For Peace and Justice,* 310.

53. U.S. Congress, Senate Committee on Military Affairs, *Hearings on S. 4164,* 73rd Cong., 3d sess. (Washington, D.C.: Government Printing Office, 1940), 262–63.

54. Clifford and Spencer, *First Peacetime Draft,* 221. Ironically, Hershey, the head of America's conscription agency for thirty years, was a descendant of pacifist Swiss Mennonites who had fled to America in part to escape conscription; George Q. Flynn, *Lewis B. Hershey: Mr. Selective Service* (Chapel Hill, N.C.: University of North Carolina Press, 1985), 4, 126, 216–309. Originally, the conscription bill prepared by a team of army and navy planners led by Hershey required that a CO be a member of a traditional peace church to qualify for alternative service. However, Hershey apparently had doubts about such a limitation, and when even a conservative such as Sen. John J. Sparkman, Democrat from Alabama, suggested expanding the definition to include all religious COs, Hershey accepted the change. George Q. Flynn, "Lewis Hershey and the Conscientious Objector: The World War II Experience," *Military Affairs* 47 (February 1983): 1–6.

55. Selective Training and Service Act of September 16, 1940, *Public Law No. 783, sect. 5 (g).*

56. For an examination of the moral and religious views of COs, see Cynthia Eller, *Conscientious Objectors;* and Patricia McNeal, *Harder than War: Catholic Peacemaking in Twentieth-Century America* (New Brunswick, N.J.: Rutgers University Press, 1992), 49–70. W. Edward Roser, "World War II and the Pacifist Controversy in the Major

Protestant Churches,'' *American Studies* 14 (Fall 1973): 5–24, surveyed mainstream Protestantism. For the experience of American Jewish conscientious objectors in World War II, see Michael Young, "Facing the Test of Faith: Jewish Pacifists during the Second World War," *Peace and Change* 3 (Summer/Fall 1975): 34–40; and Max Kampelman, *Entering New Worlds: The Memoirs of a Private Man in Public Life* (New York: HarperCollins, 1991).

57. Clifford and Spencer, *First Peacetime Draft,* 128.

58. Theodore R. Wachs, "Conscription, Conscientious Objection and the Context of American Pacifism, 1940–45," (Ph.D. diss., University of Illinois, Champaign-Urbana, 1976), 209, cited in Eller, *Conscientious Objectors,* 50, who notes that, as her interviews with former COs indicated, the language of the statute provided a strong incentive even for men who were not primarily religious to state their objection in religious terms so as to qualify for the exemption.

59. Jennifer Frost, "The Lew Ayres Case and World War II COs," paper given at the annual meeting of the Organization of American Historians, Chicago, Illinois, April 3, 1992.

60. On the Adventists, see Roger Guinon Davis, "Conscientious Cooperators: The Seventh-Day Adventists and Military Service, 1860–1945" (Ph.D. diss., George Washington University, 1970). Some Adventists used the term "conscientious cooperator" to indicate their willingness to serve their country even though they were unwilling to bear arms or kill for it. Indeed, the Seventh-Day Adventist Church withdrew from the National Interreligious Service Board for Conscientious Objectors (NISBCO) in 1967 because of the organization's opposition to conscription itself.

61. Selective Service System, *Conscientious Objection, Special Monograph no. 11,* 1:313–28; see also Flynn, *Lewis B. Hershey,* 126–34.

62. Clarence E. Pickett, *For More than Bread* (Boston: Little, Brown, 1953), 320; Lawrence S. Wittner, *Rebels against War: The American Peace Movement, 1933–1983* (Philadelphia: Temple University Press, 1984), 70–71; on the camps themselves, see Sibley and Jacob, *Conscription of Conscience,* 200–306.

63. Selective Service System, *Conscientious Objection, Special Monograph, no. 11,* 1:320.

64. Nonreligious claims made for conscientious objector status on social, political, and intellectual grounds were rejected by Selective Service and by the federal courts; see *U.S.* v. *Kauten,* 133 F.2d 703 (2d Cir. 1943); *Berman* v. *U.S.,* 156 F.2d (9th Cir. 1946); cert. denied, 329 U.S. 795 (1946); rehearing denied, 329 U.S. 833 (1947).

65. Charles Eric Lincoln, *The Black Muslims in America,* rev. ed. (Boston: Beacon, 1973), 205–6; figures in Selective Service System, *Conscientious Objection, Special Monograph no. 11,* 1:261, 264.

66. For a comparison of their treatment as draft objectors in Canada and the United States, see William Kaplan, *State and Salvation: The Jehovah's Witnesses and Their Fight for Civil Rights* (Toronto: University of Toronto Press, 1989), 214–21. Technically, the Jehovah's Witnesses are not categorized by the U.S. government as COs because they reject CO status and demand ministerial exemptions which the government denies to most of them. Yet they are, of course, objecting to military service on religious grounds.

67. Gretchen Lemke-Santangelo, "The Radical Conscientious Objectors of World War II: Wartime Experience and Postwar Activism," *Radical History Review* 45 (1989): 5–29.

68. President's Advisory Commission on Universal Training, *A Program for National Security* (Washington, D.C.: Government Printing Office, 1947), 77–88; Flynn, *Lewis B. Hershey,* 143–70; James M. Gerhardt, *The Draft and Public Policy: Issues in Military Manpower Procurement, 1945–1970* (Columbus, Ohio: Ohio State University Press, 1971), 3–122.

69. See 62 *U.S. Statutes*, 612 (1948), *Public Law 1759, ch. 625*, 80th Cong., 2d sess. (1948).

70. R. R. Russell, "Development of Conscientious Objector Recognition in the United States," *George Washington Law Review* 20 (March 1952): 409–48.

71. 65 *U.S. Statutes* 86 (1951), 50 *U.S. Code*, App. sect. 456 (j) (1951).

72. Charles C. Moskos, *A Call to Civic Service: National Service for Country and Community* (New York: The Free Press, 1988), 44–45.

73. Kohn, *Jailed for Peace*, 93; Flynn, *Lewis B. Hershey*, 162–89; Zelle A. Larson, "An Unbroken Witness: Conscientious Objection to War, 1948–1953," (Ph.D. dis., University of Hawaii, 1975).

74. The assertion that blacks were "overdrafted" is presented in Lawrence M. Baskir and William A. Strauss, *Chance and Circumstance: The Draft, the War, and the Vietnam Generation* (New York: Knopf, 1978), 8, but is rejected in Neil D. Fligstein, "Who Served in the Military, 1940–1973," *Armed Forces and Society* 6 (Winter 1979): 297. There is no doubt, however, that blacks composed a disproportionate share (25 to 30 percent) of all ground combat troops at the start of the U.S. military buildup, largely because many blacks had enlisted and reenlisted in the U.S. armed forces as a source of socioeconomic opportunity. As mentioned, blacks accounted for 25 percent of army combat deaths in Vietnam in 1965–1966. The Army took steps to reduce this figure, and by the end of the war, the casualty rate among blacks was down to 14 percent for the entire war. On this issue, see M. Zeitlin, K. G. Lutterman, and J. W. Russell, "Death in Vietnam: Class, Poverty and the Risks of War," *Politics and Society* 3 (Spring 1973); Gilbert Badillo and David Curry, "The Social Incidence of Vietnam Casualties: Social Class or Race?" *Armed Forces and Society* 2 (May 1976): 397–406; Harry G. Summers, Jr., *Vietnam War Almanac* (New York: Facts on File, 1985), 98; D. Michael Shafer, ed., *The Legacy: The Vietnam War in the American Imagination* (Boston: Beacon, 1990), 57–79, 209–32.

75. Charles DeBenedetti with Charles Chatfield, *An American Ordeal: The Antiwar Movement of the Vietnam Era* (Syracuse, N.Y.: Syracuse University Press, 1990); Michael Useem, *Conscription, Protest, and Social Conflict: The Life and Death of a Draft Resistance Movement* (New York: John Wiley & Sons, 1973); Michael Ferber and Staughton Lynd, *The Resistance* (Boston: Beacon, 1971).

76. National Interreligious Service Board for Conscientious Objectors, *Words of Conscience: Religious Statements on Conscientious Objection*, 10th ed. (Washington, D.C.: NISBCO, 1983), 9–29; Central Committee for Conscientious Objectors, *Standing with Those Who Say No, 1948–1988* (n.p. [Philadelphia]: CCCO, 1988), 3–37; E. Raymond Wilson, *Uphill for Peace: Quaker Impact on Congress* (Richmond, Ind.: Friends United Press, 1975); Stanley Rothman and S. Robert Lichter, *Roots of Radicalism: Jews, Christians and the New Left* (New York: Oxford University Press, 1982); Mitchell Kent Hall, "Clergy and Laymen Concerned about Vietnam: A Study of Opposition to the Vietnam War," (Ph.D. diss., University of Kentucky, 1987); McNeal, *Harder than War*, chaps. 4–8.

77. On African-Americans' opposition to the war and the draft, see the essay in this volume by John H. Stanfield II; see also Clyde Taylor, ed., *Vietnam and Black America* (Garden City, N.Y.: Doubleday, 1973); Clayborne Carson, *In Struggle: SNCC and the Black Awakening of the 1960s* (Cambridge, Mass.: Harvard University Press, 1981); Adam Fairclough, "Martin Luther King, Jr., and the War in Vietnam," *Phylon* 45 (March 1984): 19–39; Randall Fisher, *Rhetoric and American Democracy: Black Protest through Vietnam Dissent* (Lanham, Md.: University Press of America, 1985); and Peter Levy, "Blacks and the Vietnam War," in Shafer, ed., *The Legacy*, 209–32. In the case of Muhammad Ali, a judge initially granted him CO status. However, the U.S. government obtained a reversal of the judge's decision. In a subsequent trial, Ali was convicted of draft evasion, fined ten

thousand dollars, and sentenced to prison for five years. The prize fighter was also stripped of his heavyweight boxing title and deprived of his license to box in the ring. Eventually, the U.S. Supreme Court overturned the conviction, and when public opinion later changed against the war, Ali returned triumphantly to boxing again in the 1970s and twice regained the heavyweight title.

78. Baskir and Strauss, *Chance and Circumstance,* 5, 9, 24, 33, 39, 49–51, 64–66; David Surrey, *Choice of Conscience: The Vietnam Era Military and Draft Resisters in Canada* (New York: Praeger, 1982).

79. Kohn, *Jailed for Peace,* 89–92; Flynn, *Lewis B. Hershey,* 259–67.

80. Lawrence M. Baskir and William A. Strauss, *Reconciliation after Vietnam: A Program of Relief for Vietnam-Era Draft and Military Offenders* (South Bend, Ind.: University of Notre Dame Press, 1976), 115, 130. For examples of personal statements by Vietnam-era COs, see Alice Lynd, ed., *We Won't Go: Personal Accounts of War Objectors* (Boston: Beacon Press, 1968); and Willard Gaylin, *In the Service of Their Country: War Resisters in Prison* (New York: Viking, 1970).

81. *Seeger* v. *U.S.,* 380 U.S. 163 (1965); for a personalized account of Seeger's actions and beliefs, see Peter Irons, *The Courage of Their Convictions: Sixteen Americans Who Fought Their Way to the Supreme Court* (New York: The Free Press, 1988), 152–78. For a probing examination of the meaning of the *Seeger* decision in the light of American history, see John H. Mansfield, "Conscientious Objection—1964 Term," in *Religion and the Public Order, 1965,* ed. Donald A. Giannella (Chicago: University of Chicago Press, 1966) 3–81.

82. *Welsh* v. *U.S.,* 398 U.S. 340 (1970).

83. Selective objection merely to a particular war, such as the war in Vietnam, was rejected in *Gillette* v. *U.S.,* 401 U.S. 437 (1971). For the debate, see James Finn, ed., *A Conflict of Loyalties: The Case for Selective Conscientious Objection* (New York: Pegasus, 1968); John A. Rohr, *Prophets without Honor: Public Policy and the Selective Conscientious Objector* (Nashville, Tenn.: Abingdon Press, 1971); Michael F. Noone, Jr., ed., *Selective Conscientious Objection: Accommodating Conscience and Security* (Boulder, Colo.: Westview Press, 1989).

84. Ratios compiled by Kohn, *Jailed for Peace,* 93; see also the figures for inductions and CO exemptions reported in the U.S. Selective Service System, *Annual Report of the Director of Selective Service* for FYs 1965 to 1967, and thereafter the *Semi-Annual Report of the Director of Selective Service* for six-month periods from 1968 to 1974 (Washington, D.C.: Government Printing Office, 1966–1975). See especially the tabular compilations 1952 to 1973 in *Semi-Annual Report of the Director of Selective Service for the Period January 1 to June 30, 1973* (Washington, D.C.: Government Printing Office, 1973), 55, App. 12, 13, which disclose that in FY 1973, while the armed forces inducted 25, 273 draftees, Selective Service exempted 29,705 COs (including 16,071 classified as available and awaiting alternative civilian service and 13,724 already at work at alternative service). These figures did not include the 12,739 COs who were reclassified in 1973 as having completed alternative service.

85. David Cortright, *Soldiers in Revolt: The American Military Today* (Garden City, N.Y.: Doubleday, 1975), 15–17; see also Gerald R. Gioglio, *Days of Decision: An Oral History of Conscientious Objection in the Military during the Vietnam War* (Trenton, N.J.: Broken Rifle Press, 1989). For an internal legal critique of the military's administrative response to in-service COs, see Maj. David M. Brahms, USMC, "They Step to a Different Drummer: A Critical Analysis of the Current Department of Defense Position Vis-A-Vis In-Service Conscientious Objectors," *Military Law Review* 47 (January 1970): 1–34; see also Donald N. Zillman, "In-Service Conscientious Objection: Courts, Boards, and the Basis in Fact," *San Diego Law Review* 10 (1972): 108.

86. For opposition to the war within the military and by Vietnam veterans, see Cortright, *Soldiers in Revolt;* Cecil B. Curry ("Cincinnatus"), *Self-Destruction: The Disintegration and Decay of the United States Army during the Vietnam Era* (New York: Norton, 1981); Shelby L. Stanton, *The Rise and Fall of an American Army: U.S. Ground Forces in Vietnam, 1965–1973* (Navato, Calif: Presidio Press, 1985); and Richard R. Moser, "From Deference to Defiance: America, the Citizen-Soldier and the Vietnam Era," (Ph.D diss., Rutgers University, 1992).

87. On the end of the use of the draft, see John Whiteclay Chambers II, *Draftees or Volunteers: A Documentary History of the Debate over Military Conscription in the United States, 1787–1973* (New York: Garland Publishing, 1975), 427–646; Robert K. Griffith, Jr., "About Face? The U.S. Army and the Draft," *Armed Forces and Society* 12 (Fall 1985): 115–16; Robert K. Griffith, Jr., "The Transition of the U.S. Army from the Draft to the All-Volunteer Force, 1968–1974" (U.S. Army Center of Military History, Washington, D.C., 1988, unpublished); James Burk, "Debating the Draft in America," *Armed Forces and Society* 15 (Spring 1989): 431–48; John Whiteclay Chambers II, "The Issue of Conscription and the All-Volunteer Army in the United States since 1973," paper at the fifteenth World Congress of the International Political Science Association, Buenos Aires, Argentina, July 22–25, 1991; and George Q. Flynn, *America and the Draft, 1940–1973* (Lawrence, Kans.: University Press of Kansas, 1993).

88. Nevertheless, authorization and guidance for a standby draft as well as continued draft registration and classification were provided by Congress in the 1971 amendments incorporated as sect. 10(h) of the Military Selective Service Act, Public Law 92–129 enacted on September 28, 1971. On July 1, 1973, the president's authority to induct personnel into the armed forces expired. By action of the Congress in the passage of the FY 1974 appropriations act for the Selective Service System (Public Law 93–137), the expenditure of funds appropriated by the act for the induction of any person into the armed forces was prohibited. Thus, the lingering induction authority, in sect. 17 (c) of the draft law, was rendered inoperative. Nevertheless, the 1948 draft law, as amended, remained on the statute books, providing authority for the continuation of the Selective Service System, even though presidential induction authority was prohibited without future congressional authorization. The Selective Service Act of 1948 was adopted as Public Law 759, ch. 625, 80th Cong., 2d sess. (1948). It was recorded as 62 *U.S. Statutes,* 612 (1948). On June 19, 1951, the 1948 Draft Act was amended and retitled the Universal Military Training and Service Act, 65 *U.S. Statutes,* 75 (1951). It was subsequently amended several times and retitled in 1967, the Military Selective Service Act, Public Law 90–40, Sect. 1(l), 81 *U.S. Statutes,* 100 (June 30, 1967). The retitled 1948 law still remains the basic draft law in the United States. See 50 *U.S. Code,* App., 451ff. (1991).

89. James B. Jacobs and Dennis McNamara, "Selective Service without a Draft," *Armed Forces and Society* 10 (Spring 1984): 361–79. For the official account, see U.S. Selective Service System, *Semi-Annual Report of the Director of Selective Service, October 1, 1985 through March 31, 1986* (Washington, D.C.: Government Printing Office, 1986), 1–31.

90. In a well-publicized campaign of prosecution by the Reagan administration against selected registration refusers, eighteen young men were convicted and sentenced in federal courts in the early 1980s. The Reagan administration apparently sought no new indictments after 1985. Linda Greenhouse, "U.S. Is Upheld in Prosecuting Avowed Resisters of Draft Registration," *New York Times,* 20 Mar. 1985, A20; "Draft Resister to Spend 6 Months in House Arrest," ibid., 11 Sept. 1985, A16; Kendall J. Wills, "Draft Foe Begins Three-Year Term," ibid., 12 July 1987, A8. On the "Solomon" Amendment linking higher education assistance to draft registration and similar state laws, see Molly De Maret, "States

Continue to Legislate against Draft Nonregistrants," NISBCO, *Reporter for Conscience' Sake* 48 (July 1991): 3–4. The four states banning enrollment by nonregistrants were Colorado, Louisiana, South Dakota, and Tennessee.

91. Figures from 1985 to 1987 are from the chapter in the present volume by Michael F. Noone, Jr., "Legal Aspects of Conscientious Objection: A Comparative Analysis," and for FY 1989 and FY 1990 from a personal communication from the Department of Defense with the editors of this volume, February 1992.

92. Adam Wolman, "We're Feeling the Draft," *New York Times,* 28 Nov. 1990, Op-Ed. "Let's Be Serious When We Talk about War," ibid., 9 Dec. 1990, Letters to the Editor. "The Fairness Doctrine: Conscription?" *The Economist* (12 Jan. 1991): 35–36; "Should the U.S. Reinstate the Draft?" *Congressional Quarterly's Editorial Research Reports,* 1991, no. 2 (January 11, 1991): 18–31; Jacob Weisberg, "A Slight Draft: The Case for Occasional Conscription," *The New Republic* 204 (11 Mar., 1991): 12–14; Murray Polner, "Draft Registration Is Dumb. End It," *New York Times,* 13 Feb. 1992, Op-Ed.

93. David Gonzalez, "Some in Military Now Resist Combat," *New York Times,* 26 Nov. 1990, A7; Katherine Bishop, "Turning against the Military Life They Once Chose," ibid., 14 Jan., 1991, A5, A12, reports the Department of Defense figure of 202 applications through December 1990. The Pentagon, however, issued a "stop-loss" order, which halted the processing of discharge applications at the beginning of the deployment. According to one national survey of draft counselors, approximately 2,500 CO applications were filed by military personnel, most reservists, between August 1990 and March 1991. Michael Marsh, military and draft counselor, War Resisters League Headquarters, New York City, interview with author, March 26, 1991. NISBCO and East and West Coast CCCO reported comparable figures. See, for example, "Military COs' Catch–22 Continues," NISBCO, *The Reporter for Conscience' Sake* 48 (May 1991): 1. The Defense Department reported that between August 1990 and September 1991, some 567 military personnel filed for CO status (at least claims that were reported to Washington). Of those, 270 were approved and 203 were denied. Nearly 100 refused to report to their units and faced charges. Karen M. Thomas, "For Military Objectives, No Easy Way Out," *Chicago Tribune,* 8 Mar. 1992, A6.

94. Associated Press, "Mennonites, Quakers Join in Campaign for Peace in the Mideast," Newark (N.J.) *Star-Ledger,* 22 Feb. 1991; Laurie Goodstein, "Churches Give Resisters Shelter from War's Storm," *Washington Post,* 27 Feb. 1991, A3.

95. Of the several hundred servicemen and -women held temporarily in military confinement for refusal to go to the Persian Gulf, more than seventy-five were conscientious objectors; the Marine COs were imprisoned at the Marine Corps base at Camp Lejeune, N.C.; most of the soldiers at Fort Lewis, Wash., and Fort Sill, Okla. Michael Marsh, "Mistreated COs Prompt Movement for Change," War Resisters League, *The Nonviolent Activist,* 9 (March 1992): 13–14. Of the forty-six COs in the Marine Corps who were court-martialed and convicted of desertion or being absent without leave, thirty-two were reservists and fourteen were on active duty; of the total, twenty-four were black, eighteen Caucasian, three Hispanic, and one Burmese. There were two women, both Caucasian, among the Marine COs, a fact that received little or no publicity. Among the religious affilations of these Marine COs, twelve listed themselves as Catholic, twelve as Baptist, eight simply as Protestant, four as Methodist, two as Muslim, two as Buddhist, two as Pentacostal, and one each in a number of smaller denominations. U.S. Marine Corps, personal communication with the editors, February 1992.

For coverage of the uniformed COs by the press and CO organizations, see Laurie Goodstein, "Soldiers Must Deploy Before Seeking Conscientious-Objector Status," *Washington Post,* 28 Nov. 1990, A30; Marc Fisher, "The Army's Conscientious Question: In Germany, Soldier-Objectors Forced to Follow Units to Gulf," ibid., 9 Feb. 1991, D1; Bruce

Shapiro, "Hell for Those Who Won't Go," *Nation,* 252 (February 18, 1991): 194–98; Laurie Goodstein, "9 Who Refused to Fight Await Corps' Verdict," *Washington Post,* 16 Apr. 1991, A3; Peter Applebome, "Epilogue to Gulf War: 25 Marines Face Prison," *New York Times,* 3 May 1991, A14; "Amnesty to Sponsor CO Campaign," *CCCO News Notes* 43 (Summer 1991): 1; "Situation Still Bleak for Prisoners of Conscience," NISBCO, *Reporter for Conscience' Sake* 48 (April 1991): 1; "Gulf War CO's Cases Trickle to Federal Courts," ibid. 48 (September 1991): 1; "Answering the Call," *Commonweal* 118 (June 14, 1991): 387–88; Gordon C. Zahn, "Prisoners of Conscience, U.S. Style," *America* 165 (November 16, 1991): 360–61; Bruce Shapiro, "The High Price of Conscience," *Nation* 254 (Jan. 20, 1992): 50–54; Karen M. Thomas, "For Military Objectors;" "Clemency for Army Doctor Who Refused War Service," *New York Times,* 8 Apr. 1992, A8.

96. Ronald V. Dellums, introducing H.R. 5060, "The Military Conscientious Objector Act of 1992," in *Congressional Record,* 102d Cong., 2d sess. (May 5, 1992), vol. 138, no. 60, H 2942, E 1246–48, quotation at E 1246. The legislation, technically a bill to amend title 10 of the U.S. Code, would recognize selective objection to a specific war if the objection were based on sincerely held religious, moral, or ethical belief. It would establish a unified procedure among all the military services for processing and judging CO claims, eliminating variations such as occurred in the Marines. It would also shift the burden of proof to the military after the applicant had supplied detailed evidence that he or she was conscientious objector. While the claim was being processed, an objector would be protected against having to perform duties in violation of his or her conscience. See Michael Marsh, "Mistreated CO's Prompt Movement for Change," *Nonviolent Activist: The Magazine of the War Resisters League* 9 (March 1992): 13–14; "Dellums' Bill to Strengthen Military CO Process," NISBCO, *Reporter for Conscience' Sake* 49 (April 1992): 1, 5–6; and "The Military Conscientious Objector Act of 1992," *CCCO News Notes* 44 (Spring 1992): 8–9. On Amnesty International, see "Amnesty to Sponsor CO Campaign," *CCCO News Notes* 43 (Summer 1991): 1. On co-sponsors, *Congressional Record,* May 5, 1992, vol. 138, H 2942, and George O. Withers, legislative director for Rep. Ronald V. Dellums, telephone conversations with the author, June 9 and July 28, 1992.

97. L. William Yolton, executive director, National Interreligious Service Board for Conscientious Objectors (NISBCO), Washington, D.C., telephone interview with the author, April 5, 1991. The number of CO inquiries during the Persian Gulf deployment and war is a matter of some dispute. West Coast CCCO, with headquarters in San Francisco, estimated that it sent out ten thousand CO draft information packets in January and February 1991; Karen Jewett, a staff member at West Coast CCCO, telephone interview with author, March 27, 1991; see also the organization's periodical, *The Objector: Journal of Draft and Military Information* 11 (January–February 1991). East Coast CCCO, a separate organization, kept monthly figures on requests and mailings. Between September 1990 and March 1991, this Philadelphia-based group received requests for and distributed 16,813 "CO cards," including 8,662 in January 1991 alone. It also sold 2,243 copies of the CCCO *Draft Handbook* before it ran out of stock in January. Robert A. Seeley, executive director, CCCO, Philadelphia, telephone interview with author, March 26, 1991, and monthly publication reports in Seeley to the author, March 26, 1991. About three thousand persons filed completed "CO cards" with the Philadelphia headquarters of CCCO between January and March 1991. Robert A. Seeley, telephone conversation with author May 30, 1991. See also "Statistics from the Gulf War," *CCCO News Notes* 43 (Spring 1991): 2.

98. For some interesting earlier comparisons, see Edward R. Cain, "Conscientious Objection in France, Britain, and the United States," *Comparative Politics* 2 (January 1970): 275–308; and Nigel Young, "Conscientious Objection," in *World Encyclopedia of Peace,* 4 vols., ed. Linus Pauling et al. (Oxford, U.K.: Pergamon Press, 1986), 1:187–92.

3.
The Dilemma of Conscientious Objection for Afro-Americans

1. This observation is based on the following publications: Eugene Murdock, *Patriotism Limited, 1862–1865* (Kent, Ohio: Kent State University Press, 1967); Jonas Hartzler, *Mennonites in the World War* (Scottdale, Pa.: Mennonite Publishing House, 1919); Walter Guest Kellogg, *The Conscientious Objector* (New York Boni and Liveright, 1919; New York: Garland Publishing, 1972); Horace C. Peterson and Gilbert C. Fite, *Opponents of War, 1917–1918* (Madison Wis.: University of Wisconsin Press, 1957); Merle E. Curti, *The American Peace Crusade, 1815–1880* (New York: Octagon Books, 1965); Lawrence S. Wittner, *Rebels against War The American Peace Movement, 1933–1983* (Philadelphia: Temple University Press, 1984); Willard Gaylin, *In the Service of Their Country: War Resisters in Prison* (New York: Viking, 1970); Fred Holstead, *GIs Speak Out against the War* (New York: Pathfinder Press, 1970); J. Osborne, *I Refuse* (Philadelphia: Westminster Press, 1970); Thomas L. Hayes, *American Deserters in Sweden* (New York: Association Press, 1971); Blanche Wiesen Cook et al., eds., *Reminiscences of War Resisters in World War I* (1935; reprint; New York: Garland Publishing, 1972) Howard Newby, *Social Changes in Rural England* (Madison: University of Wisconsin Press, 1980); Nat Hentoff, *Peace Agitator: The Life of A. J. Muste* (New York: Macmillan, 1983); Howard Moore, *Plowing My Own Furrow* (New York: W. W. Norton, 1985); Caroline Moorehead, *Troublesome People* (London: Hamish Hamilton, 1986).

2. See, for example, Lt. Col. Jesse J. Johnson, ed., *The Black Soldier: Documented, 1619–1815: Missing Pages in United States History* (Hampton, Va.: Hampton Institute, 1969); Jay David and Elaine Crane, eds., *The Black Soldier: From the American Revolution to Vietnam* (New York: William Morrow, 1971). For an example in the popular press, see the feature article during Black History Month by Michael A. W. Ottey, "The Black Soldier," (N. J.) *Asbury Park Press,* 24 Feb. 1991, Cl.

3. Booker T. Washington et al., 1900; Washington, 1913.

4. See C. E. Kerman and Richard Eldridge, *The Lives of Jean Toomer* (Baton Rouge: Louisiana State University, 1987).

5. For examples, see the War Resisters League, American Section, *The Conscientious Objector,* vols. 1–6, 1939–1946, and the National Service Board for Religious Objectors, *The Reporter,* vols. 1 and 2, 1942–1944.

6. Frederick Douglass, *Life and Times of Frederick Douglass* (New York: Pathway Books, 1941), 376–85, 592; William E. B. Du Bois, *Dusk of Dawn* (1940; reprint, New York: Kraus-Thomson, 1975).

7. C. L. R. James et al., eds., *Fighting Racism in World War II* (New York: Monad Press, 1980).

8. James et al., *Fighting Racism.*

9. For recent polling data, see Isabel Wilkerson, "Blacks Wary of Their Big Role in Military," *New York Times,* 25 Jan. 1991, Al.

10. "What's Next General Powell?" *U.S. News & World Report* (18 Mar. 1991); 50–53.

11. Gunnar Myrdal, *An American Dilemma* (New York: Harper Brothers, 1944).

12. James et al., *Fighting Racism;* David J. Garrow, *Bearing the Cross* (London: Jonathan Cape, 1986).

13. James et al. *Fighting Racism.*

14. Reprinted in Michael Ferber and Staughton Lynd, *The Resistance* (Boston: Beacon, 1971), 31–32.

15. Holstead, *GIs Speak Out*.

16. Garrow, *Bearing the Cross*.

17. Statistics from a personal communication with the editors from the U.S. Marine Corps, February 1992. For press coverage of the Marine COs, see Laurie Goodstein, "9 Who Refused to Fight Await the Corps' Verdict," *Washington Post*, 16 Apr. 1991, A3; Peter Applebome, "Epilogue to Gulf War: 25 Marines Face Prison," *New York Times*, 3 May 1991, A14; for the Navy, see "Navy Orders Trial for 2," *Boston Globe*, 30 Mar. 1991, 6; "Amidst Controversy over Military Treatment of Muslims: Charges against Sailors Dropped," NISBCO *Reporter for Conscience' Sake* 48 (April 1991): 7.

18. During World War II, the Hopi tribe's aversion to all war resulted in their receiving conscientious objector status. It would be interesting to examine what the Hopi pacifist beliefs were, and to compare and contrast them with those of other native populations.

19. Another area of secularization of Afro-American culture during the last twenty years, especially in the last decade, has been the growing number of highly visible blacks outside traditional Afro-American institutions and communities. Colin Powell, Clifton Wharton, Douglas Wilder, and Charles Massey are only a few examples of the new secular black power structure in America.

4.
Alternative Service in a Future Draft

1. Charles Maresca, "Supreme Court Rules Churches May Require Faith Commitments," NISBCO, *The Reporter for Conscience' Sake* 44 (July 1987): 1.

2. U.S. Selective Service System, *Semiannual Report of the Director of Selective Service*, July 1 to December 31, 1970 (Washington, D.C.: Government Printing Office, 1971), 7.

3. U.S. Selective Service System, *Registrant Information Management System* (Washington, D.C.: Selective Service System, 1987), 15–37.

4. Michelle LeCompte, "Service Members Who Won't Fight," *Times Magazine*, 9 Jan. 1984, 10, 12.

5.
Britain: From Individual Conscience to Social Movement

1. Nigel Young, "War Resistance, State and Society" in *War, State and Society*, ed. Martin Shaw (London: Macmillan, 1984), 104. See also Richard Taylor and Nigel Young, eds., *Campaigns for Peace: British Peace Movements in the Twentieth Century* (Manchester: Manchester University Press, 1987).

2. Memorandum to Central Board for Conscientious Objections 1942, cited in Rachel Barber, *Conscience, Government and War: Conscientious Objection in Great Britain 1939–1945* (London: Routledge & Kegan Paul, 1982), 16.

3. For an analysis of the legal problems of conscientious objection in the United Kingdom in both World Wars, see John Hughes, "The Legal Implications of Conscientious Objection" (L.L.M. thesis, University of Manchester, 1971).

4. F. L. Carsten, *War against War* (London: Batsford, 1982), 67.

5. The detailed composition of these tribunals is given by Barber, *Conscience, Gov-*

ernment and War, app. 1. An analysis of their decisions, derived from *Ministry of Labour and National Service files* [Public Record Office, lab 6, pieces 405 and 337], is given as app. 3, tables 1, 2, 3(a) to 3(b), 4, 5, 6(a), 6(b), and 7.

6. Tim Evens, *Standing Up to Be Counted,* 1–2. British government policy is carefully analyzed in John Rae, *Conscience and Politics: The British Government and the Conscientious Objectors to Military Service, 1916–1919* (Oxford: Oxford University Press, 1970).

7. Barber, *Conscience, Government and War,* 17–18.

8. Calculated from Barber, *Conscience, Government and War,* app. 3, table 2, p. 145. A comparison with the statistics applicable to the First World War is given by Rae, *Conscience and Politics,* 132.

9. National Service Act, 1948: S6b.

10. Arthur Watts, "The Way to End War," March 28, 1919, cited in Carsten, *War against War,* 68–69.

11. The membership of the No-Conscription Fellowship was drawn largely from the ranks of the Independent Labour Party, with a smaller representation of those, especially Quakers, who refused on religious grounds to undertake military service. At the height of its influence, the Fellowship had some twelve thousand members, of whom about half were imprisoned. The Fellowship published a journal of considerable influence, *The Tribunal* (1916–1918).

12. Evens, in his analysis of the experience of twenty-four conscientious objectors from the Second World War, reprints the firsthand testimony of one of them of the difficulties that he faced: "Had Appellate Tribunal in Bristol, but still got no exemption—probably because I claimed to be a Christian without affiliation to any church. Dismissal of my appeal meant that I went to an army medical, but refused to undress. I was therefore arrested and sentenced to six months imprisonment." Evens, *Standing Up to Be Counted,* 23.

13. "The Position of the Conscientious Objector," leaflet in the Library of Friends' House, London, cited by Carsten, *War against War,* 68.

14. *Hansard's Parliamentary Debates,* May 4, 1939, col. 2097.

15. Minutes of a special yearly meeting of the Society of Friends, January 28–30, 1916, cited in John W. Graham, *Conscription and Conscience: A History 1916–1919* (London: Allen and Unwin, 1922; New York: Garland Publishing, 1971), 162.

16. Account of the experiences of S. M. W. in Evens, *Standing Up to Be Counted,* 21.

17. Graham, *Conscription and Conscience,* 355. In this study, the author makes reference to the analysis by Piere Ramues in *Friedenskrieger des Hinterlandes* (Warrior of Peace behind the Front) and *Erkenntniss und Befreiung* (Conscience and Emancipation) of the difficulties faced by these Christian pacifists.

18. Keith Robbins, The *Abolition of War: The "Peace Movement" in Britain, 1914–1919* (Cardiff: University of Wales, 1976),23.

19. Both of these reactions are reflected in the conclusion of the *Socialist Review* in January 1913: "With the moral, the economic, the political justification of militarism shattered, and its literary and artistic glorification gone, the task of raising armies and popularizing war politics will be too hard for governments to attempt."

20. Gwyn Harries-Jenkins and Jacques van Doorn, eds., *The Military and the Problem of Legitimacy* (London: Sage, 1976).

21. In February 1915, for example, the annual report of the ILP's City of London branch stated: "It may be taken as a good augury for the future of anti-militarist and democratic ideals that the Branch has never been as prosperous as since it took up an attitude of open hostility to the foreign and military policy of the Government and to the hysterical panic and misrepresentation masquerading as patriotism which seemed to hold undivided sway of the public mind." Among the rank and file of the ILP, more radical opinions were held.

22. Carsten, *War against War,* 57.

23. The difference in conceptual base among COs was expressed clearly in 1922 by John W. Graham in his classic study, *Conscription and Conscience*.

24. Gloden Dallas and Douglas Gill, *The Unknown Army: Mutinies in the British Army in World War I* (London: Verso, 1985), 36.

25. Caroline Moorehead, *Troublesome People: Enemies of War 1916–1986* (London: Hamish Hamilton, 1986).

26. Ibid.

27. Vera Brittain, *England's Hour 1939–41* (London: Macmillan, 1981), ch. 10.

28. Quoted in Carsten, *War against War*, 67.

29. James Burk, "Debating the Draft in America," *Armed Forces and Society* 15 (Spring 1989): 435.

30. Burk notes that concern over conscientious objectors is scarcely mentioned in Julia E. Johnson, ed., *Compulsory Military Training* (New York: H. W. Wilson, 1941). Similarly, R. J. Q. Adams and Philip P. Poirier, *The Conscription Controversy in Great Britain 1900–18* (London: Macmillan Press, 1987), note that traditional liberal resistance to conscription was based on an opposition to compulsion of the individual. A similar conclusion is reached by F. W. Perry, *The Commonwealth Armies: Manpower and Organization in Two World Wars* (Manchester: Manchester University Press, 1988). In Canada opposition to conscription was also based on political rather than religious grounds. See Frances V. Harbour, "Conscription and Socialization: Four Canadian Ministers," *Armed Forces and Society* 15 (Winter 1989): 227–47.

31. Caroline Moorehead, "Enemies of War," *The Listener* (April 16 1987): 12; see also Moorehead, *Troublesome People*.

32. By the end of 1944, 1,056 women who were liable to conscription under the provisions of the National Service (No. 2) Act of 1941 had appeared before conscientious objection tribunals. Of these, 93 were granted unconditional exemption, 771 were granted conditional exemption, 30 were liable to be called up for non-combatant duties, and the names of 162 were removed from the Register. See Barber, *Conscience, Government and War*, app. 3, table 3(h), 153.

6.
France: A Statute but No Objectors

1. The literature on this topic is immense; for a review of the philosophical-political aspects, see James Turner Johnson, *Ideology, Reason and the Limitation of War: Religious and Secular Concepts, 1200–1740* (Princeton: Princeton University Press, 1975); and Jacqueline Chanteur, *De la guerre à la paix* (Paris: Presses Universitaires de France, 1989).

2. The link between the constitution of a national armed force and the emergence and consolidation of the state has spawned a sizable literature. Less developed is conscription's relationship to the development of democratic institutions. Engels, in *Anti-Dühring*, and Mosca in *Elementi di Cienza politica*, for example, had suggested this relationship, and it later became one of the central issues in Morris Janowitz's macrosociological analyses; see especially, Janowitz, "Military Institutions and Citizenship in Western Societies," *Armed Forces and Society* 2 (Winter 1976): 185–204, and *The Reconstruction of Patriotism: Education for Civic Consciousness* (Chicago: University of Chicago Press, 1983). For further development concerning the French case see "The Citizen Soldier in France," in this chapter.

3. Literature on this question is vast, from Georg Simmel to Edward Shils; see Martin

Bulmer, "The Boundaries of the Private Realm: Limits to the *Imperium* of the Center," in *Center: Ideas and Institutions,* ed. Liah Greenfeld and Michel L. Martin. (Chicago: University of Chicago Press, 1988), 160–72.

4. T. H. Marshall, "Citizenship and Social Class," in *Sociology at the Crossroads* (London: Heineman, 1949); and Edward Shils, "The Theory of Mass Society," *Diogenes* (1962): 45–66.

5. Scholarly works on conscientious objection in France are few. Pierre Sablière, *Le Statut légal de l'objection de conscience en France* (Ph.D. diss., Librairie de Droit et de Jurisprudence, Paris, 1971); Jean-Pierre Cattelain, *L'Objection de conscience* (Paris: Presses Universitaires de France, 1973); and Jean-Paul Pancracio, "Le Nouveau statut des objecteurs de conscience," *Revue du Droit Public et de la Science Politique* 1 (January–February 1985): 105–56; Jean Duffar, "L'Objection de conscience en droit français," ibid. (May–June 1991): 655–95; and Daniel Jacquin, "L'Objection de conscience: figures d'acteurs," *Archives Européennes de Sociologie,* 31 (1990): 239–60. An exhaustive list of personal experiences by COs is included in Michel Auvray, *Objecteurs, insoumis, déserteurs: histoire des réfractaires en France* (Paris: Cerf, 1983).

6. Regarding the royal militia and its problems, see Georges Girard, *Le Service militaire en France à la fin du règne de Louis XIV: racolage et milice* (Paris: Plon, 1921); André Corvisier, *L'Armée française de la fin du XVIIIe à la fin du ministère Choiseul,* vol. 1 (Paris: Presses Universitaires de France, 1964); and D. Gillet, "Étude de la désertion dans les armées royales à l'époque de Louis XIV" (mémoire, Université de Paris, 1973).

7. For a good synthesis on this question, see the recent work of Alan Forrest, *Conscripts and Deserters: The Army and French Society during the Revolution and Empire* (New York: Oxford University Press, 1989); Jean-Paul Bertaud, *La Révolution armée: les soldats-citoyens et la révolution française* (Paris, 1973); and Richard Cobb, *Reactions to the French Revolution* (Oxford: Oxford University Press, 1972).

8. Even the rallying of deserters to the counterrevolution rarely arose from political convictions; see Forrest, *Conscripts and Deserters,* 16 and ch. 7.

9. André Philip et al., "Proposition de loi tendant à la création d'un service civil pour les objecteurs de conscience," *Documents, Assemblée Nationale,* sess. 1949, app. no. 8568, p. 2065. The issue was dealt with again in 1952 by the Christian Democrats, ibid., sess. 1952, app. no. 3738, and again by the Socialists in 1956, ibid., sess. 1956, app. no. 486.

Concerning the amnesty measures, see M. Girardot, "Proposition de loi tendant à remettre en liberté les objecteurs de conscience emprisonnés," *Documents, Assemblée Nationale,* sess. 1956, app. no. 9897, p. 860. This proposal was introduced in the form of an amendment to the amnesty bill of August 1953 by Daniel Mayer and M. Binot; it was adopted by the Assembly but rejected by the Senate.

10. The Jehovah's Witnesses refuse, however, to be called pacifists; see Hélène Roujas-Austry, "Secte et ordre social: l'exemple des Témoins de Jéhovah" (Ph.D. diss., University of Toulouse I, December 1987).

11. Pierre Messmer, "Projet de loi relatif à certaines modalités d'accomplissement du service national présenté au nom de M. Georges Pompidou premier ministre." *Documents, Assemblée Nationale,* sess. 1962–1963, app. no. 432, pp. 708–9.

12. Various proposed amendments included interdiction of hunting rights, suppression of civic rights, and political and administrative ineligibility. See the debates in *Journal Officiel* (J.O.) *Assemblée Nationale et Sénat,* July 24–December 11 1963.

13. "Loi no. 63–1255 du 21 décembre 1963 relative à certaines modalités d'accomplissement des obligations imposées par la loi sur le recrutement," *J.O., Lois et Décréts,* December 22, 1963, 11456–57.

14. Among those pointing to the paralyzing effect created by the restrictive character

of Article 2 on the application of the law was M. Longequeue, "Projet de loi portant prolongation du délai d'option pour les objecteurs de conscience," *Documents, Assemblée Nationale,* sess. 1970–1971, no. 1582. In 1971, Parliament extended the deadline to thirty days.

15. Confirmed by a written ministerial answer. *J.O., Assemblée Nationale, Questions,* January 26, 1981, 347.

16. Figures from *Le Monde,* 29 Jan. and 8 Dec. 1980.

17. "Rapport fait au nom de la commission de la défense nationale et des forces armées sur le projet de loi no. 1597 portant code du service national," *Documents, Assemblée Nationale,* sess. 1970–1971, no. 1629, p. 20.

18. "Loi no. 71–424 du 10 Juin 1971 portant code du service national," *J.O., Lois et Décrets,* June 12, 1971, 5659 and following.

19. See *J.O., Assemblée Nationale (Comptes rendus des débats),* April 7, 1971, 905–22; April 8, 1971, 943–82; *J.O., Sénat (Comptes rendus des débats),* May 7, 1971, 337–62; Pierre de Chevigny, "Rapport fait au nom de la commission des affaires étrangères et de la défense nationale sur le projet de loi adopté par l'assemblée nationale portant code du service national," *Documents, Sénat,* sess. 1970–1971, no. 206.

20. "Décret no. 72–806 du 31 août 1972," *J.O., Lois et Décrets,* September 2, 1972, 9437.

21. *Le Monde,* 6 Feb. 1974.

22. *J.O. Assemblée Nationale, Questions,* March 16, 1981, 1108.

23. On this phenomenon, see Edward Shils, "Plentitude and Scarcity: The Anatomy of an International Crisis," *Encounter* (May 1986): 37–48.

24. The journal *Objection,* for example, has become very anti-army; see Charles Deprez, "Rapport fait au nom de la commission de la défense nationale et des forces armées sur la proposition de loi no. 1537 . . . et de loi no. 1543," *Documents, Assemblée Nationale,* sess. 1980–1981, no. 2096, p. 7.

25. The number of those admitted to CO status grew from 471 in 1973 to 764 in 1978; see the ministerial response to Jean-Pierre Chevènement *J.O., Assemblée Nationale, Questions,* March 10, 1979, 1446.

26. Figures from Jean Gatel, "Rapport fait par la commission de la défense nationale et des forces armées sur le projet de loi (no. 741) portant suppression des tribunaux permanents des forces armées et modifiant le Code de procédure pénale et du Code de justice militaire," 2 vols., *Documents, Assemblée Nationale,* sess. 1981–1982, no. 758, 1:32–33. The actual percentage of objectors dodging service is much lower, 15 percent at most. Nearly 70 percent of the total are so-called administrative dodgers, those with dual citizenship or those who have inadvertently failed to notify military authorities of a changed address.

27. *Le Monde,* 8 Dec. 1980.

28. Figures quoted in Marie-Thérèse Patrat, "Rapport fait au nom de la commission de la défense nationale et des forces armées sur le projet de loi (1417) modifiant le Code du service national, les propositions de loi . . . " *Documents, Assemblée Nationale,* sess. 1981–1983, no. 1483, 49 and 51.

29. Among these were Michel Crépeau and Pierre Duraffour, "Projet de loi modifiant les articles 41 à 50 du code du service national relatifs à l'objection de conscience," Edwige Avice et al., "Projet de loi tendant à modifier certaines dispositions relatives à l'objection de conscience de loi no. 71–424 du 10 juin 1971; Yves Lancien et al., "Projet de loi tendant à une réforme du service national," all in *Documents, Assemblée Nationale,* session 1979–1980, no. 80, nos. 72, 1537, 1543, and 1843. The large number of written questions that members of Parliament sent to government ministers testifies to the interest in these issues.

30. See *Le Monde,* 8 Dec. 1980; and Charles Hernu et al., "Projet de loi tendant à la création d'une commission chargée de proposer des mesures indispensables à la réforme du

service national," *Documents, Assemblée Nationale,* sess. 1977–1978, no. 539; Edwige Avice et al., "Projet de loi sur les conditions de déroulement du service national et des droits et des libertés des appelés," ibid., sess. 1980–1981, no. 2221. Another proposal for reform was for the reduction of conscription to six months.

31. "Loi no. 83–605 du 8 juillet 1983 modifiant le Code du service national," *J.O., Lois et Décrets,* July 9, 1983; the measures concerning conscientious objection are on p. 2113. "Décret no. 84–234 du 29 mars 1984 modifiant certaines dispositions du Code du service national," *J.O., Lois et Décrets,* April, 1, 1984, 1026.

32. Pierre Mauroy and Charles Hernu, "Projet de loi modifiant le Code du service national," *Documents, Assemblée Nationale,* sess. 1982–1983, no. 1417, 3.

33. The active reserve service extends to age 35. See the ministerial responses to two written questions of members of the Parliament, *J.O., Assemblée Nationale, Questions,* September 2, 1985, 4108, and December 1, 1986, 4577.

34. Mentioned several times in the debates; see *J.O., Assemblée Nationale, Compte rendus des débats,* May 17, 1983, 1077.

35. Figures from Roger Chinaud, "Rapport général fait au nom de la commission des finances, du contrôle budgétaire et des comptes économiques de l'assemblée nationale sur le projet de loi de finance pour 1990," *Documents, Sénat,* sess. 1989–1990, no. 59, t. I11, app. 46, 39.

36. See, for example, *J.O., Assemblée Nationale, Questions,* January 1, 1984, 4340; April 26, 1984, 1793, 1799; July 23, 1984, 3408; December 10, 1984, 5395; December 16, 1985, 5725; and September 14, 1987, 5118.

37. *Le Monde,* 6 Oct. 1981.

38. Chinaud, "Rapport général," 38.

39. Deputy Jean-Pierre Kucheida, in two queries written to the defense minister, *J.O., Assemblée Nationale, Questions,* August 5, 1985, 3671, July 27, 1987, 4251.

40. Yves Dollo, rapporteur for cultural affairs, *J.O., Assemblée Nationale, Compte rendus des débats,* May 1983, 1081.

41. See, for example, the recommendation no. R (87) 8, adopted by the Council of Ministers, April 9, 1987, "Objection de conscience au service militaire obligatoire," Strasbourg: Conseil de l'Europe, June 22, 1987.

42. Charles Hernu, *J.O., Assemblée Nationale, Compte rendus des débats,* 1088; and minister's response to one written question, *J.O., Assemblée Nationale, Questions,* July 27, 1987, 4251.

43. See the parliamentary debates. The Communists were generally against too great a liberalization of conscientious objection for fear it would serve as a cover for defaulting. They favored a less generous recognition, with a service period equal to the draft.

44. Notably Jean Jaurès's famous *L'Armée nouvelle* (Paris: Jules Rouff, 1911), which inspired, for instance, Charles Hernu's *Le Soldat-citoyen: essai sur la sécurité de la France* (Paris: Flammarion, 1975).

45. The building of large armed forces incurred bureaucratic, legislative, and police innovations, in turn reinforcing the power and the range of the state's control of society. For a good analysis of the confrontation between the state and society, see Isser Wolloch, "Napoleonic Conscription, State Power, and Civil Society," *Past and Present* 111 (1986); and Forrest, *Conscripts and Deserters.*

46. This point is underlined by Eugen Weber, *Peasants into Frenchmen: The Modernization of Rural France, 1870–1914* (Stanford, Calif.: Stanford University Press, 1976).

47. See references in note 2.

48. Ibid.; see also Michel Bozon, *Les Conscrits* (Paris: Berger-Levrault, 1981).

49. Computed from Chinaud, "Rapport général, 38; for 1989, see *Le Figaro,* 16 July 1990, 7.

50. Ibid.

51. *Le Monde*, 26 May 1989, 16.

52. Ibid.

53. This point was emphasized by communist parliamentary members during the 1983 debates. See *J.O.*, *Assemblée Nationale, Compte rendus des débats*, May 16, 1983, 1091. There was a written question to the government, *J.O.*, *Assemblée Nationale, Questions*, April 24, 1988.

54. Amnesty International, *1988 Report;* Le *Canard enchaîné*, April 1990.

55. *Le Monde*, 26 May 1989, 16.

56. These figures are quoted from Patrat, *"Rapport fait au nom,"* 51–56.

57. Claude Imbert, "The End of French Exceptionalism," *Foreign Affairs* 68 (Fall 1989): 48–60.

58. *Le Monde*, 23 May 1989.

59. For accounts of pacifism and antimilitary feeling in France, see M. Meyer-Spiegler, *Antimilitarisme et refus du service militaire dans la France contemporaine* (Ph.D. diss., Fondation nationale des sciences politiques, Paris, 1969); Jean Rabaut, *L'Antimiltarisme en France, 1810–1975* (Paris: Hachette, 1975).

60. For an analysis of the different factors that have restrained pacifist developments in France, see Jolyon Howorth and Patricia Chilton, eds., *Defense and Dissent in Contemporary France* (New York: St. Martin's Press, 1984), 173–252; and *Le Monde*, 19–20 June 1983.

61. *Le Monde*, 23 May 1989; *Le Point*, 18 March 1991, 18–20.

62. For an analysis of the attachment of military officers, especially from the ground forces, to conscription, see Michel L. Martin, *Warriors to Managers: The French Military Establishment Since 1945* (Chapel Hill: University of North Carolina Press, 1981). See also *Le Monde*, 20 March 1990.

63. *Cahiers de Mars*, 122 (3rd quarter 1989), quoted by Claude LeBorgne, "Vers l'armée de métier," *Défense Nationale* 45 (January 1990): 45–52. See also his recent *Le Président et le champignon* (Paris: Albin Michel, 1991).

64. See *Le Monde*, 20 Mar. 1990. For a detailed analysis of these issues see Bernard Boëne and Michel L. Martin, eds., *Conscription et armée de métier* (Paris: La Documentation française, 1991).

7.
The Federal Republic of Germany: Conscientious Objection as Social Welfare

1. *VII*. Senat des Bundesverwaltungsgerichts am 03.10.1958.

2. For a history of conscientious objection see Dieter Maar, *Materialien zur Kriegsdienstverweigerung: Entstehungs- und Entwicklungsgeschichte des Grundrechtes* (Koblenz: ZINFU, 1989).

3. Hans-Joachim Korte, "Kriegsdienst—Wehrdienstverweigerung," in *Bundeswehr und Gesellschaft*, ed. Ralf Zoll et al. (Opladen: Westdeutscher Verlag, 1978), 151.

4. *Bundesverfassungsgericht* 13.10.1978. See also Hans-Georg Schult-Gerstein, "Staat und Gewissen," *Beiträge zur Konfliktforschung* 17 (1987): 37–52.

5. Konrad Hecker, "Kriegsdienstverweigerung—Dienen in Zivil," in *Immer diese Jugend* (Munich: Deutsches Jugendinstitut, 1985), 468.

6. Heinz-Ulrich Kohr and Hans-Georg Räder, *Image der Bundeswehr* (Munich: SOWI, 1989).

7. Dietrich Bäuerle, *Totalverweigerung als Widerstand* (Frankfurt: M. Fischer, 1989).

8. See the discussion by Jürgen Kuhlmann, "West Germany: The Right Not to Bear Arms," in *The Moral Equivalent of War?: A Study of Non-Military Service in Nine Nations,* ed Donald Eberly and Michael Sherraden (Westport, Conn.: Greenwood Press, 1990), 127–50. Also see Kuhlmann, "Linkages between Military Service and Alternative National Service in West Germany," in *International Forum vol 4: Military and Society,* ed. Kuhlmann (Munich: SOWI, 1984).

9. Klaus Steinwender, "Zivildienst vorrangig im Sozialen Bereich," in *Zivildienst nur Militärersatzdienst,* ed. EAK (Bremen: EAK, 1988); Werner von Scheven, "Das Gewissen degeneriert" in *Sicherung des Friedens* 9 (1989): 6–7.

10. Ekkehard Lippert, "Youth and Military Occupations: The Case of the Federal Republic of Germany," in *International Forum: Youth Motivation and Military Service,* ed. Jürgen Kuhlmann and Anton Bebler (Munich: SOWI, 1987).

11. Guidelines are specified in section 4 of the Law on Civilian Service.

12. A full-time ambulance person, for example, costs about DM55,000 a year. Less than 10 percent of this sum must be paid to a conscientious objector doing the same job. Christian Wernicke, "Die Helfer—oft hilflos," *Zeit,* 8 Sept. 1989, 3.

13. Jürgen Blandow, "Zivildienstleistende als Personalgruppe des Wohlfahrtswesens," in *Zivildienst nur Militärersatzdienst,* ed. EAK (Bremen: EAK, 1988); Cornelius Kraus, *Zur volkswirtschaftlichen Bedeutung des Zivildienstes* (Darmstadt: Technische Hochschule, 1988).

14. Reinhard Becker and G. A. Hoffman, "Ein Anlass zum Jubeln? 25 Jahre Zivildienst in der Bundesrepublik Deutschland," in *Sozialer Friedensdienst im Zivildienst,* ed. Evangelishe Arbeitsgemeinschaft zur Betreuung der Kriegsdienstverweigerer (Bremen: EAK, 1989), 77.

15. Klaus Puzicha and Adelheid Meissner, *Unter die Soldaten? Junge Männer zwischen Bundeswehr und Wehrdienstverweigerung* (Opladen: Leske u. Budrich, 1981), 39.

16. "Jugendwerk," in *Jugend 81* (Hamburg: SHELL, 1981), 189.

17. Puzicha and Meissner, *Unter die Soldaten?,* 86.

18. Leo Montada and Angela Schneider, *Versuch einer Charakterisierung von Kriegsdienstverweigerren im Vergleich zu Soldaten* (Bonn: BMVG, 1986); Helgard Röder, *Kriegsdienstverweigerer und Freiwillige im Vergleich* (Frankfurt: Suhrkamp, 1977).

19. Doebert Rainer and Gertrud Nunner-Winkler, *Adoleszenskrise und Identitätsbildung* (Frankfurt: Suhrkamp, 1975), 179.

20. Wolfgang Vogt and Elmar Wiesendahl, "Legitimations- und Akzeptanzprobleme der Bundeswehr-Materialien," (Hamburg: Führungsakademie der Bundeswehr, Zentrum für Innere Führung, 1989), 88.

21. *IAP-Dienst,* H. 1 (1988), 11.

22. Vogt and Wiesendahl, *Legitimations- und Akzeptanzprobe,* 146.

8.
Denmark: The Vanguard of Conscientious Objection

1. Svend Erik Larsen, *Militærnægterproblemet i Danmark, 1914–1967* (The Conscientious Objection Problem in Denmark, 1914–1967) (Odense: Odense University Press, 1977), 9.

2. Ibid., 9–10.

3. Devi Prasad and Tony Smythe, eds., *Conscription: A World Survey: Compulsory Military Service and Resistance to It.* (London: War Resisters International, 1968), 30.

4. Ibid., 13.

5. Ibid., 25.

6. Ibid., 31.

7. Bodil Hansen, Conscript Board of the Ministry of Interior, telephone interview with the author, March 11, 1990.

8. Steen Borup-Nielsen, "Conscription and Conscientious Objection in Denmark" (Paper presented at the Defense Leadership Training Center, Copenhagen, 1985).

9. In the most recent figures, forty young men registered as Jehovah's Witnesses. Of these, twenty escaped through the lottery, fifteen registered for six months, and five registered for only one month. After registering the Jehovah's Witnesses, military authorities transfer the administration of these individuals to the Civil Service Board. (Reported to the author by Maj. B. O. Riis, Conscripts Section, Defense Command, Vedbæk. The author gratefully acknowledges this helpful information.)

10. Arbejdsgruppen vedr. Vaernepligtsproblemtikken (Working Group on Conscript Problems), *Redegørelse for værne-pligtssituationen i perioden 1971–80, 3. del; Militaernægterspørgsmalet* (Statement on the Conscript Situation in the Period 1971–80, Part 3: The Issue of Conscientious Objectors) (March 1972), 6.

11. Hans J. S. Mogensen, *Militærnægterhandbogen—en bog for værnepligtige* (Manual for Conscientious Objectors—A Book for the Military Conscript) (Langeskov: Aldrig mere Krig, 1989), 13.

12. Arbejdsgruppen, *Redegørelse for værne-pligtssituationen*, 6; Borup-Nielsen, "Conscription and Conscientious Objection," 3.

13. *Gallup Poll Yearbook, 1971*, Survey 44.

14. Observa Institute, *The Danes, 1967–1977* (Copenhagen: Observa Institute, 1977), 169.

15. Larsen, *Militærnægterproblemet i Danmark*, 87, 91. Larsen cites the records of the War Resisters League as the basis for his figures.

16. Figures from 1945 to 1989 come from the Danish National Military Service Board, Værnepligtsstyrelsen, letter of March 6, 1990, j. nr. 1990/30–6. For these and other figures on conscripts and conscientious objectors, the author is indebted to Per Jensen of the Conscript Section, Civil Service Board, as well as to Maj. B. O. Riis of the Conscripts Section of the Defense Command, and Bodil Hansen of the Conscript Board of the Ministry of Interior. The numbers of conscripts each year are taken from Borup-Nielsen, "Conscription and Conscientious Objection," 5.

17. Borup-Nielsen, "Conscription and Conscientious Objection," 9.

9.
Norway: Toward Full Freedom of Choice?

The authors would like to acknowledge the assistance of Håvard Hegre in data collection and analysis, as well as word processing. Per Tonstad gave permission to quote from his unpublished thesis. A number of government agencies provided data and information, particularly the Judge Advocate General's Office and the Conscription Service. The International Peace Research Institute, Oslo (PRIO) provided financial support for the study. Jens Grøgaard let us see material from his forthcoming study of Norwegian draftees. We acknowledge comments from Tor Egil Førland, as well as participants in the 1990 Utrecht conference, on an earlier version of the manuscript. A longer version is available from PRIO in the PRIO Report series (1993).

1. Under the 1814 Treaty of Kiel, Denmark, which had sided with France in the

Napoleonic Wars, was obliged to cede Norway to the Swedish crown. Although the country technically was ruled by Sweden from 1814 to 1905, the act of union of 1814 recognized Norway as an independent kingdom with its own constitution and parliament. In 1905 the Norwegian parliament formally dissolved the union, and the Swedish government acquiesced. The second son of the future King Frederick VIII of Denmark was elected king of Norway as Haakon VII.

2. Otto Gjerpe, "Debatten om alminnelig verneplikt i Norge 1814–1821" (The Debate about Conscription in Norway, 1814–1821), (Graduate thesis in history, University of Oslo, 1953).

3. Sivert Langholm, *Stillingsretten i norsk vernepliktsdebatt og vernepliktslovgivning 1848–1876* (The *Stillingsrett* in the Norwegian Debate and Legislation for Conscription, 1848–1876) (Oslo: Norwegian University Press, 1966).

4. Ernst Lapin, "Det norske kvekersamfunnet, 1846–98: En undersøkelse med hovedvekt på Stavangermenigheten" (The Norwegian Quaker Community, 1846–98: A Study with a Main Emphasis on the Stavanger Quaker Society) (Graduate thesis in history, University of Bergen, 1983); see also Hans Eirik Aarek, "Oversikt over militærnektingens historie i Norge" (An Outline of the History of Conscientious Objection in Norway), forthcoming.

5. See Nils Ivar Agøy, "The Norwegian Peace Movement and the Question of Conscientious Objection to Military Service, 1885–1922," in *Towards a Comparative Analysis of Peace Movements,* ed. Katsuya Kodama and Unto Vesa (Brookfield, Vt.: Gower, 1990): 89–104.

6. It was not the number of COs that posed a challenge to the conscription system, but the intensity of their beliefs and their support among elements in the larger civilian community.

7. Nils Ivar Agøy, "Regulating Conscientious Objection in Norway from the 1890s to 1922," *Peace & Change: A Journal of Peace Research* 15 (January 1990): 3–25. See also Agøy, "Norwegian Peace Movement."

8. When the Labor Party split in 1923, the Communists captured control of the Labor Youth Movement. The new movement, founded by the Labor Party, renamed the "Left Communist Youth Federation," called in 1924 for a strike against the military forces. They persuaded the party to join in this action. A number of prominent Labor Party and youth leaders were jailed for inciting young men to refuse to perform military service. In 1925 the Labor Party reversed its position and called for a return to its traditional position of antimilitarist agitation in the barracks rather than objection to military service.

9. Under the 1922 and 1925 laws, a CO first had to commit a technical crime when he was drafted in order to be judged by a court and exempted as a conscientious objector. If the judicial authorities found that the defendant did not meet the criteria for being a CO, however, he would be punished for his crime. This arrangement soon came under attack, including condemnation by the Lutheran church, but the military leadership opposed any reform on the grounds that it would undermine the conscription principle and would play into the hands of the peace movement. Not until passage of the Alternative Service Law of 1937 was it possible for objectors to apply for alternative service directly to the Ministry of Justice. The key phrase remained "serious conviction" against military service of any kind.

10. Arne Haugestad, "Politisk militærnekting" (Political Objection), *Pax* 8 (1969): 44–49; Nils Kristian Sundby, "Militærnekting på politisk grunnlag" (Conscientious Objection on a Political Basis), *Lov og Rett* 10 (1968): 385–409; Anders Bratholm, "Militærnekting—lov, rettspraksis, og behovet for reform" (Conscientious Objection—the Law, Legal Practice, and the Need for Reform), *Lov og Rett* 11 (1971): 1–20.

11. Ministry of Justice *(Rode-utvalget), Utkast til lov om fritakelse for vepnet militær*

tjeneste av overbevisningsgrunner (Draft Law on Exemption from Armed Military Service on Grounds of Conscience) (Oslo: Ministry of Justice, 1955).

12. Vilhelm Aubert et al.: *Den nye militærnekterloven. Et motforslag* (Høvik: Folkereisning mot Krig, 1956).

13. For the debate on the content and goal of the alternative service program, see Tor Egil Førland, "Miljøsoldatene: en PR-bløff" (Environmental Soldiers: Window Dressing), *Vårt Land* (March 13, 1990); CO Secretariat, *Sivilarbeidernes syn. En motmelding til: Stortingsmelding 70 "Om Verneplikt"* (The View of the COs: A Counter-Report to "On Conscription," *Stortingsmelding* 70 [1983–1984]) (Oslo: Central Secretariat of the COs, 1984).

14. See, for example, *Amnesty International Report* (1986), 293. The official Norwegian position has been that neither the European Human Rights Convention nor the International Human Rights Convention has binding rules that decree that there must be an alternative to military service. Other nonbinding declarations of international law do not provide precise guidance as to what reasons for conscientious objection should be accepted. See *Stortingsmelding* 27 (1988–1989), 22–24.

15. *Amnesty International Report (1992)* (London; Amnesty International Publications), 206.

16. *Verneplikt* (Conscription). *Norges Offentlige Utredninger* 1979, no. 51(Oslo: Norwegian University Press, 1979).

17. Ministry of Justice, *Om Verneplikt* (On Conscription), *Stortingsmelding* 70 (1983–84) (Oslo: Ministry of Justice, 1984).

18. *Om militær verneplikt og sivil tjenesteplikt* (On Military Conscription and Civilian Service Duty), *Stortingsmelding* 27 (1988–1989) (Oslo: Ministry of Justice, 1989); and *Om lov om endringer i lov 19 mars 1965 nr 3 om fritaking for militærjeneste av overbevisningsgrunner og lov 17 juli 1953 nr 29 om verneplikt* (Proposal Amending Earlier Laws on Conscription and Conscientious Objection), *Odelstingsproposisjon* 39 (1988–1989) (Oslo: Ministry of Justice, February 24, 1989).

19. No such cases had reached the Supreme Court by November 1992.

20. Most public discussion of conscientious objection takes the absolute levels as its starting point. A comparison of absolute numbers of COs with relative numbers (the number of CO applications as a percentage of the cohort called up for military service in any given year) discloses that this error is not too serious because the broad outlines of the curves over time are the same. The rate of conscientious objection in the early 1950s, however, is seriously underestimated by using absolute rather than relative figures. The rise in conscientious objection in the early 1970s also was less dramatic than the absolute numbers might suggest. The peak rate in 1975 was barely 1.5 percentage points above the 1951 peak rate. On the other hand, the relative figures show that the rate of conscientious objection in the 1980s was higher than ever before (between 8 and 9 percent, as contrasted to a peak of 7 percent in 1951), a fact obscured by the absolute figures.

21. In the initial phase of very low conscientious objection, the absolute number of COs may be the most meaningful index of activity. At the higher levels, however, the fluctuations to a large extent reflect variations in the size of the population called up for military service in any given year. Norway now practices general conscription for all males, rather than a draft based on lottery or systematic selection criteria. Conscripts drew lots until 1910 and again in 1926–1935, but the lottery was abolished because it was viewed as unfair. Without a mechanism to regulate the intake, the size of the relevant cohort influences the number called up for military service and thus affects the number of COs. In addition, administrative practice may vary. For example, an increasing frequency of military exercises may boost the number of call-ups. The rapid rise in the number of COs before 1922 was partly a result

of the practice of repeatedly calling up religious objectors. Because they had not discharged their service obligations, they were called up every year until they had done so. Their numbers grew so rapidly because new objectors were added to the pool every year.

22. Ministry of Justice, *Stortingsmelding* 27 (1988–1989), 11.

23. S. Moene, personal communication with Nils Ivar Agøy, January 1990. See also Ministry of Justice, *Stortingsmelding* 27 (1988–1989), 18.

24. Letter from the Ministry of Justice, September 15, 1989.

25. Nils Ivar Agøy, *"Kampen mot vernetvangen": Militærnekterspørsmålet i Norge 1885–1922* (The Struggle against Forced Conscription: The Conscientious Objection Issue in Norway, 1885–1922) (Graduate thesis in history, University of Oslo, 1987), 34, 134; revised version forthcoming.

26. *Statistics Yearbook* NOS B 774 (Oslo: Central Bureau of Statistics, 1988), 100.

27. Membership figures reported by the organization.

28. Standard sources on the Pentecostals in Norway are Nils Bloch-Hoell, *The Pentecostal Movement* (Oslo: Norwegian University Press, 1964) and Tor Edvin Dahl and John-Willy Rudolph, *Fra seier til nederlag: Pinsebevegelsen i Norge* (From Victory to Defeat: The Pentecostal Movement in Norway) (Oslo: Land og Kirke/Gyldendal, 1978). These sources are virtually silent on the issue of conscientious objection; consequently the authors' assertions are based largely on scattered personal experiences and on conversations with present and former Pentecostals.

29. Nils Bloch-Hoell, "Smiths venner: En eiendommelig norsk dissenterbevegelse" (Smith's Friends: A Curious Norwegian Dissenters' Movement), *Tidsskrift for Teologi og Kirke* 27 (1956): 165–77.

30. In a study of the 1902–1922 period, occupational data were available only for a minority (30 percent) of the COs. Among both religious and nonreligious COs, a sizable majority belonged to the working class. Some 47 percent listed their occupation as "worker" and 21 percent as "artisan" and "apprentice." The third largest category was that of preacher (9 percent). Only a small minority (5 percent) of COs came from the primary sector, which made up about 45 percent of the population during this period (Agøy, *Kampen mot vernetvangen*, 160).

31. Johan Galtung, *Hva mener sivilarbeiderne? En undersøkelse på Havnås leir for vernepliktige sivilarbeidere* (What are the Opinions of the Conscientious Objectors? A Survey at Havnås Camp) (Oslo: University of Oslo, Department of Sociology, *Stensilserie*, 1957).

32. CO Secretariat, *Sivilarbeidernes syn. En motmelding til*, 75.

33. Per Tonstad, *Militærnekting og verneplikt: En studie av militærnektingens omfang og militærnekternes sosiale og geografiske bakgrunn* (Conscientious Objection and Conscription: A Study of the Extent of Conscientious Objection and the Social and Geographical Background of the Conscientious Objectors) (Bergen: Department of Sociology, University of Bergen, 1976).

34. They also can lead to changes in administrative practice. For example, the rate of denials of CO applications reached a peak in 1953, two years after the peak in applications; the same phenomenon occurred in the early 1970s and the 1980s, suggesting that officials were trying administratively to reduce the net rate of objection at a time of dramatically increasing conscientious objection.

35. Agøy, *Kampen mot vernetvangen*.

36. Nils Petter Gleditsch, "The Rise and Decline of the New Peace Movement," in *Towards a Comparative Analysis of Peace Movements*, ed. Kodama and Vesa, 73–88.

37. Tonstad, *Militærnekting og verneplikt*, analyzed conscientious objection in Norway during the Korean and Vietnam War eras.

38. See Ådne Cappelen, Nils Petter Gleditsch, and Olav Bjerkholt, "Guns, Butter,

and Growth: The Case of Norway," in *Defense, Welfare and Growth,* ed. Steve Chan and Alex Mintz (London and New York: Routledge and Kegan Paul 1992), ch. 4.

39. The one difference between the two curves is that the peak in conscientious objection in 1908 has no parallel in rising military expenditure.

40. This line of thinking was advocated by the member of the public commission, appointed in 1974 to study conscription, who was generally regarded as the representative of the COs, but it gained support from the entire civilian faction of on the commission. The military, however, held to a more traditional interpretation of "conscription" as it appeared in the Constitution. See the commission report, *Verneplikt: Norges Offentlige Utredninger, 1979,* No. 51.

41. Tasks such as peacekeeping in the Middle East, cleaning up mines in the Persian Gulf, and international disaster relief might make use of military training and organization and give the military new and challenging tasks.

42. Tor Egil Førland, "Siviltjeneste som miljøverntjeneste" (Civilian Service as Environmental Service), International Peace Research Institute (PRIO), *PRIO Report* 3 (1989).

43. See, for example, Charles C. Moskos, *A Call to Civic Service: National Service for Country and Community* (New York: Free Press, 1988) and Donald Eberly and Michael Sherraden, eds., *The Moral Equivalent of War? A Study of Non-Military Service in Nine Nations* (Westport, Conn.: Greenwood Press, 1990).

10.
South Africa: From Laager to Anti-Apartheid

1. Writings on conscientious objection constitute a tiny fraction of the modest literature on the armed forces in South Africa. In most instances, conscientious objection emerges in a larger context, such as assessments of the organizational growth and activities of the South African military.

2. Union of South Africa, *Defense Act, no. 13 of 1912;* see also "South Africa," in *Conscription: A World Survey: Compulsory Military Service and Resistance to It,* ed. Devi Prasad and Tony Smythe (London: War Resisters International, 1968), 117–18.

3. John de Gruchy, *The Church Struggle in South Africa* (Cape Town: David Phillip, 1979), 14.

4. Philip H. Frankel, *Pretoria's Praetorians* (London: Cambridge University Press, 1984), 1–28.

5. A mix of anti-British colonialism and republicanism informed the objection of many Afrikaners. See Jaap Durand and Dirkie Smit, "The Afrikaner Churches on War and Violence," in *Theology and Violence: The South African Debate,* ed. Charles Villa-Vicencio (Johannesburg: Skotaville, 1987), 32–42; Dian Joubert, *Oorlogsverklaring 1939 Drama in die Volksraad* (Cape Town: Tafelberg, 1972), 12–97; Deon F. S. Fourie, "The Evolving Experience," in *Defense Policy Formation,* ed. James Roherty (Durham, N.C.: Carolina Academic Press, 1980), 67–85; Kenneth W. Grundy, *Defense Legislation and Communal Politics: The Evolution of a White South African Nation as Reflected in the Controversy over the Assignment of Armed Forces Abroad, 1912–1976* (Athens, Ohio: Ohio University Center for International Studies, 1978); and Deon Geldenhuys, *South Africa's Search for Security Since the Second World War* (Johannesburg: South African Institute for International Affairs, 1978). Not all Afrikaners were hostile to Great Britain. Jan Christian Smuts, general and prime minister, supported Britain in both world wars.

6. When the principle of military service was challenged, the courts held that military

service is "a general obligation of universal application." Exemption was to be narrowly and strictly applied as it otherwise would "cast an unfair burden upon the more patriotic of the country's citizens." *S. V. Lovell* 1972 3 SA 760 (A) 765H.

7. R. Louw, ed., *Detention Barracks* (Cape Town: Mission of the Churches for Community Development, 1984); and M. T. Steyn, *Compendium Juris Religionis* (1985), 8.

8. Harald E. Winkler and Laurie Nathan, "Waging Peace: Church Resistance to Militarization," in *War and Society: The Militarization of South Africa*, ed. Jacklyn Cock and Laurie Nathan (Cape Town: David Philip, 1989), 324–25.

9. Stephen Bennet Anderson, *The End Conscription Campaign in Cape Town, 1983–1989* (Honors diss., University of Cape Town, 1990), 8.

10. Justice and Peace Commission of the Catholic Church of South Africa, *The Call to End Conscription* (Randburg: Justice and Peace Commission, n.d.), 1.

11. Catholic Institute for International Affairs, *War and Conscience in South Africa: The Churches and Conscientious Objection* (London: Catholic Institute for International Affairs, 1982), 78–79.

12. Center for Inter-Group Studies, *Conscientious Objection* (Rondebosch: University of Cape Town, 1984), 5. *The Argus* of Cape Town conducted a survey that indicated that 81 percent of whites supported conscription.

13. Winkler and Nathan, "Waging Peace," 327.

14. These descriptions are based on the cases of Anton Eberhardt, Peter Hathorn, Peter Moll, and Richard Steele.

15. Many draft resisters against apartheid's wars went into exile. In 1978 they formed the Committee on South African War Resisters, which sought to upgrade objectors' diplomatic position to entitle them to political asylum; it also provided support for exiled objectors and linked up with other anti-apartheid organizations in putting pressure on the South African government. Anderson, *End Conscription Campaign*, 15. See also the COSAWR journal *Resister*.

16. Interview with William Dommeris, an original member of COSG, November 11, 1986.

17. Duran and Smit, "The Afrikaner Churches," 45.

18. Frankel, *Pretoria's Praetorians*, 129.

19. If a CO applicant belonged to a religious denomination not represented on the board, a theologian from his denomination could be appointed to the board for the hearing.

20. J. A. Robinson, "Hartman *v.* Chairman, Board for Religious Objection 1987 1 South Africa 922 (O)," *De Jure* 20/1 (1987): 374.

21. M. T. Steyn, *Compendium Juris Religionis*, 169.

22. Ibid., 172.

23. "Hartman *v.* Chairman, Board for Religious Objection, and Others," *South African Law Journal* (1987): 1.922

24. Ibid.

25. The case of Peter Hathorn is one noteworthy example.

26. Such as that of David Bruce.

27. Winkler and Nathan, "Waging Peace," 332–33.

28. *Weekly Mail*, 9–15 Mar. 1990.

29. Anderson, *End Conscription Campaign*, 31–38, and Laurie Nathan, "Marching to a Different Beat: The History of the End Conscription Campaign," in *War and Society*, ed. Cock and Nathan, 312.

30. Cape Supreme Court, *ECC v Minister of Defense, Judgment* (Case 2870 of 1988).

31. Regulation 1 (vii) b (v).

32. See especially the trial of Philip Wilkenson.

33. On the first anniversary of that decision, President de Klerk announced plans to repeal remaining laws on which South Africa's ideology of racial discrimination rested. They included the Land Acts of 1913 and 1936 (which reserved most of the country's land for the white minority), the Group Areas Act of 1966 and Black Communities Act of 1984 (which entrenched the separate status of black townships), and the Population Registration Act (which classified all South Africans into four racial groups: blacks, whites, people of mixed race, and Asians). Christopher S. Wren, "South Africa Moves to Scrap Apartheid," *New York Times,* 2 Feb. 1991.

11.
Switzerland: Questioning the Citizen Soldier

1. Theodor Wyder, *Wehrpflicht und Militärdienstverweigerung* (Berne, 1988) 68.

2. For the figures on and motives for conscientious objectors in Switzerland, 1914–45, see Schweizerischer Friedensrat, *Dienstverweigerung aus Gewissensgründen* (1948); Ernst Altdorfer, *Die Dienstverweigerung nach schweizerischem Militärstrafrecht* (Zurich, 1929).

3. For development of the strength of the Swiss militia army in different periods see Ernst Wetter, *Schweizer Militär Lexikon* (Frauenfeld, 1985), 70.

4. Walter Real, *Ausreissen und unerlaubte Entfernung nach schweizerischem Militärrecht* (Ph.D. diss. Zurich, 1948).

5. Altdorfer, *Die Dienstverweigerung,* 202.

6. These military courts consist of a law colonel (usually a judge or lawyer by civilian profession) and four judges.

7. For discussion of the introduction of a civilian alternative service for COs in and shortly after World War I see Peter Hug, "Die Geschichte des Zivildienstes in der Schweiz bis zum Ende des Zweiten *Weltkrieges in Auseinandersetzungen mit Bestrebungen für eine* Arbeitsdienstpflicht" (Seminararbeit, University of Berne, 1982); Alex Kugler, *Zivildienst und Abrüstung, Pazifismus und Antimilitarismus in der Schweiz vom Ende des Ersten Weltkrieges bis in die Mitte der Zwanziger Jahre* (Ph. D. diss., University of Basel, 1979), 48; and Rudolph Epple-Gass, *Friedensbewegung und direkte Demokratie in der Schweiz* (Frankfurt am Main, 1988), 69–116.

8. Motion by Hermann Greulich in the federal parliament.

9. Kugler, *Zivildienst und Abrüstung,* 32–72.

10. See the report of the Swiss government to the federal parliament, September 12, 1924, 396–97.

11. Order of the Chief Medical Officer of the Swiss Army, April 4, 1966.

12. Motions and postulates in the federal parliament: 1946 Oltramare, 1955 Borel, 1964 Borel and Sauser, 1967 Petition of the Schweizerischen Friedensrat.

13. In Switzerland, the initiative process requires that at least one hundred thousand registered voters sign a petition to bring to a public vote proposed amendments to the Federal Constitution. The initiators are given a limited period of eighteen months to collect the signatures. Since 1891 when the right of partial revision of the Constitution by means of an initiative was introduced, only a few such initiatives have been approved by the voters in the final plebiscite on the measure. There are two kinds of initiatives, the "general request," which requires Parliament to formulate an amendment, and the "precisely formulated amendment" to which Parliament can make no changes. In both cases, however, Parliament can bring to public vote its own version of an amendment on the same matter alongside the one demanded by the authors of the initiative.

Text concerning the two initiatives is according to Ruth Meyer/Hans-Jorg Schweizer, "Conscientious Objection in Switzerland," *Forum International*, 5 (Munich: Sozialwissenschaftliches Institut der Bundeswehr, 1987): 299–301. Figures on COs are from Devi Prasad and Tony Smythe, eds. *Conscription: A World Survey: Compulsory Military Service and Resistance to It* (London: War Resisters International, 1968), 126.

14. See the report of the Swiss Government to the federal parliament, August 25, 1982, 11–44.

15. See the report of the Swiss Government to the federal parliament, May 27, 1987.

16. Amnesty International, "The Right Not to Fight: A Guide for AI Activists," internal document of Amnesty International, U.S.A., published in March 1992.

17. Better-educated COs, who can generally express themselves better than those objectors with less education, are thus at an advantage. See Karl W. Haltiner, *Milizarmee-Bürgerleitbild oder angeschlagenes Ideal?* (Frauenfeld, 1985), 170–72.

18. *Neue Züricher Zeitung*, 18 May 1992. On the same ballot, Swiss voters also recommended that Switzerland join the World Bank and the International Monetary Fund.

19. Karl W. Haltiner and Ruth Meyer, "Aspects of the Relationship between the Military and Society in Switzerland," *Armed Forces and Society* 6 (Fall 1979): 49–81; Haltiner *Milizarmee-Bürgerleitbild*, 27–60; and Ruth Meyer and Hans J. Schweitzer, "Conscientious Objection in Switzerland," paper presented at the Eleventh World Congress of Sociology, August 18–22, 1986.

20. Surveys: 1976 by R. Meyer; 1983 by K. Haltiner; 1988 by Riklin-UNIVOX; 1989 by K. Haltiner and ISOPUBLIC Zurich, member of Gallup-International; 1991 by C. Buri, K. Haltiner, K. R. Spillmann.

21. Karl W. Haltiner, "Switzerland," in *The Military—More Than Just a Job?*, ed. Charles Moskos and Frank R. Wood (Washington, D.C., 1988), 260.

22. Surveys by Karl Haltiner and others cited in n. 20.

12.
Israel: Conscientious Objection in a Democracy under Siege

1. David Biale, *Power and Powerlessness in Jewish History* (New York: Schocken Books, 1986).

2. Edward Bernard Glick, *Between Israel and Death* (Harrisburg, Pa: Stackpole Books, 1974). See also Yoram Peri, "Coexistence or Hegemony: Shifts in the Israeli Security Concept," in *The Roots of Begin's Success,* ed. Dan Caspi, A. Diskin, and E. Gutmann (London: Croom Helime, 1984), 191–218.

3. Edward Luttwak and Dan Horowitz, *The Israeli Army* (London: Allen Law, 1975).

4. Moshe Lissak, *Boundaries and Institutional Linkages between Elites: Some Illustrations from Civil-Military Relations in Israel* (Florence: European University Institute, 1982).

5. Dan Horowitz, "The Israel Defense Forces: A Civilianized Military in a Partially Militarized Society," in *Soldiers, Peasants and Bureaucrats,* ed. Roman Kolkowicz and Andrzej Korbonski (London: Allen and University, 1982), 77–105.

6. Leon Sheleff, *The Voice of Honor: Civil Disobedience and Civil Loyalty* (Tel Aviv: Ramon, 1989).

7. C. Cohen, *Civil Disobedience: Conscience, Tactics, and the Law* (London: London University Press, 1971).

8. *Proceedings of the Supreme Court*, September 24, 1980.

9. Ibid.

10. Rubik Rosenthal, ed., *Levanon: Hamil Chama Haacheret* (Lebanon: The Other War) (Tel Aviv: Sifriat Poalim, 1983).

11. Reuven Gal, *A Portrait of the Israeli Soldier* (Westport, Conn.: Greenwood Press, 1986), 181–86.

12. Ishai Menuchin and Dina Menuchin, *The Limits to Obedience* (Tel-Aviv: Yesh Gvul and Siman Kria Books, 1985).

13. Ruth Linn, "Conscientious Objection in Israel during the War in Lebanon," *Armed Forces and Society* 12 (1986): 489–511.

14. Ofra Meizels, Reuven Gal, and Eli Fishoff, (World Views and Political Opinions of High School Students on Issues of Army and Defense) (Zichron Yaakov: Israeli Institute for Military Research, 1990).

15. E. Yuchtmann-Ya'ar, "The Israeli Public and its Institutions," *Israeli Democracy* (Fall 1989), 7–11.

16. Moshe Negbi, *Above the Law: The Constitutional Crisis in Israel* (Tel Aviv: Am Oved, 1987), 127–42.

17. Ibid.

18. Alex Fishman, "Yechida 101" (Unit 101), *Monitin* (March 1990), 32.

13.
The German Democratic Republic: Dissidence That Prevailed

1. Vladimir Tismaneanu, "Nascent Civil Society in the German Democratic Republic," *Problems of Communism* 38 (1989): 92.

2. Wilfried von Bredow, *Moderner Militarismus* (Stuttgart: Kohlhammer Verlag, 1983), chapter on Prussian Militarism.

3. *Frankfurter Allgemeine Zeitung,* Mar. 23 1990. A valuable source for the legal texture of the late regime is Wolfgang Heinrich, ed., *Wehrdienstgesetz und Grenzgesetz der* DDR. *Dokumentation und Analyse* (Bonn: Urheber Verlag, 1983).

4. *Gesetzblatt der DDR,* September 16, 1964, 129–30.

5. This was also true for service in the units of the civil defense, units of the ministry of interior who live in barracks, as well as the notorious ministry for state security.

6. See Bernd Eisenfeld, *Kriegsdienstverweigerung in der* DDR—*Ein Friedensdiesnt?* (Frankfurt: Haag & Herchen, 1978), 7.

7. In one of those ironies of history, a former conscientious objector became the last minister of defense of the GDR. Rainer Eppelman was drafted in the late 1960s, but refused to take the oath of allegiance to communism. He was jailed for eight months and got out only by agreeing to work for eighteen months with an army construction brigade. In yet another irony, the pacifist pastor was seen as a strong supporter of the Nationale Volksarmee during his term in the ministry. *Wall Street Journal,* 25 June 1990, 1.

8. Bernd Eisenfeld, "Wehrdienstverweigergung: Jugendlichen in der DDR schwer gemacht," in DDR-*Jugend Heute,* ed. G. Zitzlaff (Stuttgart: J. B. Metzler, 1986), 71.

9. Ibid.

10. See "Bausoldaten," in DDR-*Handbuch,* 3rd ed., ed. H. Zimmerman (Köln: Verlag Wissenschaft und Politik, 1985), 152.

11. Klemens Richter, "Kirchen und Wehrdienstverweigerung in der DDR," *Deutschland-Archiv* 12 (1979): 44.

12. See Klau Ehrig and Martin Dallawitz, *Schwerter zu Pflugscharen, Friedensbewegung in der* DDR (Rinbeck: Rowohlt, 1982), 1982; also Helmut Zander, *Die Christen und die Friedensbewegungen in den beiden deutschen Staaten* (Berlin: Dunker & Humboldt, 1989);

and Eberhardt Kuhrt, *Wider die Militarisierung der Gesellschaft: Friedensbewegung und Kirche in der* DDR (Melle: Verlag Ernst Knoth, 1984).

13. A useful account of this episode is Zander, *Die Christen,* 259–62; see also Joyce Marie Mushaben, "Swords to Plowshares: The Church, the State, and the East German Peace Movement," *Studies in Comparative Communism* 17 (Summer 1984): 123–35.

14.
Socialist Countries of Eastern Europe: The Old Orders Crumble

1. I wish to acknowledge the useful information on conscientious objection that I have gained from the unpublished papers of Miklos Toma on Hungary, Jerzy Wiatr and D. Kociecka on Poland, and Nikita Chaldymov and Alexander Korokin on the Soviet Union. I am also indebted to Amnesty International for the information found in their periodic reports on conscientious objection.

2. In the second oldest socialist state, Mongolia, there was a parallel to the tolerance of conscientious objection during the Leninist era. The traditional military exemption of Buddhist monks was maintained from 1922 until the early 1930s. The abolition of this exemption coincided with the introduction of the Stalinist mode in Mongolia.

3. *Zolnierz Wolnosci,* July 14, 1988.

4. *Delo,* January 7, 1987.

5. *Amnesty International Report 1990* (London: Amnesty International, 1990), 264. See also the statement by the Federal Executive Council, *Delo,* February 6, 1990.

6. Statement of Col. General Milan Daljevic, *Delo,* January 7, 1987.

7. Nikita Chaldymov, personal communication as relayed by Charles Moskos, Moscow, November 1991.

15.
Legal Aspects of Conscientious Objection: A Comparative Analysis

1. *The Life of Henry V,* act 4, sc. 1.

2. Summarized in the 1982 report edited by Asbjorn Eide and Chama Mubanga-Chipoya, *Conscientious Objection to Military Service: A United Nations Report Prepared in Pursuance of Resolutions 14 (XXXIV) and 1982/30* of the UNESCO commission on Human Rights, Subcommission on Prevention of Discrimination and Protection of Minorities, *U.N. Document E.CN.4/Sub.2/1983/30* (New York: United Nations, 1988). Subsequent reports by country are filed under the same document number; hereafter, references to these submissions will be cited as *U.N. Doc.,* December 20, 1988.

3. National reports to the International Society for Military Law and the Law of War as a result of its 1987 questionnaire; the reports are summarized in François Godet, "L'Objection de Conscience," *Revue de droit militaire et de droit de la guerre* 29 (1990): 13, which appends twelve national reports: from Austria, Belgium, Brazil, Canada, the United States, France, Israel, Norway, the Netherlands, the Federal Republic of Germany, Sweden, and Switzerland. Hereafter, references to these reports will be cited as *Soc. Doc.,* 1990. All statistics included in my work are drawn from these national reports unless otherwise indicated.

4. *U.N. Doc.,* December 20, 1988. In addition, *The Military Balance 1990–91* (London: International Institute for Strategic Studies, 1990) lists eighty countries that rely on some form of military conscription. The difference, although not significant, illustrates the

difficulty of gathering current comparative statistics. For an earlier effort see Roger W. Little, *A Survey of Military Institutions* (Chicago: Inter-University Seminar on Armed Forces and Society, 1969).

5. See n. 24.

6. Recommendation R (87), April 8, 9, 1987, *U.N. Doc.*, December 20, 1988, 19–26.

7. Guatemala concluded that conscientious objection was contrary to the national will, *U.N. Doc.*, December 20, 1988, 15. In the same report, both Israel and Cuba pointed to external threats to justify their failure to recognize conscientious objection.

8. Lawrence M. Baskir and William A. Strauss, *Chance and Circumstance: The Draft, The War, and the Vietnam Generation* (New York: Knopf, 1978), 41, 280, n. 10, estimated that fifty thousand conscientious objectors had dropped out of the alternative service system by 1969.

9. George Q. Flynn, "Selective Service and the Conscientious Objector," in *Selective Conscientious Objection: Accommodating Conscience and Security*, ed. Michael F. Noone, Jr. (Boulder, Colo.: Westview Press, 1988), 46–47.

10. France National Service Code, Article 116–1 (see also chapter by Michel L. Martin in this book).

11. This is the position taken by Italy (n. 13) and apparently by the Federal Republic of Germany (see text accompanying n. 14).

12. This is apparently the position taken by United States and the former Warsaw Pact nations.

13. Petruzzellis, "L'Obiezione di Coscienza al Servizio Militare," *Rivista Militare* 2 (1986): 106, citing Council of State Judgment 16, May 16, 1985. See also Giorgio Giannini, *L'Obiezione di Coscienza al Servizio Militare* (Naples: Edizione Dehoniane, 1987).

14. R. McCartney, "West German Conscientious Objectors Now Legion," *Washington Post*, 11 Oct. 1988, A12, A14, gave the example of a successful essay that was used by eight objectors. The same report stated that 80 percent of the objectors relied on religious grounds.

15. D. Raymond, "Objecteurs de conscience: l'avis de la société suisse des officiers," *Revue Militaire Suisse* 1 (January 1986): 52–54.

16. *Soc. Doc.* 1990, Belgian response, citing Articles 3 and 4, Law of February 20, 1980.

17. *Soc. Doc.*, 1990, citing Articles 17, 18, and 19, Law of February 20, 1980.

18. *Soc. Doc.*, 1990, France.

19. Case #66.820, October 11, 1985; Case #65.422, February 19, 1986; Case #74.564, November 21, 1986; Case #77.757, February 11, 1987.

20. In two Dutch cases, objectors who sought exemption from serving in United Nations peacekeeping operations were denied at the national level, but won their cases before the European Court of Human Rights. See n. 50 and accompanying text.

21. For example, Italy has a liberal system for excusing objectors (n. 13). Yet during debates over the continuing need for peacetime conscription, Italian military authorities stated that NATO commitments and budgetary constraints mandated a conscript army ("Italy: Mama's Boys," *The Economist*, 4 Oct. 1986, U.S. edition, 4).

22. During the Vietnam War, U.S. draft boards required personal hearings in conscientious objector cases. A disproportionate number of the men excused (42 percent) had university degrees. See Peter Karsten, ed., *Soldiers and Society: The Effects of Military Service and War on American Life* (Westport, Conn.: Greenwood, 1978), 83.

23. Caroline Moorehead, *Troublesome People: Enemies of War 1916–1986* (London: Hamish Hamilton, 1986), 34.

24. Those countries whose constitutions require service in defense of the homeland but that do not constitutionally recognize conscientious objection must somehow justify alternative (nonmilitary) service. The Italian Constitutional Court's reasoning is as follows: Although defense is a fundamental duty under Article 52 of the Constitution, the duty may be rendered either by military service or by service of equal weight (Decision no. 164 of May 24, 1985). Similarly, it has been argued that Article 18 of the Swiss Constitution, which imposes a duty, can be interpreted to permit alternate service as long as it is "*en faveur de la défense générale.*" Both formulations seem to strain the plain language of the constitution, much as the U.S. Supreme Court did when it interpreted the "religious exemption" in the U.S. Selective Service Act to encompass deeply held moral and ethical beliefs of the irreligious (*United States* v. *Seeger,* 380 U.S. 163 [1965]; *Welsh* v. *United States,* 398 U.S. 333 [1970].

25. France, *Decree of 29 March 1984,* chap. 3, includes very specific regulations.

26. Belgium provides for imprisonment of three months to three years if a conscript fails to report for military duty without an excuse. French law provides for imprisonment of up to two years.

27. In Switzerland, the offense of failing to serve has been treated as a crime and appeared in a police record, but with a note that the person sought conscientious objector status.

28. Ruth Linn, "The Moral Judgment, Action, and Credibility of Israeli Soldiers Who Refused to Serve in Lebanon (1982–85)," *Selective Conscientious Objection,* ed. Noone, 129 at 145. Norwegian law provides that offenders will be tried in the civil courts, where they can expect to receive three months' imprisonment. The objector then is called up again; if he refuses to enter the military, he will be sentenced to a year's imprisonment, of which he can expect to serve three to four months.

29. Belgian law, unlike that of the Federal Republic of Germany, makes no special provisions to exempt ministers of religion, but in practice ministers are assigned to the medical services as "ecclesiastical stretcher bearers." French law does not make special provisions for seminarians or ministers. When the Netherlands completed the 1987 questionnaire, the status of persons holding spiritual or religious offices was under review by the government.

30. Individual states' responses to the United Nations survey rarely discuss Jehovah's Witnesses. Responses to the 1987 questionnaire of the International Society for Military Law and the Law of War indicate a wide divergence in national law and practice. Belgian law, for example, provides that conscripts who refuse to report for duty are automatically inducted. Thereafter they are subject to military law. Until recently they were subject to the same penalty as a serviceman for disobedience of an order to report for duty. In 1987, however, Brussels issued a decree providing for the punishment of recalcitrant Jehovah's Witnesses by weekday work in a penitentiary between 8:00 A.M. and 5:00 P.M. Whether the Witnesses will accept that alternative remains to be seen. Norway confines Jehovah's Witnesses if they refuse to perform the alternative service that apparently is granted to them automatically. The confinement, however, is not treated as a term of imprisonment. In the Federal Republic of Germany, Jehovah's Witnesses are routinely exempted; if they refuse to perform alternative service, they are permitted to do hospital work for an extended period (exceeding civilian alternative service by at least one year). Bonn's response to the 1987 questionnaire states that Jehovah's Witnesses who refuse hospital work are "subject to prosecution." This statement suggests that in practice, few, if any, are prosecuted. When the questionnaire was filled out in the Netherlands, the status of Jehovah's Witnesses was under review by the Parliament.

31 J. Diehl, "Antigovernment Groups Thrive on Polish Campuses," *Washington Post,* 16 Nov. 1988, A21, A23.

32. J. Diehl, "Poland Bows to Dissent, Proposes Alternative to Military Service," *Washington Post,* 20 Jan. 1988, A1.

33. NEXIS search, *Reuter Library Report,* March 1, 1989.

34. L. Berat, "Conscientious Objection in South Africa: Governmental Paranoia and the Law of Conscription," *Vanderbilt Journal of Transactional Law* 22 (1989): 127–86. In the universal conscription statute for white male citizens, enacted in 1967, conscientious objectors were not excused, although authorities were authorized to assign members of peace churches to non-combatant duties. Jehovah's Witnesses were recognized as members of a peace church, but were required to undergo basic military training and were imprisoned if they failed to report for duty. Penalties for refusal to serve were doubled (to three years) in 1978, and repeated prosecutions after release were common. Subsequently the maximum period of confinement was extended to six years.

35. *Hartman* v. *Chairman, Board for Religious Objection,* 1987 (1) *S. Afr. L. Rep.* 922 (Orange Free State Provincial Division). The South African Court simultaneously rejected, as had the U.S. Supreme Court, claims that selective conscientious objection warranted recognition. See *Gillette* v. *United States,* 401 U.S. 437 (1971).

36. In 1985—the last year in which statistics were available—the military board granted objector status to all but 11 of 758 applicants. Berat, "Conscientious Objection in South Africa," 167.

37. NEXIS search, *Reuter Library Report,* February 1, 1990.

38. In 1988 the South African government had stated that peace negotiations in Angola and the Namibian independence would not bring any *immediate* change in the conscription system (emphasis added). See NEXIS search, *Reuter Library Report,* August 15, 1988.

39. 32 *C.F.R.* Part 75 (1989). A somewhat dated but still useful analysis of the Directive is found in Donald N. Zillman, "In-Service Conscientious Objection: Courts, Boards, and the Basis in Fact," *San Diego Law Review* 10 (1972): 108.

40. In responding to the latter question, one must recognize the competing interests at work. On the one hand, military personnel planners would prefer that there be no limitations (other than skill and rank) on assignment policies. On the other hand, civilian financial management experts might be willing to accept some constraints on assignment (such as refusal to serve in a unit assigned to a nuclear weapons mission) in order to preserve the investment made in the soldier's training. I have the impression that the personnel planner's position is generally accepted because the institution does not want to appear to have legitimated objection by making provision for it. United States Army policies (law as product) regarding serving members who develop scruples regarding the use of nuclear weapons are described in Mary Eileen McGrath, "Nuclear Weapons: A Crisis of Conscience," *Military Law Review* 107 (Winter 1985): 245–47. U.S. Air Force policies, which permitted officers with ethical qualms to withdraw without penalty from nuclear weapons training are identical. In practice (law as process) officers who withdraw are administratively separated for lack of leadership qualities. *Tilley* v. *United States,* 19 Cl. Ct. 33 (1989), *Gifford* v. *United States,* 1991 WL 60640 (Cl. Ct.).

41. The typical religiously motivated uniformed military objector has undergone a conversion and advises the authorities that he can no longer serve in good conscience. In the British and American systems of military justice, he will still be punished for failure to report for duty or refusal to wear the uniform, although his reasons may affect the amount of punishment imposed. See, generally, Michael Noone, "Rendering unto Caesar: Legal Responses to Religious Nonconformity in the Armed Forces," *St. Mary's Law Journal* 18 (1987): 1234–94.

42. Linn, "Moral Judgment," relates that Israeli reservists who objected on moral grounds to service in occupied Lebanon were not court-martialed but were punished by their battalion commanders, who had authority to confine disobedient soldiers for as long as thirty-five days. In some instances, soldiers were confined for less. Presumably, if a commander had thought that the refusal was due to cowardice, the soldier would have been court-martialed. Alternatively, commanders might decide that a court-martial and its attendant publicity would direct adverse public attention to the problem. I have been told that during the Vietnam War, several air crew members of the Strategic Air Command who refused to bomb North Vietnam were administratively released from active duty. The incident was never publicized, so no rationale was offered. If the objector sought to publicize his opposition to the war, however, court-martial followed. See *United States* v. *Noyd*, 40 C.M.R. 195 (C.M.A. 1968); *Culver* v. *Secretary of Air Force*, 559 F.2d 622 (D.C. Cir. 1977).

43. See, for example, C. Cohen, "Conscientious Objection," *Ethics* 58 (1968): 269; J. C. Murray, "War and Conscience," in *A Conflict of Loyalties: The Case for Selective Conscientious Objection*, ed. James Finn (New York: Pegasus, 1968), 27.

44. See C. H. Clancy and J. A. Weiss, "The Constitutional Objector Exemption: Problems in Conceptual Clarity and Constitutional Considerations," *Maine Law Review* 17 (1965): 155.

45. See, for example, *U.S.* v. *Austin*, 27 M.J. 227 (CMA 1988). But see also N[avy] C[ourt] M[artial] 66 0804 *Minnix* (1966), in which a military appellate court concluded, "Even though the accused [a Jehovah's Witness] is of no value to the naval service and his separation from the service is indicated, the circumstances of this case are such that a punitive discharge is not warranted" (ibid., 4).

46. See *McCullough* v. *Seamans*, 348 F. Supp. 511 (D.C. Cal. 1972).

47. See, for example, Marina Nuciari, "Value Change in New Social Movements and Military Problems in the Italian Young Generation" (paper presented at the Inter-University Seminar on Armed Forces and Society Conference, Chicago, 1987).

48. In regard to West Germany and uniformed COs, Robert Dillman's "Des rapports avec un militaire qui invoque sa conscience," *Revue de Droit Pénal Militaire et de Droit de la Guerre* 22 (1988): 3–4, apparently based on experiences with members of the Bundeswehr, suggests topics to be discussed with the soldier expressing scruples against war but offers no information on the number of cases experienced in the Federal Republic of Germany.

49. *N.* v. *Sweden*, App. No. 10410/83, 40 European Commission on Human Rights, Dec. & Rep. 203 (1985). One author has characterized the decision as "anomalous." See L. Helfer, "Finding a Consensus on Equality: The Homosexual Age of Consent and the European Convention on Human Rights," *New York University Law Review* 65 (1990): 1044 at 1067 n. 151. Compare *Arrowsmith* v. *United Kingdom* (1981), 3 *European Human Rights Reports* 218 (concluding that pacifism was a right protected by the European Convention).

50. (1986) 8 EHRR (European Human Rights Reports), 20.

51. *Final Act of the Conference on Security and Cooperation in Europe, Dept. State Pub. No. 8826* (Gen'l For. Pol. Ser. 298), reprinted in 14 I.L.M. 1292 (1975). Article VII concerns respect for human rights and fundamental freedoms, including the freedom of thought, conscience, religion, and belief. At follow-up conferences in Vienna in 1976 and in Paris in 1989, proposals to include conscientious objection as a fundamental right were rejected, but they were adopted in modified form at the CSCE Conference in Copenhagen in 1990.

52. *Commission on Human Rights: Report of the Forty-Fifth Session* (March 1989) 139–42; *U.N. Doc.*, December 20, 1988, 61; see also M. Lippman, "The Recognition of

Conscientious Objection to Military Service as an International Human Right," *California Western International Law Journal* 21 (1990–1991): 31.

16.
Conclusion: The Secularization of Conscience Reconsidered

1. A methodology for cross-national research based on qualitative case studies is presented by sociologist Charles C. Ragin, *The Comparative Method* (Berkeley: University of California Press, 1987).

2. Although the Netherlands was the first European nation to establish a broad and continuing program of alternative civilian service, tsarist Russia was paradoxically the first country in Europe to adopt a program of civilian service as an alternative to military service—at least for a small selected group of religious pacifist COs. This anomaly—of liberal treatment by an autocratic regime—resulted from particular historical circumstances. In the mid-eighteenth century, under Empress Catherine, German Mennonites had been invited to Russia with exemption from compulsory service. When modern universal mass conscription was first imposed in Russia in 1874, thousands of the descendants of these Mennonites fled to the United States. This exodus led the Russian government to initiate a program that allowed Mennonites who remained to undertake alternative service in hospitals or in the forestry service. Other pacifist sects in Russia, however, such as Doukhobors, Tolstoyans, Evangelicals, Baptists, and Quakers, were not exempted, and many members of these groups were imprisoned for refusal to serve in the military.

Other countries also encouraged Mennonites to move there. Mennonites in Mexico were the only citizens eligible for recognition as conscientious objectors following the revolution of 1910. In Paraguay a privilege granted in 1921 states that all Mennonite settlers and their descendants, whether members of the church or not, are exempt from obligatory military service. Ralph Potter, "Conscientious Objection to Particular Wars," in *Religion and the Public Order,* ed. Donald A. Giannella (Ithaca, N.Y.: Cornell University Press, 1974), 96.

3. In some other ways, Switzerland is not so advanced; women only recently obtained the franchise there, and still could not vote in some cantons of the Swiss Federation.

4. For a discussion of anti-militarism in the early twentieth century, see the essays in John R. Gillis, ed., *The Militarization of the Western World* (New Brunswick, N.J.: Rutgers University Press, 1989). Although the continental socialist traditions were antimilitaristic, they were not, strictly speaking, pacifistic. Socialists opposed standing professional armies as instruments of capitalist rule, but in several of the continental European nations, the socialists supported militia systems of citizen-soldiers precisely as antimilitarist measures. See George J. Neimanis, "Militia vs. the Standing Army in the History of Economic Thought from Adam Smith to Friedrich Engels," *Military Affairs* 44 (February 1980): 31–33.

5. *New York Times,* 18 May 1990, A14.

6. For a review and critique of the relevant literature, see Edward A. Tiryakian, "Modernization: Exhumetur in Pace," *International Sociology* 6 (June 1991): 2165–80. On the broad and controversial literature on "modernization" and "modernity," see Roy Boyne and Ali Rattansi, *Postmodernism and Society* (New York: St. Martin's Press, 1990); Scott Lash, *Sociology and Postmodernism* (London: Routledge and Kegan Paul, 1990); Nathan Rosenberg and L. E. Birdzell, Jr., *How the West Grew Rich: The Economic Transformation of the Industrial World* (New York: Basic Books, 1986), which describes and evaluates the process without using the controversial term "modernization"; Alex Inkeles, *Exploring Individual Modernity* (New York: Columbia University Press, 1983); Seymour Martin Lipset,

ed., *The Third Century: America as a Post-Industrial Society* (Stanford, Calif.: Hoover Institution Press, 1979); and Alex Inkeles and David H. Smith, *Becoming Modern: Individual Change in Six Developing Countries* (Cambridge, Mass.: Harvard University Press, 1974). See also Wolfgang Schluchter, *The Rise of Western Rationalism: Max Weber's Developmental Theory,* translated with an introduction by Guenther Roth (Berkeley: University of California Press, 1991).

7. Lawrence M. Friedman, *The Republic of Choice: Law, Authority, and Culture* (Cambridge, Mass.: Harvard University Press, 1990), 2–3, 188–213, and passim. On the transformation of the concept of individualism, see also Nicholas Abercrombie, Stephen Hill, and Bryan S. Turner, *Sovereign Individuals of Capitalism* (London: Allen and Unwin, 1986); Robert N. Bellah et al., *Habits of the Heart: Individualism and Commitment in American Life* (Berkeley: University of California Press, 1985); Norval D. Glenn, "Social Trends in the United States: Evidence from Sample Surveys," *Public Opinion Quarterly* 51 (Winter 1987): 109–26; and Jerry G. Pankhurst and Sharon K. Houseknecht, "The Family, Politics, and Religion in the 1980s: In Fear of the New Individualism," *Journal of Family Issues* 4 (1983): 5–34.

8. See, for example, Charles S. Maier, ed., *Changing Boundaries of the Political: Essays on the Evolving Balance between State and Society, Public and Private in Europe* (Cambridge: Cambridge University Press, 1987).

9. For example, see the classic modern statement in American legal thought on the balanced relationship between rights and duties: Wesley N. Hohfeld, "Some Fundamental Legal Conceptions as Applied in Judicial Reasoning," *Yale Law Journal* 23 (November 1913): 16–59.

10. On the need for a re-emphasis on duties and civic responsibilities, see, for example, Benjamin R. Barber et al., "Forum: Who Owes What to Whom? Drafting a Constitutional Bill of Duties," *Harper's* 282 (February 1991): 43–54; Mary Ann Glendon, *Rights Talk: The Impoverishment of Political Discourse* (New York: Free Press, 1991); Christopher Lasch, *The True and Only Heaven: Progress and Its Critics* (New York: Norton, 1991); Lawrence M. Mead, *Beyond Entitlement: The Social Obligations of Citizenship* (New York: Free Press, 1985); Morris Janowitz, *The Reconstruction of Patriotism: Education for Civic Consciousness* (Chicago: University of Chicago Press, 1983); Alan Wolfe, *Whose Keeper? Social Science and Moral Obligation* (Berkeley: University of California Press, 1989); and William A. Galston, *Liberal Purposes* (New York: Cambridge University Press, 1991). The new "communitarian thought" is reflected in the journal *The Responsive Community,* under the editorship of Amitai Etzioni.

11. Thomas Luckmann, *The Invisible Religion* (New York: Macmillan, 1967), 99–102; see also Friedman, *Republic of Choice,* 164–69.

12. For descriptions of these trends, see Jeffrey K. Hadden, ed., *Religion in Radical Transition* (New York: Aldine, 1971); and Edwin Scott Gaustad, *A Religious History of America* rev. ed. (New York: HarperCollins, 1990), 264–83, 331–71.

13. Recent sympathetic scholarly studies of twentieth-century peace movements in various countries include Charles Chatfield and Peter van den Dungen, eds., *Peace Movements and Political Cultures* (Knoxville, Tenn.: University of Tennessee Press, 1988), and Katsuya Kodama and Unto Vesa, eds., *Towards a Comparative Analysis of Peace Movements* (Brookfield, Vt.: Gower, 1990).

14. Secular currents in Christian denominations, are discussed in Martin E. Marty, *A Nation of Believers* (Chicago: University of Chicago Press, 1976); Robert Wuthnow, *The Struggle for America's Soul: Evangelicals, Liberals, and Secularism* (Grand Rapids, Mich.: William B. Eerdmans, 1989), and Ari L. Goldman, *The Search for God at Harvard* (New York: Random House, 1991). On the rise of secular humanism within American Judaism,

see Irving Kristol, "The Future of American Jewry" *Commentary* 92 (August 1991): 21–26.

15. *European Churches and Conscientious Objection to Military Service,* proceedings of an international conference hosted by the German Protestant Association for the Care of Conscientious Objectors (EAK) and held at Loccum, Germany, September 25–28 1989, ed. EAK, (Bremen: EAK, 1991, English edition), 18.

16. Ibid., 26 (emphasis in the original).

17. For an example of the concern over the evasion of military service by the middle and upper classes in the United States, see Arthur T. Hadley, *The Straw Giant: Triumph and Failure: America's Armed Forces* (New York: Random House, 1986), 30–33, 283–84.

18. *Washington Times,* 20 May 1991, A4; statistics from USMC personal communications with the editors, February, 1992.

19. Although Jehovah's Witnesses contribute more incarcerated draft objectors than any other religious body, most scholars and other commentators on the subject have given this group little attention in regard to conscientious objection. Technically, many countries do not classify the Jehovah's Witnesses as COs because the young men reject that status and demand draft exemption as ministers. Yet they are, of course, objecting to military service on religious grounds.

20. United Nations, Commission on Human Rights, Resolution 1987/46 on Conscientious Objection as a Human Right, adopted March 10, 1987, U.N. Document E/CN.4/1987/L.73. On March 8, 1989, the Commission on Human Rights adopted resolution 1989/59, reaffirming the right to conscientious objection and appealing to states to alter existing legislation, if necessary, to permit conscientious objection. U.N. Document E/CN.4/1989/L.69. The Commission addressed the question again in 1991, and groups such as Amnesty International sought then and in 1992 to obtain further steps by the United Nations to strengthen protection for the right of conscientious objection. The United Nations' position was based on Articles 3 and 18 of the Universal Declaration of Human Rights, which proclaim the right to life, liberty, and security of person, and the right of freedom of thought, conscience, and religion, as well as the implementing statute, the International Covenant on Civil and Political Rights. The covenant was adopted by the U.N. General Assembly in 1966. It has subsequently been ratified by treaty by numerous nations. See Amnesty International, *Amnesty Report 1991,* (London: Amnesty International, 1991), 290 and app.

21. European Parliament, resolution on conscientious objection and alternative civilian service, adopted October 13, 1989, Document A2—0433/88/A and A3/15/89 reprinted in EAK, *European Churches and Conscientious Objection to Military Service,* 107–109.

22. Document of the Copenhagen Meeting, June 29, 1990, of the Conference on the Human Dimension of the Conference on Security and Cooperation in Europe (CSCE), Sec. 18, reprinted in EAK, *European Churches and Conscientious Objection to Military Service,* 109–10.

23. See, for example, M. Lippman, "The Recognition of Conscientious Objection to Military Service as an International Human Right," *California Western International Law Journal* 21 (1990–1991): 31; and also Amnesty International, *Conscientious Objection to Military Service* (London: Amnesty International, 1991), 1–5.

24. The "decline of secularism" argument is made in Robin Gill, *Competing Convictions* (London: SCM, 1989). See also Martin E. Marty and R. Scott Appleby, eds., *Fundamentalisms Observed* (Chicago: University of Chicago Press, 1991).

25. On the intersection between democracy and Christianity, see Samuel P. Huntington, *The Third Wave: Democratization in the Late Twentieth Century* (Norman: University of Oklahoma Press, 1991). Irving Louis Horowitz, "The Glass is Half Full and Half Empty,"

Society 28 (July/August 1991): 17–22, notes a strong correlation between political participation and religiosity.

The editors think it is important to note that whatever current signs portend for the future, conscientious objection, new or old, should be kept in perspective. To be sure, people of love and goodwill give conscientious objection and pacifism a substantial moral justification. Humanity cannot be maintained without an ideal of the sanctity of human life and a vision of universal peoplehood. Although pacifists' goal of a completely warless world may be unattainable, their efforts to eliminate the causes of war and violence are not in vain.

But there is another perspective on pacifism and conscientious objection that should be noted. That is the view that the acceptance of the right of conscientious objection is greater in a liberal democratic society than in a repressive or totalitarian society, and that it is sometimes seen as necessary to employ armed forces to protect the former against the latter. Absolute pacifists reject such an argument. By rejecting war as an acceptable means of settling disputes, they reject the idea of being party to the use of organized violence. Furthermore, with some significant exceptions, defense of liberal democracy and human rights has not generally been the main purpose of either side in most wars. Still, we are left with a paradox: People who bear arms in defense of democracy and human rights can be seen as also protecting the right of conscientious objectors not to bear arms.

26. For historical and contemporary coverage of national youth service in the United States, see Charles C. Moskos, *A Call to Civic Service: National Service for Country and Community* (New York: Free Press, 1988). For a cross-national study on nonmilitary youth service, see Donald Eberly and Michael Sherraden, eds., *The Moral Equivalent of War? A Study of Non-Military Service in Nine Nations* (Westport, Conn.: Greenwood Press, 1990). A conservative addition to the call for national service is William F. Buckley, Jr., *Gratitude: Reflections on What We Owe to Our Country* (New York: Random House, 1990). A summary of the recent debate is found in Wiliamson M. Evers, ed., *National Service: Pro and Con* (Stanford, Calif.: Hoover Institution Press, 1990). Extensive treatments of the connection between citizenship and military service may be found in Eliot A. Cohen, *Citizens and Soldiers: The Dilemmas of Military Service* (Ithaca, N.Y.: Cornell University Press, 1985); John Whiteclay Chambers II, *To Raise an Army: The Draft Comes to Modern America* (New York: Free Press, 1987); and David R. Segal, *Recruiting for Uncle Sam: Citizenship and Military Manpower Policy* (Lawrence, Kans.: University Press of Kansas, 1989).

27. William James' seminal essay on national service, "The Moral Equivalent of War," reprinted in his *Essays on Faith and Morals* (New York: Longman, Greens, 1942), 311–28, was published originally in 1910.

28. For evidence of President-elect Bill Clinton's commitment to a voluntary national service program, linking educational financial support to advance or subsequent public service work, see Ruth Marcus, "Clinton, Hill Leaders Hail New Teamwork," *Washington Post*, 17 Nov. 1992, Al, A12; and a segment on voluntary national service in *All Things Considered*, National Public Radio, 20 Nov. 1992.

29. "Text of a Letter by Bill Clinton on His R.O.T.C. Deferment," *New York Times*, 13, Feb. 1992, p. A8.

Select Bibliography

Adams, R. J. Q., and Philip P. Poirier. *The Conscription Controversy in Great Britain, 1900–18.* London: Macmillan Press, 1987.

Amnesty International. *Conscientious Objection to Military Service.* London: Amnesty International, 1991.

Anderson, Martin, ed. *Conscription: A Select and Annotated Bibliography.* Stanford: Hoover Institution Press, 1976.

———, ed. *The Military Draft: Selected Readings on Conscription.* Stanford: Hoover Institution Press, 1982.

———, ed. *Registration and the Draft.* Stanford: Hoover Institution Press, 1982.

Axelrad, Albert S. *Call to Conscience: Jews, Judaism, and Conscientious Objection.* Nyack, N.Y.: Jewish Peace Fellowship, 1986.

Bainton, Roland H. *Christian Attitudes toward War and Peace: A Historical Survey and Critical Re-evaluation.* Nashville, Tenn.: Abingdon Press, 1960.

Barber, Rachel. *Conscience, Government and War: Conscientious Objection in Great Britain, 1939–1945.* London: Routledge and Kegan Paul, 1982.

Baskir, Lawrence, M., and William A. Strauss. *Chance and Circumstance: The Draft, the War, and the Vietnam Generation.* New York: Knopf, 1978.

Biale, David. *Power and Powerlessness in Jewish History.* New York: Shocken Books, 1986.

Bowman, Rufus D. *The Church of the Brethren and War, 1708–1941.* Elgin, Ill.: Brethren Publishing House, 1944.

Brock, Peter. *Freedom from Violence: Sectarian Nonresistance from the Middle Ages to the Great War.* Toronto: University of Toronto Press, 1991.

———. *Freedom from War: Nonsectarian Pacifism, 1814–1914.* Toronto: University of Toronto Press, 1991.

———. *Pacifism in the United States: From the Colonial Era to the First World War.* Princeton: Princeton University Press, 1968.

———. *The Quaker Peace Testimony, 1660–1914.* Syracuse, N.Y.: Syracuse University Press, 1991.

———. *Twentieth-Century Pacifism.* New York: Van Nostrand Reinhold Co., 1970.

Carsten, F. L. *War against War.* London: Batsford, 1982.

Catholic Institute for International Affairs. *War and Conscience in South Africa: The Churches and Conscientious Objection.* London: Catholic Institute for International Affairs, 1982.

———. *Out of Step: War Resisters in South Africa*. (London: Catholic Institute for International Affairs, 1990).

Ceadel, Martin. *Pacifism in Britain, 1914–1945: The Defining of a Faith*. Oxford: Oxford University Press, 1980.

Central Committee for Conscientious Objectors. *Standing with Those Who Say No, 1948–1988*. Philadelphia: CCCO, 1988.

Chambers, John Whiteclay II. *To Raise an Army: The Draft Comes to Modern America*. New York: The Free Press, 1987.

———. *The Tyranny of Change: America in the Progressive Era, 1890–1920*. 2d ed. New York: St. Martin's Press, 1992.

———, ed. *Draftees or Volunteers: A Documentary History of the Debate over Military Conscription in the United States, 1787–1973*. New York: Garland Publishing, 1975.

———, ed. *The Eagle and the Dove: The American Peace Movement and United States Foreign Policy, 1900–1922*. 2d ed. Syracuse: Syracuse University Press, 1991.

Chatfield, Charles. *The American Peace Movement: Ideals and Political Activism*. New York: Twayne, 1992.

———. *For Peace and Justice: Pacifism in America, 1914–1941*. Knoxville: University of Tennessee Press, 1971.

———, and Peter van den Dungen, eds. *Peace Movements and Political Cultures*. Knoxville: University of Tennessee Press, 1988.

Childress, James F. *Moral Responsibility in Conflicts*. Baton Rouge: Louisiana State University Press, 1982.

Clifford, J. Garry, and Samuel R. Spencer, Jr. *The First Peacetime Draft* [1940]. Lawrence: University Press of Kansas, 1986.

Cock, Jacklyn, and Laurie Nathan, eds. *War and Society: The Militarization of South Africa*. Cape Town: David Philip, 1989.

Cohen, C. *Civil Disobedience: Conscience, Tactics, and the Law*. London: London University Press, 1971.

Cohen, Eliot A. *Citizens and Soldiers: The Dilemmas of Military Service*. Ithaca, N.Y.: Cornell University Press, 1985.

Cook, Blanche Wiesen, Sandi E. Cooper, and Charles Chatfield, eds. *The Garland Library of War and Peace* 360 vols. New York: Garland Publishing, 1970–1980.

Cooper, Sandi E. *Patriotic Pacifism: Waging War in Europe, 1815–1914*. New York: Oxford University Press, 1991.

Cortright, David. *Soldiers in Revolt: The American Military Today*. Garden City, N.Y.: Doubleday, 1975.

Cortright, David, and Max Watts. *Left Face: Soldier Unions and Resistance Movements in Modern Armies*. Westport, Conn.: Greenwood Press, 1991.

Cromartie, Michael, ed. *Peace Betrayed: Essays on Pacifism and Politics*. Washington, D.C.: Ethics and Public Policy Center, 1990.

DeBenedetti, Charles (Charles Chatfield, assisting author). *An American Ordeal: The Antiwar Movement of the Vietnam Era*. Syracuse, N.Y.: Syracuse University Press, 1990.

———. *The Peace Reform in American History*. Bloomington: Indiana University Press, 1980.

———, ed. *Peace Heroes in Twentieth-Century America*. Bloomington: Indiana University Press, 1986.

Decosse, David, ed. *But Was It Just? Reflections on the Morality of the Persian Gulf War*. Garden City, N.Y.: Doubleday, 1992.

Defense and Foreign Affairs Handbook, 1990–1991. Alexandria, Va.: International Media, 1990.

Doty, Hiram. *Bibliography of Conscientious Objection to War*. Philadelphia: Central Committee for Conscientious Objection, 1954.

Doughterty, James, and Robert Pfaltzgraff, eds. *Shattering Europe's Defense Consensus: The Antinuclear Protest Movement and the Future of* NATO. London: Pergamon-Brassey's, 1985.

EAK. *European Churches and Conscientious Objection to Military Service*. Proceedings of an International Conference Hosted by the German Protestant Association for the Care of Conscientious Objectors (EAK), held in Loccum, Germany, September 25–28, 1989. English edition. Breman: EAK, 1991.

Eberly, Donald, and Michael Sherraden, eds. *The Moral Equivalent of War? A Study of Non-Military Service in Nine Nations*. Westport, Conn.: Greenwood, 1990.

Edmonds, Gwyn Martin. *Armed Services and Society*. Leicester: Leicester University Press, 1988.

Eide, Asbjorn, and Chama Mubanga-Chipoya, eds. *Conscientious Objection to Military Service. A United Nations Report Prepared in Pursuance of Resolutions 14 (XXXIV) and 1982/30* of the UNESCO Commission on Human Rights, Sub-Commission on Prevention of Discrimination and Protection of Minorities, *United Nations Document E.CN.4/Sub.2/1983/30*. New York: United Nations, 1988.

Eller, Cynthia. *Conscientious Objectors and the Second World War: Moral and Religious Arguments in Support of Pacifism*. New York: Praeger, 1991

Evers, Williamson M., ed. *National Service: Pro and Con*. Stanford, Calif. Hoover Institution Press, 1990.

Ferber, Michael, and Staughton Lynd. *The Resistance*. Boston: Beacon Press, 1971.

Ferguson, John. *War and Peace in the World's Religions*. New York: Oxford University Press, 1978.

Finn, James, ed. *A Conflict of Loyalties: The Case for Selective Conscientious Objection*. New York: Pegasus, 1968.

Flynn, George Q. *America and the Draft, 1940–1973*. Lawrence: University Press of Kansas, 1993.

———. *Lewis B. Hershey: Mr. Selective Service*. Chapel Hill: University of North Carolina Press, 1985.

Forest, James H. *Catholics and Conscientious Objection*. New York: Catholic Peace Fellowship, 1981.

Forrest, Alan I. *Conscripts and Deserters: The Army and French Society during the Revolution and Empire*. New York: Oxford University Press, 1989.

Frankel, Philip H. *Pretoria's Praetorians*. London: Cambridge University Press, 1984.

Gal, Reuven. *A Portrait of the Israeli Soldier*. Westport, Conn.: Greenwood Press, 1986.

Gara, Larry. *War Resistance in Historical Perspective*. New York: War Resisters League, 1983.

Gaylin, Willard. *In the Service of Their Country: War Resisters in Prison*. New York: Viking Press, 1970.

Gerhardt, James M. *The Draft and Public Policy: Issues in Military Manpower Procurement, 1945–1970*. Columbus: Ohio State University Press, 1971.

Giannini, Giorgio. *L'Obiezione di conscienza al Servizio Militare*. Naples: Edizioni Dehoniane, 1987.

Gillis, John R., ed. *The Militarization of the Western World*. New Brunswick, N. J.: Rutgers University Press, 1989.

Gioglio, Gerald R. *Days of Decision: An Oral History of Conscientious Objectors in the Military during the Vietnam War*. Trenton, N.J.: Broken Rifle Press, 1989.

Godet, François, "L'Objection de Conscience," *Revue de droit militaire et de droit de la guerre* 29 (1990): 13ff.

Gold, Philip. *Evasions: The American Way of Military Service.* New York: Paragon House Publishers, 1985.

Gooch, John. *Armies of Europe.* London: Routledge and Kegan Paul, 1980.

Harries-Jenkins, Gwyn, and Jacques van Doorn, eds. *The Military and the Problem of Legitimacy.* London: Sage, 1976.

Hartmann, Albrecht, and Hartmann, Heidi. *Kriegsdienstverweigerung im Dritten Reich.* Frankfurt am Main: Haag and Herchen, 1986.

Howlett, Charles F. *The American Peace Movement: References and Resources.* Boston: G. K. Hall, 1991.

Howorth, Jolyon, and Patricia Chilton, eds. *Defense and Dissent in Contemporary France.* New York: St. Martin's Press, 1984.

International Institute for Strategic Studies. *The Military Balance, 1990–1991.* London: Brassey's, 1990.

Janowitz, Morris. *The Reconstruction of Patriotism: Education for Civic Consciousness.* Chicago: University of Chicago Press, 1983.

Johnson, James Turner. *Can Modern War Be Just?* New Haven: Yale University Press, 1984.

———. *Just War Tradition and the Restraint of War: A Moral and Historical Inquiry.* Princeton: Princeton University Press, 1981.

Johnson, James Turner, and John Kelsay, eds. *Cross, Crescent, and Sword: The Justification and Limitation of War in Western and Islamic Tradition.* Westport, Conn.: Greenwood Press, 1990.

Josephson, Harold, ed. *Biographical Dictionary of Modern Peace Leaders.* Westport, Conn.: Greenwood, 1985.

Kaplan, William. *State and Salvation: The Jehovah's Witnesses and Their Fight for Civil Rights.* Toronto: University of Toronto Press, 1989.

Keegan, John, ed. *World Armies.* 2d ed. London: Macmillan, 1984.

Keim, Albert N., and Grant M. Stoltzfus. *The Politics of Conscience: The Historic Peace Churches and America at War, 1917–1955.* Scottdale, Pa.: Herald Press, 1988.

Kellogg, Walter Guest. *The Conscientious Objector.* With a new introduction by John Whiteclay Chambers II. New York: Garland Publishing, 1972 (orig. New York: Boni and Liveright, 1919).

Kodama, Katsuya, and Unto Vesa, eds. *Towards a Comparative Analysis of Peace Movements.* Brookfield, Vt.: Gower, 1990.

Kohn, Stephen M. *Jailed for Peace: The History of American Draft Law Violators, 1658–1985.* New York: Praeger, 1986.

Land, Gary, ed. *Adventism in America: A History.* Grand Rapids, Mich.: Eerdmans, 1985.

Lewy, Guenther. *Peace and Revolution: The Moral Crisis of American Pacifism.* Grand Rapids, Mich.: Eerdmans, 1988.

Linn, Ruth. *Not Shooting and Not Crying: Psychological Inquiry into Moral Disobedience.* Westport, Conn.: Greenwood Press, 1989.

Little, Roger W., ed. *Handbook of Military Institutions.* Beverly Hill, Calif.: Sage, 1971.

Lynd, Alice, ed. *We Won't Go: Personal Accounts of War Objectors.* Boston: Beacon Press, 1968.

MacMaster, Richard K., Theron F. Schlabach, and James C. Junke. *The Mennonite Experience in America.* 3 vols. Scottdale, Pa.: Herald Press, 1985–89.

Marrin, Albert, ed. *War and the Christian Conscience: From Augustine to Martin Luther King, Jr.* Chicago: Henry Regnery Co., 1971.

Martin, David A. *Pacifism: An Historical and Sociological Study*. London: Routledge and Kegan Paul, 1965.

Martin, Michel L. *Warriors to Managers: The French Military Establishment since 1945*. Chapel Hill: University of North Carolina Press, 1981.

Mayer, Peter. *The Pacifist Conscience*. New York: Holt Reinhart and Winston, 1966.

McNeal, Patricia. *Harder Than War: Catholic Peacemaking in Twentieth-Century America*. New Brunswick, N.J.: Rutgers University Press, 1992.

Moorehead, Caroline. *Troublesome People: Enemies of War, 1916–1986*. London: Hamish Hamilton, 1986.

Moskos, Charles C. *The American Enlisted Man: The Rank and File in Today's Military*. New York: Russell Sage, 1970.

————. *A Call to Civic Service: National Service for Country and Community*. New York: The Free Press, 1988.

————. *Peace Soldiers: The Sociology of a United Nations Military Force*. Chicago: University of Chicago Press, 1976.

————, ed. *Public Opinion and the Military Establishment*. Beverly Hills, Calif.: Sage Publications, 1971.

Moskos, Charles C., and Frank R. Wood, eds. *The Military: More Than Just a Job?* Washington, D.C.: Pergamon-Brassey's, 1988.

Musto, Ronald G. *The Catholic Peace Tradition*. Maryknoll, N.Y.: Orbis Books, 1986.

National Council of Catholic Bishops, *The Challenge of Peace: God's Promise and Our Response, A Pastoral Letter on War and Peace*. Washington, D.C.: United States Catholic Conference, 1983.

National Interreligious Service Board for Conscientious Objectors. *Words of Conscience: Religious Statements on Conscientious Objection*. 10th ed. Washington, D.C.: National Interreligious Service Board for Conscientious Objectors, 1983.

Niebuhr, Reinhold. *Christianity and Power Politics*. New York: Archon Books, 1940, reprint, 1969.

Noone, Michael F., Jr., ed. *Selective Conscientious Objection: Accommodating Conscience and Security*. Boulder, Colo.: Westview Press, 1989.

O'Sullivan, John. *From Voluntarism to Conscription: Congress and Selective Service, 1940–1945*. New York: Garland Pub. Inc., 1982.

O'Sullivan, John, and Alan M. Meckler, eds. *The Draft and Its Enemies: A Documentary History*. Urbana: University of Illinois Press, 1974.

Perry, F. W. *The Commonwealth Armies: Manpower and Organization in Two World Wars*. Manchester: Manchester University Press, 1988.

Prasad, Devi and Tony Smythe, eds. *Conscription: A World Survey: Compulsory Military Service and Resistance to It*. London: War Resisters International, 1968.

Rae, John. *Conscience and Politics: The British Government and Conscientious Objectors to Military Service, 1916–1919*. Oxford: Oxford University Press, 1970.

Reid, Charles J., Jr., ed. *Peace in a Nuclear Age: The Bishops' Pastoral Letter in Perspective*. Washington, D.C.: The Catholic University of America Press, 1986.

Rohr, John A. *Prophets without Honor: Public Policy and the Selective Conscientious Objector*. Nashville, Tenn.: Abingdon Press, 1971.

Russell, Frederick H. *The Just War in the Middle Ages*. Cambridge: Cambridge University Press, 1975.

Schlissel, Lillian, ed. *Conscience in America: A Documentary History of Conscientious Objection in America, 1757–1967*. New York: E. P. Dutton, 1968.

Segal, David R. *Recruiting for Uncle Sam: Citizenship and Military Manpower Policy*. Lawrence: University Press of Kansas, 1989.

Shaw, Martin. *Post-Military Society*. Philadelphia: Temple University Press, 1991.

——, ed. *War, State and Society*. London: Macmillan, 1984.

Sheleff, Leon. *The Voice of Honor: Civil Disobedience and Civil Loyalty*. Tel Aviv: Ramon, 1989.

Sibley, Mulford Q., and Philip E. Jacob. *Conscription of Conscience: The American State and the Conscientious Objector, 1940–1947*. Ithaca, N.Y.: Cornell University Press, 1952.

Smith, Hugh. "Conscience, Law and the State: Australia's Approach to Conscientious Objection since 1901." *Australian Journal of Politics and History* 35 (1989): 13–28.

——. *Conscientious Objection to Particular Wars: The Australian Approach* Working Paper No. 116. Canberra: Strategic and Defence Studies Centre, Australian National University, 1986.

Solomonow, Allan, ed. *The Roots of Jewish Nonviolence*. Nyack, N.Y.: Jewish Peace Fellowship, 1981.

Stayer, James M. *Anabaptists and the Sword*. 2d ed. Lawrence, Kans.: Coronado Press, 1976.

Surrey, David S. *Choice of Conscience: The Vietnam Era Military and Draft Resisters in Canada*. New York: Praeger, 1982.

Taylor, Richard, and Nigel Young, eds. *Campaigns for Peace: British Peace Movements in the Twentieth Century*. Manchester: Manchester University Press, 1987.

Thomas, Norman. *The Conscientious Objector in America*. New York: B. W. Heubsch, 1923.

U.S. Selective Service System. *Conscientious Objection*. Special Monograph no. 11. 2 vols. Washington, D.C.: Government Printing Office, 1950.

Useem, Michael. *Conscription, Protest, and Social Conflict: The Life and Death of a Draft Resistance Movement*. New York: John Wiley & Sons, 1973.

Vellacott, Jo. *Bertrand Russell and the Pacifists in the First World War*. Brighton, Sussex: Harvester Press, 1980.

Walzer, Michael. *Just and Unjust Wars: A Moral Argument with Historical Illustrations*. New York: Basic Books, 1977.

Wamsley, Gary L. *Selective Service and a Changing America: A Study of Organizational-Environmental Relationships*. Columbus, Ohio: Charles E. Merrill Pub. Co., 1969.

Wittner, Lawrence S. *Rebels against War: The American Peace Movement, 1933–1983*. Philadelphia: Temple University Press, 1984.

Wright, Edward Needles. *Conscientious Objectors in the Civil War*. Philadelphia: University of Pennsylvania Press, 1931.

Zahan, Gordon C. *War, Conscience and Dissent*. New York: Hawthorne Books, 1967.

Contributors

Nils Ivar Agøy is a research fellow in history under the Norwegian Research Council for Science and Humanities (NAVF). He is currently working on a study of the Norwegian military establishment and "the enemy within" in the period 1910–1940.

Anton Bebler is professor of sociology and political science at the University of Ljubljana, Slovenia, where he heads the Defense Research Center. He has been a fellow at the Aspen Institute for Humanistic Studies and a visiting scholar at the Swedish Institute of International Affairs. His books include *Military Rule in Africa* (1976), *Youth Motivation and Military Systems* (1988), and *Contemporary Political Systems* (1990).

John Whiteclay Chambers II is professor of history at Rutgers University, New Brunswick, N. J. A former president of the Council on Peace Research in History, he has been a Fulbright scholar and a Rockefeller Humanities Fellow. His books include *To Raise an Army: The Draft Comes to Modern America* (1987); *The Eagle and the Dove* (1976, 1991), and *The Tyranny of Change: America in the Progressive Era* (1980, 1992).

Donald J. Eberly is executive director of the National Service Secretariat in Washington, D.C. His books include *National Service: A Promise to Keep* (1988), *National Service: A Global Perspective* (1992), and, with Michael Sherraden, *National Service: Social, Economic, and Military Impacts* (1982) and *The Moral Equivalent of War: A Study of Non-Military Service in Nine Nations* (1990).

Nils Petter Gleditsch is editor of the *Journal of Peace Research*, a senior research fellow at the International Peace Research Institute (PRIO) in Olso, and chairman of the board for the Center of Peace and Conflict Research in Copenhagen. His books include *Arms Races: Technological and Political Dynamics* (1990).

Karl W. Haltiner is lecturer of sociology in the Department of Military Sciences at the Swiss Federal Institute of Technology in Zurich. His books include (in

German) *The Citizen Army—Still a Model for Citizenship or an Antiquated Ideal?* (1985).

Gwyn Harries-Jenkins is director of the department of adult education at the University of Hull, England. His books include *The Army in Victorian Society* (1977) and *Armed Forces and the Welfare Societies* (1982). He is past president of the Research Committee on Armed Forces and Conflict Resolution of the International Sociological Association.

Jürgen Kuhlmann is a senior research fellow at the German Armed Forces Institute for Social Research (SOWI) in Munich, Germany. He serves as the executive secretary of the Research Committee on Armed Forces and Conflict Resolution of the International Sociological Association. He has published widely on civil-military relations, organization behavior, and leadership.

Ekkehard Lippert is a senior scientist at the German Armed Forces Institute for Social Research (SOWI) in Munich, Germany. He is the coeditor of the quarterly journal *Sicherheit und Frieden* (Security and Peace) and his books include (in German) *Females in Arms* (1980), *Political Psychology* (1983), and *Peace Handbook* (1988).

Michel L. Martin is professor of political science and public law at the University of the Antilles and Guyane, where he heads the Center of Geopolitical and International Analysis, and at the Institute of Political Studies of Toulouse, France. He has been a visiting scholar at the University of Chicago and is president of the Seminar on Armed Forces and Society in Paris. His books include *Warriors to Managers: The French Military Establishment since 1945* (1981), (in French) *The African Soldier in Politics* (1990), and, as editor, *The Military, Militarism, and the Polity: Essays in Honor of Morris Janowitz* (1985).

Charles C. Moskos is professor of sociology at Northwestern University, Evanston, Ill., and chairman of the Inter-University Seminar on the Armed Forces and Society. He has been a Guggenheim Fellow, a Fellow at the Woodrow Wilson International Center for Scholars, and the S. L. A. Marshall chair at the Army Research Institute for the Behavioral Sciences. His books include *The American Enlisted Man* (1970), *Peace Soldiers* (1976), *The Military* (1988), and *A Call to Civic Service* (1988).

Stephan E. Nikolov is on the staff of the Institute of Sociology of the Bulgarian Academy of Sciences. He is also an editor of *Armiya i Obshchestvo* (Army and Society). He has written widely on issues of civil-military relations and political sociology. He has been visiting scholar at the John F. Kennedy Institute in Berlin and George Mason University in Virginia.

Michael F. Noone, Jr. has been a law professor at The Catholic University of America in Washington, D.C. since 1978. Prior to his faculty appointment, he was a judge advocate in the United States Air Force, retiring as a colonel. He has been distinguished visiting professor in the Law Department of the United States Military Academy, West Point, and is coauthor of the text *Constitutional and Military Law* (1992). He also edited *Selective Conscientious Objection: Accommodating Conscience and Security* (1989).

Marina Nuciari is professor of sociology at the University of Torino and professor of military sociology at the Italian Army Academy. Her books include (in Italian) *Effectiveness and the Military* (1990), *Military Unions in Italy* (1991), and *Changing Values: Security, Development and Defense* (1991).

Yoram Peri is editor-in-chief of the daily *Davar*, published in Tel-Aviv. He has been a professor of political science at Tel-Aviv University and follow at the Jaffe Center for Strategic Studies. He is the author of *Between Battles and Ballots: Israeli Military in Politics* (1983).

Annette Seegers is associate professor in the department of political studies at the University of Capetown, South Africa. She has published in the area of civil-military relations and African politics. She has been a fellow at the Woodrow Wilson International Center for Scholars.

Henning Sørensen is director of the Institute for Sociological Research, Lyngby, Copenhagen. His books include *The Military Profession* (1982) and (in Danish) *The Danish Officer* (1988), *Introduction to the Sociology of the Military* (1988) and, as editor, *Non-Offensive Defense: An Introduction* (1990) and *Defense in Change* (1991).

Hugh Smith is senior lecturer in politics at the University College, University of New South Wales, Australian Defense Force Academy. His books include *The Military Profession in Australia* (1988) and *Australia and Peacekeeping* (1990). He has also written on defense and foreign policy, officer education, and moral issues in international politics.

Dimitrios Smokovitis is professor of sociology and management at the Technological Educational Institute of Piraeus, Greece. His books include (in Greek) *Armed Forces as a Special Social Group* (1977), and he has published in international professional journals on issues of civil-military relations and Greek national security. He has been a visiting scholar at the Center for International Affairs at Harvard University.

John H. Stanfield II is the William Taylor professor of sociology at the College of William and Mary, Williamsburg, Va. His books include *Philanthropy and Jim Crow in American Social Sciences* (1986).

J. G. van de Vijver is on the staff of the Armed Forces and Society Foundation in the Hague. He also serves as first secretary of the Social Council for the Armed

Forces and teaches at military staff schools in the Netherlands. He has written articles on military law, criminal law, and national service.

Wilfried von Bredow is professor of political science at the Phillips University, Marburg, Germany. He has been a Research Fellow at St. Anthony's College, Oxford, and a visiting professor at the University of Toronto, the University of Toulouse, and the University of Saskatchewan. His books include (in German) *Modern Militarism* (1983), *Germany: A Provisional Arrangement* (1985), *Origins and Elements of the West European Peace Movements* (1987), and *The* CSCE *Process* (1992).

Index

Absolutists: definition of, 5; World War II, 14; in
U.S.A., 34, 38; in Britain, 70; in Germany
(F.R.G.), 100, 204; in the Netherlands, 223
Adventists. *See* Seventh-Day Adventists
African Americans, 38, 40, 47–56, 240, 243
Agøy, Nils Ivar, 17
Aid to Conscientious Objectors (France), 84
Albania, 173
Algazi, Gadi, 151, 152
Ali, Muhammad, 40, 54, 240–41
All Quiet on the Western Front (film), 37
All-Volunteer Force (USA), 4, 43–45
Allen, Clifford, 76
Alternative service, 13; in U.S.A., 57–64; in Britain,
71, 75; in France, 90; in Germany (F.R.G.), 101–3,
186–187; in Denmark, 107–9; in Norway, 125; in
South Africa, 131–33; in Switzerland, 142, 203–4; in
Greece, 216; in Italy, 218; in the Netherlands, 221,
224
Alternativist COs, definition of, 5
American Civil Liberties Union (ACLU), 34–35
American Peace Society, 29
Amish, 10, 25
Amnesty International, 8, 118, 171; survey of
conscientious objection (1990), 226
Anabaptists, 10, 11, 13, 25, 136
Apartheid, 18, 129–34
Aquinas, Thomas, 9
Aren, Moshe, 153
Association of Conscientious Objectors (Denmark), 109
Australia, 209–11; and noncombatants, 209; and
religious origins of COs, 210; and Vietnam War,
210; selective COs in, 211; and Persian Gulf War,
211
Austria, 181, 184, 187
Ayres, Lew, 37

Baker, Newton D., 32, 34
Baldwin, Roger, 34
Banks, Douglas, 132
Bausoldaten, 161, 164, 204
Bebler, Anton, 19
Begin, Menachem, 152
Belgium, 183, 186

Bell, J. Franklin, 33
Ben-Gurion, David, 149
Bergman, Hugo, 150
Blacks (South Africa), 127–34. *See also* African
Americans
Black Muslims, 6, 38, 40, 52, 54
Bond, Julian, 54
Botha, P. W., 132
Brethren, 6, 10, 26, 27, 30, 31, 34, 45, 57, 58, 200
Britain: COs in World War I in, 12, 185; and legal
basis of COs, 68–70; in World Wars I and II, 69;
absolutists in, 70; noncombatants in, 70, 72;
alternative service in, 71, 75; secularization of COs
in, 73; selective COs in, 73–74; British Independent
Labour Party, 74; and rates of COs, 75, 77; and COs
as political movements, 78–79
Buber, Martin, 150
Buddhism, 9, 131, 189
Bulgaria, 168, 169, 173, 212–14; Muslim minority in,
213; *stroitelni voiski* (construction battalions) in, 213;
stages of conscientious objection in, 214
Burk, James, 76
Bush, George, 43

Campbell, John A., 31
Carmichael, Stokley, 54
Carnegie Endowment for International Peace,
32
Carter, Jimmy, 43, 59
Cecko, Ivan, 171, 172
Center of Defense of the Objectors (France), 84
Central Board of Conscientious Objectors (Britain), 71
Central Committee for Conscientious Objectors (CCCO),
40, 44, 203
Chamberlain, Neville, 71
Chambers II, John W., 3, 15, 23, 196, 273, 278
Chaplain, role of regarding military objectors (U.S.A.),
190
Christian IV, King of Norway, 114
Christianity and conscientious objection, 9–12, 200–
201, 205
Civilian Conservation Corps (CCC), 207
Civilian Public Service Camps (U.S.A.), 13, 38
Clinton, Bill, 207

282